Carolly Erickson has a PhD in medieval history from Columbia University, New York, which led to six years as a college professor, then to a career as a full-time writer. Her many books include biographies of Empress Josephine, Catherine the Great, Bloody Mary and Elizabeth I.

Praise for *Alexandra: The Last Tsarina*

'This biography ... is by one of the most accomplished of biographers ... [It] takes one through her life at a good pace and makes use not only of the established sources but of the wealth of new information made available by the collapse of the Soviet Empire.' **Contemporary Review**

'Using material previously unavailable, the author presents a closely observed and enthralling biography.'

Ilysa Magnus, *Historical Novels Review*

D0988218

ALEXANDRA
The Last Tsarina

Carolly Erickson

ROBINSON
London

Constable & Robinson Ltd
3 The Lanchesters
162 Fulham Palace Road
London W6 9ER
www.constablerobinson.com

First published in the US in hardback
by St Martin's Press, 2001

This paperback edition is published by Robinson,
an imprint of Constable & Robinson Ltd, 2003

Copyright © Carolly Erickson 2001

The right of Carolly Erickson to be identified as
the author of this work has been asserted by her in accordance
with the Copyright, Designs and Patents Act, 1988

All rights reserved. This book is sold subject to the condition
that it shall not, by way of trade or otherwise, be lent, re-sold,
hired out or otherwise circulated in any form of binding or cover
other than that in which it is published and without a similar condition
including this condition being imposed on the subsequent purchaser.

A copy of the British Library Cataloguing in
Publication Data is available from the British Library

ISBN 1-84119-782-3 (pbk)
ISBN 1-84119-464-6 (hbk)

Printed and bound in the EU

10 9 8 7 6 5 4 3 2 1

We are born in a clear field and die in a dark forest

Russian Proverb

Illustrations

1

In the darkened bedroom of the new palace in Darmstadt, Alice, Grand Duchess of Hesse, lay dying. She was only thirty-five, but looked fifty, her white face with its sharp features gaunt, her eyes deeply sunken in their sockets, her heaving chest narrow and bony.

For the past month Alice had exhausted herself nursing her family through an epidemic of diphtheria, sitting beside their beds through the long nights, holding their hands, coming when they called out to her. The weakest and youngest of the children, her four-year-old daughter May, had been the most severely ill, and when she died, the pain Alice felt, she wrote to her mother Queen Victoria, was 'beyond words'.

Her other stricken children – fifteen-year-old Victoria, twelve-year-old Irene, ten-year-old Ernie and six-year-old Alicky – had all survived, though Ernie had for a time been given up for dead; her husband Louis, robust and thickset, had lain in bed for several weeks in a semiconscious state, unable to eat and barely able to speak, until gradually, under her unceasing care, he began to recover his strength.

Though most of her family and many of her servants succumbed, Alice herself had at first seemed immune to the terrible disease, as if willing her body to resist it so that she could spend herself in nursing the others. But after several weeks of overwork, lost sleep and anxiety she too experienced the painful sore throat, fever and throat-tightening constriction that were the hallmarks of diphtheria, and she took to her bed, unable to do anymore for her ravaged family.

They stood by her bedside now as she struggled for breath, clutching the bedclothes and straining to fill her congested lungs.

She had had a severe attack, and Louis had felt it necessary to notify the state officials and to request prayers in all the churches of the small German principality of Hesse. A telegram had been sent to Queen Victoria at Windsor telling her that Alice's condition was worsening. And the children had been summoned to stand by their mother's bed, and to say their prayers for her.

The youngest of the children, sweet-faced, golden-haired Alicky, stood next to her brother Ernie, her mainstay and closest companion, watching the events in the silent room. Her expressive grey-blue eyes were troubled, for all was loss and confusion in her world – her little sister dead and in her small coffin, her mother near death and beyond her reach, her governess Orchie, always so self-possessed and calm, upset and in tears. Even the nursery itself, spare and homely, was particularly sad and bare, for all the toys had been taken away to prevent their carrying infection.

Several crosses hung from the walls in the sickroom, together with verses from the Bible. There were pictures of Balmoral and of Windsor Castle and its grounds and portraits of Alice's sisters and brothers, and several tapestries in the fashionable William Morris style. Dominating the room was a stained glass window, dedicated to the memory of Alicky's brother Frederick, or 'Frittie', who at the age of three had fallen from that very window to his death on the terrace below. Alicky was too young to remember Frittie, she had been an infant when he fell, but she knew that her mother grieved for him and she and the other children went every year to visit his grave. On Frittie's memorial window were the comforting words from the Bible, 'Suffer the little children to come unto me.' Alicky, lonely and fearful, had much need of comfort, for as the hours passed her mother grew weaker, her every breath an effort.

Throughout Hesse prayers were being offered up for Alice, the Landesmütter (Mother of the Country), who had earned the respect of her husband's subjects by nursing the sick, visiting the poor and founding hospitals and schools. Since her marriage to Grand Duke Louis, Alice had thrown herself into the cause of social betterment, never satisfied with what she had done and always striving to do, as she said, 'the little good that is in my power'.

Alice had created a stir in quiet Darmstadt, introducing the Art Nouveau style in the grand ducal palace, playing duets with Johannes Brahms (Darmstadters preferred Mozart), substituting informality for formal etiquette at court, even holding daring religious views that aimed, as she said, to separate the historical Jesus from such 'later embellishments' as the resurrection. Though her outraged mother-in-law called Alice 'a complete atheist,' and the quiet Darmstadters clucked their tongues over her outspokenness ('Providence, there is no Providence, no nothing!' Alice burst out when her favourite brother Bertie was gravely ill, 'and I can't think how anyone can talk such rubbish,'[1]) Alice maintained her opinions truculently, and dared others to refute them.

A new and more liberal spirit had come to Hesse with Alice, but in her effort to make changes and to air her advanced views she had brought disruption and controversy, and even as she lay on her death-bed there were whispers – respectful, quiet whispers – that her demise would restore a welcome peace to the community.

For Alice's rigorous commitment to modernity was rooted in a mental and spiritual restlessness that made others uneasy. There was something hard and flinty at her core, an icy toughness of mind, that was seemingly at odds with her overall charitableness. She was unforgiving. Demanding a great deal of herself, she demanded as much of those around her, and constantly found them wanting – especially her warm-hearted, stolid husband Louis, who disappointed her at every turn.

Alicky, young as she was, understood something of her mother's uniqueness. Alice was not like other mothers; she did not adorn herself or curl her hair or wear colourful gowns. Her gowns were always black, and her only ornaments were a large gold cross on a chain and a mourning brooch with locks of her father's hair and Frittie's inside. Her pale face bore a perpetual expression of pre-occupation and sorrow, a haunted look. She was often very tired. Even when she took the children on a vacation to the seaside, as she

had only a few months before they had all come down with
diphtheria, she did not rest or play with them, but went to visit
hospitals and schools, taking Alicky with her to give away nosegays
of flowers.

She was always helping people, and she was always full of sorrow.
This much Alicky knew of her suffering mother.

The following morning Louis sent another telegram to Queen
Victoria at Windsor. 'I see no hope,' Louis wrote his mother-in-law.
'My prayers are exhausted.' The queen's own physician Jenner, whom
she had sent from England to treat Alice, added his terse assessment.
'Disease in windpipe extended, difficulty of breathing at times con-
siderable; gravity of condition increased.'

The date on the telegrams, December 13, carried an ominous
implication. Seventeen years earlier Alice's adored father Prince
Albert had died of typhoid on December 14, and ever since the
anniversary of his death had been marked with prayers and
solemnities by his ever-grieving widow and their children. December
14 was feared as a fateful day, and though Alice herself was unaware
of the date, or of much else, she did rave in her delirium that she saw
her dead father, along with May and Frittie, standing together in
heaven welcoming her in.

A little after midnight, early on the morning of the fourteenth,
the patient began to cough and choke. The swollen membrane in
her mouth was so thick she could no longer swallow, and could barely
talk. Her face, even though bathed in warm candlelight, was chalk-
white, her lips bloodless. Her attendants heard her whisper 'May
. . . dear Papa' before becoming unconscious. By sunrise she was
dead.

To the beat of muffled drums the Grand Duchess of Hesse's funeral
procession made its slow way along the narrow, cobblestoned streets
of Darmstadt to the chapel in the Old Palace. There were many
mourners, each carrying a lighted torch. Alicky, her brother and sisters
did not follow the coffin but were allowed to watch from a window
as the mourners assembled in the courtyard below. Later, the children
were told how hundreds of people came to see their mother in the

chapel, taking off their hats as a sign of respect and leaving flowers and wreaths. The tributes were eloquent, the tears heartfelt.

A letter arrived from Windsor Castle.

'Poor Dear Children,' Queen Victoria wrote, 'you have had the most terrible blow which can befall children – you have lost your precious, dear, devoted Mother who loved you – and devoted her life to you and your dear Papa. That horrid disease which carried off sweet little May and from which you and the others recovered has taken her away from you and poor old Grandmama, who with your other kind Grandmama will try to be a mother to you.'

The queen sent particular wishes to 'poor dear Ernie', who was bound to suffer acutely since he was so close to Alice. 'God's will be done,' she concluded. 'May He support and help you all. From your devoted and most unhappy Grandmama, VRI [Victoria Regina Imperatrix, Victoria Queen Empress].'[2]

Alicky and her sisters were measured for mourning clothes, and wore identical black dresses, stockings and shoes. Their fourteen-year-old sister Elizabeth, or Ella, who had been spared sickness and who had spent the last month away from the palace, now rejoined the family, and together the five children and their father spent a mournful Christmas.

Snow drifted down over the narrow streets of Darmstadt, settling on the gabled roofs and piling in deep drifts in the palace park. Orchie let the children play in the snow, bundled warmly against the cold, their ears covered with fur hats and their hands encased in mittens. As the days passed, though they continued to grieve, there were hours in which their sorrow lifted, and they remembered how to skate and build snow forts and ride their sleds down the gentle slopes of the hills.

One day in January Alicky, Irene and Ernie were playing in the garden, and Alicky began to chase the two older children, who ran across an area where seedlings were growing under glass. Ernie and Irene knew how to avoid the glass, but Alicky, too young to be cautious, crashed through it. Blood began to pour from her lacerated legs, and she screamed in pain and fear.

Later, bandaged and soothed by Orchie, Alicky ceased to sob, but her injured legs healed slowly, and she could not run without limping. Over the following weeks she continued to cry every night for her mother, and to say her prayers for her. All in all it was a season of scars, emotional and physical, and it would be a long time before the deepest of them would begin to heal.

2

In the Europe of the late 1870s, the Grand Duchy of Hesse was a very minor principality, and the death of its grand duchess a very minor event.

The leading power of the age was Britain, and Alicky's grandmother Queen Victoria was by any reckoning the most powerful monarch in the world. Britain's navy dominated the seas, Britain's goods – many of them stamped with the Queen's inimitable image – flooded the world. Britain's ideals of high-minded probity in government, gentlemanly honour and social betterment (ideals often honoured in the breach) were much admired, as were such humbler products of British industry as Norfolk jackets and Sheffield pottery, Pears soap and Cadbury's chocolate.

But Britain's dominion was being challenged by the rising power of Prussia. For the better part of two decades the Prussian state had been consolidating its influence among the various German-speaking states and principalities. Prussia's large, efficient armies had proven effective against Austria and France, Prussian manufacturing had mushroomed rapidly until, by the late 1870s, the ruler of Prussia, William I, had become German Emperor and his chancellor Bismarck was declaring, much to the annoyance of Queen Victoria, that England had 'ceased to be a political power'.

Compared to the might of Britain and Germany, Hesse was a virtually powerless entity with a perennially depleted treasury. But the ruling family had important dynastic ties. Not only had the late Grand Duchess Alice been Queen Victoria's daughter, but Alice's sister Victoria – always called Vicky in the family – was married to

Crown Prince Frederick ('Fritz') who would one day inherit the German imperial throne. Alice's brother Edward ('Bertie') was heir apparent to the throne of Britain. Another brother, Alfred ('Affie'), had married into the Russian imperial family. Indeed the five Hesse children were related to virtually every royal house in Europe, and could be counted on, in their turn, to make dynastically advantageous marriages as soon as they reached marriageable age.

Always the matchmaker, Queen Victoria had had her eye on Alice's daughters as prospective brides almost since birth, and had singled out Ella ('a wonderfully pretty girl') and Alicky ('a most lovely child') as likely candidates for marrying well. When in January of 1879, a month after Alice's death, Louis brought his son and daughters to England, the queen was prepared not only to console them for the loss of their mother but to inspect them to make certain they were growing up to be well-mannered, well-spoken and obedient.

Victoria was concerned that the children's father, kindly but passive, would not show sufficient rigour in attending to their futures. She had always been fond of Louis, ever since she had brought him to England, a handsome boy in a smart uniform, to meet Alice in the hope that the two would marry. But she had never been blind to his limitations, and she felt certain that without Alice to look after him he might fall under questionable influences. Louis had never been one to deny himself; as a lonely widower he could, she feared, be enticed into improper liaisons which would be harmful for the children.

To prevent this, Victoria had a plan. Her youngest daughter Beatrice, twenty-one and single, would make a capable stepmother; Louis had known her since she was a child of three and would surely feel comfortable with her. It might not be a love match, but then, what could Louis expect at his age? In her mind's eye Victoria could see a satisfying future. A quiet wedding, with Beatrice slipping easily into the place Alice had vacated. Long visits to England each year by the entire family. A future Victoria could supervise and control. And a marriage for unattractive Beatrice, instead of the spinsterhood that presently seemed to be her fate.

In mid-January of 1879 the Hesse children made the journey from Darmstadt to Flushing, where their Uncle Bertie met them and took them aboard the royal yacht. They made the crossing to Cowes, stayed for a time at the seaside mansion of Osborne, then travelled to Windsor where the queen awaited them.

The draughty corridors of Windsor Castle were full of noise and bustle that January, for the wedding of the queen's son Arthur was only weeks away and the many members of Victoria's large family were gathering to attend it. Vicky and Fritz and their children arrived from Berlin, Bertie and his family came from Sandringham, and Victoria's daughter Helena and her husband and children who lived on the Windsor grounds joined the others for meals and excursions. In addition, relatives of Arthur's bride, Princess Louise of Prussia, arrived – in all, at least three dozen visitors, plus their entourages of servants.

Despite Arthur's insistence that his sister Alice's death had 'thrown a sad gloom' over his approaching marriage, the wedding promised to be a magnificent affair, celebrated with a degree of pomp not seen at the old castle since the Prince Consort died. Arthur was Victoria's favourite son; of her other three, Bertie was an ageing roué, Alfred a stodgy nonentity who had had the audacity to marry the daughter of the Russian emperor ('The murder is out!' the queen exclaimed when she heard of his engagement), and young Leopold, intellectual and engaging, was afflicted with the bleeding disease which earned him the epithet 'child of anxiety'. For Arthur, her 'good' son, the queen would have a grand celebration, and would, for the first time since the start of her widowhood, add a long white train to her black gown, to be held up by train-bearers.[1]

To six-year-old Alicky and her sisters, brought up on plain food and taught to sew and cook and wait on themselves, entering the opulent precincts of Windsor Castle was akin to entering fairyland. The vast, high-ceilinged halls and spacious salons, the endless corridors decorated with imposing art works, trophies from colonial wars, and regimental insignia overawed them and all but forced on them an awareness of their Hanoverian roots. When all the relatives gathered at the long dining table laid with gleaming silver, polished candelabra and banks of hothouse flowers, and with the queen, her ample chest adorned with flashing diamonds and sapphires, presiding at its head, the sense of dynastic force was strong indeed.

To little Alicky, however, who disliked crowds and always sought isolation and quiet, the bustle of Windsor was uncongenial. There were too many faces, too much stimulation. She much preferred spending time alone with her cousin Marie-Louise, Helena's daughter, or with Ernie, or with her benevolent sister Ella, talking and playing games. The animals on the Windsor grounds attracted her, and as the weather was mild that winter she was able to go walking and riding in a pony cart through the extensive park – though she could not walk far, for her injured legs were weak and tired easily.

What little time she spent on her own with her royal grandmother, 'Gangan', was agreeable, for when not presiding over a family occasion or enforcing family discipline Gangan could be very loving and comforting. Alicky was one of Gangan's favourites among her twenty-seven grandchildren; the little girl's cheerful if somewhat reserved nature, her good manners and the beauty of her delicate features were all pleasing. To Gangan Alicky was a 'dear little thing', to be hugged and joked with, fed on biscuits and chocolate sponge cake. To be sure, the queen subjected Alicky, as she did all her grandchildren, to considerable scrutiny. She had to be certain that the child's education and character formation were progressing satisfactorily. But once Alicky passed those tests, she was rewarded with approval and affection, and she had the pleasure of basking in Gangan's warm smile and hearing her rich, deep-throated laugh.

Setting aside a time for solemnity amid all the family activity, the queen took her grandchildren and their father to see the memorial she had commissioned for their mother, then in the process of being carved. It was a tall granite cross, plain and austere, with the inscription 'To the dear memory of Alice, Grand Duchess of Hesse, Princess of Great Britain and Ireland, . . . by her sorrowing mother Queen Victoria.' No doubt she took them to visit Albert's tomb as well, for she visited it herself often and insisted that all her grandchildren, most of whom had never known their grandfather, pay their respects to his cherished memory.

The weeks went by, and the day of the wedding came. Arthur and Louise were joined together in St George's Chapel, fêted in the dining hall, and sent off in a carriage with congratulations and trunkloads of gifts. The wedding had been splendid, though the ever-critical queen had detected minor flaws – the bride's rotted teeth and 'ugly' nose, her father's vulgarity, the embarrassing estrangement between her parents – and Victoria's temper seemed to worsen after she discovered that the other wedding she had hoped to arrange, that between Grand Duke Louis and her daughter Beatrice, was destined never to take place. Under British law, it was prohibited for a man to marry his deceased wife's sister.

In mid-March the visitors to Windsor began to disperse. Queen Victoria sent her Hesse grandchildren back to Darmstadt, escorted by their Uncle Leopold, and promised to send their Aunt Helena to Hesse to visit them later in the year. She had obtained from Louis a guarantee that the children would return to England for their summer holiday. In the interim she had given instructions to their English governess, Margaret Jackson, to send her frequent written accounts of their activities, and to notify her at once of any untoward behaviour.

By the next time there was a large family gathering, in the spring of 1884, Alicky was nearly twelve years old and her place within the large circle of her extended family was much better defined. In an era in which women were valued primarily for their looks, little Alicky was attracting much admiration. She was slender and tall for her age, with thick reddish-blonde hair, a smooth fine complexion and grey-blue eyes whose direct, intelligent gaze was both intriguing and daunting. By any measure, she was a beautiful child, and it was clear that she would soon become a beautiful young woman. Most observers thought that her sister Ella, whom she closely resembled, had a lovelier face, but both sisters were exceptional, eclipsing their numerous cousins, and Alicky's full loveliness had yet to unfold. Where Ella was cheerful and outgoing, Alicky was inward-turned, with a wistfulness that added to her appeal.

Alicky drew and sketched well, and played the piano with skill –
though she cringed and suffered terrible 'torment' whenever her
grandmother insisted that she play for others. (Her 'clammy hands
felt literally glued to the keys', the adult Alexandra told her biographer and lady-in-waiting Sophie Buxhoeveden. It was 'one of
the worst ordeals' of her life.[2]) A good and disciplined student, she
was quick to learn her lessons in literature, history and religion.
Though she showed only average ability in French, her English was
fluent (albeit spoken with a strong German accent) and she excelled
at needlework.

Beyond the exercises she wrote out in the schoolroom, Alicky
was being taught other lessons: from strict yet loving Mrs Orchard
('Orchie'), with her starched, ironed caps and aprons, she learned
the importance of orderliness, tidiness, punctuality and cleanliness;
from her governess Margaret Jackson ('Madgie'), an irascible but
liberal and cultivated woman who believed in the then progressive
idea that girls should have access to the same education as boys, she
learned how to speak her mind and arrive at her own opinions.

By Baroness Wilhelmine Grancy, her spare, elderly lady-in-
waiting, Alicky was taught self-reliance and strict attention to duty.
One must never waver, Baroness Grancy frequently said; one must
never let down one's guard, never relax, always be self-disciplined
and 'not give in, either physically or morally'.[3] Where another child
might have rebelled against such strictures and the rather grim view
of life they bore, Alicky absorbed Baroness Grancy's teachings, with
their attitude of granite self-control. They reinforced the philosophy
of life she had observed in her sainted if overburdened mother, who
had taken on duty after duty and had never spared herself, never
wavered, never given in.

Alicky was turning out to be an idealist like her mother, one who
perceived that larger truths and richer beauties lay beyond the
appearances of things – truths and beauties to be glimpsed through
art, faith and the power of deeply felt emotion. She was carried away
by the music of Wagner, which she 'adored', into realms beyond the
quotidian. She was greatly affected by the power of the sacred, as

impressed on her with considerable forcefulness by her religious teacher Dr Sell. Unlike more extroverted children, Alicky tended to dwell on serious things, to strive after what she saw as nobler, higher pursuits – and, in the process, to be hard on herself if she did not live up to her ideals.

What brought the Hesse and Hanover relatives to Darmstadt in April of 1884 was yet another wedding, that of Alicky's oldest sister Victoria to their cousin Louis of Battenberg. Queen Victoria approved of the match, for although Louis lacked a distinguished title and his parentage was a disgrace – his father, Alicky's uncle Alexander, had married a woman of no social rank, causing a scandal – still his personal qualities were outstanding and he was a serving officer in the British navy. For some time the queen had believed that the oldest of the Hesse girls was 'so talented' that she should marry an extraordinary man, not merely one who was a 'good match'.[4] The handsome, charming Louis was in every way appropriate.

The queen had long since decided whom Ella and Alicky would marry. Her grandson Willy, who would one day inherit the German imperial throne, was in love with Ella; as his wife she would occupy a splendid position at the pinnacle of continental royalty. And Alicky would make the ideal bride for Bertie's oldest son Eddy, who would one day be King of England.

Queen Victoria arrived in Darmstadt prepared to celebrate the wedding of Victoria of Hesse and to further her other matrimonial projects. But she was not only thwarted but severely vexed to discover that Ella, with her father's full consent, had turned her back on her arrogant, bombastic cousin Willy and become engaged to Serge Alexandrovich Romanov, brother of Tsar Alexander III.

There had been close connections between the court of Hesse and that of St Petersburg for generations. Romanov rulers had a preference for brides from small Protestant German states, for such marriages were unlikely to involve either major political entanglements or religious conflicts. (The Protestant women invariably converted to Orthodoxy.) In the previous generation, Tsar Alexander II had married the Hessian princess Maximiliane Wilhelmine, who took the name Maria Alexandrovna, and Serge, Ella's fiancé, was their fifth son.

So in choosing to marry Serge, Ella was fitting into a long established dynastic pattern, and was moreover marrying a familiar relation, for both Serge and his mother, the former Princess Maximiliane, were frequent visitors to Darmstadt.

But in Queen Victoria's eyes Ella was making a disastrous mistake. German princesses, she insisted, withered and suffered in frigid Russia, where the Romanovs and their courtiers were as icy as the long hard winters. Had not Maximiliane been miserable in her marriage to Tsar Alexander II? Was it not common knowledge that the tsar, having been excessively in love with his wife in his youth, had subsequently made her miserable with his infidelities, and had even moved his mistress Princess Dolgorukoy into the Winter Palace, humiliating the poor tsarina and virtually forcing her to seek refuge with her Darmstadt relations?[5]

It was common knowledge, the queen said, that marriages between Russians and Germans were doomed. Her own son Alfred, who had married Serge's sister Marie, had lived to regret his choice and Marie too was unhappy.

Behind the queen's fulminations was a deep and intense personal dislike and distaste for all things Russian – including the reigning tsar himself, Alexander III, who heartily returned her dislike and called Victoria a spoiled, self-indulgent old woman.[6] Given this antipathy, Ella's decision to marry Serge seemed extremely ill-advised.

Hardly had the queen begun to recover from her aggravation at Ella than she was given cause for fresh outrage. She learned that her heretofore favourite son-in-law Louis, Alice's devoted but wayward widower, had had the audacity to marry his mistress Alexandrine von Kolemine, a beautiful divorcée nearly twenty years his junior.

Word of the clandestine marriage leaked out and spread like an infection through the family gathering. The fact that Madame von Kolemine was a charming person and much liked by Louis's children made no difference to Louis's relations, all of whom regarded his secret wedding – held under their very noses – as an insult to family honour and reacted angrily. The German empress ordered Vicky and Fritz to leave Darmstadt immediately and return to Berlin. Others among the wedding guests departed hurriedly as well, leaving Louis in no doubt that from then on he would be *persona non grata* at their courts and homes. Queen Victoria, taking it upon herself in her role of matriarch to repair the damage the foolish Louis had done, sent Bertie to Louis to inform him that he had no choice but to separate from the woman with whom he had disgraced himself and seek an annulment of his marriage. To Madame von Kolemine the queen sent a much harsher message, before leaving Darmstadt for calmer climes.

All the family turmoil must have been confusing to soulful, sensitive Alicky, who was just on the threshold of young womanhood and whose idealistic, Wagnerian sensibility drew her towards love as towards a magnet. But love – whether it was her father's rebellious love for Alexandrine von Kolemine, or Ella's sensible, safe love for the avuncular Serge, or the love she knew her grandmother expected her to develop for her cousin Eddy – love was so upsetting. There were so many unhappy marriages, so much pain arising from mismatched husbands and wives, so much bitterness created within the extended family when love refused to follow the dictates of social etiquette. And the consequences of love and marriage that Alicky observed among her relations were so different from the nobler love stories she saw on the operatic stage, where romance took on a sacred, doomed quality and became the central element in the characters' lives.

While ruminating on these complexities, Alicky prepared to make an important journey. She was to go with her sisters and brother and father to St Petersburg, to attend Ella and Serge's wedding.

It was to be by far the longest journey she had ever made, much longer than her trips to Balmoral. For three days the train rode eastwards along the sparsely populated Baltic seacoast, where the air was chilly even in June and a damp mist hung low over the villages. Gradually the coastal plain gave way to low-lying swampland, cratered with small lakes, the only vegetation thickets of rough marsh grass and tall reeds. Many years later, the adult Alexandra recalled riding 'up the long ugly stretches of country from the Russian frontier to Petersburg', an interminable expanse of barren waste and marshland, the bleak landscape turned a silvery grey in the eerie northern summer light.[7]

The desolate landscape mirrored the sadness Alicky felt in losing her 'greatly beloved Ella', the sister she was closest to. Tall, beautiful blonde Ella, always the peacemaker in the Hesse family, must have been something of a surrogate mother to her much younger sister Alicky. Ella's outgoing nature and generosity – she was, as the adult Alexandra remembered her, 'the personification of unselfishness' – strengthened the bond between the sisters, and the thought that after her marriage Ella would be living very far from Darmstadt must have deepened Alicky's habitual melancholy.[8]

But the splendours of St Petersburg, with its flowing canals and immense baroque palaces, the entire city bathed in a unique watery luminescence, quickened Alicky's aesthetic sense and the excitement with which the Petersburgers greeted Serge's bride-to-be helped to raise her subdued spirits.

Ella's wedding, held in the high-ceilinged chapel of the Winter Palace amid white pilasters crowned with gold, far surpassed any royal event Alicky had ever witnessed, even those at Windsor Castle. The wealth in jewels, gowns and furnishings was of an opulence she had not known existed, while the richness of the Orthodox service surpassed any religious ceremony she had ever seen. Long-bearded, golden-robed priests in tall headgear presided over the lengthy ceremony, during which the vast room was filled with the scent of incense and the ethereal sound of choral singing.

Ella, in her bridal gown of shining silver, her long fur-trimmed train and white veil, seemed already transformed from a relatively humble Hessian princess into a fairytale Russian grand duchess. Her heavy necklace of large jewels had belonged to Catherine the Great, and there were other reminders of the Romanov imperial past throughout the room. Alicky, standing and watching in her white muslin dress, a wreath of roses in her hair, was thoroughly caught up in the mystique of the ceremony; afterwards, taking out her diary, she made a sketch of herself dressed in a long bridal gown.

For a few days following the wedding the Hesse children went to stay with Tsar Alexander and his family at the imperial palace of Peterhof on the Gulf of Finland. The palace was a playground of gardens, fountains, lakes and small ornate summer houses, and Alicky and her brother Ernie spent time wandering through the grounds with the tsar's children Georgy, Xenia and Michael, aged fourteen, nine and six, and even with the oldest of the tsar's children, sixteen-year-old Nicky, who recorded in his diary some of what they did together.

'The weather today was wonderful,' he wrote. 'We lunched as usual with all the Darmstadts. We jumped with them on the net. At three o'clock we all went out in the four-horse break. Papa led the way in the family charabanc with Aunt Marie and Victoria [Alicky's sister].' They made an excursion to a peasant village and rode through the low-lying countryside, stopping to dine on black bread and milk. Later, at supper, Nicky noted that 'sweet little Alix' came to join them.[9]

The shy, warm, charming Nicky felt drawn to his twelve-year-old second cousin, whom he called Alix; she too was shy and reserved, though when they went sight-seeing she was the one most eager to see and do everything, and she laughed heartily at Georgy's practical jokes. For her part, Alicky too was captivated, though when Nicky gave her a gift, a brooch, she felt she could not keep it, and gave it back.

The brooch had been a keepsake, a token of affection. And there was another token of their mutual affection: their names, scratched into a pane of glass in the Italian summerhouse. By the time Alicky and her sisters and brother left for Hesse, a pact had been sealed. 'We love each other,' Nicky wrote in his diary. Alicky's diary was filled with page after page of sketches, all of brides in white veils and long white gowns, marching to imagined music.

3

Officers in the imperial army told a story about the tsar's son Nicholas. When he was born, so the story went, he was such a tiny, puny baby that his father Alexander III, who was six feet, six inches tall, muscular, tall and strong was certain that there was something terribly wrong with him. He summoned a doctor, who examined the child and confirmed the tsar's fears. 'Your son's no use,' the physician said. 'You must have him shot.' Instead the doctor was shot, and the baby's physical shortcomings were never again discussed.[1]

Many people, not only army officers, looked askance at the heir to the imperial throne for, having been a puny baby, he grew to be an undersized boy and then, at sixteen, a short, thin young man. When he stood near his father and his uncles, all of whom towered over him, there seemed to be something wrong; how could such a small person, with such slender shoulders, one day carry the burden of the entire Russian empire?

Had Nicky possessed a more forceful personality, a loud voice, a domineering manner, his physical slightness might have seemed less significant. But his manner was gentle, simple, and direct; in contrast to his blustering father and dignified uncles there was nothing authoritative about him, nothing that inspired fear. He did not carry himself with the air of command to be expected in a young man who would one day inherit a vast empire. Indeed, far from possessing an air of command, he had what one astute contemporary called 'an almost feminine delicacy' about him, a sensitivity to the moods and feelings of others that was as remarkable as it was, from a political point of view, unfortunate; Nicky's sensitivity was seen as weakness, and weakness in a future sovereign, everyone agreed, was certain to prove a dangerous liability.

Of course, it was precisely Nicky's sensitivity, along with his sandy-haired, boyish good looks, that attracted Alicky to him. Above all, it was the look in his eyes.

'Of the most delicate shade of blue, they looked you straight in the face with the kindest, tenderest, the most loving expression,' wrote Sydney Gibbes, who was to know Nicky well later in life. 'His eyes were so clear that it seemed as if he opened the whole of his soul to your gaze, a soul that was so simple and pure that it did not fear your scrutiny.'[2]

If Nicky was subdued, it was in part because he had had a great shock. Only three years earlier, one afternoon at the Winter Palace, he had heard two enormous explosions, and had at once turned white with fear, for a terrorist bomb had gone off in the palace not long before, blowing up the dining room and killing forty soldiers. Shortly after hearing the explosions Nicky saw his grandfather the emperor, his beloved Anpapa, carried into the palace more dead than alive, and laid on a sofa in his study. He had been attacked by a bomb on a St Petersburg street. Twelve-year-old Nicky, in his blue sailor suit, watched with his weeping father and hysterical grandmother as the emperor, his legs mangled and bleeding, lay dying. The ghastly vigil lasted well over an hour, as thousands of Petersburgers gathered in front of the palace, shouting and crying out.

Only those present in the study ever knew the ghoulishness of that final hour. The dying tsar, shivering, white-faced and in terrible pain, tried to speak, tried to make the sign of the cross. Frantic physicians worked over his broken body but there was no hope, he had lost far too much blood. Everyone in the room, an eyewitness remembered later, was numb with shock and terror. 'The horror showed in their faces, they sobbed like little children.' Finally the tsar gasped out his last breaths.

The event marked young Nicky. Every year thereafter on the anniversary of his grandfather's assassination, March 1, he paused to remember Anpapa's 'excruciating death'. The memory of the two terrible explosions, and their fatal aftermath, never left him.[3]

In an effort to protect his family from further harm the new tsar, Alexander III, had moved them to the huge, fortress-like suburban palace of Gatchina, whose nine hundred rooms surrounded two immense courtyards and whose many acres of park, wood and water gave ample space for recreation. Moats and watch towers offered protection against assault, and soldiers surrounding the palace compound were on guard night and day. Nicky and his sisters and brothers had been virtually sequestered at Gatchina ever since their grandfather's murder, yet even there they could not feel safe. Rumours of revolutionaries carrying mines and bombs intended to destroy the imperial family continued to reach Gatchina, and trenches had to be dug all around the palace to prevent sabotage from underground. Even within the palace itself there was menace, for no one could be certain that all of the thousands of servants were trustworthy; everyone, from the butlers to the janitors, was suspected of being a secret revolutionary. Furthermore, the servants were themselves in a constant state of dread, for they firmly believed that the ghost of the murdered Emperor Paul I walked the corridors of Gatchina, and many of them swore they had seen it.[4]

Immured in the gloomy, low-ceilinged rooms of medieval Gatchina, troubled by an unspoken dread of his dynastic future, Nicky took his pleasures where he could find them. He liked walking with his father in the palace grounds in the summer, wading into muddy ponds to look for tadpoles or wandering into orchards and picking apples off the trees. It amused him when his father, who had a vehement dislike of foreign royalty, once turned the hose on the king of Sweden. Nicky enjoyed watching his cleverer brother Georgy, with whom he had his lessons, embarrass their tutors with his pointed questions. (Once Georgy cornered the pompous geography tutor and demanded to know whether he had personally seen the lands and seas he described to them; the poor man had to admit that he had not.) When Georgy's green parrot Popka imitated their hated English tutor Mr Heath, jumping up and down on his perch and speaking with an exaggerated British accent, Nicky could not stop laughing.[5]

Indifferent to the workings of government, and left largely in ignorance of them by his father, Nicky was happiest when outdoors, occupied in building snow houses in winter, or chopping wood or planting trees. He was often preoccupied, his cousin Alexander ('Sandro') thought, his mind wandering to far-off things, his clear blue eyes fixed on some distant reverie.[6]

Whether, and how frequently, Nicky thought about his young cousin Alicky in Darmstadt during his moments of reverie is difficult to say, but certainly she thought of him very often. By the time she was thirteen, she knew that she loved him, and confided her feelings to her best friend Toni Becker when the latter came to the palace for gymnastic and dancing lessons.[7] Toni's father, who had once been private secretary to Queen Victoria and Albert, had come to Darmstadt as private secretary to Alicky's mother; he stayed on after Alice's death and his daughter was at the palace nearly every day.[8] Reserved as she was with others, Alicky told her secrets to Toni: that she loved her cousin Nicky, that she would soon be a bridesmaid for the first time, at the wedding of her Aunt Beatrice who was to marry Henry of Battenberg, that she did not like her cousin Eddy at all, though her grandmother wanted her to marry him.

Eddy, Uncle Bertie's oldest son, was among the least appealing of Alicky's cousins. Despite being tall and good-looking, he seemed both backwards and clinging; unlike his younger brother George he never seemed to leave his mother's side, and followed her, often with one arm draped around her neck, wherever she went. Lazy and list-less, with little intelligence and much evident sensuality, Eddy was a disappointment to his father, and even his stoutly loyal grandmother Queen Victoria could not help speculating that he might soon be lost to a life of vice. Of course, marriage to a strong, patient woman would be an antidote to this, and as Alicky grew older her inner strength and patience seemed more and more in evidence. The queen continued to hope that Alicky would in time accept the obvious honour of becoming Eddy's wife and future queen.

Alicky – now more and more known as Alix, as she reached her mid-teens – continued to nurture her infatuation with her Russian cousin Nicky, and continued to hear about him in her sister Ella's letters.[9] But they did not meet, and meanwhile her social world widened to include a variety of other young men. There were the officers of the Hesse regiments, there were her brother Ernie's friends from the university, there were the young men who attended the tea dances given at Darmstadt for her sister Irene, who at twenty was still unmarried. When Alix went with her father and sister to London to join in the celebrations surrounding Queen Victoria's Jubilee in 1887, she was reunited once again with most of her many cousins, although she was still too young to attend the balls and parties given for the sixty-eight-year-old queen.

By the time Alix turned sixteen, in the year following her grandmother's Jubilee, she had grown into a complex young woman with austere tastes, romantic aspirations and a unique nature that was too challenging for most of those who knew her to fathom. Her cousin and childhood friend Marie-Louise, Aunt Helena's daughter, described her as 'a most wonderful person' with 'a curious atmosphere of fatality' about her. 'I once said in the way that cousins can be very rude and outspoken to each other: "Alix, you always play at being sorrowful; one day the Almighty will send you some real crushing sorrows, and then what are you going to do?"'[10] The response was not recorded.

Sir George Buchanan, who knew Alix well in her youth, wrote of her as 'a beautiful girl, though shy and reserved', and took note of the 'sad and pathetic expression' her face took on at times.[11]

But her shyness, reserve and melancholy were counterbalanced by a strong strain of impetuousness and passion, a capacity for stony anger and iron resolve, and at the same time a gift for levity, even frivolity. With a close friend, or with her brother Ernie, she could be bright and cheerful, full of light conversation. One girlhood friend, Minnie Cochrane, remembered that Alix liked to play the banjo, and that the two girls sang duets by the hour.[12] Sunshine and shadow seemed to alternate in Alix's ardent nature, and she withheld herself warily from anyone she did not know well, repressing the more vulnerable and appealing side of her personality and becoming ill at ease. Signs of this discomfort were evident; a flush spread across her face and down her neck, and her cheeks became blotched with red.

Alix's sixteenth birthday arrived, in May of 1888, and with its advent she crossed an important threshold. Once a girl reached sixteen she underwent a series of rituals marking her formal entrance into adulthood. For the first time, she pinned up her hair; she abandoned her girlish clothing for low-necked full-skirted gowns; she became confirmed in the church; and, if she was of high birth or wealth, she was formally presented to society at a ball or party. It was understood that at sixteen a girl was ready to become engaged, preferably as quickly as possible so that she did not risk appearing undesirable.

With Orchie's help, Alix began pinning up her long, thick reddish-gold hair each day and wore the new gowns her dressmakers provided. Coached by Dr Sell, she prepared successfully for her confirmation in the Lutheran church and by Ella, who came from Russia for the occasion, and by her new lady-in-waiting Gretchen von Fabrice, she prepared for her coming-out ball.

Perhaps because the many guests at the ball were all familiar to Alix, she was at ease on that evening – or, if she was not at ease, no one recorded her anxiety. Dressed in a simple gown of white tulle, with a string of pearls around her neck and fresh orange blossoms arranged like a crown in her hair and scattered on her gown, she made her entrance into the ballroom and was much admired, presiding alongside her father at the banquet and dancing to the music of the seventy-piece Darmstadt theatre orchestra.

No one who saw Alix that night could have been in any doubt that she would soon become engaged, for she had beauty, breeding, taste and accomplishments, chief among which was her musical ability. Over the following months, from autumn 1888 to spring 1889, Darmstadt society waited for the expected announcement that the grand duke's daughter Alexandra had agreed to become the wife of some fortunate man.

But no announcement was made, and by summer it was beginning to appear as though, against all odds, Alix might actually have to enter her second social season unattached, bearing the stigma of looming spinsterhood.

Queen Victoria now stepped in in an effort to prevent that disaster. It was the queen's habit, when she intended to promote a match, to invite both members of the potential couple to one of her residences for a visit at the same time; during the course of their stay, with the queen as chaperone, they were expected to fall in love (or at least acquire a liking for one another) and come to an understanding about their future.

She invited Alix and Eddy to Balmoral in hope that, under the influence of the wild and romantic Scottish countryside and the almost equally potent influence of their determined grandmother, they would at last do what had long been expected of them by many in their families, including Eddy's parents. (Many – but not all. Ella had strong reservations about Eddy as a husband for Alix; he was physically feeble and of only mediocre intelligence, and the fact that he would one day be king of England and emperor of India made him no more attractive.)

For Alix the time at Balmoral must have been awkward at best, and at worst extremely uncomfortable. She listened to Eddy's protestations of love, she endured her grandmother's scrutiny and, most likely, her pointed lectures on what a fine husband Eddy would make, how few eligible men there were of appropriate social rank for her to choose from, how her chances of marriage were certain to diminish even further if she waited until she was any older (she was then seventeen) to make up her mind.[13] In the end, Alix refused Eddy's proposal – but neither he nor Queen Victoria quite gave up hope that she would change her mind. 'We have just a faint lingering hope,' the queen wrote to her granddaughter Victoria; as for Eddy, he was to be sent abroad to recover from his disappointment.[14]

What neither the queen nor Eddy knew was that Alix had acquired a Russian language exercise book, and was applying herself to learning Russian in preparation for her forthcoming visit to Ella – a visit during which, she was certain, she would see a great deal of her cousin Nicky.

Thick ice crusted the Neva in January of 1890, and deep snowdrifts lined the long, straight boulevard of Nevsky Prospekt where Ella and Serge's massive red palace stood, squat and four-square, opposite the far grander Anitchkov Palace where the tsar and his family were in residence for the season. The city was in darkness most of the time; a feeble sun rose just above the horizon for a few hours at midday, but its pale wintry light, glowing on the snow, was almost spectral, and in order to provide enough light along the canals and walkways, lanterns had to be kept lit even at noon.

Horses slipped on the icy streets, the jingling of their harness bells a constant noise from morning until late into the night. For St Petersburg in winter came alive in the evening, when the city's elite, elegantly gowned and jewelled, drove to one another's mansions to attend grand soirées. Lines of carriages filled Nevsky Prospekt every night, jostling as they clogged the broad avenue, the drivers in their thick greatcoats shouting and swearing and urging the horses forwards, the thick reins clutched in gloved hands.

Foreign observers noted a carnival atmosphere among the crowds at St Petersburg dances and receptions, a spirited gaiety that distinguished the highborn Russians from the decorous, ponderous Germans or the homely albeit ceremonious British. The Russians had style, bravado, dash; their mansions, their clothing, their banquets, the very livery of their servants had a splendour that was almost gaudy by comparison with the high society of Western capitals. It was, in part, a lavishness of scale; everything in Russia was large, in keeping with the vast land itself – the fortunes, the aristocratic estates, the style of living. Extravagance and profligacy, among the aristocratic class, were all but taken for granted, an exception being the eccentric tsar himself, who lived quite modestly in his grand palaces and had raised his children on plain food and amid simple furnishings.

When Alix, her brother and father arrived in the imperial capital the social season was under way, and Ella, an eager hostess who particularly enjoyed giving balls, entertained often. Taking her younger sister under her wing, she showed Alix off in the best drawing rooms and ballrooms of the city, and often took her to the dances given by the tsarina, Maria Feodorovna ('Minnie') at the Anitchkov Palace.

Alix was content to follow her sister's lead, despite her dislike of crowds and her wariness among strangers. She was aware that she was being studied and judged, especially by Minnie and the tsar himself, and their scrutiny must have made her self-conscious; she knew that she did not truly fit in, that her manners were considered provincial and her inexpensive clothes almost shabby beside the elaborate gowns of the Russian court ladies. To an extent she lost her self-consciousness when sitting in the theatre, enjoying the delights of the ballet and especially the opera, where she was swept away by the grandeur of the music. But every time she was introduced to new people or stood in a long reception line, her unease was apparent to those around her. They took note of her clumsy curtsy, her inability to make light conversation, her stiffness and uncontrollable blushing. They called her a haughty German, and dismissed her from their thoughts.

If the reception of the Petersburgers caused Alix strain, the continued pressure she felt to agree to marry her cousin Eddy was an equal source of stress. Throughout the winter of 1890 Queen Victoria kept up her campaign to bring about the match, writing letters to Alix herself and to other family members. Far away though she was, the queen maintained a nervous watch on Alix in Russia, aided by letters from Minnie to her sister the Princess of Wales, Bertie's wife Alexandra. (Minnie and Alexandra were Danish princesses, daughters of King Christian IX.)

What Minnie told Alexandra was uncompromising and rather harsh. A wife would soon have to be found for Nicky, Minnie told her sister in England, but it would not be Alix. For one thing, it would never do for the youngest daughter of an undistinguished grand duke to marry the heir to the Russian throne. Besides, Alix was not personally suited to be tsarina. She was too hard, she lacked grace and tact, she did not have the gift of making people like her.

Alexandra passed on to her mother-in-law Queen Victoria all that Minnie told her, adding that Minnie was 'very annoyed' that an attachment had been allowed to develop between Alix and Nicky. She had in mind another young woman to be Nicky's wife: Hélène, daughter of the Count of Paris, who was the pretender to the French throne. Hélène would be preferable in every way, and a Franco-Russian union would reinforce prevailing diplomatic currents.

While their elders worried and schemed, Alix and Nicky met frequently, often when Ella brought them together at social gatherings. For if the Russian sovereigns and Queen Victoria were vehemently opposed to any thought of marriage between the two young people, Ella and Serge were enthusiastically in favour of it.[15] Nicky and Alix skated together, sometimes battling winds so forceful that they could hardly move. They met at tea parties, they attended church services together. They played badminton, built snow fortresses, and slid down immense ice hills on sledges. Ella staged a performance of *Eugene Onegin* at her private theatre and persuaded Nicky to play a small part; whether Alix had a part is unknown, but doubtless she watched the rehearsals and chatted with Nicky during them.[16]

Alix and Nicky were falling in love. For Alix it was a deepening of the feeling she had cherished for five years, while Nicky's desire for his beautiful cousin grew 'stronger and more tender', he afterwards wrote, during their winter in St Petersburg. The fact that both were being strongly influenced to choose other marriage partners must have intensified their bond, and made it more romantic.

On the last Sunday of the carnival season, a small end-of-season party was held at Tsarskoe Selo, the imperial estate some thirteen miles south of St Petersburg, for Nicky's family and close friends. The dancing began in the afternoon, followed by a dinner of blinis with fresh caviar, then a cotillion, with gifts for all the guests and more dancing until late into the evening. Most likely Alix was not able to dance all evening, her legs were not strong enough, and knowing that she would soon be leaving Russia may have saddened her.

Carnival was in its last waning hours and Lent, the long season of austerity, was about to begin. At midnight a signal was given and immediately the musicians stopped playing and the dance floor cleared. The mood in the ballroom turned solemn. The dancers sat down to a Fasting Meal of mushrooms, cabbage and potatoes, their minds adjusting to the swift change of atmosphere.

For Alix and Nicky, who had spent so many intense hours in each other's company, it was almost their last evening together. A long season of deprivation had begun.

4

Shortly after she returned home to Darmstadt, in April or May of 1890, Alix sat down to write a letter to her cousin Eddy. She knew that she had to give him a final, definitive answer. In her own mind, there was nothing but certainty that Nicky was the one she wanted to marry – though after her disapproving reception by his parents during her stay in St Petersburg, she must have wondered if her hopes were futile.

Alix told Eddy, in kind but firm language, that although it 'pained her to pain him', she had to say once and for all that she could not marry him. She was sure that they would not be happy together. She urged him to put her out of his mind, assured him of her cousinly affection, and closed her letter.[1]

To her grandmother she put her case somewhat differently, saying that if she were 'forced' by the family to go against her inclinations and her better judgment, she would do her duty and marry Eddy, but that if she did, in the end both of them would be miserable.

The queen, who was after all humane and reasonable, was apparently convinced that Alix was right, or at least that she was unshakable in her feelings and opinions, and gave in, though her disappointment and that of Eddy's parents was considerable, and Eddy himself was crushed. She decided that Alix had shown 'great strength of character' in holding firm against so much family persuasion, though she thought it a shame that her stubborn granddaughter was refusing what she considered 'the greatest position there is'.[2]

Alix was headstrong, Ella was very eager for her to marry in Russia, Nicky was lovesick: it was all but inevitable that Alix would return to Russia, and soon.

As for Alix's father Louis, although Queen Victoria admonished him to be 'strong and firm' in directing his daughter's future, he was at best passive; he had become an unhappy man, and was unwell. After his disastrous marriage to Alexandrine von Kolemine (a marriage quickly annulled, with Madame von Kolemine given a large cheque and sent away), Louis was scorned by all his in-laws and lonely in Darmstadt. He took refuge with Queen Victoria in England for a while, but even there he was harassed by his former mistress, and could find no peace.[3] Russia was one of the few places where he was beyond the reach of the vengeful Alexandrine von Kolemine, and was not made to feel a pariah. Thus when Ella invited him to return there, to stay with her and Serge at their country estate of Illinsky near Moscow, he was only too glad to accept her invitation.

When Alix, her brother and father arrived once again in Russia in the summer of 1890 the snow had melted and, in the immense expanses of agricultural land around Moscow, fields of green flax and golden wheat stretched away towards the horizon. The vast stretches of meadow and plain were broken here and there by groves of birch and deep pine forests, and as the travellers made their way along the rutted roads, they passed through dozens of small villages. Each village, it seemed, had its own blue-domed church, its own pond or stream; the small wooden houses, many of them intricately carved with patterns of stars and flowers, garlands and arches, clustered along a single narrow unpaved refuse-clogged street. Here and there along the road, planks were laid down to cover deep mud-holes. In some places the wooden bridges crossing streams had been swept away by swollen waters, and the travellers had to take long detours.

The quiet of the countryside, the long stretches of road between villages and the expansive forest glades, where the white trunks of the birches rose out of clumps of blooming forget-me-nots, moss and thick grass, were soothing to the spirit; Alix, who craved quiet and solitude, must have felt refreshed by her surroundings, despite her nervousness at the prospect of seeing Nicky again.

Ella and Serge's summer house at Illinsky was a rambling, rustic structure with wide balconies skirting the large inner rooms. Light, flowery English prints covered the furniture and curtained the windows, and fresh flowers brightened the wood-panelled rooms. They kept open house; friends came and went, sometimes staying for weeks at a time. The atmosphere was informal, and on fine days everyone stayed outside as much as possible, taking a picnic lunch into the forest, hunting for mushrooms, swimming in the cool ponds or simply reading in the shade of a large tree. The long hours of daylight encouraged wakefulness. Sometimes, on warm starry nights, gypsy choruses came to serenade in the garden, and all the neighbours gathered to listen, afterwards waiting up together to watch for the break of dawn.

Always in the background of Alix's thoughts was what Ella had told her, that Nicky would probably come to Illinsky to join the rest of the family in celebrating Ella's name day, September 18. She daydreamed about him, longing for September to come. Yet in her soberer moments she 'thought she would never get him', and must have confided her anxieties to Ella.[4]

Meanwhile Nicky had told his father that he was in love with Alix and wanted to marry her, and was fighting an urge to go to Illinsky even earlier than Ella's name day celebration. He was prevented from going, for the time being, by having to be present for army manoeuvres, but he confided to his diary that if he didn't go, he would miss his chance to see her and would have to 'wait a whole year, and that's hard!!!'[5]

As heir to the throne Nicky was not free to go where he liked, when he liked. His parents guarded his movements, as they kept close watch on whom he saw and where he went. They were still pressuring him to marry the French princess Hélène, and he was still resisting. And there was a new complication in his emotional life. His father, thinking that it was time his twenty-two-year-old son had a mistress, arranged for Nicky to meet the eighteen-year-old Matilda Kchessinsky, the newest star graduate of the Imperial Ballet School. The dark, lithe Matilda, vibrant and charming, immediately appealed to Nicky, who fell 'passionately in love' with her while at the military camp in the summer of 1890. They were not yet lovers – that would come in time – but, much to Nicky's surprise, he now cherished two loves at once.

'The heart is a surprising thing!' Nicky wrote in his diary. He never stopped thinking about Alix, yet he yearned for Matilda as well. 'Should I conclude from all this that I am exceptionally amorous? To a certain extent, yes.'[6]

Amorous Nicky was – partly because of his age, partly because of his emotional, sensitive nature, and partly, one suspects, because he was given too little to do. All but prevented by his father from preparing for his future role as tsar – Alexander III had little respect for Nicky, and preferred his son Michael – Nicky lived the feckless life of a young officer with very light military duties, staying out too late at night, drinking too much, whiling away his days socializing and his nights in dining, gambling and flirting. He often felt lethargic; his mind was perpetually underoccupied and although he occasionally attended a session of the imperial council, he was inattentive and emerged unenlightened.

His education had been poor – a smattering of science, a whiff of law and economics, a heavy concentration on the basics of military strategy and command – artillery training, surveying and topography, the art of fortification. He had an interest in history, but hardly pursued it, beyond leafing through a historical journal on occasion. He was bored, understimulated, often on the verge of falling asleep. At times, reduced to complete inactivity, he gazed out through the railings of the palace grounds 'for something to do'.[7]

In his idleness he daydreamed about Alix, about Matilda Kchessinsky – and, before many months had passed, he acquired a new love, Olga Dolgoruky.[8]

Unaware of the course Nicky's emotional life was taking, caught up in her own infatuation for him, Alix counted the days until September 18, while in the fields around Illinsky the grain ripened and in the orchards the branches of the trees drooped low, heavy with apples, pears and plums. Ella took Alix and Ernie to Moscow – their first sight of the wondrous city of the golden domes and clanging bells – and led them on expeditions through country markets, where old toothless women sold green, yellow and pink mushrooms in homemade birchbark baskets and choruses of red-shirted peasant boys sang and danced to the accompaniment of accordions and tambourines. The rich exuberance of peasant life, the abundance and variety of the crops, the warm late-summer evenings lit with coloured lanterns and enlivened with dancing bears and twirling gypsies, all delighted her. This was Russia, Nicky's inheritance. This was where she hoped to make her home, as Ella had.

But Ella, she was forced to acknowledge, had made a flawed bargain. Serge, who on his visits to Darmstadt had always seemed to be a benign, avuncular presence, was turning out to be someone else entirely. Now that he was Ella's husband, Serge had become her jailer. He controlled where she went, whom she saw, how she spent her time. His jealousy of her companions made him hateful, even cruel. Ella could not write a letter or read a book without running the gauntlet of his suspicions. Tolstoy's *Anna Karenina*, with its Russian background and theme of adulterous love, was forbidden to Ella because, according to Serge, it might arouse 'unhealthy curiosity and violent emotion'.[9]

Even more troubling was the way Serge criticized Ella, sometimes in front of others, calling her 'my child' in a scathing voice. Strained in each other's presence, Ella and Serge appeared to avoid spending time together, especially when Serge was in one of his surly moods. Alix watched her tall, gaunt brother-in-law, his eyes cold and his lips pressed tightly together, nervously turning a jewelled ring he wore on his little finger, and was thoughtful. This too was a part of Nicky's inheritance: haughty, scornful Serge, and the others in Nicky's very large extended family. What would it be like to live among these people?[10]

Although Ella professed to be content with her life, and Serge's fearsome, domineering side was not always in evidence, what Alix could observe of the troubled relationship between her sister and her husband must have given her pause. Ella, walking out with Alix on fine days, her complexion shaded by a green-lined parasol, appeared lovelier than ever, her grey-blue eyes unclouded. She occupied herself with her religious devotions – she had become a communicant of the Orthodox church – and in designing and sewing her own gowns and making her own face-lotions from cucumber juice and sour cream. After six years of marriage she and Serge still had no children, but she did not appear at all distressed by her childless state. Her one aim seemed to be to make things so that Alix too could live in Russia, as the wife of the heir to the throne.

September 18 came, and, greatly to Alix's disappointment, Nicky did not arrive at Illinsky. Quite possibly he was prevented from going there by his parents, for there was a great deal of gossip that summer about Nicky and Alix, and the tsar and tsarina had decided to send their son on a long trip abroad to broaden his mind and experience and ensure that he didn't see his cousin Alix for a long time.

With his sickly brother Georgy, his cousin George of Greece and a travelling party of young officer friends under the supervision of Prince Bariatinsky, Nicky went aboard the frigate *Memory of Azov* in Trieste in November of 1890 and embarked upon a round-the-world journey.

During his prolonged odyssey the tsarevich rode donkeys along the Nile, steamed down the Suez Canal, went on crocodile hunts in Java and attended balls, banquets and receptions held in his honour by local dignitaries throughout the tropics. Apart from the bazaars, Nicky found most of the local culture tiresome; his diary entries reveal that he and his young companions were much more interested in the Egyptian dancing girls, who 'undressed and got up to all sorts of tricks', and performing geishas (with whom they had 'a very jolly time') than they were in visiting museums or temples.[11] They drank heavily, caroused at night and generally behaved like the fun-loving, immature young men they were. In Japan, however, something went wrong. Gossip afterwards said that, in their pursuit of uninhibited pleasures, the Russians visited male brothels; according to the rumour, George of Greece, who was homosexual, had made offensive advances to a Japanese boy.[12] The result was swift and unexpected.

Nicky was in a rickshaw in the town of Otsu, travelling from a temple back to his hotel, when suddenly a burly policeman attacked him with a sabre, striking two blows which, had they been slightly better aimed and had Nicky not been wearing a thick felt hat, might have killed him. Nicky leaped nimbly out of the rickshaw, calling out, 'What are you about?' while George, who was riding in another rickshaw immediately behind Nicky's, knocked the assailant down with several swift blows of his cane. The rickshaw drivers subdued the policeman, bound his wrists and legs, and dragged him to a nearby house where they left him while they ran for help.

The wounds Nicky received penetrated to the bone, and blood poured down his face. He was rushed to the governor's house, his frightened companions terrified that he would die. Fortunately his wounds, though serious, were not fatal. He had a long red gash on the top of his head, and would suffer permanently from chronic severe headaches.

'I was very touched by the Japanese,' Nicky wrote in a letter to his mother, 'who knelt in the street as we passed and looked terribly sad.' The peaceable, law-abiding Japanese were shocked that such a violent assault against the heir to the Russian throne could occur in their country – though in fact this was not the first attack on Europeans. Recuperating in Kyoto, Nicky received hundreds of telegrams from all over Japan expressing polite regret. Emperor Meiji himself came to visit, with his entourage of princes. 'I felt sorry for them,' Nicky wrote, 'so stricken were they.'[13]

While Nicky was seeing the world, Alix too was travelling. She wintered at Malta, where her sister Victoria had leased a house. Her sister, and her grandmother in England, hoped that Alix might find a husband among her brother-in-law Louis of Battenberg's fellow naval officers. But though Alix flirted, danced and sipped tea with the eligible young men, and even singled out one of them, a handsome Scot, for special friendship, she was not swayed from her bond to Nicky, and went back to Darmstadt unattached.

There were other trips: to Kiel, to visit her sister Irene, who had married Henry of Prussia, brother of Emperor William, and to Italy, where she joined Queen Victoria and toured the museums of Florence and Venice.

Most of the time, however, Alix stayed in Darmstadt and served as her father's hostess and as the 'Landesmütter' of Hesse – a role she apparently relished. It is worthy of remark that in all the social-izing Alix did at this time, whether welcoming guests at banquets, or making speeches to open charity events, or visiting hospitals or delivering largesse from the court to poor families, no one recorded that she was shy or ill at ease. Meeting new people, being highly visible, suited her – particularly if the event had an altruistic purpose. In reaching towards the larger goal of helping others, including helping her father socially, she lost her self-consciousness.

In the spring of 1891, Alix was nineteen. Three social seasons had come and gone and she was still without a fiancé. She was rapidly becoming an old maid, and her grandmother, concerned that she had 'so few choices', and worried that before long Ella would arrange a match for her sister in Russia, once again decided to intervene in an effort to direct Alix's future.

Among Alix's few choices, Queen Victoria thought, was Prince Max of Baden, an ill-favoured, charmless but otherwise suitable prospective husband. She wrote to Louis, emphasizing the urgency of the situation and asking him to invite Max to Darmstadt as soon as possible.

Max duly arrived in Darmstadt, and a startled Alix was informed that he intended to propose to her. 'I vividly remember the torments I suffered,' Alix told an informant many years later. 'I did not know him at all and I shall never forget what I suffered when I met him for the first time.'[14] Threatened with the danger of marrying without love or even affection, she recoiled inwardly. She had already refused Eddy. Nicky was being kept from her. Now she was being asked to accept this unappealing stranger, who might very well be her last hope.

It was an awkward and painful situation. Max, it appears, had been led to believe that he would be accepted. With the aid of her sister Victoria, Alix managed to convince him otherwise, and grand-mother Victoria was appeased. But Alix knew that it was only a matter of time before another stranger was sent to Darmstadt, or was invited to Balmoral when she was there, or was placed in her path during some other visit to relatives. The matchmaking would not cease, she knew, until everyone in the family was convinced that it was too late for her to marry at all.

Meanwhile life in Darmstadt was quite pleasant, if uneventful. Alix sat beside her bearded, balding father at stiff formal dinners and travelled with her beloved brother Ernie, handsome, dapper and devil-may-care, whose cheerful companionship she enjoyed. Like Alix herself, Ernie had artistic tastes, and his nature also included a strong vein of whimsy. She spent time with her effervescent new friend Julia Rantzau, whom she met through her sister Irene at Kiel. She played her banjo and piano, danced at the winter balls, kept up her large correspondence – and thought, sadly, of Nicky, occasionally exchanging letters with him and receiving the small gifts he sent.[15]

Nicky, back in Russia after his global wanderings and suffering severe headaches from his slowly healing head wound, was confiding to his diary that marriage to Alix had become 'the dream and the hope by which I live from day to day'. He was quite bewitched by Matilda Kchessinsky, who had become his mistress, but his feelings for Alix were of another order entirely. 'I resisted my feelings for a long time,' he wrote in December 1891, 'trying to deceive myself into believing that my cherished dream could not be realized.' But the more he thought about her, the more he began to believe that his cherished dream was not impossible. She had not become engaged to anyone else. He was 'almost convinced' that she felt as strongly about him as he did about her. 'The only obstacle or gulf between her and me is the question of religion,' he wrote, and while his parents never ceased to emphasize that obstacle, it had never been a problem in the past; whenever a Protestant had married the tsarevich, she had always converted to Orthodoxy.

'Everything is in the will of God,' Nicky wrote. 'Trusting in His mercy, I look to the future calmly and resignedly.'[16]

Alix was becoming concerned about her father. As winter closed in on Darmstadt in January 1892, and the snow began to pile high in the palace park, Louis was often short of breath, his face pale and his gait unsteady. The cold seemed to bother him more than usual, and many days he did not leave his room. He had always been physically strong, though far from fit; his uniforms had had to be made larger year by year, as his paunch expanded, but he still wore them proudly, with his array of medals and ribbons gleaming across his broad chest.

On a March afternoon as he sat eating lunch with his family, he collapsed. Alix, anxious and tense, sat by his bedside for the next nine days, sleeping very little, keeping vigil along with Ernie. Telegrams were sent to Irene and Victoria, who arrived quickly. Only Ella was missing.

No one expected Louis to die. It seemed impossible that so robust a man could succumb so suddenly. 'Death is dreadful without preparation,' Alix recalled long afterwards, 'and without the body gradually loosening all earthly ties.' She watched in vain for some flicker of recognition on her father's wan face, but he did not regain consciousness. On the tenth day after his attack, his pulse ceased. Alix, haggard from her long vigil and inconsolably grief-stricken, was now an orphan.

5

A small, carefully wrapped package arrived from Windsor, from Grandmama Victoria, for Alix's twentieth birthday in June 1892. It was a decorative enamel, with a whiskery portrait of the late Grand Duke Louis – a sad memento.

Pale and thin, and in pain from her sore legs, Alix had suffered a good deal in the aftermath of her father's death. The strain on her nerves was considerable, and she was not resilient; for months she had been tearful and slept badly, while her hardier sisters Victoria and Irene, sombre in their black mourning gowns, had hovered around her and her brother Ernie, who now assumed the title Grand Duke of Hesse, made vain efforts to comfort and cheer her.

Orchie too hovered around Alix, muttering that she ought to get married as soon as possible, indeed that she ought to have married Max of Baden while she had the chance, and Baroness Grancy, spry and elderly, counselled Alix to pull herself together and think only of doing her duty, not of her grief. Only Gretchen von Fabrice struck the right note; she was sympathetic, warm and retiring.

But Alix, gazing at the enamel likeness of her father and confined to bed, was slow to recover despite the ministrations of those around her. She had lost her 'precious one', the father she had loved and clung to, the dear papa whose handsome face and solid bulk were in her earliest memories.[1] She had lost him before confiding in him fully about her great desire to marry Nicky and her qualms about adopting his Orthodox faith – qualms that had recently begun to grow stronger. She could no longer turn to her father for advice, indeed there was no one she could turn to who could speak to her in a genuinely disinterested way, and this, combined with her sorrow over being apart from Nicky for so long, deepened her grief.

Like it or not, she was ensnared in the dynastic politics of the Russian court, where Alexander III hated Queen Victoria and all her German relations and Alexander's wife Minnie sought a princess of the blood royal for her son.

The tension between the Russian and British courts played itself out, not only in the real world but in Alix's lively imagination. One night she dreamed of being in a hospital surrounded by dying men, among them her brother-in-law Louis of Battenberg. Her sister Victoria stood by. All of a sudden Queen Victoria entered the room and a shot was fired at her. The shooter, Alix discovered in her dream, was a Russian, someone she had met in St Petersburg. With a smile and a bow the would-be assassin walked away.[2]

To distract Alix and speed her healing Ernie took her to a health resort to 'take a cure' and then to England in August, where they visited cousins, aunts and uncles and drank tea every afternoon with grandmama, a shrunken, ageing figure but still mentally agile and protective of her family's and England's interests. After Ernie left for Darmstadt, Alix stayed on with her grandmother, who took her to Wales, to visit the mining districts. There, amid the grime, in a landscape marred by huge black slag-heaps and towering smoke-stacks, Alix was drawn out of her melancholy. Her curiosity was aroused. She took notice of the miners and their families, of the hardships in the mining towns and the ragged children, the many men crippled by accidents in the mines, the worn sunken-cheeked women in shabby dresses who lined the roadways to welcome the queen. Alix insisted on going down into one of the mines, descending in a metal cage into the dark and emerging, blinking, her dress coated with flecks of earth and coal-dust, an hour later.

In the autumn Queen Victoria took Alix to Balmoral, where she could breathe what the queen firmly regarded as 'the finest air in the world' and benefit from long walks and carriage rides. But in the queen's view the air proved 'rather too bracing' for her grand-daughter, and Alix did not flourish. Nor was her health improved or her spirits raised when, journeying to Berlin for a family wedding (her cousin Frederick Charles of Hesse married Margarethe, her brother-in-law Henry's sister), she saw Nicky, had a family tea and dinner with him, but did not spend time with him alone.[3]

Back in Darmstadt, the short days were windy, grey and exceptionally cold. Deep snowdrifts accumulated around the palace and in the park, the branches of the leafless trees drooped with their burden of snow. Alix, listless and despondent, developed an ear inflammation and had to stay in bed.

Alone of all her friends, she was still unmarried at twenty-one. While they were having babies, she was adrift, in love with a man she felt she could not marry, yet unwilling to consider any other. She knew that her relatives gossiped about her, for she stuck out awkwardly in the family. All of her cousins were married, even the unattractive ones; she alone remained single, without a home and husband of her own, given a temporary home by her brother.

And she was uncomfortably aware that even this arrangement was bound to end before long. Ernie, as Grand Duke of Hesse, would soon have to bow to the pressure of his relatives and courtiers and get married himself. And when he did, Alix would no longer be needed as his hostess. She would be in the way.

The prospective change in Ernie's status must have made Alix very ill at ease, not only for her own sake, but for his. For Ernie, handsome, blithe, whimsical Ernie, was homosexual, and Alix must have known, or strongly suspected, that he was.[4] Ernie had never had a girlfriend; he spent his time with a circle of artistic male friends. Thwarted in his desire to become a painter, he was forced to content himself with designing stage sets for the palace theatre and redecorating the halls and salons in Art Nouveau style. His effervescent, rather brittle cheeriness endeared Ernie to his sister, and their bond, strong since childhood, deepened in adulthood. Still, the knowledge that before long there would be a grand duchess, an official Landesmütter, in the palace must have worried Alix for Ernie's sake and her own, and made her situation seem even more tenuous.

On the advice of the court physician, who was concerned about Alix's ear inflammation, in January of 1893 Ernie and Alix left the darkness and cold of Darmstadt for Florence, where their grandmother had rented a grand house, the Villa Palmieri. The queen's villa was full of other relatives escaping the harsh winter, and each day they went out in groups to visit museums and churches and to tour the lovely countryside. For Alix, who had never before been to the warm south, Italy was, as she wrote to her old governess Madgie, 'a dream of beauty'. The views delighted her, the paintings and sculpture overawed her, and the thought that she could walk, in January, in green fields and along cobble-stoned streets free of snow seemed both startling and wondrous.

'We have been favoured with the finest weather,' Alix wrote, 'so that you can imagine how enjoyable it all has been. It is like a dream, so different to anything one has ever seen.'[5]

Venice Alix found to be even more enchanting. She wrote of 'the delightful sensation of being rowed in a gondola and the peace and quiet.' The magnificent, weathered palazzos lining the canals, the old churches and bridges bathed in pearly aqueous light, the twisting, malodorous streets with their quaint shops, all captivated Alix. 'Now we have once been here,' she wrote to Madgie, 'I fear that we shall always long to come again.'

Though Alix did not yet know it, there had been a significant change in the attitude of Nicky's parents toward his marriage. Possibly because Alexander III had been ill, and his illness reminded him of his mortality, he had decided to drop his objections to Alix as a prospective bride for his son. Minnie too acquiesced. Early in January, 1894, Nicky was given permission to make enquiries about Alix with a view to proposing to her. He was stunned. 'I never expected such a suggestion, especially not from Mama,' he wrote in his diary. He began his enquiries immediately – and, over the following few months, said his goodbyes to his mistress Matilda Kchessinsky, though not without some sentimental regrets. ('I am completely under her spell,' he wrote in his diary. 'The pen is trembling in my hand!'[6])

With Ella, in Russia, as an encouraging go-between, Nicky approached Alix and an exchange of letters began. What he soon discovered, much to his chagrin, was that Alix now clung to her Lutheran faith with the tenacious fervour of a martyr in Roman times being sent into the arena to face the lions. The thought of having to abjure the confession in which she had been raised in order to embrace Orthodoxy stung her conscience, and she had not been able to bring herself to see the merits of Nicky's church. In 1890, Serge had sent her a book about Russian Orthodox belief, and for three years she had kept it, and no doubt studied it. It was not ignorance about the Orthodox creed that led to her attitude, rather it was a very deep loyalty to Lutheranism. Leaving the Lutheran church felt, to Alix, like abandoning a dearly loved childhood companion, like 'a wrongful thing', as she told Nicky in a letter.

'I thought [about] everything for a long time,' she said, 'and I only beg you not to think that I take it lightly for it grieves me terribly and makes me very unhappy. I have tried to look at it in every light that is possible, but I always return to one thing. I cannot do it against my conscience.' She told Nicky she thought it was a sin to change her belief, and that if she were to renounce her Lutheranism, she would be miserable for the rest of her life.

'I am certain that you would not wish me to change against my conviction,' she went on. 'What happiness can come from a marriage which begins without the real blessing of God?. . .I should never find my peace of mind again.'[7]

Alix's letter was heartfelt, and full of sadness, but very firm. She could not 'act a lie', she could not go against her conscience. She would never abjure her faith and adopt his. 'I am certain that you will understand this clearly and see as I do, that we are only torturing ourselves, about something impossible and it would not be a kindness to let you go on having vain hopes, which will never be realized.'[8]

Nicky received Alix's letter on a raw November day when a storm was beginning to blow. He walked out into the storm, his hands in his pockets, leaning in against the wind, his thoughts in such turmoil that he was hardly aware of the violent weather. 'I walked about all day in a daze,' he wrote later in his diary. 'It's so hard to appear calm and happy when an issue affecting the whole rest of your life is suddenly decided in this way!'⁹ To numb his shattered feelings, he drank himself into a stupor, and continued to drink heavily for four days.¹⁰

He knew, for Ella had told him, that behind Alix's carefully phrased, discouragingly adamant letters was a wounded, grieving heart. She loved him, with a love, Ella assured him, that was 'deep and pure'. She was 'utterly miserable', indeed she had confided to Ella, when Ella was visiting in Darmstadt, that she would 'die for her love'.¹¹ Nicky wanted to meet with Alix, certain that he could sway her if only they could talk about the thorny issue of religion together. But if they were to meet – and this Alix dreaded – word would be sure to leak out to the press, and for some time there had been speculation in the newspapers about a possible engagement. The last thing she wanted was to endure what was certain to be a painful personal interview with Nicky, made more tense by persistent reporters stalking them, waiting for news.

Shortly before Christmas Nicky wrote to Alix from Gatchina, asking her to forgive his long delay in responding. 'I could not write to you all these days on account of the sad state of mind I was in,' he said. 'Now that my restlessness has passed I feel more calm and am able to answer your letter quietly.' He had been, he admitted, 'lonely and beaten down', but was not without hope.

He felt certain that if only she could learn, from an Orthodox believer, the richness and depth of his faith, her objections to entering his church would fall away. He trusted in God's mercy to make it so.

'Oh! do not say "no" directly, my dearest Alix, do not ruin my life already!' was his closing plea. 'Do you think there can exist any happiness in the whole world without you! After having INVOLUNTARILY! kept me waiting and hoping, can this end in such a way?'¹²

So the issue rested as the new year of 1894 began.

The transition in the grand ducal household at Darmstadt for which Alix had been preparing herself was well under way. Ernie had yielded to family and social pressure and agreed to marry his cousin Victoria Melita, daughter of Uncle Alfred and Aunt Marie, known in the family as 'Ducky'. She was seventeen, he twenty-five; they had a common interest in art, and were reasonably companionable. Ernie was handsome, outgoing and flamboyant, Ducky spirited and strong-willed. Both were highly intelligent. The engagement was a compromise, and each partner knew it. Ernie would have much preferred to remain a bachelor, while Ducky, young as she was, had already met the love of her life – her Russian cousin Cyril, son of Nicky's uncle Vladimir – only to discover that she could not marry him because the Orthodox church forbade marriage between first cousins.

Doing their best to lay aside their inner misgivings, Ernie and Ducky were proceeding with the wedding arrangements, with Alix's help. She busied herself overseeing the preparation of their suites at the palace and at the summer residence at Wolfsgarten, and she corresponded with Ducky in order to find out her tastes and also to cement their friendship. She met with members of the staff and arranged the hiring of new servants. She conferred, rather wistfully, with Ernie, who, she wrote, was 'always running into her room at every hour of the day', as the wedding day approached.

Though she did her best to remain cheerful, presiding as usual as Ernie's hostess and looking after his household, she was overcome at times by sadness. She missed her father. She knew that she would soon miss her brother, for after he married their relationship would not be the same. She even found herself thinking about the little sister she had lost so many years earlier, little May, who had she lived would have turned twenty in this year of 1894.[13]

She wrote to Queen Victoria asking if she could come to England for a few months after the wedding, for she did not want to be in the newlyweds' way. She was beginning to withdraw, tactfully, from the world of married couples, to enter that limbo occupied by spinsters. Accustomed to keeping busy – attending her brother's formal audiences, seeing to the comfort of visiting dignitaries, entertaining friends, even on occasion picking flowers and arranging them in the palace chapel when a wedding was to be held there – she expected to become idle once Ducky took her place and assumed all her responsibilities.

As the new year 1894 opened, Alix was apprehensive. 'I cannot help always dreading the coming of the New Year,' she wrote to her grandmother, 'as one never knows what is in store for one.'

In fact Alix could foresee only too clearly what was likely to be in store for her. Not marriage, for she could not imagine marrying anyone but Nicky, and that was impossible. And besides, Nicky would no doubt marry someone else before long. Not a home of her own, for without a husband there could be no real home, only temporary stays with her sisters Victoria and Irene (not Ella, it would be too painful to go to Russia again) and, if she and Ducky got along well enough, a marginal role in Ernie's household. Before long her grandmother would die, possibly quite soon, and then she could no longer count on long stays at Windsor or sojourns at Balmoral.

She was already the subject of much gossip. She was known as the grand duke's beautiful sister who had turned down two glorious thrones, rejecting first the heir to the British imperial title (poor Eddy, who had died in 1891) and then the heir to the Russian Empire. She was something of a mysterious figure, her attitudes hard to fathom. In time, as her beauty faded, she would be labelled an eccentric. She would float from one relative to another, watching her nieces and nephews grow up, treated (she hoped) with kindness touched with pity. She would fill her time with charitable works, reading and embroidery. She would play the piano and make polite conversation, while bearing the painful burden of a constant sense of emptiness and waste.

Such was the constrained and narrow life Alix foresaw for herself as she spent yet another bleak winter in Darmstadt, nursing her wounded heart and expecting, before long, to have a great deal of time on her hands.

6

Military bands played and a guard of honour stood smartly to attention beside the track as Nicky, in uniform, stepped out of the imperial train onto the platform at Coburg, flanked by his Uncles Paul, Serge and Vladimir. He smiled affably as Alfred, Duke of Saxe-Coburg-Gotha, came forwards to embrace him and the others on the platform greeted him in their turn. Ernie and Ducky, whose wedding day was only three days away, were also on the platform to greet Nicky, and Alfred's sister Vicky and brother Bertie, Ducky's sister Missy and her husband, Crown Prince Ferdinand of Rumania, and a score of others. But the only one Nicky wanted to see was Alix, and he greeted her warmly, all but ignoring the others, intent on her response.

He had almost decided not to come to Coburg, for his sister Xenia had told him that Alix remained fixed in her opposition to any thought of marriage to him. Xenia had recently written to Alix to say that she was 'ruining Nicky's life' by her refusal; Alix had written back to say that Xenia's accusation was cruel, and that, no matter what, 'it NEVER can be'.[1] For emphasis, Alix had sent a telegram saying the same thing, and when he heard about it, Nicky had been very upset. But his mother had convinced him not to give up so quickly, and by the time the train arrived he had regained his courage. He would speak to Alix, alone, and all would be well.

He was so convinced that all would be well, in fact, that he had brought along a chaplain, Father Yanishev, to instruct Alix in the Orthodox faith, and a tutor, Fräulein Schneider, to teach her Russian.

But when on the following day Nicky had his first private conversation with Alix, he found her to be resolute, though emotional. He too was keyed up, his emotions in turmoil; this was the crucial talk which for months he had longed to have with her, his chance to sway her with the force of his love and his reasoned arguments. For two hours he tried to persuade her to give in, to drop her objections and agree to marry him, alternately arguing and pleading, while she wept and repeatedly whispered, 'No, I cannot.'

Deeply moved, part of her wanting nothing more than to yield to his pleas, still Alix resisted. She could not forgo her loyalty to the Lutheran church, she could not be false to it. Fidelity to her church loomed in her mind as the ultimate test of her character, the defining core of her personal honour. Again and again she shook her head, tears rolling down her cheeks, and whispered, 'No, I cannot.'[2]

Finally Nicky gave up, and went out into the rainy afternoon and took a drive with Ella and Serge, then a long walk with Uncle Vladimir to the old Coburg castle on the hill.

No record remains of what Alix did that afternoon, but inwardly she had clearly come to a crossroads. Ella, Serge and now even Ernie were bringing pressure to bear on her to accept Nicky, probing her attitudes and feelings, looking for a way around her adamant objections. Tsar Alexander and Minnie were inviting her into the family, and would be affronted if she refused their invitation. She was about to lose the only home she had, and enter the featureless land of spinsterhood. Her will was strong, but her heart was breaking under the strain, with the man she loved holding out his arms to her, offering her all his sweetness and warmth – if only she would take one hallowed step, across the threshold of Orthodox Christianity.

Alix's firm and independent stance on the marriage issue was, if not unheard-of, very rare. Women in 1894 were not masters of their own destinies; they did not assert their desires in opposition to the strong urgings of their suitors and relatives. To do so was considered unfeminine, even unnatural. Deference to others was the expected norm for a woman of any age in that era, especially where marriage and family were concerned, and the force of convention was exceedingly strong.

So Alix, standing at her crossroads, showed remarkable power of will, assailed as she was by prevailing social expectations, by the threat of lifelong loneliness, by her family, by her adored Nicky.

Thus assailed, she did not capitulate – but she began, tentatively, to search for a way out of her dilemma.

In conversations with Ella and Serge and Ernie it slowly began to be apparent to Alix that what troubled her conscience so deeply was not the prospect of being baptized into the Orthodox church: it was forswearing Lutheranism. She had always assumed that the two things would have to go hand in hand. But perhaps they need not. Ella, when voluntarily adopting the Orthodox faith, had not been required to abjure her Lutheranism. And other German princesses, facing the same difficulty Alix faced, had, it now appeared, arrived at compromises that allowed them to continue their loyalty to the Lutheran creed while entering into their new church.

One such princess was Aunt Marie, Maria Pavlovna, born a Princess of Mecklenberg-Strelitz – known in the Romanov family as 'Auntie Miechen' – the wife of Uncle Vladimir. (Not to be confused with Aunt Marie, the sister of the late Tsar Alexander II and wife of Duke Alfred of Saxe-Coburg-Gotha.) Alix went to visit Auntie Miechen, at her brother's urging, presumably to talk about her conversion. To Nicky, Ernie gave an encouraging message – that 'there was hope of a happy outcome'.[3]

Two days now remained before Ernie and Ducky's wedding, and more and more family members were arriving at the Coburg station. There were excited greetings, tearful hugs. When passing one another in carriages, the affectionate members of Queen Victoria's large family sometimes got out and 'started kissing in the middle of the road', much to the amusement of the visiting Russians. The official topic of conversation within the family was the forthcoming marriage, what a handsome couple Ernie and Ducky made, how enviably tiny Ducky's waist was, where the newlyweds would go on their honeymoon, what a cheery, ebullient fellow the grand duke was, so debonair and artistic. How surprising it was that he had never married until now.

But at the same time, much attention was focused on the drama between Nicky and Alix. Would they become engaged? Why was she hesitating? Had Queen Victoria said or done something to prevent the two from marrying?

In the evenings, after the theatre, when champagne was served in the billiard room and the men gathered to smoke and drink and talk, Nicky was asked about Alix. How did things stand? What could be done? His cousin Willy, German Emperor, was especially solicitous. He would talk to cousin Alix, Willy said. He would take command of the situation. Alix could not hold out against him. All would be well. The champagne flowed freely, and Nicky, who confided to his diary that he was suffering 'great fears and doubts', did not go to bed until the early hours of the morning.[4]

The arrival of Queen Victoria provided a temporary respite from these preoccupations. Clutching a thick black cloak around her, she drove in her carriage from the train station through the town, shivering in the northern chill – she had just come from warm Florence – and smiling her endearing shy smile at the cheering Coburgers. The elderly queen felt a strong nostalgic attachment to the duchy of Coburg, for her beloved late consort Prince Albert had been raised there and she viewed everything associated with Albert through a haze of sentiment and regret. She had taken to wearing a miniature of Albert around her neck, and speaking to it on occasion. One imagines that she had much to say to his image on this April afternoon, as her carriage, escorted by an entire battalion of guardsmen, clattered along the cobble-stoned streets. Handfuls of flowers were flung in front of her carriage wheels as they rolled under an enormous triumphal arch of welcome. In the palace square, in front of Schloss Ehrenburg, she paused to receive her official welcome.

All the relatives had assembled to greet the family matriarch, the women in formal afternoon attire, the men in freshly pressed uniforms. They took tea with her, but could not all dine together as there were far too many to fit around the long dining table. The queen, white-haired and benign, her lumpy figure (Nicky unkindly referred to her as 'belly-woman' and 'a round ball on shaky legs') encased in an old-fashioned dress of black bombazine, her Indian servant at her side, presided comfortably over all, content that her matchmaking had succeeded in bringing Ernie and Ducky together. Alone of those present, the queen was unaware of the gossip about Nicky and Alix; she was under the impression that, having done her best to prevent any engagement between them, the possibility of their union no longer existed.[5]

The wedding day came, and in the royal chapel of the palace, amid masses of flowers and garlands of fir branches, Ernie and Ducky stood to repeat their vows. The ceremony had hardly concluded before a violent thunderstorm broke, drenching the newlyweds as they drove off in their carriage and forcing the mayor to cancel the evening fireworks display.

The rain continued all that night, and Alix, her head by now spinning with excitement, cannot have slept well. The ray of hope she had begun to glimpse two days earlier had broadened into a beacon. There was a way, it seemed, to square the demands of her conscience with her heartfelt desire, she could enter the Orthodox church without formally abjuring the Lutheran faith. She could be true to herself – and marry Nicky.

On the following morning two more hasty conversations were held – the first between Alix and cousin Willy, the second another discussion with Auntie Miechen. She was no longer in any doubt. No obstacles remained in her path. She was ready to accept Nicky.

'[She] came into the room where I was sitting with the Uncles,' Nicky wrote, describing the scene in a letter to his mother. 'They left us alone and . . . the first thing she said was . . . that she agreed! Oh God, what happened to me then! I started to cry like a child, and so did she, only her expression immediately changed: her face brightened and took on an aura of peace.'[6]

Later Alix would castigate herself for being so stubborn for so long. She asked Nicky to forgive her. She had not been able to see clearly, she had imagined barriers where none existed. Now all restraint fell away, and the lovers embraced, their fervour all the greater for the long season of frustration that had kept them apart. 'I went about all day dazed,' Nicky wrote in his diary. 'I could not believe that all this had happened to me.' Alix wrote her friend Toni Becker that she was 'endlessly happy,' and when she and Nicky burst into the adjoining room to announce to Willy and the aunts and uncles that they had agreed to marry, she was radiant.

Queen Victoria was the next to be told – and great must have been her astonishment! – then Aunt Marie and Uncle Alfred and the hosts of other relatives who indulged, Nicky wrote, in 'an orgy of kissing'.[7] Telegrams were sent to Russia and elsewhere, and by evening many more telegrams had begun to pour in, congratulating Alix and Nicky and wishing them happiness.

'Please tell your dear fiancée from me,' Tsar Alexander telegraphed to Nicky, 'how much I thank her for at last consenting, and how I wish her to flourish for the joy, comfort and peace she has given us by deciding to agree to be your wife!' Xenia too sent her congratulations, and Alix wrote her an ecstatic note. 'I cannot describe my happiness – it is too great . . . And what an angel the dear boy is.'[8] Alix and Xenia had long been on the most affectionate terms. Now they would be sisters-in-law – and would be brides together, as Xenia was soon to marry her cousin Sandro.

Over the following few days the engaged pair were together most of the time, eating their meals together, driving out in a pony carriage, having photographs taken, sitting together at the opera and afterwards, late into the night, staying up together in the privacy of Alix's sitting room with only Gretchen von Fabrice as chaperone. As one by one the wedding guests departed, Alix and Nicky seemed to have Coburg to themselves, the lilac-scented gardens, the crooked narrow streets and quaint houses, the small opera house and wooded environs. The intensity of those romantic days, the joy each of them felt in the presence of the other, were beyond description. 'I am more happy than words can express,' Alix wrote to her old governess Madgie. 'At last, after these five sad years!'[9] 'My soul was brimming with joy and light,' Nicky wrote, referring to those 'golden days' following his engagement.[10]

It was as if every detail of their rapturous days stood out with special significance: an operatic aria they both loved ('Once again, once again, once again, O nightingale!'), the pink flowers Alix habitually wore, and Nicky came to love, the house on the road from Coburg to Ketchendorf where they shared an erotic interlude. Time hung suspended, or so it seemed – though on rainy afternoons they both managed to attend to their correspondence and to answer each of the more than two hundred telegrams that came for them.

Plans for the future had to be made, but there would be time for this in the summer. Nicky was to return to Russia, then come to visit Alix in England. While they were apart they agreed to communicate by telegram, in a special code. After a last day spent in Darmstadt, where they visited Ernie and Ducky, they said their reluctant goodbyes, and Alix left for Windsor.

She arrived looking happy but tired, and with pain in her legs. Over the course of only a few short weeks an immense change had been wrought in Alix's life, and the strain of it was apparent. After a visit with family and a conference with the Bishop of Ripon – no doubt a discussion of her conversion – she went to Harrogate to treat her pain with a course of sulphur baths and rest.

Hoping to avoid attracting the attention of journalists and the curious, she adopted the incognito 'Baroness Starckenburg', and settled into a routine of immersing herself in the waters and studying Russian with her teacher Catherine Schneider, the Baltic Russian Nicky had engaged to instruct her. ('It is amusing, but certainly not easy!' Alix wrote to Madgie, describing her Russian lessons.[11]) She made progress, but soon lost all her privacy. Her true identity was discovered. People crowded around her lodgings, bothering her very pregnant landlady, trying to peer in at the windows, observing her every coming and going.

The British were enthralled by the story of this beautiful granddaughter of Queen Victoria who, having waited so long to marry, had at last become engaged to the future tsar of Russia. They were curious about every detail of her future. What would her wedding gown be like? Her trousseau? When was the wedding to be? Just how rich would she be, as the wife of the Russian tsar? Was it true she had rooms full of diamonds?

'Of course it is in all the papers that I am here,' Alix wrote to Nicky, 'and all the tradespeople send epistles and beg of one to order things, even a piano and tea were offered. The rude people stand at the corner and stare; I shall stick my tongue out at them another time.'[12]

The speculation mounted, the crowds grew. People stared through their windows at her lodging, opera glasses in hand. Every time Alix drove out they congregated and got in the way, forcing her to go in and out through a back entrance; once they discovered the back entrance they clogged it too, and some ran behind her carriage when it went out. It became impossible for her to enter a shop without drawing a group of onlookers, who gawked quite rudely and called out, 'That's her.'

When Alix's landlady gave birth to twins, and asked her celebrated guest to be godmother to the babies, the church was full of noisy strangers attending the christening service, watching as the infants were given the names Nicholas and Alexandra, their attention fixed on the godmother and not on the babies or their parents.

'If I were not in the bathchair I should not mind,' Alix told Nicky, and tried to make light of the annoyance. She was vulnerable, however, for the wheeled chair was unwieldy and, had she ever felt herself in danger she could not have run away, not on her sore legs.

There was one woman in the crowd who stood out. She was always there, wherever Alix went. She came closer than the others, peering at Alix, her manner suggesting mania or mental imbalance. Alix wondered whether it might be the same woman who had annoyed Nicky earlier in the year, stalking him and writing him letters.[13] Watching out for the woman kept her nerves on edge, and the atmosphere of constant surveillance made rest and healing impossible. The sulphur baths failed to ease her pain, and seemed to increase her fatigue. Her attitude was fatalistic. 'It does not matter so, suffering pain,' she told Nicky. 'I daresay it is even good to have to bear pain.'[14]

Towards the end of June Nicky arrived from Russia, and Alix left Harrogate with its beleaguering crowds and travelled to Walton, to her sister Victoria's house, to meet him. They grew closer than ever during Nicky's month-long visit, picnicking, going for long drives together in the hot summer afternoons, breakfasting at Frogmore with Queen Victoria, paying calls on Uncle Bertie and Aunt Beatrice and all the numerous English cousins.

From Walton Alix and Nicky went on to Windsor, where Nicky good-humouredly adapted to the formalities and protocols of the old palace, putting on old-fashioned knee breeches, tight shoes and the Windsor coat with red collar and wristbands to please 'Granny'. He also helped to commemorate an important family event – the birth of a son to Bertie's son and heir George (brother of the late Eddy); this child, who would grow up to be King Edward VIII, ensured the continuity of the dynasty into the next generation, and Nicky was asked to be his godfather.

In the intervals between garden parties, family luncheons, visits to the theatre and opera, Alix and Nicky were often alone together. During their private hours Nicky wrote in his diary, and Alix interrupted him to write in her own notes and loving thoughts. 'God bless you my angel,' she wrote in the margin. 'All's well that ends well.' She drew a heart, and within it wrote 'You you you' in French. 'I dreamed that I was loved, I woke and found it true,' went another of her interpolations, 'and thanked God on my knees for it. True love is the gift which God has given – daily stronger, deeper, fuller, purer.'[15]

Nicky's confession to Alix of his long affair with Matilda Kchessinsky drew from her a longer passage in the diary.

'My own boysy dear,' she wrote, 'never changing, always true. Have confidence and faith in your girlie dear, who loves you more deeply and devotedly, than she ever can say.' She assured him that 'what is past, is past, and will never return and we can look back on it with calm. We are all tempted in this world and when we are young we cannot always fight and hold our own against temptation, but as long as we repent and come back to the good and on to the straight path, God forgives us.

'I love you even more since you told me that little story,' she added, 'your confidence in me touched me, oh, so deeply, and I pray to God that I may always show myself worthy of it.'[16]

Thunderclouds gathered in the hot, humid air and sudden squalls drove everyone indoors during the long afternoons. 'We were dying from the heat,' Nicky noted in his diary. Week after week of incessant, crowded social events left both Alix and Nicky longing for privacy. Her leg pains continued to bother her, though she did not complain. As for Nicky, he had had enough of 'the fat aunts and their husbands', and was becoming irritated with Beatrice's naughty children, his patience frayed by constantly having to 'sit with hands folded and always to wait without end' while Granny took her time getting ready for the next tea party or special exhibition.[17] Nicky was energetic; if he didn't get his daily walk he chafed and grew restless. He distracted himself buying jewels for Alix from the jewellers who, he complained, 'camped in his room'.

He had already given her a beautiful pink diamond engagement ring, along with a necklace of jewels so dazzling that she 'nearly fainted' when presented with it. Now he added other engagement gifts: a pink pearl necklace and ring, a bracelet with an enormous emerald, a sapphire and diamond brooch. Some of the jewellery sent to Alix from the tsar's court was very costly, and the queen, when she saw the fabulous display, was quick to chide her granddaughter. 'Now do not get too proud, Alix,' Victoria said, perhaps unaware that her own humility and lack of material greed or pretension had made a far more lasting impression than any words she could say.

To judge from her letters and other written comments, Alix in fact gave little thought to the high state she would one day occupy as Nicky's wife. Exalted status and position were not important to her; love was. And love she certainly had, and gave – a love that seemed to grow daily, and to flower into a rich, perfectly satisfying compatibility. She and her fiancé were of one mind, one outlook. Being together was enough to make them rapturously happy.

They were tender with each other, they were teasing, they laughed and joked and, none too kindly, made fun of other people. They laughed together over an English phrase book Nicky was studying, compiled by Russians, *'English as She Is Spoke.'* ('At what o'clock dine him?' 'It must never to laugh of the unhappiest.' 'Dress your hairs!')

Alix told Nicky that her 'most earnest desire and prayer' was to make him happy, and he, equally devoted, made it clear to her that her happiness was his prime object. 'I love you, my own darling, as few persons can only love!' Nicky had written shortly after their engagement. 'I love you too deeply and too strongly for me to show it; it is such a sacred feeling, I don't want to let it out in words, that seem meek and poor and vain!'[18]

When towards the end of July the day came for him to go aboard the yacht *Polar Star* to return to Russia, he was mournful and depressed. Parting, even for a little while, was painful. 'The sadness and longing have made me feel faint,' he wrote in his diary. 'Was exhausted from sadness and longing.'[19]

The separation would not be long, Alix assured him. They would meet in two months, at the end of September, at Wolfsgarten. Meanwhile Alix would go on with her religious instruction, training for her formal ceremony of acceptance into the Orthodox church, and with her Russian lessons. She had ordered her trousseau from Madame Flotov, a fashionable designer, and there would be many boxes of gowns, hats, undergarments and nightgowns to try on and approve.

'Ever true and ever loving, faithful pure and strong as death,' Alix wrote in Nicky's diary on the night before he left. Nothing could separate them now, not the cold of the North Sea, not the passing of time, not accident or fate. 'Once again, once again, once again, O nightingale!' Alix sang to herself after watching the departure of the *Polar Star*. She limped back down the landing stage towards the shore, turning her engagement ring on her finger. Her legs hurt, but what was a little pain, when such happiness lay just beyond the horizon?

7

Tsar Alexander, that giant of a man with a look as cold as steel, that much admired ruler whom his subjects called Alexander Mirotworetz, Creator of Peace, had collapsed suddenly, and his doctors insisted that he be taken to his estate at Livadia, on the Black Sea, and given a complete rest.

It was the end of September, 1894, and Nicky, having agreed to meet Alix at Wolfsgarten, was just preparing to leave to join her there. Startled by his father's sharp decline, and made uneasy by the firmness of the imperial physicians' directives, he felt he had to accompany the family to Livadia rather than go to Hesse, and cancelled his plans.

The tsar had not been well for some months. His huge, cumbersome body swayed ominously when he walked, his immensely broad shoulders had become somewhat stooped and the skin of his round, black-bearded face had taken on an unhealthy pallor. At times he had difficulty breathing. He was only forty-nine, and until this year his health had always been exceptionally good, his physical strength phenomenal. But some said he would not survive this abrupt collapse, and there were murmurs of concern about the succession, for it was generally assumed that Nicky, with his clear, kind eyes and gentle manner, his slight frame and sensitive mien, would be shoved roughly aside by his domineering uncles once the tsar was dead, and there would be a struggle for power.

Frightened and ill-equipped to cope with the crisis, Nicky asked for permission to bring Alix to Livadia, and his parents agreed. He missed her: he needed her support to steady him. Though the doctors did not say that his father was dying, Nicky had only to look at him to sense that, if he did not die, he would at least be incapacitated, and for a long time; already the government papers sent in a steady stream to Livadia from Petersburg were being given to Nicky to read and sign, and he was finding this work a great strain.

He had always feared and dreaded the day when he would become tsar, and taken comfort from his father's relatively young age and robust health.[1] To be sure, there was the ever-present danger that Alexander might be assassinated, as his father had been, and attempts on his life had been made. But Nicky, ever the fatalist, was not overly concerned about that, and had always made the assumption that he would not have to take on the burden of the throne himself for a very long time to come.

Now, though, watching his dearly loved father, that Hercules who had once been able to tie an iron poker into knots, who could bend a solid silver rouble with his thumb, slip daily more and more into enfeeblement, Nicky was forced to confront the probability that the terrifying task of rulership would soon become his.

If Alexander III were to die before he was fifty, he would indeed be an anomaly, but then he had always been an anomaly, not only in the strength and girth of his outsize body but in his manner of living. He looked, many thought, like a very large Russian peasant, and within his palaces he lived in peasant style, simply and without formality, wearing whenever possible the baggy trousers, soft bloused shirt and sheepskin jacket of a Russian villager. He wore his clothes, in fact, until they tore at the seams, and then he asked his valet to patch them.

All his life Nicky had watched his father working at his big desk, his dog at his feet, tall stacks of papers before him. He had worked doggedly, frequently angrily, scribbling insults to his ministers ('Fools! Idiots!') in the margins of the documents he signed, muttering to himself about the perfidy of the European states and condemning Queen Victoria in particular as a 'nasty, interfering old woman'.[2] He had made the task of rulership seem gruelling and distasteful – not an honour and a privilege to be cherished but a cross of martyrdom, to be carried while in a mood of constant irritation. And Nicky was well aware that his father would have preferred to pass on that cross, that obligation, to his favourite son Michael, and not to Nicky himself, who had the misfortune to be the firstborn. Michael was still an adolescent, but in the tsar's opinion he alone, of the three imperial brothers, displayed the self-confident, frank manner of one born to rule; Nicky was too soft and self-effacing, too easily swayed by others, and the third son Georgy, clever but shallow, lacked the seriousness to take on the imperial authority.

Alix received Nicky's telegram at Wolfsgarten, telling her of the tsar's grave illness and asking her to come to the Crimea, and immediately she made plans to join her fiancé. She knew he would be in anguish, worrying about his father and grieving at his suffering and at the same time dreading the looming probability of having to step into his shoes. He was bound to need her comfort, reassurance and strength, and she had to be with him.

She had worries of her own just then, for she had discovered, once she returned to Hesse from England, that a rift had developed between Ernie and his wife. Ducky was pregnant, miserable and full of grievances. She poured out those grievances to Alix – 'in her open way she speaks about everything', Alix told Nicky in a letter, implying that Ducky's revelations concerned her intimate life with Ernie. Alix took pride in her own sophistication, in her knowing things 'others don't till they are grown up and married'.[3] She could listen without being shocked, and she could understand. But the rift, though not entirely unexpected, was upsetting. Ernie had tried, against his nature, to make a conventional marriage, and the effort was failing. There would be an heir to inherit his grand ducal throne, but if Ducky continued to be outspoken, there would also be a scandal.

Alix set out from Wolfsgarten, accompanied by Gretchen von Fabrice, Baroness Grancy, and her sister Victoria, who travelled with her party as far as Warsaw. From there the others went on alone, across the Ukraine, the air growing warmer as they made their way southwards.[4] Frosty mornings gave way to mists and fog as their train carried them past rain-soaked fields from which the grain had been harvested, only the pale stubble remaining. For days they journeyed on through the flat plains, with longer and longer stretches of track between towns and villages. Cut off from word of what was happening in Livadia, Alix must have worried over what she would find when she arrived.

At Warsaw Ella joined Alix and her party, and brought news. The tsar was still alive, but his condition was worsening. Bertie had been sent for from England, and would make the journey as soon as he could. Meanwhile, no one was in charge at Livadia, and all was in disorder.

When Nicky came to meet Alix, Ella and the others at the mountain town of Simferopol he looked stricken. It was all too much for him, having to fend off his father's ministers with their contradictory advice and suggestions and to struggle to keep his equilibrium while the loud-voiced Uncle Vladimir and the strong-willed, sinister Uncle Serge tried to influence, if not control, his every move. His mother was beside herself with anxiety. The doctors, all but helpless, offered neither comfort nor hope. And Nicky himself, torn between attending to his father's governmental affairs and sitting by his bedside, listening to his increasingly shallow breathing, watching his vitality ebb, was tense and miserable.

The long slow drive from Simferopol to the southern coast of the Crimea wound through mountain passes, along swift rivers and in among green hills. Thick oak forests led to a high, twisting, boulder-strewn pass, then to a plateau beyond which the land sloped away towards the broad bay. On high cliffs overlooking the brilliant expanse of dark blue sea were perched an array of handsome large whitewashed villas set in gardens blooming with oleander, wisteria and abundant roses. Flowering vines covered the walls, even in October, and the warm sun shone down on green lawns and groves of cypress, and left a golden wake across the deep blue of the water. The air was full of the scent of grapes and there were vineyards and orchards set in among the mansions, giving the entire panorama a lush Mediterranean atmosphere.

When Alix and Nicky drove up to the imperial mansion, they were given a formal welcome. With old-fashioned politeness Tsar Alexander had insisted on dressing up in uniform to meet his future daughter-in-law, though the effort left him prostrate afterwards. It was all he could do to recline on a sofa brought out onto a balcony, his huge bulk swathed in a blanket despite the balmy weather, his oxygen tank by his side. He was sleeping much of the time during the day, waking fitfully at night and suffering severe nosebleeds and attacks of nausea. Every new attack brought his children, Minnie, and all the doctors to his bedside, while the other relatives, ministers and servants congregated nearby, listening and waiting for the latest medical pronouncement. In the intervals between crises the family went into the chapel to pray, while the court officials huddled in panic-ridden clusters and the servants, sorrowful and lost, wandered aimlessly from room to room, many with tears running down their cheeks.

Nicky took refuge from all the strain and chaos in Alix's room, where she sat, outwardly composed, and embroidered a chalice cover to be used in the rite when she joined the Orthodox church. They prayed together, and he told her of his difficulties. They went for walks and drives together, though with each passing day the tsar's crises seemed to come more often and Nicky could not afford to be away for long.

'A sad and painful day!' Nicky wrote in his diary a week after Alix's arrival. 'Dear Papa did not sleep at all and felt so bad in the morning that they woke us and called us upstairs. What an ordeal it is.'[5] No one was in charge, not the doctors, not Nicky, not even Uncle Vladimir, whose bluster added to all the agitation.

'Darling boysy,' Alix wrote in Nicky's diary, 'me loves you, oh so very tenderly and deeply. Be firm and make the doctors, Leyden or the others, come alone to you everyday and tell you how they find him. Don't let others be put first and you left out.' She urged him to 'show his own mind' and not let others forget who he was – the heir to the throne.[6]

It was now clear that Nicky was only days, perhaps hours, away from succeeding his father. Yet the closer he came to entering his inheritance, the weaker and less assertive he grew. Only in Alix's presence could he find relief from the emotional turmoil that ate away at him, and that was apparent to all who saw him. The tsar was dying, the tsarevich was sinking under the weight of his fear and suffering. The entire edifice of settled life seemed to be tottering, and chaos loomed.

Finally, on November 1, the long ordeal ended. 'My God, my God, what a day,' Nicky recorded. 'The Lord has summoned our adored, dear, deeply beloved Papa to Him. My head is spinning, I don't want to believe it – the awful reality seems so unjust.' After a traumatic morning during which the exhausted patient was continually given oxygen, he mustered the energy to take communion, then repeated a short prayer and kissed his wife. Soon afterwards, with a priest holding his head and his sons and daughter nearby, he went into convulsions and died.

'It was the death of a saint!' Nicky wrote. 'Lord, help us in these terrible days!' Now the full weight of all he faced seemed to fall on Nicky, as he wept for his father, for himself, for the unknown future. According to his brother-in-law Sandro, Nicky 'could not collect his thoughts'. He took Sandro to his room and collapsed in grief, his raw suffering painful to see.

'What am I going to do?' he cried out. 'What is going to happen to me, to you, to Xenia, to Alix, to mother, to all of Russia? I am not prepared to be a tsar. I never wanted to become one. I know nothing of the business of ruling. I have no idea of even how to talk to the ministers. Will you help me, Sandro?'[7]

Help was needed, and immediately, for the funeral arrangements had to be made, the world had to be told of the passing of the tsar, the ministers reassured and guided. Nicky's first actions as tsar would set the tone for his reign. He had to make decisions, delegate responsibilities, oversee arrangements, all the while assuming the role of patriarch of the large and unruly Romanov family.

He did none of this. Hours passed, and the chaos in the house mounted. Frightened servants cowered in dread, or ran from room to room, unable to carry out their duties. No one was in charge.

Throughout the huge sprawling mansion there was a feeling of emptiness and loss, of a world coming to an end. By his death Alexander Mirotworetz, Creator of Peace, had become the destroyer of order and calm, the sower of desolation. Suddenly there was no order, no solid ground, all was unravelling.

As if to underscore the emotional devastation the weather abruptly changed. The air turned cold, and a gale blew up from the sea, churning the bay into frothy waves and blowing fiercely along the flower-covered balconies and whitewashed terraces of the imperial mansion. The wind tore at the gardens, lashed the branches of the trees and moaned under the eaves, its sonorous, eerie voice an echo of the bewildered sadness and disorientation felt by the entire household.

It was all Nicky could do, late that night, to drag himself through the Prayers for the Dead, held in the death-room by the clergy. 'I felt as if I were dead also,' he recorded.[8] It was all he could do to hold himself together, buoyed up by Alix, whose constant reassurances and promises of help made the terrible pain he felt bearable – but only just. He could not comfort his mother, whose grief all but incapacitated her, or reach out to his sisters and brothers in their sorrow. Save for Alix's nurture, he was alone. And he was now Tsar Nicholas II, Emperor of Russia.

He was now the tsar – yet his uncles, feuding with the agitated imperial ministers, ignored him in the days after Alexander III's death. Vladimir and Serge bullied and commanded, trying to organize the funeral cortege. A temporary casket had to be made, the imperial train ordered. Officials in Petersburg had to be given detailed instructions about the funeral so that they could make preparations. The body could not be transported over the mountains, it would have to go by sea to Sebastopol. The Black Sea Fleet had to be contacted, with orders to despatch a vessel to Livadia at once. So much had to be done, and so quickly.

Meanwhile the imperatives of nature had begun to assert themselves. The corpse stank horribly and had to be carried by Nicky and his uncles out of the house and into 'a little corner' where it could be embalmed. As if making a grotesque comment on the dark absurdity of all that was occurring, the face of the dead tsar, which was turning black with corruption, appeared to be smiling, as if it were about to laugh.[9]

On the second day after the tsar's death Bertie arrived from England, and under the influence of his imposing yet warm and fatherly presence, things began to right themselves. The blustering uncles backed off, the ministers, ashamed to reveal their confusion and incompetence before the heir to the English throne, began to find their focus again. Gradually the household began to return to normal; meals were served, beds made, horses fed and watered, provisions bought. Quickly perceiving that Nicky was unable to make the necessary arrangements for his father's transport and burial, Bertie himself undertook to organize the funeral, and to lead the family on their long sad trek to Petersburg where their patriarch would be laid to rest.

Alix, meanwhile, observed all that was going on and tried her best to remain tactfully uninvolved, while lending her sympathy and strength to her fiancé. Everything was happening too fast, there was no time to adjust to the sudden changes. Nicky was urging her to marry him immediately, in a quiet private ceremony in the Livadia mansion, with only the immediate family present. Uncle Vladimir and Uncle Serge objected: such a wedding was not suitable for a tsar of Russia, they said, the tsar had to be married in Petersburg, with appropriate grandeur and solemnity, and in the presence of the entire court.

The argument went back and forth, with the weak, anguished Minnie supporting Nicky and Alix attempting to avoid taking sides. To marry in a season of mourning, with a sombre trousseau and with the wedding guests wearing black, was far from what she had been expecting only a few weeks earlier. To have her wedding be the occasion of family conflict was equally unforeseen – and dismaying. She had to feel her way through the labyrinth of conflicting loyalties, trying not to give offence, aware that sharp criticism, even ostracism, by other family members was the risk she ran.

She observed that Sandro, Xenia's husband, was treated with coldness by the rest of the family. Minnie in particular disliked him, and had done so ever since his wedding to Xenia a few months earlier. He had given offence by making demands, making himself and his needs conspicuous. He had not been able to ease himself gracefully, self-effacingly, into the family community. He was being punished, silently but unmistakably. The feeling against him was strong and unpleasant.[10]

The last thing Alix wanted was to trigger the same reaction among those who were about to become her in-laws. She made an effort to hold herself aloof from the struggles and conflicts – only to be criticized, behind her back, for her hauteur.[11]

The effort to be both helpful and self-effacing cost Alix a good deal, for her leg pains had returned and she was suffering. Another young woman, in pain and surrounded by turmoil, suddenly finding herself on the threshold of marriage to a weak, hesitant ruler who seemed incapable of fulfilling his responsibilities might have had second thoughts and fled. But Alix stood firm. Nicky's weakness, which she saw only too clearly, made her strength all the more necessary. Or, rather, she would be his strength. Where he faltered, she would step into the breach. She had given him her pledge. To love him, to help him was her sacred duty. She would follow him into the maw of hell itself.

If Alix pondered, as the funeral journey got under way, what the future was likely to hold for her as wife of the new tsar, she seems to have kept her thoughts to herself. To voice misgivings would after all have been disloyal. But she must have perceived, in that November of 1894, the depths of her fiancé's ineffectuality, and she must have wondered how, if he was unable even to manage the arrangements for his father's funeral, he would be able to govern Russia.

The imperial train carrying the late tsar's body made the journey from Sebastopol to Petersburg in slow stages, stopping often so that prayers could be repeated and services held. In Moscow, the emperor's remains were on view for three days, while his mourning subjects came to pay their respects. Then it was on to Petersburg for the final lying in state in the cathedral in the Peter and Paul Fortress.

There in the dim interior of the vast cathedral, amid the thousands of glowing candles, Alix knelt in her black crepe veil to repeat the service for the dead. Her legs were stiff and sore, her hands and face cold – for there was no heat in the draughty church, apart from that given off by the candles. The services went on for hours, and more than one worshipper, including Alix's waiting lady Gretchen von Fabrice, fainted. But Alix held on, moved by the dramatic rise and fall of voices in the choir, by the chanted prayers and the overpowering scent of incense.

She was a daughter of the Orthodox church now, she had made her formal profession of faith. She was one with Nicky in faith, as she would soon be one with him in marriage. In a week she would become his bride – the 'funeral bride', they were calling her in the streets of Petersburg.

The choir began the singing of the funeral dirge, 'Eternal Memory', and the imperial grenadiers took their places around the coffin. One by one, each member of the family filed past, bending over to kiss the black, wizened face of the dead tsar with its hint of a smile. Wincing, Alix limped along, placing her reverent kiss on the stinking, shrivelled cheek.

It was an unpleasant duty, kissing the corpse, but Russian custom required it of her. She was after all about to become tsarina, and she had to follow the traditions of her adopted country. Solemnly, dutifully, and with only a slight feeling of chill and pain, Alix stood holding Nicky's unsteady arm as the grenadiers slowly lowered the heavy coffin into its final resting place.

8

A soft blanket of new snow had cleansed Petersburg, covering every dirty cornice and grimy windowsill, every roof, turret and chimney with a thick layer of gleaming whiteness. Above the city the skies were dull grey, threatening more snow, and the air was very cold, but along the streets, and especially along Nevsky Prospekt, thousands of black-clad Petersburgers waited eagerly. For this was the new tsar's wedding day, and they looked forward to the spectacle that always accompanied such imperial occasions. By eleven o'clock the streets were choked with onlookers, and as each golden coach carrying wedding guests passed, making its slow way to the Winter Palace, the dark throng had to part to allow the horses to proceed.

All Petersburg was still in mourning for the late tsar, and many in the crowd, wanting a memento of his passing, had purchased a cheap reproduction of a painting commemorating his death. It showed the tall, broad-shouldered tsar, in uniform, ascending into heaven, borne aloft by four winged angels, his arm raised as if in a final salute to his people. Another angel bore his crown. His weeping widow clung to his ascending figure. The painting captured the prevailing mood, which was one of sorrow and desolation. Yet on this day the public grief was dispelled somewhat by the excitement of the wedding, and the gossip about the 'Funeral Bride', Tsarina Alexandra, the German princess who was rumoured to be beautiful and suspected, because of the known weakness of Tsar Nicholas, of being ambitious for power.

The grand salons of the Winter Palace too were abuzz with rumour, for most of the thousands of aristocrats and dignitaries gathering there had never seen the new tsarina and knew of her only through the bits of gossip they had heard. In the huge Hall of the Armorial Bearings, the women of Petersburg society had assembled, wearing traditional Russian caftans of heavy embroidered cloth and tall velvet headdresses with pearls and long white veils; they stood, uncomfortable in their finery, waiting for the bride and groom to pass through on their way to the wedding chamber. The Hall of the Field Marshals too was crowded with guests, Tartar merchants in long silk jackets vivid with colour, mayors and town councillors, journalists representing not only the Petersburg papers but the major papers of foreign capitals. The largest of the immense halls, the Hall of Nicholas I, was full of military officers, while the Concert Hall contained the leading officials of the imperial household, the Dames de Portrait or bedchamber women of the empress, and the maids of honour and ladies-in-waiting of the Dowager Empress and Empress Alexandra.

The new empress's Russian ladies were especially curious about her, and the chief waiting maid, Martha Mouchanow, wrote down her initial view of her new mistress.

'My first impression was that of a tall, slight girl, with straight long features, a classical profile, and a lovely figure,' she wrote. 'She had fair hair that shone like gold in the sun, whilst at times it appeared quite dark, according to the light which played upon it.'

'I remember thinking that I had never yet seen anyone more beautiful than this girl,' Mouchanow went on. 'The general impression she produced was that of a superb woman.' But the lovely face of the empress was flawed, Mouchanow thought, by the 'determined expression' of her mouth, set in a hard unpleasant line.[1]

The grim set of Alix's small mouth on her wedding day was a symptom of the strain she was under. She had kept her familiar German maids around her for as long as she could, but on her wedding day the Germans withdrew and were replaced by an entirely new staff of Russian personal servants, chosen by Minnie, and a new and very large household staff. The eight Russian waiting maids, themselves nervous, no doubt curious, and unaccustomed to the formality their German predecessors had observed, must have made Alix uncomfortable as they went about the task of helping her dress and prepare herself for her wedding.

'It was very difficult for the servants to attend to the many details accompanying a complicated toilette,' Mouchanow wrote, 'and to make decisions for an utter stranger.'[2] To Alix, of course, everything was strange: the enormous palace with its hundreds of outsize rooms, gilded walls and costly furnishings; the elaborate protocol of the imperial court; the lavishness of everything, from her extensive trousseau to the wedding gifts that filled several large rooms; even the Russian language, which she was learning but which was still largely foreign to her. She was nervous, isolated, in dread of committing some fatal faux pas that would put her forever at odds with her new household.

Alix had come to the palace by coach early in the morning from Serge's mansion, and had been escorted to the room set aside for the dressing of imperial brides. Awaiting her there were her new Russian maids and all of her mother-in-law's waiting ladies, a keen-eyed, chilling reception line, all of the women outwardly deferential but inwardly full of sharp scrutiny. Under their exceptionally watchful eyes the tsarina had to make her complicated toilette, putting on her lacy undergarments, her court dress of silver tissue with its ermine-trimmed, eight-foot-long train, her long diamond earrings and splendid necklace, finally her shining mantle of cloth of gold.

Every garment, every jewel was handed to her with great solemnity on a tray or a red velvet cushion, a ceremonious silence prevailing. Around her was displayed the venerable gold toilette service that had belonged to the Empress Anna, and that had been used by every subsequent empress and grand duchess. It was as if her every gesture, her every movement was charged with symbolic significance.

One of the imperial dressers approached Minnie with the dazzling, diamond-studded crown on its velvet cushion. By custom the dowager empress placed the crown on the new empress's head at the climax of the garbing ceremony, then the hairdresser arranged the coiffure and fixed the bridal veil in place.

But when it was time for the hairdresser to come forward, he could not be found. The waiting maids sent the imperial footmen and valets to look for him. After a delay they reported that he was nowhere in the palace. Now a susurration arose in the garbing room, a treble murmuring. The bride could not go to her wedding without her crown and veil, and no one but the hairdresser could fasten them on properly. What would happen? Would there be no wedding?

The women began circling Alix, who was seated before the huge gold-framed mirror, waiting for the final touches to be added to her coiffure. She said little, she maintained an almost unnatural calm. More tense minutes passed. The wedding was to begin at eleven-thirty, but the time came and was gone. No one seemed to know what to do, or how to find the one man without whom the bride could not be wedded to her groom.

Out in the grand salons, the guests and dignitaries began to fidget and to wonder what was happening. Watches were consulted, eyebrows raised. Had there been a sudden change of plan? Was it the new empress who was keeping so many thousands waiting, and all because of some whim?

Mouchanow watched her new mistress during the tense hour that ensued. Alix continued to sit unmoving before her mirror, 'saying hardly a word, but with tears in her eyes which, however, she bravely tried to conceal'. Mortified, increasingly irritated, on edge, she waited in the greatest uneasiness for the impasse to resolve itself. The others, trying and failing to attract her attention, interpreted her marmoreal calm as hauteur, and felt themselves silently chastised. The gulf between mistress and servants widened, and began to be corroded by resentment.

Minnie, well-meaning but ineffectual, fluttered anxiously about with the others, unable to offer Alix any reassurance. There was no bond between the two women, though Alix found her future mother-in-law to be 'sweet and patient'. 'She touches one with her gentleness,' Alix wrote in a letter to one of her sisters.[3] But Minnie was still struggling with her great grief at the loss of her husband, and was despondent at losing two of her children, first Xenia and now Nicky, to marriage within a few months of one another. After years of opposition, Minnie had reconciled herself to having Alix as a daughter-in-law. But her long opposition would never be forgotten by either woman, and the most that could be hoped for between them was civility and a wary affection. Minnie was no help to Alix now.

At last, to Alix's enormous relief, the door of the room opened and the hairdresser, overheated and excited, rushed in. He had been refused entrance to the palace by the police, as it turned out, and it had taken him an hour to straighten out the confusion. Swiftly he pinned Alix's diadem in place, and her long lace wedding veil. Now the wedding procession could begin.

At twelve-thirty, the doors of the Concert Hall were thrown open and the first of a long line of servants in scarlet livery made their slow way through the first of the grand salons, traversing a narrow pathway marked out by guards of honour with sabres drawn. At the same moment the great guns of the Peter and Paul Fortress across the river began firing, each renewed burst so loud that it seemed as if the windows of the hall would shatter. One hundred and fifty gentlemen of the chamber marched past the assembled notables, then came Prince Trubetskoy, marshal of the court, with his gold staff seven feet high.

Behind the marshal walked Minnie, her pale face nearly as white as her dress, on the arm of her father the king of Denmark. Behind them came Nicky, in the crimson tunic and fur-lined cloak of a colonel in the Life Guard Hussar regiment. On his arm walked Alix, moving, an observer thought, 'quite simply and with great dignity', a magnificent vision in her silver gown and glittering diamonds, her shimmering mantle, held by four chamberlains, flowing out behind her like a river of gold.

'She looked the perfection of what one would imagine an Empress of Russia . . . would be,' the English visitor Lord Carrington thought.[4] As the imperials passed all the men bowed low, the women dipped in a curtsy, silks and satins rustling, ceremonial swords rattling. All the thousands of eyes were on the bride – and Alix felt the force of their gaze – but after appraising her, all eyes seemed to turn to Minnie.

For it was the Dowager Empress, not the bride, who was the true centre of attention that day. Everyone at court knew that it was her birthday – a very sad birthday because of her bereavement. All their sympathies were directed towards Minnie, for she had made herself beloved and the affections of the courtiers, built up over many years, were intensified by recent events. She was given the first position in the procession, ahead of her son and his wife-to-be, she was deferred to, admired – for she was still, at forty-seven, in her prime, and was very pretty – and accorded a great degree of sympathy. It was clear to all that she was suffering that day; Nicky's relative Constantine, his father's cousin, known in the family as 'K.R.', wrote in his diary that Minnie looked frailer than usual, 'like a victim being led to the slaughter'.[5]

It was not in Alix's nature to be envious of Minnie's pre-eminence, and besides, her own happiness at the prospect of marrying Nicky overshadowed any prickings of envy she might have been tempted to feel. Her good sense told her, however, that there was a potential danger to her caused by the courtiers' strong allegiance to her mother-in-law; it would be easy for them to perceive her, Alix, as an interloper, an outsider bent on supplanting the Dowager Empress, vying with her for power and influence. Should that perception become widespread, it would lead to factionalism, and to a poisonous prejudice against her, reinforcing the natural prejudice felt by Russians against all foreigners. So it must have been with some trepidation that Alix took note of the primary attention accorded to Minnie, and the primary place she was given in the wedding procession.

Once the ceremony began, however, the focus shifted back to the bridal pair, and to the wedding liturgy itself. Bride and groom held lighted tapers in their hands, the priest swung the gilded censer, filling the chapel with pungent incense. The rings were exchanged, the vows were repeated. 'The servant of God, Nicholas, betroths himself to the servant of God, Alexandra,' the priest announced, and the attendants held crowns over the heads of the bride and groom while they walked three times around the lectern – Alexandra's attendants having difficulty keeping her long train from upsetting the candelabra and starting a fire. At last it was over, and the newly married pair

kissed the icons and turned to accept the blessings and congratulations of their guests.

Outside the palace, the morning's layer of soft white snow had
turned to black slush beneath the feet of the huge crowd that continued to wait patiently yet in mounting excitement for the tsar and
tsarina to reappear in their carriage. Pressing in on the palace gates,
squeezed in among buildings, jammed tightly together along the
roadway, the people kept arriving, all wanting a glimpse of the newly
married imperial couple.

More and more of them arrived, until Nevsky Prospekt was a
solid mass of bodies in dark clothing. From the windows above the
street, where the city's more affluent citizens watched the spectacle,
the street appeared clogged, and the small number of mounted police,
who here and there attempted to invade the wall of packed onlookers,
found the wall to be impenetrable.

The overcast afternoon had given way to dim twilight by the time
the palace gates were opened and the imperial carriage, accompanied
by a military escort, attempted to pass through. Cheering and shouting, the waiting Petersburgers greeted Nicky and Alix enthusiastically, pressing in around their carriage in a swarm, making it all
but impossible for the coachman to force the horses forward.

Inch by inch, with the deafening shouts and exclamations of
thousands of voices on all sides, the carriage made its way towards
Kazan Cathedral, where after what seemed an eternity Nicky and
Alix got out and, under guard, entered the church to kiss the revered
icon of the Mother of God. But when with difficulty they got back
into the vehicle, they could not proceed. The military escort had not
been able to hold back the surging crowd. Mobbed on all sides, the
coach was as if enmired in the morass of people, and the tsar and
tsarina, clinging to one another, must have felt fearful.

Where were the police? Why didn't they intervene to force the
crowds back? Why had there been no plan, no precautions taken to
safeguard the imperial coach?

'Little Father, Little Father,' the people cried, nearly swamping
the delicate carriage with its painted panels and intricately carved

woodwork. Those closest to the windows peered in, and were rewarded with a glimpse of Nicky in his crimson uniform and Alix in her diamonds, her beautiful features firmly set, a look of terror in her eyes.

At length, after much angry shouting, the coachman laying about him with his whip, a narrow gap appeared in the sea of wildly waving hands and clustered bodies. Gradually the coach began to move, foot by slow foot, along the broad avenue, until it turned into the courtyard of the Anitchkov Palace – Minnie's palace. Servants were waiting with lit torches to welcome the bride and groom and lead them to their new home, a small suite of apartments on the ground floor.

Minnie too was waiting, and presented her son and daughter-in-law with the traditional Russian gifts of bread and salt.

The long, trying day was nearly over. Nicky and Alix, having divested themselves of their finery, sat before the fire in their little sitting room and began to answer the hundreds of telegrams that had arrived for them.

Alix had a terrible headache, brought on by the frightening carriage ride, the tense ordeal of the robing ceremony, the strain of the wedding itself. 'We dined at eight o'clock and collapsed into bed early,' Nicky wrote in his diary.[6] They belonged to each other now, they could never again be parted. Clasped in each other's arms, they forgot all else, even the clamour of the crowd that went on, growing louder and more raucous, a harsh charivari, until the early hours of the morning.

9

In the early 1890s, the years just prior to the wedding of Nicholas II and Alexandra, Russia suffered a series of disastrous famines. In province after province, the crops withered and died before they could be harvested, cattle died, what scant reserves of food there were were soon used up and, in village after village, starvation resulted. The peasants were hardy and stoic; they took a long time to die. They grew thin, and watched their children grow thin and sad-eyed. Gradually what vitality they had ebbed; they no longer had the strength to complain, to seek aid, even to pray. They buried their children, then sat down and waited for the end.

Some help arrived. Local charity, organized by the popularly elected assemblies, the zemstvos, allowed some villages to survive. Here and there a wealthy landowner bought food abroad and imported it to distribute among the emaciated villagers. But these efforts were insignificant in the face of the monumental want that swept region after region, causing many to say that God was angry with his people, that they were being chastised for their sins.

The terrible ongoing famine was all the more overwhelming in that it was followed by devastating outbreaks of cholera and typhus, in which hundreds of thousands of survivors of the famine perished. A curse lay upon Russia, it was said – and whether it was the curse of divine displeasure, or climatic change, or, as many said, the curse of the tsar's ministers interfering in people's lives, it was ruinous, and it was causing a great wave of angry discontent.

Certainly those in the population educated enough and aware enough to comprehend the force and range of recent government policies believed those policies to be punitive and misguided, marked by indifference to the plight of peasants and large landowners alike. The tsar's Finance Minister, Sergei Witte, and his predecessor Ivan Vyshnegradsky, had forced the peasants to sell their grain at such low prices that they took large losses, and were driven deeper into poverty; at the same time the ministers made it much more difficult, through the imposition of high tariffs, for landowners small and large to buy machinery and fertilizer from Europe, without which they could not improve their yields and raise their incomes. Most critics of the finance ministers could not comprehend the mounting pressures the ministers themselves were under: the fluctuations of the global economy, the panic in the West over dwindling gold reserves and the oversupply of wheat and rye and barley worldwide that led prices to fall drastically and threatened the stability of the entire monetary system. They only knew that the immediate effect of the harsh policies was to cause widespread misery.

And there was something else askew in the economy, another cause of misery that ought to have been, educated observers felt, a cause of prosperity and improvement in the lot of the poor. Russia was rapidly becoming industrialized. Vast fortunes were being made as steel poured from new plants, coal was drawn in unprecedented amounts from newly worked mines, oil flowed from new wells. The country contained great wealth in oil and mineral deposits, enough wealth, perhaps, to abolish poverty altogether, provided the revenues were shared. But of course they were not being shared; rather, foreign investors and a small group of Russian speculators were taking all the profits – and exploiting the labourers from whose toil the profits arose.

Over the course of a single generation, from the period after the end of the Crimean War to the accession of Nicholas II, hundreds of new factories had been built in Moscow and Petersburg. The number of factory workers had more than doubled. And with the growth of the factories had come an increase in suffering, for the workers, whose days averaged from fourteen to seventeen hours, were paid very little and housed in overcrowded, unheated slums full of the stench of rotting rubbish and open sewers.

The contrast between the luxury of the imperial court and the ragged populace of the capital was glaring. Visitors inevitably commented on it. Alix's aunt Victoria, Dowager Empress of Germany, saw Russia as 'another world', with 'something so squalid and sad, suggesting poverty and loneliness, about the landscape and population' and extremes of wealth and poverty far more exaggerated than in any western European country.[1] The Romanovs in their palaces possessed untold millions of roubles, and spent them lavishly, while the factory workers in the districts across the river struggled to survive on ten roubles a month. On the streets of Petersburg, and in the provincial towns, the sharply defined economic gradations of society were evident, as was the very high proportion of peasants; for every uniformed military officer or dark-suited civil servant one saw, there were dozens of peasants, looking like shaggy beasts in their long locks and woolly sheepskin coats, strips of dirty cloth wrapped around their feet and bark sandals worn in place of shoes. The peasants, and the city workers who had migrated from the countryside in search of jobs, constituted the great majority of the population, and were bearing the brunt of Russia's distress.

It had been only thirty-three years since the peasants – formerly serfs legally bound to the land, subject to being bought and sold by their masters – had been granted their freedom by Nicholas's grandfather Alexander II. The 'Tsar-Liberator', as he was known, had dissolved the bonds of serfdom and decreed that all former serfs were free men, able to own land themselves and carry on business enterprises, beholden only to the other members of their village communities.

The euphoria that followed emancipation had been short-lived, however, for the tsar himself, ambivalent about the wisdom of granting freedom to the uneducated, unruly, potentially disorderly majority of his subjects, had as it were hobbled their liberty by hedging it in with restrictions and limitations. Unlike other free men, the former serfs had to carry passports and could not go where they liked, when they liked; they were judged in special courts, subject to special taxes. And if one of them defaulted on a tax obligation, the others in his community were obligated to make up for the shortfall. These were onerous restrictions, made more onerous by the alarming fall in peasant prosperity that followed emancipation. Everywhere the former serfs eagerly bought land – only to discover that, having taken on the burden of a heavy mortgage payable to the government, the amount of land they could own was much smaller than the amount they had farmed as serfs. They had acquired personal liberty, and had become property owners, but at the price of an ever-deepening poverty.

It was a bewildering dilemma, this bitter outcome of emancipation. How, the peasants asked themselves, could their Little Father the Tsar allow his children to undergo such harsh privation? Surely he wanted what was best for them. Surely he wished to aid them – yet when the famine came, it was their own organizations, the zemstvos, which had come to their aid, not the tsar.

Thus as the 1890s opened, the traditional reverence for the tsar – a reverence still overwhelmingly present, almost as automatic as a reflex – was being diluted, even reversed, by the restless, angry mood born of catastrophe. Most of the time, among most of the people, as at the imperial wedding in Petersburg, the reverential, even worshipful attitude was uppermost. ('Their majesties are to people here what the sun is to our world,' an American visitor to Russia wrote in 1895, addressing an American correspondent. 'I do not expect you to understand it, it must be seen and felt.'[2]) But increasingly often the worshipful reaction gave way to hostility, and once again, as in the era of Nicky's grandfather Alexander II, revolutionary groups began to expand in numbers and influence and political radicals, who advocated the overthrow of the tsar's government, found among factory workers a receptive audience for their views.

If, indeed, a curse lay upon Russia, if the twin scourges of famine and disease were flaying the countryside and causing unprecedented anguish and upheaval, one would not know it from reading the new tsar's diaries, which were full of references to long walks and bicycle rides around the palace garden, reading (he liked to read historical journals and memoirs; early in his reign Nicky recorded enjoying 'a new French book about Napoleon's time on the island of St Helena' and Countess Golovin's 'interesting memoirs for the time of Catherine the Great'[3]), and above all, spending time with his new wife.

'It's a shame work takes up such a lot of time that I would so much like to spend alone with her,' Nicky wrote candidly. Nothing pleased him more than having a 'day of rest', with no reports to read and no audiences to hold.[4] Then he could spend a quiet, idle afternoon with Alix, reading while she did her embroidery, hanging pictures, pushing her in her wheeled chair when she was suffering sciatic pain and could not get out on her own.

If Nicky's subjects were in anguish, that anguish was far away, contained in the dry words of a ministerial report on agricultural conditions or a few paragraphs in a newspaper article on an outbreak of cholera. Apart from visitors to the palace or casual encounters with servants, Nicky rarely saw his people at all, other than on state occasions. Once, in the early weeks of his reign, he left the Anitchkov Palace unescorted one afternoon, and went out along Nevsky Prospekt. He strolled past the shops, looking at the window displays, attracting no more attention than would any other good-looking young man in military uniform. He had not gone far, however, when a passing carriage halted and an older man – the prefect of Petersburg, General Von Val – got out and approached him.

'This is not possible, Your Highness,' the general said.

The tsar protested that he was perfectly safe, that no one had bothered him.

'It is not possible, Your Highness,' the general repeated, truly concerned. 'I pray you to return to the palace.'

By now a small crowd had begun to gather, and someone recognized the tsar. Immediately there were shouts of 'Hurrah!' and gestures of reverence. Soon, Nicky could tell, there would be pandemonium. Reluctantly he allowed himself to be taken back to the palace in the general's carriage.

Once there, Minnie scolded him for risking his life in such a dangerous fashion. Didn't he realize that the entire future of Russia was on his shoulders? Why, he didn't even have a son yet – if he were to be killed, the throne would pass to his brother Georgy, and Georgy was ill. What had he been thinking of? Or, rather, why had he not been thinking at all?

Minnie's reprimand had its effect, and the tsar did not go out alone again. In this, as in many other areas of his life, Nicky looked to his mother to guide him. It was noted that he sometimes interrupted the reports of his ministers and asked them to wait while he consulted with his mother. His dependence on her, along with his passivity and his shyness, were universally perceived. He never stood up for himself or asserted his own views.

'He did not like to argue,' one observer wrote, 'partly through a lack of self-confidence, and partly through a fear that he might be proved wrong or that others would perceive the error of his opinions. He realized that he was incapable of defending his own point of view, and found the idea of this quite demeaning.'[5]

Paralyzed with indecision, withdrawn and insecure, Nicky deferred to his strong-willed mother, and in fact her overweening influence was apparent in every aspect of Nicky's life – and Alix's too – in the early weeks and months of the new reign. The dowager empress had decided where the newlyweds would live, how their tiny suite of rooms would be furnished, and what servants would wait on them there. They dined with her at every meal, obtained her permission before going anywhere or seeing anyone. Because they had so few rooms of their own, Alix had to borrow her mother-in-law's sitting-room to receive her own guests, which led to increased strain, for Minnie and Alix were uncomfortable in each other's presence. Alix, diffident and deferential at first, chafed under the restrictions placed on her, while Minnie, still grieving and deeply disturbed over the transfer of power from her husband to her ineffectual son, tried to control her son and daughter-in-law's lives to an inordinate degree.

That the six cramped, shabbily decorated rooms assigned to them in the Anitchkov Palace – rooms Nicky had once shared, as a boy, with his brother Georgy – were inadequate was abundantly clear, yet Nicky did not demand larger ones. It did not seem to him important enough to argue about that there was no space for Alix's clothes, that the rooms were badly ventilated and cold, or that as tsar, he deserved the finest suite of apartments in the palace, not the meanest.

Coping as best she could with the overall situation, Alix went along with her husband's attitude at first. But before long she discovered that an insidious intrigue was going on around her, and this eventually forced her to change her stance.

The servants, she soon discovered, were reporting everything that she did and said to Minnie – everything from her preferences in food and dress to her casual remarks to the misbehaviour of her little terrier dog to her bathroom and boudoir habits. She had no privacy, and an attempt was clearly being made to rob her of her dignity.

She reacted. She began to dress up, to garb herself 'with great magnificence', as her principal waiting maid Martha Mouchanow remembered, from early morning until late at night. Disregarding the designs her court dressmakers proposed, she sketched gowns of her own design, ornate, elaborate ones, in sharp contrast to the simpler tailored gowns her mother-in-law favoured. If she dressed like an empress, Alix seems to have reasoned, she would be treated with respect.

But the tactic achieved the opposite result. The ill-judged opulence in dress led to much smothered laughter, and unflattering comparisons between Alix and the undeniably more elegant, more simply dressed Dowager Empress. The dressmakers fumed, the servants sneered and complained to Minnie that Alix overworked them by asking them to bring out three or four different gowns, complete with hat, gloves, shoes, stockings and other accessories, each time she changed her clothes during the day so that she could choose from among them.[6]

The complaints about Alix's fussiness reached Minnie, and she chastised Alix, adding, with a hint of snobbery, that 'when she [Alix] was at Darmstadt she would not have dared to display such a capricious temper'.[7] The reference to her lower status and relatively modest upbringing wounded and offended Alix, who soon found herself barraged with criticisms.

The whispering campaign on the part of the servants had only been the start of a much wider assault of censure that spread within the imperial family and among the courtiers. The empress was said to be capricious, extravagant, always avid for new gowns and especially new furs. Her bills from the Paris couturiers Worth and Paquin were said to be enormous – though in fact they were far smaller than Minnie's – and Aunt Miechen dismissed Alix's taste as that of a parvenue, unused to having costly things and shamelessly eager to acquire and flaunt them.[8] And to an extent, Aunt Miechen was right.

But the imputation of extravagance was only one of many reproaches. If the servants reported that the empress had a headache, and appeared pale, the family said it was because she was upset over something Minnie had said or done. If she smiled, she was assumed to be mocking others in the family. If she frowned, she was being disagreeable. If she was merely thoughtful, she was said to be angry. If she ordered English-style bacon for breakfast, she was said to be expressing scorn for Russian food. If her terrier snapped at the heels of a member of the family, Alix, and not the dog, was blamed.

All but smothered under the avalanche of gratuitous opprobrium, Alix took a stand against it. She persuaded Nicky to take her away to Tsarskoe Selo for a week. While there, temporarily out of Minnie's control and removed, at least a little, from the relentless condemnation of the immediate family, she stiffened her backbone and armoured herself, inwardly, to face the assaults. When she and Nicky returned from those few days away, Mouchanow noticed the change immediately. There was, she wrote, an alteration in the empress's 'manners and bearing, much of her former diffidence and shyness having disappeared'.[9] She began giving orders, making decisions on her own, acting without consulting Minnie first.

She summoned Mouchanow into her presence and instructed her that from now on, there would be new rules for the waiting maids to follow – rules which would protect her privacy and prohibit tale-bearing. When Mouchanow began to protest, Alix silenced her, telling her 'most peremptorily' to obey her instructions and not to offer any contradiction or advice.[10] Stunned, Mouchanow set about implementing the new rules, knowing that they would create hostility among the servants where before there had merely been disrespect and ridicule.

No doubt Alix too could predict the harshly disagreeable outcome of her new rules and firm attitude, but the former situation was untenable, and could not be endured. She had to assert herself – there was no other way, since Nicky would never stand up for her or defend her interests and peace of mind. He looked to her for constant support and reassurance, but she knew she could not look to him for protection in the maelstrom of court intrigue. To survive in its midst, she had to provide her own defence.

Meanwhile Nicky, doing his best to meet his responsibilities as tsar, was suffering from what he called 'terrible emotions', knowing that he had soon to appear before a deputation of his subjects and make a brief speech. His natural diffidence made such an appearance a torment to him. He would have to enter a crowded hall, mount a dais, receive the worshipful greeting of those present, and then make his remarks – nothing lengthy, only a few sentences. Still the dread of it ate away at him, making him withdrawn and nervous.

'The tsar does nothing. He is a sphinx,' one of the courtiers wrote, observing the new ruler. 'He has no kind of personality.' He was not often seen and, though affable enough on social occasions, he did not seek company outside of his family. Beneath his sphinx-like exterior Nicky was full of nervous dread; he smoked, he had a habit of stroking his beard in a preoccupied way, he sought release in physical activity. But the dread persisted.

Grieving for his father, he laboured under the burdensome certainty that he would never live up to his example. He would try, of course. He would honour Alexander III's memory by continuing his policies, by being diligent in controlling irresponsible tendencies towards self-government on the part of his people. He would keep ever sharp in his memory the terrible afternoon when he had watched his grandfather die, slain by revolutionary advocates of 'the people,' who were in truth enemies of the state. He would not listen to the views of any minister who discussed, even in the abstract, the idea that Russia might one day adopt a constitution, or that he himself might become a constitutional monarch, subject to legal restrictions.

Nicky turned for advice to the man who had tutored and advised his father, and who had tutored him: the lawyer Constantine Pobedonostsev, head of the Church Synod. Pobedonostsev held strong views on the need to preserve inviolate the old political order: the absolute autocracy of the tsar, the absolute subordination of his subjects, the rejection of harmful Western ideas about constitutional reform. Pobedonostsev gave Nicky some notes to refer to when he made his speech; fortified with these notes, which he concealed in his lambskin hat, Nicky prepared to meet the deputation.

In the Nicholas Hall, members of the nobility, representatives of the zemstvos and other city groups were waiting on January 17, 1895, to be addressed by Tsar Nicholas. Many in the audience were enthusiastic, eager for encouragement from the new young tsar. Their expectations reflected their circumstances; the harvest of 1894 had been good, the first adequate harvest in four years. It had helped to weaken their discontent and revive their hopes. Perhaps, after all, there was no curse on Russia, other than the curse of ill-advised ministers. And perhaps Tsar Nicholas, after reading the petitions they had sent him, would realize that his ministers were wrong and that he needed the advice of his people.

They had urged him, in their petitions, to listen to their collective voice, the voice of the people, and having heard it, to protect them against the evils of poverty and overtaxation, punitive tariffs and low grain prices, to broaden their rights, consult with them, entrust them with more of their own decisions. There must be no more vast famines, no more epidemics, no more needless misery.

Nicky took Pobedonostsev's notes out of his hat and prepared to speak to his subjects. Though he trembled inwardly, his voice was unwavering, even harsh as he delivered his short message.

'I shall maintain the principle of autocracy just as firmly and unflinchingly as it was preserved by my unforgettable dead father,' he told them. Any other course would be unthinkable. As for their hopes, their expectations that he might include them in any fashion in the work of government, these were nothing but 'senseless dreams'.

It was his own phrase, and a memorable one. 'Senseless dreams.' What Pobedonostsev had written in his notes was 'unrealizable dreams,' but Nicky, either because of his nervousness or because, on the spur of the moment, looking out over the sea of upturned faces, he saw fit to amend it, spoke the words 'senseless dreams' instead.[11]

The import of his words spread through the vast crowd, and almost in an instant their hopes were turned to dismay. The vision of a slow, orderly progression towards political reform that so many of them had imagined – increasing civil liberties, governmental efficiency, the advance towards constitutionalism – began to dissolve. Instead there came a vision of darkness, of monumental want, crushing misery, perpetuated indefinitely into the future. The tsar did not want to help them. He did not care that they were suffering. He was a man of iron, with a stone for a heart. There was indeed a curse on Russia, God's curse, and nothing anyone could do or say would ever take it away.

10

A satirical drawing of the emperor and his mother was passed from hand to hand in the imperial court. Some laughed at it, but most were shocked – and even more shocked when they learned that the emperor's wife had drawn it.

The drawing showed Nicky as a naughty baby sitting in a high chair, refusing a plate of soup his mother was handing to him. Minnie, fierce and scolding, was reprimanding him. Both figures were exaggerated, caricatures of themselves, Nicky made comically infantile and Minnie made into a farcical nagging mother.

The cartoon was clever, but had a malicious edge to it that was unmistakable to all who saw it. And as Alix's chief waiting maid Martha Mouchanow pointed out, the empress was oblivious to the harm it was bound to do.

For Alix, Mouchanow wrote, was 'inclined to be satirical, and had a keen sense of humour, that was not destined to add to the pleasures of her existence'. She not only drew caricatures, of everyone from members of the imperial family to ministers and leading society figures, she was 'fond of showing them'. Naturally, the people she drew were offended (except for Nicky, probably), and those who had not yet been the subject of her sketches feared that they soon would be. The public, meanwhile, was 'scandalized to see the tsar made fun of by his own wife', Mouchanow thought, 'who ought to have been the first person to show him respect and deference'.[1]

Disregarding, probably even welcoming, the unpleasant stir she was causing, Alix went on drawing her caricatures. She drew her in-laws: the matronly, authoritarian Aunt Miechen, who referred to her as 'that stiff Englishwoman'; she drew the loud, hectoring Uncle Vladimir, who disliked her and had opposed Nicky's marriage to her, and who was, due to the compulsions of protocol, her frequent escort on formal occasions, Nicky having to escort his mother.[2] She drew Countess Lamsdorff, one of her maids of honour to whom she took a 'violent dislike,' and Minnie's ageing, hypochondriacal, triple-chinned lady-in-waiting Countess Kutuzov, a descendant of the great Napoleonic Field Marshal Kutuzov, who complained that she had suffered a heart attack after seeing a mouse.

There were so many characters at the imperial court who lent themselves to mimicry and exaggeration – eccentric old servants; Minnie's muscular Circassian bodyguard Omar, a former bandit, with dark flashing eyes and a dishonest smile; the elderly gentleman who wore an old-fashioned white wig and claimed the right to live in the imperial palace by virtue of his descent from the poet Zhukovsky; the crippled Countess Marie Kleinmichel, among the leaders of Petersburg society, rich, haughty, and full of gossip.

The more Alix showed her drawings to those around her the more she laid herself open to rebuke. It was said that she was not only unkind and spiteful, but domineering. When one night she and Nicky dined at the barracks of Nicky's Hussar regiment, she found the company tedious, and was overheard to say to her husband, 'Now come, my boy, it's time to go to bed!'

That she addressed her husband in the casual manner of a brisk English governess giving orders to a young child caused still more remarks to fly through the court, and Minnie, calling her daughter-in-law into her presence, lectured her on the proper way to address the sovereign – as 'Sir' or 'Your Majesty'. Alix bristled; court protocol was one thing, but her relationship with Nicky was her own business, their own business.[3] No one could dictate to her what the nature of that tender, intimate, jokey, deeply loving tie ought to be.

Alix was retrenching, drawing her battle lines. Through her caricatures she was launching an assault, albeit a misguided and ultimately futile one, against the family and court that was rejecting her. The effort was emotionally costly. It meant that she had to become two selves: the warm, vulnerable self she liberated when with Nicky, and the hardened, flinty self she showed to others. It was noticed that the empress pinched her lips almost convulsively when under stress. Her voice when addressing servants or family members was low and constrained, her movements nervous and unsure.[4] The flinty public self was fundamentally unconvincing, and frayed around the edges.

A page in the imperial household described his first encounter with the empress. She was 'beautiful and majestic', but when she offered her hand for him to kiss, it was with 'an awkward and embarrassed gesture', he wrote. 'A sense of unease was thus the first thing you noticed on meeting the young empress, and this impression she never managed to dispel. She was so obviously nervous of conversation, and at moments when she needed to show some social graces or a charming smile, her face would become suffused with little red spots and she would look intensely serious.'

The page was particularly struck by Alix's eyes, which 'promised kindness, but instead of a bright spark, they contained only the cold embers of a dampened fire. There was certainly purity and loftiness in the look, but loftiness is always dangerous; it is akin to pride and can quickly lead to alienation.'[5]

Others noted the same unease, the same tell-tale physical signs of nervousness, the same chilliness in the empress. 'One could not say that the superficial impression she produced was favourable,' wrote a court observer. 'Despite her wonderful hair which lay like a heavy crown on her head and large dark-blue eyes beneath long lashes, there was something about her exterior that was cold, even repellent.' If only she had kept still, her marmoreal beauty would have remained fascinating. But she broke its spell as soon as she moved. 'Her majestic stance gave way to a maladroit bending of the legs resembling a curtsy at greeting or parting. When she was conversing or grew tired, her face became covered in red blotches; her hands were red and fleshy.'[6]

Many memoirists who met Alix in her first months in Russia recorded similar impressions, of a beautiful young woman, stiff and ill at ease, who mumbled in a barely audible voice and was physically awkward, even clumsy. She seemed to know nothing of the art of putting others at their ease. Instead she infected them with her own self-conscious uncertainty, and made them recoil with her unsmiling aloofness. The odd blotches on her skin, and her beet-red hands, embarrassed others and added to their discomfort.

Unlike her vivacious mother-in-law, whose girlish face was full of smiles on social occasions, Alix appeared never to smile in public. Her expression often conveyed a discontented impatience.

'As she was easily embarrassed,' Ernie wrote about his sister, 'and honest to a fault, she would unsmilingly tilt her head to one side if something displeased her, with the result that people often thought that she was unhappy, or bored, or simply capricious.'[7]

Aware that there was a strong current of anti-German feeling in Russia, and that the aristocracy was steeped in French culture, Alix knew that if she were ever to be accepted, she would have to present herself as a cultivated, French-speaking German. French was the language of the Russian court, but Alix rarely spoke it, since she and Nicky spoke English with one another. Alix's French was full of mistakes, and though Nicky tried to help her improve it by reading French novels aloud to her, she never mastered the idiom, and the courtiers laughed at her efforts, and criticized her for pretending to be something she was not.[8]

She dreaded social functions, knowing in advance that her linguistic errors would lead to laughter and censure, and that her nervousness would itself make her tongue-tied and worsen her command of the language. When it came time to circulate among the guests, she froze; she could hardly speak. She began to blush and look uncomfortable and to 'long to disappear into the ground'.[9] She managed to get through the suppers at the Winter Palace by seeking out the Turkish ambassador Husny Pasha and sitting beside him. He was a dull, prosaic old-fashioned diplomat, with no pretensions to wit or social prestige. He did not criticize her French, and she found his leaden conversation a relief.[10]

That the new empress was in actuality a complex person with high ideals who held herself to an elevated standard of conduct (with a few exceptions, as in the drawing of unkind caricatures) was not at all apparent to her detractors. They would have been very surprised to learn how empathetic she could be, how, when any of her servants suffered a loss or an illness, she responded immediately with kindness and solicitude.[11] They would never have guessed, from her reserve, that her capacity for friendship was very great and that, as her lady-in-waiting Sophie Buxhoeveden wrote, she was always 'ready to do literally anything for her friends'. Their interests became hers; she assumed their burdens. 'She would take up things and people with violent enthusiasm,' according to Buxhoeveden. 'The first enthusiasm might wane with time, but her friendships were lasting.'[12]

The empress was in fact a baffling combination of warmhearted-ness and reserve – the latter seeming to mask the former. The paradox of her nature could not be understood unless one got to know her well, or spent time with her alone.

'I must have a person to myself, if I want to be my *real* self,' Alix wrote to a member of her household, Marie Bariatinsky, who in time became her friend. 'I am not made to shine before an assembly – I have not got the easy nor the witty talk one needs for that. I like the *internal being*, and that attracts me with great force.'

Alix's deep capacity for aesthetic enjoyment, and for religious feeling, qualities of little account in the public sphere, went un-appreciated.

'As you know,' she told Marie Bariatinsky, 'I am of the preacher type. I want to help others in life, to help them to fight their battles and bear their crosses.'[13] Her natural arena was the battleground of conscience, where scruples warred with temptations, and the impulse to fulfil one's duties was at odds with the contrary impulse to seek pleasure and ease.

This warfare of conscience – the product of a Protestant upbringing – though not unknown in Russia, was something of a rarity in court circles, where venality, ambition and vanity were pre-eminent, and self-aggrandizement the norm.

Alix's intellectuality too was unappreciated, but this was probably just as well, since, had it been known at court that she read and studied a good deal, and attacked problems analytically, this tendency would have been condemned as unfeminine and come under suspicion as a symptom of plotting and intrigue. In truth the empress dedicated herself not only to improving her Russian – something she evidently found easier than improving her French – but to translating Russian writings and studying Russian music. With Nicky, she read the novels of Tolstoy and other classics, as well as formal histories and historical novels. Her tastes were refined, her views thoughtful. Yet though there were intellectuals among Nicky's relatives, notably Grand Duke Nicholas Michaelovich, Nicky's 'Uncle Bembo', a historian and biographer who had written studies on diplomacy and genealogy, and 'Uncle' Constantine, 'KR', who was a poet, playwright and translator, Alix was not able to form any connection with them through her pursuit of learning, and in fact she counted Uncle Bembo among her severest critics.

The servants who watched the empress closely in order to report everything she did to her mother-in-law were beside themselves with speculation late in December, 1894. At a church service during which she had had to stand for several hours, Alix fainted. It was the second time she had fainted in church; clearly her physical stamina was lowered. Could she be pregnant?

By mid-January another symptom appeared – illness in the morning. Now they were certain. The empress was indeed pregnant. There was going to be an heir to the throne.

Suddenly there was a change in the atmosphere. Alix might be mean-spirited, dominating, socially gauche and aloof – but she was going to be the mother of the next tsar. She was fulfilling her primary duty. She and her child had to be protected, hovered over, guarded against every possible harm. For a brief time, her critics were silenced, and there was rejoicing at the court.

Winter settled in, and Alix gave herself the task of making the baby's layette, sewing and embroidering tiny lace-trimmed gowns and caps and bibs and blankets. She enjoyed hard work; according to her chief maid of honour, Alix was 'one of those industrious women whose hands are never at rest, and who require to be always occupied in someway or another, either mentally or with some manual work which keeps their attention'.[14] As her body grew heavier her spirits began to lift, for her oppressive living situation was about to change. New apartments were being prepared in the Alexander Palace at Tsarskoe Selo, complete with a nursery for the baby, and Alix was sending away to England for furniture, along with chintz for curtains and cushions. She ordered that many of the paintings and bas-reliefs in the renovated rooms be removed, and replaced by mahogany woodwork, tall hutches and shelving. When complete the imperial apartments would be cosy, unpretentious, comfortable, with none of the outsize magnificence of the Winter Palace or the Catherine Palace at Tsarskoe Selo, with its hundreds of immense rooms and monumental statues.

Alix was attempting to re-create, within the vast, coldly palatial expanses of the Russian court, an oasis of charm and homeliness – a replica of her grandmother's taste, in fact. Within the circuit of this homely refuge she and Nicky and their child would live, away from the hostility and machinations of the courtiers, away from Minnie and her spies, away from the drawing rooms of Petersburg.

The baby was expected in October, and as the time drew near little was talked of but the coming birth. Calculations were made, reckoning from the first reports of morning sickness in January. When November began and still the empress had not given birth, dark rumours began to spread. It was said that the empress was very ill, and might not survive. There was another story that she had been unable to conceive, that the entire pregnancy was a sham. Still others said that she was indeed pregnant, but could not be delivered normally; the doctors would have to cut her open to remove the baby.[15] On one thing alone everyone was agreed: the child, assuming there was indeed a child, was sure to be a boy.

The imperial nursery was ready, the accoucheur Professor Ott and his assistants had installed themselves in the palace and made their preparations, as had the imperial surgeon Dr Girsh. Queen Victoria, much experienced in matters of childbirth, having had nine children herself, had sent a detailed list of instructions for the baby nurse, and these had been followed. As the empress was several weeks overdue, the baby was expected to be large, and Alix was slim and narrow in the hips; her delivery was sure to be difficult.

At last the birth pains began. Alix was awakened by them at one in the morning on November 15, 1895, and could not get back to sleep. 'All day she lay in bed suffering strong torments – the poor thing!' wrote Nicky in his diary. 'I could not help feeling for her.'

Ella and Nicky sat beside the bed, the doctors and nurses watched the progress of the labour as, hour after hour, the pains continued to grow stronger and more frequent. At two o'clock Minnie arrived and took her place in the bedside vigil. By this time Alix had been struggling for thirteen hours, and her strength was waning. After another three hours of fruitless suffering, Dr Ott declared that forceps would have to be used; the baby was too large to come through the birth canal unaided.

'At exactly nine o'clock a baby's cry was heard and we all breathed a sigh of relief!' Nicky wrote. 'When all the anxiety was over, and the terrors had ceased, there was simply a blessed feeling at what had come to pass!'[16]

Nicky was ecstatic, if exhausted. The doctors were relieved, Alix very tired but pleased. The servants, however, who were given the task of carrying the news of the birth to the gunners in the Peter and Paul Fortress, looked dismayed. And when the guns began firing, and the citizens of Petersburg stopped to listen, all held their breath. Three hundred shots were to be fired for a boy, one hundred and one for a girl.

At the hundred and first volley a terrible silence fell over the city, and the joy went out of the faces in the street. It was a girl.

11

In the clear blue skies above Moscow crows drifted and circled in the warm May air, rising high over the gleaming golden domes, white stone monasteries and vivid blue and green and red rooftops of the vast and sprawling city. Their cawing was all but lost amid the noisy clamour of the city's bells, ringing to herald the coming coronation of Tsar Nicholas II, and the sounds of hammering and sawing, the clatter of hoofs and the shouting of workmen carrying out renovations and decorating the houses and public buildings for the celebration to come.

In a flowering meadow just outside the city walls, wooden stalls, reviewing stands and temporary stages for theatrical performances were being built, along with wooden bridges to span the deep pits in the meadow's uneven surface and barricades to control the crowd of several hundred thousand Muscovites expected to attend the outdoor festivities. Here in Khodynka Field, the popular celebration would be held, and the tsar would come to watch the parade and greet his people.

Alix too was preparing for the coronation, learning the order of the lengthy ceremony, being fitted for new gowns, readying herself mentally for the weeks of banquets, luncheons and other gatherings.

She was a happy woman. Ever since the birth of her fair, fat little daughter Olga – named after the character in Pushkin's *Eugene Onegin* – her life had been full of contentment, despite the ongoing carping of her in-laws. At six months old, Olga was flourishing, breast-fed by Alix, occasionally bathed by Nicky, supervised by the rather grim English nanny Queen Victoria had sent – 'a stubborn woman,' Nicky thought, with 'something hard and unpleasant in her face' – and in general, growing into a healthy childhood. Far from being disappointed that Olga was not a boy, Alix and Nicky rejoiced in their daughter, and indulged shamelessly in what Queen Victoria would have called 'baby-worship'. Behind her back, the imperial family called Alix 'Mère Gigogne' – the French equivalent of 'the old woman who lived in a shoe.'[1]

Alix was happy – in part because she believed herself to be pregnant again.[2] This time, surely, the baby would be the son and heir the realm required. No one but Nicky, her waiting maid Martha Mouchanow, her doctor and possibly her brother Ernie, to whom she wrote daily, knew of this pregnancy, and she did not want it generally known just yet; she wanted to avoid for a while longer the scrutiny and avalanche of overconcern that had accompanied her last pregnancy.

Her life at Tsarskoe Selo had settled into a comfortable routine of long morning and afternoon walks with Nicky, time spent with Olga, quiet family lunches and dinners – with time in between for writing long letters and meeting with her private secretary in an effort to find a cause to devote herself to, either a state charity or a school. She wanted to make a personal contribution; her rescuing instincts were unfulfilled. But so far no opportunity had emerged, and in the meantime life at Tsarskoe Selo was so pleasant, with the extensive gardens just coming into bloom and the inviting woods full of new spring green. It was gratifying to linger in the family rooms of the Alexander Palace, which Alix kept filled with orchids and white lilacs, to lie on the sofa in the mauve boudoir – her favourite room – surrounded by watercolours of English and Hessian scenes, photographs of family, dozens of icons and a striking painting of the Annunciation.

Enjoyable distractions beckoned: embroidery, playing duets with Nicky on the wonderful Erard piano Minnie had given her for a wedding present – Alix's favourite of all her pianos – visiting the nursery (though the nanny complained that Alix made too many unannounced visits).[3] And there was the other fashionable distraction of the era, occultism.

So many upper-class people were drawn into the pursuit of truth through metarational means, outside the Orthodox faith: attending seances, studying the Cabbala, reading journals called *From There* and *The Spiritualist*, visiting mediums and acquiring obscure books of hermetic wisdom. Self-proclaimed spiritual teachers sprang up in Petersburg, gathered worshipful followers into cultlike societies, and made fortunes offering advice, healing and the cachet of possessing hidden learning.

Within the imperial family itself, Nicky's relative Grand Duke Nicholas Nicholaevich was, in the words of the highly sceptical Count Witte, 'one of the chief, if not the chief initiator of that abnormal mood of Orthodox paganism and searching for miracles, into which they obviously strayed in the highest circles'.[4] The desire to glimpse a world beyond the limits of ordinary reality, to know something of the unknown, tantalized many in the family, including Nicky himself, who was tempted to try to communicate with his late father.[5]

These preoccupations interested Alix as well, though she was chiefly absorbed in Olga, and was beginning to be troubled with morning sickness – which she did her best to hide. Throughout the celebrations in Moscow, Alix continued to nurse Olga, while doing her best to control her nausea and appear self-possessed and regal at all times. The days preceding the coronation were long, and full of events: breakfasts for two hundred guests, meetings with special foreign envoys sent to Russia for the festivities, nightly banquets and balls, state visits and musicales, a visit to the Bolshoi Ballet where (against the Dowager Empress's wishes) Matilda Kchessinsky was the featured dancer in a new ballet, *The Pearl*.

There were touching displays of loyalty to the tsar – immense cheering crowds, banners proclaiming 'God Save the Tsar' and 'Glory, Glory to Our Russian Tsar', open-air concerts by massed choirs thousands strong, singing the National Anthem with heartfelt passion. But there were disturbances as well, notably a massive workers' strike that spread from Petersburg to Moscow, with tens of thousands of wage earners refusing to go back to their machines unless their employers reduced the work day to ten and a half hours. The populace, thrilled by the coronation, particularly excited by the prospect of the carnival to be held on Khodynka Field, was stirred up and restive. Their sovereign was showering them with favours – money gifts for everyone, amnesty for unpaid taxes, freedom for prisoners and relief from many penalties and fines – yet these favours, far from having a pacifying effect, seemed to contribute to a sense of giddy assertiveness among those assembled in Moscow, a loosening of constraints in the relations between tsar and people.

The crowds that gathered to watch each of the coronation events were volatile, now heatedly loyal, now expressing disapproval. And their disapproval, unfortunately for Alix, was in part directed towards her. On the day of the tsar's formal ceremonial entry into Moscow, Alix rode in a coach of her own some distance behind her husband, and also behind that of her mother-in-law. Loud shouting greeted the tsar, vociferous hurrahs rang out when Minnie passed. But Alix's coach was greeted with a hush – an eloquent silence that stung like a blow, reducing her to tears.[6]

Silence – an ominous silence. Not open jeering, or insults, but the quiet of rejection. Among her husband's subjects, as among his relatives, her efforts were unappreciated. The Muscovites, after all, knew nothing of her attempts to understand Russian culture, her hours of study of the Russian language, her sincere desire to devote herself to some charitable activity. Nor did they know that she was carrying the heir to the Romanov throne. Once they knew more about her, and once her son was born, their reaction would change. They would be grateful.

The long ordeal of coronation day began very early in the morning, with cannon booming from the Kremlin walls and bells ringing ceaselessly. Inside the Cathedral of the Assumption, its twilit interior aglow with shimmering gold and gleaming gems from the wall paintings, the icons, the uniforms and gowns of the glittering spectators, the endless ceremony droned on, and Alix, feeling faint, had to struggle against dizziness. She watched as her husband, his face expressive of 'piety and supplication', received the crown and the imperial purple mantle was fastened around his shoulders. With the other onlookers she was startled to see his diamond-studded chain break and fall with a clatter to the tiled floor, just at the climactic moment in the ceremony. Then it was her turn to kneel before him and receive, with a kiss, her own crown.

The mass, the long sermon, the sung psalms and prayers – in all the formalities took nearly five hours, and were followed by another several hours of banqueting in the Palace of Facets, where a feast of meats and piroshki, borscht and pickled cucumber was spread out on long tables.

The heat of the day, the smell of food, the maddening cannonades and incessant peals of bells, the crowds of people everywhere must have made Alix feel dizzy and weak. Long before evening she must have been exhausted, and by the time the illumination of the city began, at ten o'clock, and thousands of glowing lights outlined the houses, shops and public buildings, even the trees in the park, she must have long since gone to her bed.

Three days later, the public celebration, the outdoor fair for the Muscovites, was to take place. The night before, tens of thousands of people began arriving on the outskirts of Khodynka meadow, camping out in the open, waiting for dawn, when the turnstiles would open and they would be allowed to enter the designated area of the fair to claim their gifts and food and begin their merrymaking.

The last time there had been a public festival on this meadow, thirteen years earlier on the occasion of Alexander III's coronation, two hundred thousand people had attended; now, however, there were at least twice that many, and a rumour began to spread through the immense throng that there would not be enough gifts or food to go around. They had been promised sausage, bread rolls, sweets, nuts, gingerbread and a precious keepsake – a pink enamel mug bearing the arms of the city of Moscow and the words 'In memory of the Holy Coronation', all wrapped together in a coloured kerchief stamped with the tsar and tsarina's pictures.[7] They had also been promised as much free beer and mead as they could drink, along with entertainment to last all day.

Throughout the brief night hours, people waited anxiously, made uneasy by the rumours of shortages, and made increasingly uncomfortable by the pressing in of the crowd itself, as more and more people came and pushed their way towards the barricades that guarded the entrance to the meadow in order to be first in line when the turnstiles opened.

A reporter for the *Russian Gazette*, Vladimir Giliarovsky, was among the waiting fairgoers, and he wrote afterwards of the terrible crush that resulted from so many massed bodies.

'Steam began to rise,' he recalled, 'looking like the mist over a swamp ... Many felt faint, some lost consciousness.' All around him people were fighting for breath, vomiting, succumbing to the irresistible pushing and jostling. There was no wind, no moon. Only the suffocating congestion, which worsened as dawn approached.

Just when the barriers began to fall no one was ever certain, but it was very early in the morning, long before the officially scheduled opening of the meadow. The patrols designated to control the crowd – a hundred mounted Cossacks – could not begin to hold the people back, and within minutes a vast dark wave of humanity poured out across the meadow, trampling the flowers, knocking over fences, rushing towards the wooden stalls where the gifts and food were kept.

'A mass of people half a million strong,' wrote a survivor of the surge, 'staggered with all its unimaginable weight in the direction of the buffets. People by the thousand fell in a ditch and ended standing literally on their heads at the bottom. Others fell straight after them, and more, and more ... ' People fell into abandoned wells, trenches, muddy troughs. Those behind them, unable to stop their forward progress, simply walked or ran across the mounds of writhing bodies towards the next set of deadly cavities in the earth, into which they themselves fell.

The screams of the trapped, helpless and dying, were horrible, and those in charge could only stand by in confusion, watching the carnage, unable to arrest the onrushing multitude.

Khodynka Field had become a deathtrap, but the authorities, including the Governor of Moscow, Grand Duke Serge, were so overwhelmed by the magnitude of the disaster that their first reaction was to try to cover it up.

Instead of informing the tsar and his ministers of what had happened, Serge and his subordinates rounded up as many carts and wagons as they could find and attempted to remove all evidence of the carnage. Mangled bodies, severed limbs, bloodstained clothing were loaded onto carts, then covered with tarpaulins and hauled off to the mortuaries – and when the mortuaries were full, to be emptied into the river, into hastily dug mass graves, anywhere distant from the meadow itself.

The ghastly procession of blood-stained wagons moved along streets gaily decorated with banners and flags hailing the newly crowned tsar. Onlookers became curious, then recoiled in horror. For in their haste the labourers who had endeavoured to clear away the human debris had been less than thorough; bloody arms and hands dangled down below the edges of the tarpaulins, and a terrible, unmistakable stench rose from the carts – the stench of blood and death.

Then too there were the survivors, thousands of them, walking glassy-eyed and filthy towards their homes, limping and bleeding, some clutching their coronation gifts and mugs. Seeing them, and wanting to help, some aristocrats drove in their carriages to Khodynka, and took the wounded to hospitals.

By ten-thirty in the morning news of the terrible catastrophe was spreading through Moscow, and it was no longer possible to keep it from the palace. The tsar was informed that many of his subjects were dead, though the estimates of the dead and wounded were much lower than the actual numbers.[8] He was asked whether, out of respect for the victims, he would cancel the day's activities, which included not only his appearance at Khodynka Field but a ball at the French embassy. Most likely influenced by his advisers, Nicky said no, that he would go ahead.

When Alix learned, from one of her ladies, of the events at Khodynka she was shocked, and sorrowful. That the coronation should have occasioned such suffering and loss seemed a monstrous wrong. No doubt she could not help thinking, as many others did, of the ominous breaking of her husband's diamond chain at the moment of his crowning. It had been a portent of calamity – and now the calamity had arrived.

For the head of state to appear in public in the aftermath of the Khodynka disaster seemed to her a serious mistake; for herself, she would have preferred to spend the day visiting the hospitals. (Here, albeit under sad circumstances, was her opportunity to be of help.) But she could not go against Nicky's official decision, and besides, she knew that that decision had a political dimension. Had she not shown herself at the French Embassy ball, it would have been said that her absence was due to her pro-German sympathies.

Besides, the public did not seem, at first, to want the festivities to be cancelled. Throughout the morning, fairgoers continued to stream onto the meadow by the thousands, enjoying the warm sun, ignoring the sight of corpses being dug out of the trenches and laid out on the ground, and swarming around the pavilion where the tsar was to make his appearance that afternoon. It was a ghoulish spectacle, with bands playing, people milling about, eating and drinking, while quite nearby, improvised mortuaries were being created, with bodies hastily covered with tree branches, linens, banners torn down – anything to hide the grisly remains. It was not possible, however, to hide the crows that gathered over the meadow, eager for carrion, or to disguise the units of the fire brigade, small horse-drawn trucks, which continued to come and go all afternoon, carrying the dead from the field.

The blaring of the National Anthem announced the arrival of the tsar, and when he appeared on the balcony of his pavilion, with Alix beside him, the crowd cheered lustily. He made a brief speech, but did not allude to the loss of life. (In his diary, however, Nicky conscientiously recorded noticing the presence of corpses near the pavilion.[9]) The pageantry went forward as planned, regiments of soldiers marching past in smart order, guns firing salute after salute, people singing, delegations of peasants coming before the tsar to pay their respects and receive his blessing. The parade of pageant cars bumped their way across the uneven plain, carefully avoiding the deep ditches and craters, and the long afternoon spun itself along, or so it appeared, towards a satisfactory ending.

Alix, however, was tired and emotionally drained, and although she went to the French Embassy ball, and danced the opening dance with the ambassador, she and Nicky did not stay for the midnight supper and returned home relatively early.

By now the long eventful days were catching up with her, the disappointing reception she had received, the tiring ceremonies and banquets, the hours of standing, the heat, the excitement – and the wrenching calamity on Khodynka Field. Her stomach churned, and she was often close to tears.[10] She still did not disclose her pregnancy; there was too much turmoil in the family. Serge was blamed for having failed to forestall the tragedy, and when he offered to resign as Governor of Moscow, Nicky was blamed for refusing to accept his resignation.[11] Rifts between Sandro and Serge, Aunt Miechen and Minnie resurfaced. KR noted in his diary that 'muted antagonism' arose between Minnie and Alix, and the latter, pale and ill, looked as though she was badly in need of rest.

As the days passed, the mood in the city darkened. The workers' strike continued. Muscovites dressed in black for the Khodynka victims, some twenty thousand of them, so it was believed, and blamed the police, the city officials, even the doctors for the huge loss of life. Serge was called 'The Prince of Khodynka', the tsar 'Bloody Nicholas'. Alix became 'The German Bitch', and it was said that she had laughed and danced in heartless abandon at the French ambassador's ball, heedless of the suffering of the people.

Alix faded, suffered, and in the end, succumbed to her weariness and anxiety. Her body rebelled, and she miscarried her baby.[12]

What had begun in joy and celebration was ending in a season of disaster, with the crown of the Romanovs tarnished by tragedy and the heir to the throne, the boy whose existence Alix had kept as her secret, lost in a swirl of blood.

The warm June sun continued to shine down over the domes and rooftops of Moscow, but now it was a city in mourning, and the crows, bloated and sated, floated like dark wraiths in the cloudless blue sky.

12

In the summer of 1896, Empress Alexandra made a serious effort to launch a charitable project. She called it 'Help Through Handwork', and envisioned a vast number of workshops all across Russia where, under the leadership of aristocratic women, poor women would come to learn to sew and to do other handcrafts. A committee, of which she would be the head, would supervise this network of workshops and direct its operations.[1]

It was an ambitious project, modelled on charitable enterprises in Germany and England and inspired by Alix's own fine needlework, which she wanted to teach others to imitate, with the ultimate aim of raising money through the sale of embroidered garments, the money to be distributed to needy families. Her aims were high-minded and unselfish; she wanted no glory, only the chance to undertake a project that could improve the lives of the poor, and to satisfy her need to contribute to the alleviation of want.

As soon as she announced the start of 'Help Through Handwork', many women, among them quite a number of aristocratic women, came forward to join the sewing guild. There were also women from the merchant class, living in the village of Tsarskoe Selo or nearby, who wanted to join, and soon the meetings were organized and the sewing began. Alix presided, offered guidance and correction to the sewers, and began making plans for the expansion of the guild and for the distribution of the first group of garments.

She hoped to go further in her charitable efforts, to establish a school for nurses and housemaids, like the one founded by her Aunt Helena in England. She wrote to Helena's school asking for help in initiating her project, and anticipated beginning it soon, within months if possible.

But Alix had no sooner launched her efforts than obstacles arose. In Russia, she discovered, there was virtually no private charity; all charitable enterprises were controlled by the government, and most government charities were headed, at least nominally, by the Dowager Empress. Wherever Alix turned, it seemed, Minnie stood, arms folded, barring the way.

What was worse, she quickly discovered that the highborn women who joined her guild had done so in the expectation that in return they would receive her special patronage; they expected advancement to positions at court, or promotions or positions for their husbands or sons – some immediate, concrete quid pro quo. When they discovered that the empress had no expectation of rewarding them for joining her charitable enterprise, they withdrew – with many a bitter comment about 'imperial ingratitude'.[2] Some wives of merchants and tradesmen remained, proud to belong to an undertaking headed by the empress. But they too, Alix realized, were far from disinterested. They were seeking the social cachet of association with the court, and this mattered far more to them than any benefit their sewing might bring to the poor.

The failure of her scheme was disillusioning to Alix, and the scoffing of the women she had tried to recruit wounded her. In the aftermath of the Khodynka disaster, the brief lull in criticism had ended. The gossiping against the empress now grew more scurrilous. It was being said that she had been pregnant by a lover, and had deliberately aborted the foetus to hide her transgression – a malevolent distortion of the reality of her miscarriage.[3] The members of her household were pestered for details of her private life in the hope that scandalous stories could be built upon them. It must have seemed to Alix as though a web of malice was being woven around her; everywhere she turned, she found petty meanness and spite. If she wore white on a festival day – as she had been told was the correct thing to do – all the other women wore dark gowns, so that she stood out awkwardly. If she gave one of her rare receptions, and struck off the invitation list married women she suspected of 'loose manners', all the invited women pointedly refused to attend.

'The whole of Petersburg rose up in arms against its empress,' Martha Mouchanow recalled.[4] Hardly anyone would speak to her. Behind her back, court and society alike criticized her for being dull, for dressing badly, for having declared, with unpardonable hauteur, 'that she was going to reform the morals of her empire'.[5] Her tastes, her sensibilities were not theirs. She bored them – and she made it plain that they bored her.

Thwarted and angered, and wounded to be, as she thought herself, so misunderstood, Alix prepared for a far wider social challenge. In August of 1896, she and Nicky left for a European tour.

Despite all her reading and study about Russia, it is doubtful whether Alix had even a rudimentary understanding of her adopted country's actual position among the European states, or of Russia's vulnerability as a great power. No one in the Foreign Ministry attempted to instruct her – indeed the only message she received from the foreign minister before leaving for the West was that she must take along certain magnificent necklaces from among the Crown Jewels and wear them to impress the rulers and dignitaries at the foreign courts.

Russia was in fact in a precarious condition as the nineteenth century drew to its close for, although it had traditionally been among the leading states of Europe, it no longer possessed either the wealth or the military strength to compete with the phenomenally expanding German Empire. Russia was advancing economically, its industrialization spreading but, compared to the Western European states, it was still a backward country with a medieval agricultural system where illiterate peasants lived in poverty and ignorance.

And it was still overwhelmingly autocratic, ruled by the will of one man, the tsar. What movements there had been to promote constitutional government had been short-lived, and brutally suppressed. Observers in Europe watched with interest to see whether the new tsar Nicholas would finally bring his backward realm out of what they saw as its benighted, barbaric condition and into the light of modernity – or whether, as it seemed, he was intent on preventing change, which meant continued stagnation in the government and continued unrest among his subjects.

Here Russia's newly forged link with France, formalized by the signing of an agreement in 1892, was crucial. For there was increasing tension between Russia and Germany, with the German government imposing high tariffs on Russian goods and threatening to expand militarily into Russian territory; only the protection of an alliance with France – and the friendship of Britain – could hold the might of Germany at bay. Meanwhile the Russian treasury was being shored up by loans from French banks, French entrepreneurs were doing more business than ever before in Petersburg, and French investors were funding the growth of Russian industry, growth vital to the country's viability as a great power with aims of its own in Asia and the Balkans.

It was essential, if the path the Russian government had decided to pursue was to succeed, that the sovereigns aid in cementing the bond with France, while helping to prevent further deterioration of relations with Germany through preserving the tie of cousinage with the German emperor. Beyond this, the effect of press reports and public opinion on the relations between states was significant; if Nicky and Alix managed to make themselves liked and admired on their tour, if they projected magnanimity, confidence and majesty, and an aura of wealth and glamour, if they said the right thing at the right time, then the public would be favourably disposed towards Russia and would influence their governments accordingly.

Alix went to great trouble over her clothes for the trip, sending detailed instructions to Worth in Paris, who supplied her gowns. Worth sent a team of seamstresses to Petersburg for the final fittings. It was an era of excess in dress, when upper-class women wore wide hats piled a foot high with swathes of gauze and luxuriant clusters of artificial flowers and curling ostrich feathers, parasols with many flounces, long draping feather boas and gowns and mantles in delicate, perishable white crepe and pink satin and pale mauve velvet. There were layers upon layers of ornament, rows of lace, frills, ribbon bows and beadwork. Collars and mantles were embroidered in silver and gold thread, ball gowns were trimmed with sequins and thickly encrusted with pearls. Flowers and fur were heaped generously upon garments already overdecorated with adornments of other kinds, and long ropes of pearls were worn looped many times around the neck or dangling from neck to ankle.

Alix, who had a weakness for beautiful clothes, and wore them to striking effect, being tall and having a stately posture, indulged her pleasure in finery when ordering her travelling wardrobe. The trunks arrived from Worth, and were loaded onto the imperial train, along with dozens of cases and boxes filled with linens, lace and bed sheets, jewels and lingerie, and Alix's large heavy gold toilette service, which filled several large trunks in itself. There was an entire travelling nursery for baby Olga, along with her nursery staff – minus the sour English nurse, who had recently been sent away – and hundreds of servants and officials, among them doctors, cooks, laundresses, waiting maids and valets.

It quickly became apparent, once Nicky and Alix arrived in Breslau for the start of their tour, that Alix was not prepared to play her part in promoting Russian diplomatic interests. Partly out of nervousness, partly because she was still aggrieved over the failure of her handcrafts project and the ugly rumours in Petersburg that she had a lover, she was defensive and oversensitive; her focus was not on acting with discretion and tact but on herself and the respect due her as the newly crowned empress of Russia. She became touchy, moody, demanding; she was peremptory with her servants, insisting that they go to much extra trouble to change the costly Argenton and Brussels lace trimmings on her dressing table everyday, just as they did at home, and that it match exactly the lace on her bed sheets and nightgowns. She argued with Martha Mouchanow, and told her curtly to be quiet and do as she was told. Worst of all, she clashed with her cousin Willy.

Alix had never liked her imperial German cousin, and had always responded to his overbearing, domineering personality with mockery and disdain. She could not bring herself to establish a more mature relationship with him, as their formal positions now demanded. When Willy provided Alix with an antique silver toilette service that had once belonged to Queen Louise of Prussia, instead of accepting it graciously she took offence, feeling slighted instead of honoured. Only her gold service would do for an empress; she put the silver one aside.

Willy, highly insulted, responded with a cutting remark to the effect that in lending Alix the silver service he was 'paying her a great compliment'.

Alix, incensed, retorted that 'it seemed to her that her cousin William still thought her the little Hessian princess of as little importance as she had been before her marriage'.[6]

Egos were bruised, feathers ruffled. Willy's grandmother, the Dowager Empress Augusta, turned her back on Alix and pronounced her 'frivolous', and no doubt she wrote a letter to her great friend Queen Victoria criticizing the Russian Empress for light-mindedness and vanity. Soon the entire German court had made up its mind to dislike Alix, and when she appeared at a state dinner wearing a fortune in sapphires and pearls, and in a gown strewn with gold threads, it was whispered that she cared for nothing but impressing others with her wealth.[7]

When Alix and Nicky sailed aboard the new yacht *Standart* from Copenhagen to Scotland, her mood did not soften, even though she must have been aware, in the presence of her aged grandmother Victoria, that this would probably be the last time she would see her. For ten days rain poured down and a cold wind wrapped itself around the draughty castle of Balmoral, confining the family to the chilly interior with its eccentric decoration of animal heads, mounted antlers and tartan-covered furniture. Alix, Victoria declared, was changed; she had become distant and all but unapproachable. When the queen attempted to talk to her about her tactless behaviour in Germany, and her conflicts with her Russian court and relations, Alix became noticeably cool. In Scotland, as in Germany, press and public reacted badly to the Russian Empress's costly gowns and were affronted that she did not choose British tweeds.[8]

Even in Paris, where enthusiastic crowds shouted wildly 'Vive l'impératrice!' and where Alix was judged to be very pretty and most welcome, she responded with frostiness to the embrace of the French. The beauty of the city, specially adorned in honour of the imperial visitors, with even the bare chestnut trees covered with artificial flowers, left Alix unmoved, while the constant cheering and praise with which she was surrounded only brought out her flinty side; she 'felt embarrassed', Martha Mouchanow wrote, 'at what she considered to be exaggerated expressions of admiration'.[9]

In Paris, as in Breslau, Alix seemed almost perversely bent on destroying rather than cementing good relations. In a clumsily mistaken effort to align herself with the Republican government, she pointedly ignored some aristocratic women who had been invited to lunch at the Russian embassy. The snub was effective and devastating; the French public and press withdrew their approbation and decided that Alix was not after all very chic, that her personality was not likable, and that perhaps she did not deserve the privilege, which had been allowed her, of sleeping in Marie Antoinette's former apartments at Versailles. After all, Marie Antoinette had not been a good Republican either.[10]

It was noted that the empress was quite lethargic: she was in fact pregnant, having conceived another child in the early days of her tour. By the time she reached Paris she was yielding to the torpor of her condition. Once she returned to Russia she took to her bed, and stayed there, without interruption, for nearly two months, until the danger of another miscarriage was past.

Along with the entire court, she was hoping for a boy, and confided her hopes to her sister Irene when she came to visit. Irene, the calmest and most undemanding of Alix's three sisters – she and her husband Prince Henry of Prussia were known among their relatives as 'the Very Amiables' – may have come to Russia partly to soothe her younger sister and calm her anxieties. For apart from worrying that she might miscarry again, and that the child might be another girl, Alix was troubled by renewed threats of danger to the imperial family from revolutionaries.[11]

Although no actual attempts had been made on the life of the tsar during the first two years of his reign, the constant menace of assassination was never far from his thoughts, with detectives in attendance at the palace around the clock and armed guards surrounding Nicky everywhere he went. While Nicky and Alix were in England, Scotland Yard sent information that a plot had been uncovered to dynamite the train they would ride to Ballater, near Balmoral. The conspiracy was international, with Belgian, French and Irish terrorists as well as Russians involved; bombs were being made in a secret laboratory near Antwerp. The imperials were put aboard their train, but many extra precautions were taken to ensure its safe arrival. The line was cleared by a second engine, travelling on ahead, and on the train itself were special British constables and railway agents, checking every passenger and searching every compartment.

The Khodynka disaster had stirred up a fresh wave of antagonism among the public and, throughout the winter and spring of 1897, death threats were received by the Russian court. Murders of police chiefs and other officials in provincial cities led to the arrest and imprisonment of hundreds of suspected enemies of the regime. One of those arrested, a young woman student named Maria Vetrova, was the object of much talk and sympathy in Petersburg when her story became known in February. Imprisoned in the Peter and Paul Fortress for urging government reform, she was raped by one of her captors, following which she poured kerosene on her dress and lit it. News of her self-immolation, and of the crime that prompted it, sent a shudder of horror through the capital and triggered yet another wave of strong feeling against the tsar and his ministers, radicalizing more students.

Nervous and beleaguered, made more anxious by the tides of hostility that radiated from Petersburg, Alix sewed and embroidered the layette for the new baby, praying that it would be a son. She was often ill in the final months of her pregnancy, and her chronic leg pains returned, but she forced herself to give four balls and invite guests to four plays at the Hermitage Theatre – all of which were sparsely attended. Society was snubbing the empress, with Minnie's tacit approval (for a word from the dowager empress would have reversed this trend) and Nicky's passive acquiescence.

When in late May Alix's birth pains began, only Irene, Nicky and Nicky's Danish grandmother Queen Louise were present. Significantly, Minnie stayed away – possibly at the accoucheur's request. Minnie's presence would certainly have increased Alix's nervousness, and made her labour more burdensome.

Because of Alix's apprehension about the baby's gender – her exaggerated hope for a son, her dread of a second daughter – it had been agreed that, at the moment of birth, the accoucheur would give a silent signal to Nicky to indicate the baby's sex. That way Alix would be spared any shock, and could be left to recover from the effects of the chloroform without the added strain of either elation or disappointment.

The labour pains came on in the evening, and continued throughout the night. The court was alerted; once again word went out that the empress was about to give birth. At eight in the morning, Alix was moved into the bedroom Queen Louise was occupying during her stay, so that in tribute to her, the baby could be born there. Now the chloroform was administered, and the pains became more intense.

'The second bright happy day in our family life,' Nicky wrote in his diary later that day. 'At 10:40 in the morning the Lord blessed us with a daughter – Tatiana . . . This time it all went quickly and safely, and I did not feel nervously exhausted.'[12]

As at Olga's birth, Nicky was elated. Little Tatiana was a large and beautiful child, weighing nearly nine pounds, and looked very much like Alix. Nicky was overjoyed, but the others present were glum. 'When the child came into the world,' Martha Mouchanow wrote, 'there was a profound silence in the room.' Everyone was disappointed, no one wanted to voice that disappointment.

When after a moment or two Alix opened her eyes and knew where she was, she saw anxiety and distress on the faces of her sister and the others. She knew at once that she had had another daughter. Her sobs were louder than the crying of the newborn, and lasted long into the afternoon.

13

It was noticed by those in close contact with her that the empress had become increasingly preoccupied with the orderliness in which her possessions were kept. She had keys to all her trunks, wardrobes and cupboards, and kept them close at hand, so that at any moment she could open the container and inspect its contents, becoming very angry at her servants when anything was out of place or disarranged.

At least once a month she went through every one of her hundreds of drawers and dozens of wardrobes, making certain that every gown, every hat, every pair of gloves was exactly where it should be. She checked her very extensive jewel collection, her cabinets of baubles and gifts, and especially her lace cabinet, for which she wrote out a catalogue in her own hand, every bit of lace entered in its own space and checked off as being present in its proper space. So conscientious was she about her lace, in fact, that she had her seamstresses remove all the lace trims from her hundreds of gowns and her lingerie in order to inventory it carefully; after she completed her inspection, the trims were laboriously sewn on again.

When she discovered that a particular crystal and gold writing set, supposed to be stored on a special shelf, had been moved so that part of it was on another shelf, she became livid. She summoned all her maids of honour and lectured them harshly for keeping things 'in such disorder', and redoubled her surprise inspections.

She turned the same obsessive attention to the keeping of the household records. Much to the annoyance of the stewards, she insisted upon inspecting the books in which household expenses were recorded, and criticized any expenditures that seemed to her excessive. Having managed her brother's household in Darmstadt, Alix may have believed that she was competent to evaluate the capability of the palace staff, though she freely admitted that she had no idea how much an egg or a potato cost in the markets of Tsarskoe Selo or Petersburg. The stewards complained – for in fact Alix's understanding of the management of the huge, intricate system of palace administration was very limited, and her criticism was caustic – and Aunt Miechen, Uncle Vladimir and others in the family began to laugh over the 'German housekeeper' who made such a fuss about the price of potatoes.

Alix's increasing intolerance of disorder and mismanagement extended to her use of time. 'Things had to be done at a certain hour,' Martha Mouchanow wrote, 'and if not, had to be put off until the next day. She would not for anything in the world have sacrificed five minutes of the time appointed for something else to finish what she was doing at the moment.'[1] When she sat at her desk to write letters, she always stopped when her clock reached precisely the hour of five in the afternoon, even if she was in mid-sentence, leaving the written sheets strewn on the desk to be put in order the next day.

The overconcern with orderliness, expenses and the management of her time were symptoms of a deep feeling of powerlessness that bedevilled Alix in the wake of Tatiana's birth. If she could not control the sex of her children, the hostility of her in-laws and her husband's subjects, she could at least attempt to govern how her possessions were kept and how her household was run. And if her excessive focus on these things bordered on an unhealthy fixation, she could not help it; that was part of her nature.

Nor could she prevent the growing rift between herself and her mother-in-law, a rift that widened in the year of Tatiana's birth. Relations between the two women had gone from cordial distance to an uneasy truce, and then to polite estrangement and muted antagonism. They did not exchange sharp words, but Alix complained that Minnie found other ways to make her feel inadequate in her role and to emphasize her provincial upbringing and the fact that she was not of royal birth.

Minnie insisted that she, as a dowager empress and the daughter of a king, ought to be prayed for in the church liturgy immediately after the tsar himself, and that Alix's name should follow hers. (The Synod disagreed, and Alix had a moment of triumph when it was decreed that her name would precede her mother-in-law's; according to Mouchanow, Alix was 'not wise enough to hide her joy' at this turn of events, and Minnie took deep offence.)[2]

Relations curdled over the matter of the crown jewels, a treasure hoard of white, yellow and pink diamonds, emeralds and sapphires and other ornaments of rare quality worth hundreds of millions of roubles. Minnie believed these were hers by right, and kept them in her possession, but soon after Nicky's accession the treasury demanded the jewels, causing 'painful scenes' when Minnie, standing on her rights, tried to refuse entrance to her private apartments by the treasury officials. Ultimately Minnie was forced to give in and surrender the jewels, and every time Alix wore any of them Minnie took it as an affront. Alix, for her part, cared little for the brilliant stones in their old-fashioned settings, preferring her own pearls, amethysts and aquamarines, which Nicky showered on her in abundance and which the royal jewellers, Bolin and Fabergé, offered to her at frequent intervals.[3] Much to Minnie's chagrin, Alix let it be known that she actually disliked the crown jewels, and resented the fact that, at special court functions, she had to wear Catherine the Great's huge and heavy pearl and diamond tiara, or another celebrated piece, a necklace worth twenty million roubles that had in fact been one of Minnie's favourite possessions.

Adding to the friction was the elaborate ritual surrounding the protection of the imperial jewels, which had to be escorted to and from the strong room by a detachment of soldiers every time they were worn, and handed over with an exchange of forms. Alix found all the fuss and paperwork tiresome, while Minnie, who continued to covet the jewels and who would gladly have filled out a dozen forms if only she could wear them, criticized her for complaining.

By far the greatest source of conflict between the two women was the nursery. It was not just that Alix had had two daughters and no sons – while Xenia, Nicky's sister, was producing only sons, and many of them – it was that she spent so much time with her daughters, nursing them herself (which everyone but Nicky considered ludicrously inappropriate for an empress), playing with them and supervising their care every morning and evening. Minnie and others remarked cuttingly that Alix 'wasted all her time looking after little girls whose existence was of no interest at all to the Russian Empire', when she ought to have been putting all her efforts into her imperial duties.[4] If she could not give the realm an heir, at least she could act like an empress and not like a bourgeois Hausfrau.

The nursery itself, to which an entire wing in the Alexander Palace at Tsarskoe Selo was devoted, was a sunny, well-run domain of its own with spacious rooms and large windows framed in curtains of flowered cretonne. Lemonwood furniture, ordered from Alix's favourite furniture supplier, Maple's in England, lined the walls, which were hung with icons and lamps. A well-scrubbed English head nurse in a starched uniform ran the nursery establishment, with a staff of many Russian nurses and chambermaids, two of them dressed in regional Russian costume, the rest in crisp white skirts and shirtwaists with tall caps of white tulle.

Baby Tatiana, a beautiful infant who was reportedly 'always happy', slept in her lemonwood cradle, while Olga, nearly two years old, tottered through the rooms or down the corridor, chattering alternately in Russian and English, gazing up at the guards and soldiers posted in the hallways. Both girls had an abundance of toys, including a special doll with her own large, fashionable wardrobe of gowns and hats and slippers, even a tiny comb and brush and mirror – a gift from the French president.

The nursery was a healthy, well-run environment – but to Minnie it was just another of Alix's many failures. Minnie criticized Olga, who had a broad forehead, for being ugly, found fault with the nursemaids for being too fond of drink or too eager to fraternize with the palace Cossacks. She found Alix as inadequate as a mother

as she was as a wife and an empress. Indeed Minnie let it be known – and she took no pains to hide her view from anyone – that she would have preferred to have her son Michael, her late husband's favourite, inherit the throne. With Michael as tsar, there would have been no starchy English nursery, no unwanted little girls, no awkward, inept empress.

Michael was just nineteen in 1897, tall and handsome and genial, physically much more in the traditional Romanov mould than Nicky. Where Nicky was very much a home-lover, Michael was dashing, an able swordsman and a daring rider, a gunner in the Horse Guards artillery, much at home in society and attractive to women. On the surface at least, there was much in Michael that was lacking in Nicky. He was unproven, but promising. And even as she was complaining about Alix's lack of a son, Minnie was rejoicing at the thought that, until Alix produced one, Michael was next in line for the throne after his sickly brother Georgy, a consumptive who was not expected to live much longer.

In 1897 Minnie was given yet one more reason to regret her daughter-in-law. The 'Hesse scandal', as it came to be known, spread from court to court, darkening Alix's reputation by association.

Ernie's marriage to Ducky was in ruins, and all Europe knew why. The incompatibility between the spouses had become more severe and, earlier in the year, Ducky had spent several months travelling, glad to be away from her husband. While she was gone, Ernie had let his secret life become public, and had indulged his homosexual preference indiscriminately – and most indiscreetly. On Ducky's return to Darmstadt she discovered Ernie in bed with a young kitchen boy – and soon learned that, as she wrote afterwards, 'no boy was safe, from the stable hands to the kitchen help. He slept quite openly with them all.'

Ducky was ill, the Darmstadt court was shrouded temporarily in dishonour, and the Romanovs discovered a fresh reason to be contemptuous of Ernie's sister Alix, who could not, they supposed, have been ignorant of her brother's unmentionable proclivities.

Another member of Alix's large extended family, her childhood friend and cousin Helena Victoria, came to Russia for a visit in the winter of 1897–98, and in her cousin's presence some of Alix's perpetual social discomfort seemed to abate. For a few weeks Alix and Nicky took Helena Victoria out into Petersburg society, introducing her at embassy parties, escorting her to balls and suppers. But then Alix caught the measles, and had to go into seclusion for many weeks, cutting short her participation in the winter season.

Illness came again in the summer of 1898 when Olga developed scarlet fever and Alix, giving the new English nurse complete charge over Tatiana, devoted herself for many days and nights to Olga's care.

'I can remember her so well during these days and nights sitting by the cot in which her small daughter slept,' Mouchanow recalled, 'clad in a dressing gown of white flannel . . . her fair head resting on her hand, absorbed in her thoughts, and with that sweet but anxious expression on her beautiful face.'[5] The Madonna-like image was striking, but even more striking was Alix's sudden burst of candour. Until this time she had treated her chief waiting maid only as a servant, never as a confidante; now, made wretched by her worry about her daughter, her loss of sleep and general depression, she opened her heart.

What tormented her was that her mother-in-law, Aunt Miechen and her other in-laws, far from commending her for watching by Olga's bedside, scolded her for exposing herself to the very contagious disease of scarlet fever when the possibility existed that she might be pregnant – and with a son. Olga would live or die, they seemed to be saying, the outcome of her disease was of no consequence, and therefore Alix ought not to hover over her. All that mattered was that Alix keep herself healthy so that she could give the realm the all-important heir.

'As if that mattered,' Alix burst out to Mouchanow. 'Even if I died . . . the Emperor would always find another wife who perhaps would be luckier than I have been, and able to give him an heir. No one would miss me, with the exception perhaps of these children.' She broke down and wept, and her maid of honour, taken aback, tried to reassure her that she was wrong, that Nicky loved her as 'no woman had ever been loved'.

'Ah, my dear,' Mouchanow remembered her replying, 'what good does it do me to be loved by my husband when all the world is against me?'[6]

That Alix and Nicky were bound by a very deep, enduring intimacy was beyond question. Later in the year, after Olga had recovered from her illness and the family had gone to Livadia to spend the autumn months, Nicky was suddenly summoned to Denmark, to attend the funeral of his grandmother Queen Louise.

'My own precious Darling,' Alix wrote to him on the day he left, 'you will read these lines when the horrid train will be carrying you always further and further away from poor Wifie. Our first separation since the marriage – I am frightened of it, I cannot bear the idea of your going away so far without me.' Bereft of her husband's company, Alix felt the full force of her isolation, her dependency. 'I cannot bear to think what will become of me without you – you who are my one and all, who make up all my life.'

Her letter went on and on, covering many sheets of notepaper. She promised to sleep in Nicky's cabin on the yacht *Standart*, moored at the foot of the steep whitewashed steps leading from the palace terraces to the bay below, so that she would feel nearer to him in his absence. She was, as always, anxious. She believed that she might be pregnant, but couldn't be sure. 'God grant it may be so,' she wrote, ever convinced that the key to her restoration to favour in the eyes of her in-laws and her husband's subjects lay in her finally giving birth to a son.[7]

Her sister Irene had come once again for a visit, and she relied on Irene in Nicky's absence, and on Martha Mouchanow and also on her maid of honour Marie Bariatinsky, who had become her 'true and devoted friend', as she called Marie, a valued ally in a poisonous court environment where Alix felt that all the world was against her.

Not long after Nicky's return from Denmark, late in 1898, Alix became certain that she was pregnant once again. Her morning sickness was severe in the early months and, when it subsided, she began having such crippling sciatic pain that she could not walk at all, and had to be in a wheelchair all day. Nicky insisted on pushing her himself, and took her out each afternoon in the hunting sleigh along the cleared sleigh paths at Tsarskoe Selo.

Despite Nicky's diligent efforts to care for Alix and raise her spirits, she became ill and gloomy and, as winter retreated and the first leaves began to appear on the trees in the palace park, she felt pessimistic, not only about the sex of the child she was carrying, but about her own future. The depression that had attacked her during her last pregnancy returned, with thoughts that she was replaceable, that another woman in her place might well be luckier, and even darker ruminations.

'I never like making plans,' she wrote to her oldest sister Victoria early in April, 1899. 'God knows how it will all end.'[8]

Her labour began in late June. Weakened by months of illness and immobility, Alix had a very difficult and painful time, wrestling for many hours with the arduous task of delivering her child. For a few hours the accoucheur seemed to lose hope, and his doubts alarmed the nurses, the waiting women, and the other palace servants. If Alix should prove unable to expel the baby, then Nicky would be faced with the terrible, and at that era all too common, decision many husbands had to make: should he save Alix, at the risk of having the child be stillborn, or should he tell the doctor to perform a caesarean delivery at great risk to Alix's life?

Fortunately Alix rallied; both mother and child were saved, and just after noon on June 26, 1899, the third daughter of Nicholas II and Alexandra came into the world. Whether, as at Tatiana's birth, the accoucheur was instructed to give a secret signal indicating the baby's sex, sparing Alix shock and disappointment, is unknown. Perhaps the sheer relief that both mother and child came through the ordeal alive was all that counted – at least for the moment. In any case, the word that another daughter had been born was spread from the birth room out into the corridors beyond, the courtiers informed one another, shaking their heads in frustration and disbelief, and a courier was dispatched to Petersburg to instruct the gunners in the Peter and Paul Fortress to begin their cannonade.

Another girl! The Petersburgers heard the guns go off, counted each boom eagerly, then groaned in discouragement when only one hundred and one shots were fired. The German bitch had failed again.

The new baby, a rosy, robust child – the strongest Alix had yet produced – was named Marie, after her grandmother, and all the Romanovs went to church to give thanks for her birth.

Telegrams of congratulation arrived from all over Europe, and Alix, as she began to recover her strength, addressed herself to the task of answering them. It was a bittersweet task, for she well knew that an unspoken disappointment lay behind every telegram, every good wish. The securing of the Russian succession was a matter of great concern to every court, the stability of Europe was affected by it; bound up with Alix's private sorrow was a public problem of growing seriousness.

And it became more serious when, two weeks after Marie's birth, Nicky's brother George succumbed to illness following a bicycle accident and died, making Michael heir and tsarevich.

Almost immediately there was a change in the atmosphere of the court. Michael was now sought-after, his views solicited, his activities regarded and imitated. There was a tacit acceptance of the fact that he would become the next tsar; after three unsuccessful tries, Alix was not expected to have a son any time in the future.

Michael's new-found pre-eminence began to cause difficulties. To the existing rift between Minnie and Alix was added the complication of Michael's probable succession, and Minnie's preference for him. Old factions were strengthened, new factions formed. Michael was courted and supplicated and approached for favours, which undermined the already fragile support Nicky enjoyed among his officials and ministers.

At foreign courts, queries were made about Michael, who began to be entertained by diplomats and invited abroad. Queen Victoria, shrewdly assessing the situation in Russia, invited Michael to visit her at Balmoral and, liking him, saw to it that he enjoyed himself while in the Highlands and went home with a favourable view of the English.

She had sent Alix a telegram of congratulations when Marie was born, noting tartly, 'I am so thankful that dear Alicky has recovered so well, but I regret the third girl for the country.'

No one regretted the third girl more than the empress. She began to speak of herself as a 'Pechvogel', a 'bird of ill omen', who was bringing bad luck to Russia. Her tired mind, desperate for an explanation and worn out with analyzing and reanalyzing her unhappy situation, cast about for answers outside the sphere of reason. Her strong Lutheran upbringing had taught her to trust in Providence; her adopted Orthodoxy induced a deeper, more superstitious reverence for the power of the unseen. With all the fervour of her romantic nature she began to reach out, with expanding faith, into the realm of the occult.

14

In the dim interior of the tiny Kremlin church of the Exaltation of the Cross, the emperor and empress knelt before the iconostasis. All was quiet save for the shuffling of feet across the mosaic floor, as pilgrims passed in and out to kiss the wounds of Christ and prostrate themselves before the holy icons.

The walls of the church glowed golden in the candlelight, their painted images of Saint Michael and Saint Sergius, of Christ the Redeemer and the Virgin Mary shining as if lit from within. The wide golden haloes of the holy figures, radiant bands in which were embedded flashing emeralds and rubies, their facets reflecting every shimmer of the flickering candles, gave the dark interior an unearthly quality, making the pale faces of the painted saints look almost animate.

It was Holy Week, the week before Easter, 1900, and Alix and Nicky had been observing the Great Fast, living on mushrooms, cabbage and fish, taking no food at all some days, attending two- and three-hour services every morning and evening and, between services, making the rounds of the ancient Kremlin churches. They watched reverently the rite of brewing the Holy Chrism, the fragrant oils stirred by priests in huge silver cauldrons while Biblical texts were read aloud by candlelight. They repeated the Eastertide prayers, joined processions, spent time in private devotions. They immersed themselves in the richness of medieval liturgies and traditional ceremonies, feeling, as the days passed, that in the words of the proverb, 'there is nothing above the Kremlin except heaven'.

With Ella, Alix had taken on a large sewing project, embroidering velvet hangings for a church of which Ella was patron. She felt 'like an ancient Tsaritsa', Alix told her biographer years later, 'sitting in her rooms in the Kremlin with her sister and their ladies', working away at the intricate designs, surrounded by heavy antique furnishings, dark stonework and crackling fires. In contrast to the classical austerity of baroque Petersburg, Moscow was intimate, mysterious, half-Asiatic, full of shadows and enigmas. It ignited the soul.

Focused as they were on the old rites of the Moscow Easter, the tsar and tsarina gave scant notice to the swiftly changing contours of the old city, whose sprawling suburbs, greatly enlarged since the start of Nicky's reign, were home to tens of thousands of factory workers newly arrived from the countryside. They had endured a hard winter, made harsher by food shortages and chronic unemployment; now, in Holy Week, they stood in long lines outside soup kitchens and shelters, waiting in the snow for small rations of food. Had Alix seen these long lines, and looked into the faces of the desperate, she would surely have done what she could to alleviate their distress. She had contributed to famine relief in the previous year, and she was tender-hearted and generous. But her attention was fixed elsewhere, on the dim, incense-filled churches with their rich atmosphere of hidden mysteries and infinite possibilities, and on her own fervent, heartfelt prayers.

In particular, her attention was fixed on the wonder-working icons, those glowing holy pictures with their haunting lifelike quality, their almost speaking presences. They had been known to cure the sick, to bring rain or stop floods, even to turn back armies. Icons focused the power of God. Bearing the images of His saints and of Christ and the Virgin, they were more than slabs of wood and smears of paint; they were nothing less than fragments of the divine, and as such, they could be supplicated, and were capable of working miracles.

Each day in Holy Week, Alix and Nicky watched the procession of priests and servants accompanying the icon of the Miraculous Virgin of Mount Athos, mounted in a carriage, wind through the Kremlin, on its way to the homes of the sick and dying. Many gravely ill people claimed to have been revived by coming near this holy icon. The sacred Icon of the Redeemer rose above them when they passed through the Spassky Gate; this icon too was believed to have brought about miracles. They kissed the wonder-working icon in the tower of the Church of the Annunciation, and knelt before the image of the Virgin of Vladimir, the Virgin of Tenderness, in the Church of the Assumption, that holiest of images, before which Tamerlane the Great, the Sword of Islam, had cowered and retreated in fear.

They prayed to the icons for an heir for Russia.

It was partly at Ella's urging that they prayed, for Ella, having converted voluntarily to Orthodoxy, was undergoing a deepening of her piety and was convinced that God would hear and answer her sister's and brother-in-law's prayers.

Because Ella and Serge lived in Moscow, Alix did not see Ella often. However, Ella had been sending her sister gifts, letters, and emissaries – in particular, nuns with whom she talked and prayed.[1]

Partly due to Ella's influence, partly because of the strong interest at court in mystical faith and occult experimentation, Alix and Nicky had begun inviting self-styled mystics and religious teachers to the Alexander Palace. Some of them, such as the Austrian healer Schenk and the French psychic Papuce, were Europeans, but most were Russians, for holy men with extraordinary spiritual gifts were a fixture of Russian religious tradition.

It was as if there existed in Russia two streams of religious inspiration: the church, with its hierarchy of priests and higher clergy, and another more amorphous body of teachers and masters, bound by no community or discipline and answerable to no superior. To this body belonged the stranniki, the Holy Wanderers who roamed from village to village, casting spells and praying over barren fields and dying cattle, claiming to be able to see the future and to cure ills in the present. Holy Fools also wandered from place to place, and it was thought that the voice of God spoke through them. Startsy, or elders, were spiritual teachers or mentors gifted with clarity of vision; they offered guidance to the faithful who came to them and submitted themselves to the startsy's will and insight.

Russians held stranniki, Holy Fools and startsy in awe. Though they often had the appearance of dirty, deranged outcasts, their clothing threadbare, their hair filthy and uncombed, their manner wild-eyed and intimidating, still they were believed to possess a rare holiness – to be, by their very nature, channels for the divine. Many cures were ascribed to them, and they were believed capable of foreseeing the future. The credulous gathered around stranniki and Holy Fools with unreasoning fervour, but even the sceptical, among them educated, sophisticated people who questioned the existence of God, conceded that these shabby, half-incoherent holy beggars possessed authentic and inexplicable powers.

So when Alix and Nicky welcomed the holy Matrena, a wandering fortune-teller, and Vasya Tkachenko, another strannik, and Antony the Wanderer to the palace they were following an established Russian custom, which called for well-off people to provide charity to 'God's slaves', as the wanderers were sometimes called. And when they took in the Holy Fool Mitya Kozelsky, a mute simpleton with deformed legs who 'talked' by means of hand gestures, they were seeking a blessing, a glimpse of God, a message of comfort.

For there existed at court, as the new century opened, a tight circle of seekers into hidden teachings, explorers of occult mysteries, and the emperor and empress were among their most eager members.

Organizers of this circle were Nicky's cousins by marriage, Militsa and Anastasia of Montenegro, daughters of King Nicholas of Montenegro, Militsa married to Grand Duke Peter Nicholaevitch, younger son of Emperor Alexander II's brother Nicholas, and Anastasia married to Duke George of Leuchtenberg.[2] Alix had a family connection to the Montenegrin sisters also. Her cousin Prince Francis Joseph of Battenberg was married to Militsa and Stana's sister Anna, and Francis Joseph and Anna lived in Darmstadt.

The two vivacious sisters, of whom Militsa was the more colourful and unconventional, galvanized the thirst for supernatural explorations and the excitement that arose whenever a psychic or spiritual healer was brought to court. Anastasia, or Stana, held spiritual meetings in her mansion at Znamensky, and Militsa gathered the devotees in a secluded tower in her garden at Sergeyevsky.

Alix, alternately tearful and depressed over her lack of a son and expansively hopeful and prayerful, saw more and more of Militsa and Stana, drawn to Militsa's formidable intellectuality as well as to the promise of secret learning.[3] For the first time since she came to Russia, Alix felt welcomed and accepted. The group of fellow seekers brought together by the Montenegrins provided Alix with the sense of community she had long looked for in vain. She took her place in the circle, not as a German outsider, nor as empress, but merely as a pilgrim among pilgrims, a spiritual explorer, one in need of divine help. It must have come as an immense relief to her to be able to sit quietly in the group, relaxed and expectant, forgetting herself in the collective hush and anticipation of revelations to come.

In the early months of 1901, Alix had several reasons for participating in the spiritual circle. First, she had lost two people who were dear to her: her closest friend Juju Rantzau and her grandmother Queen Victoria, both of whom had died at the beginning of the year.

Along with her friendship, Juju had served as a sort of confessor to Alix, a moral guide. 'She was a rare flower, too delicate for this world,' Alix wrote of her friend, 'but rejoicing others with her fragrance and cheering them on the way. She understood the difficulties of this world and the different temptations, and always encouraged one in the right, and helped one to fight one's weaknesses.'

The weekly diary that Alix and Juju exchanged had been a valued psychological anchor to the empress. Now that it was discontinued, she felt adrift.

'It came so naturally to speak about one's faith to her, that now I feel her loss greatly. Only her dear writings have remained to me. I pray to God to make me as worthy, as she was, of a new and more perfectly happy life in yonder world.'[4]

The afterlife was much on Alix's mind that winter, with Queen Victoria also in 'yonder world'. The great queen, who had been a seemingly eternal fixture in Europe for three generations, died on

January 22, 1901, and Alix's first reaction was to make plans to go to England with Ernie for the funeral. She regretted not having gone to visit Victoria in England the previous year; she had had the feeling then that she would never see her grandmother's 'dear old face' again, and, now that she was dead, Alix wanted one more glimpse of her.

'How I envy you,' Alix wrote to her sister Victoria after abandoning her initial impulse to make the journey to Windsor, 'being able to see beloved Grandmama being taken to her last rest. I cannot believe she is really gone, that we shall never see her any more. It seems impossible.'[5] Alix told her friend Marie Bariatinsky that the queen had 'been as a mother to me, ever since mama's death'. Even though a distance had grown between Alix and her grandmother on her last visit to Balmoral, Alix's underlying affection remained very strong. According to Nicky's sister Xenia, when Alix learned of Queen Victoria's death she was 'in despair'. 'She did so love her grandmother!'[6]

But perhaps, within the circle of believers, it was not after all impossible. For among the gifts of the teachers and advisers sought out by Militsa and Stana were some who claimed to be able to communicate with the dead, or to place those of sincere faith in a state in which they themselves could receive messages from the other world.

Alix's other pressing motivation for taking part in the Montenegrins' circle was that she was once again pregnant, and was vacillating between hope and anxiety over the sex of her unborn child.

Much to her surprise and delight, this pregnancy felt different from the three previous ones. She was not constantly ill, she looked and felt bursting with health and, although stout, appeared 'very beautiful', according to KR.[7] The most obvious explanation for the difference was that this time she was carrying a boy. And why not? She knew that she was capable of conceiving a son; had she not miscarried one? And she knew that some women had boys after a long series of girls. And if her baby was not a boy, perhaps it could become one. There were spiritualists who claimed to be able to influence the sex of a child in utero.

Alix visited Stana and Militsa nearly every day throughout the winter of 1901, and with the coming of spring she continued to be intermittently hopeful. She spent hours talking with her new intimates, and also with Militsa's diffident, cultivated husband Peter. Besides joining the spiritual circle, Alix and Nicky spent social time with the Montenegrins, reading together and discussing what they read, the talk often turning to theology and philosophy. Militsa, a strong personality who liked to hold forth before small audiences, lectured the others on her particular specialty, Persian literature, along with Hindu and Confucian teachings. Though Militsa's actual knowledge was probably quite shallow, her observations were stimulating to Alix, who had a quick intelligence and who liked conversing about ideas. She had been reading on her own since coming to Russia, studying the writings of Augustine and Jerome, investigating what her biographer Sophie Buxhoeveden called 'French and English philosophical books'. She had virtually no one to talk to about these books and the abstract concepts they elucidated. Now she had found a satisfying discussion group, an outlet for her vigorous if largely untrained intellect.

Alix's fourth baby was born in mid-June, another girl whom she named Anastasia. The birth was as easy as the pregnancy had been, with a relatively short labour. 'We both had a feeling of calm and solitude,' Nicky wrote in his diary, adding that 'Alix felt quite cheerful.'[8] The contrast to her dismay at the births of her three other daughters was striking. It seems likely that Alix owed her calm and cheer to the effects of her deepening spiritual questing, and in particular, to a new influence in her life: the hypnotist Philippe Vachot.

The small, black-haired Vachot, a man of fifty, 'very unsightly in appearance', according to the sceptical KR, had become the leader of the Montenegrins' circle. Despite his unprepossessing appearance, Vachot had a powerful effect on the devotees, who knelt and kissed his hand when he came to them and listened attentively, their faces aglow with inspiration, when he spoke to them in his soft voice with its southern French accent.

'Are you all listening to me?' Vachot would ask once they had settled down in the dimly lit room.

'We all hear you, O Master,' they would respond in unison.

'I am nothing in myself,' he reminded them, meaning that he was nothing more than a channel through which the divine force entered the world.

Groans of denial met this remark as Vachot made the rounds of the room, bending down to listen as each member of his audience confided his or her difficulties and desires to him.

'Believe and you will be cured,' he told each of them, pausing at times to pass his hands over their heads and bodies, tracing complex patterns in the air.[9]

'Our friend Philippe,' as Alix and Nicky came to call him, claimed to be able to cure nervous diseases by means of manipulating invisible magnetic forces with his hands. Reportedly he made many other claims as well: that he could conjure the spirits of the dead (it was said he had summoned the ghost of Alexander III, who gave Nicky advice), that he could make himself invisible at will, along with anyone who was with him, and that he could control the sex of an unborn child.

Philippe was certainly an accomplished charlatan, and the more suspicious members of the court and government, alarmed by the central place he was coming to occupy in the emperor's and empress's lives, and by the lengths to which they went to keep their association with him a secret, set about exposing his deceit. What they discovered was that in his native France he had been a butcher and had experience as a medical assistant, and that he had begun practising his magnetic healing there only to be arrested several times for fraud. The Russian secret police, operating in France, were well aware of Philippe and his illegal activities; they had a dossier on him and knew when he left the country to go to Russia, though they made no effort to detain or control him.

What Philippe's opponents could not assess, however, was his genuine power to influence the thinking and strengthen the belief of those who sought him out. Herein lay his value to these seekers; he was a catalyst for their own increasing trust and positive thought – and positive thinking can bring about somatic change, as Alix was soon to demonstrate.

Through the summer of 1901 Nicky's diary is full of references to 'our friend' and to the many evenings he and Alix spent in the company of the hypnotist. Sometimes they visited him after the theatre, staying until two-thirty in the morning; sometimes they went to Znamenka immediately after dinner and listened to Philippe lecture all evening. 'We all prayed together,' Nicky wrote.[10] They prayed, they entered a collective trance, they tasted what one member of the circle called the 'sacred joy' of Philippe's presence.

For what Philippe told his followers was that he had been sent to earth on a divine mission, and that that mission was in its last days. Soon he would lay his earthly body aside, but the mission itself would not end, for his spirit would inhabit the body of another man, and this man would continue his work.

Though he spoke of endings, and of death, his hearers were rapt, caught up in the idea of his divine mission, feeling themselves to be somehow part of it, filled with certainty that, having received the benison of his soothing words, their own lives too would become infused with holy purpose. According to KR, who was well informed, Nicky and Alix 'had fallen into a mystical frame of mind'. They returned from Znamenka, and their long evenings with Philippe, 'in an exalted state, as if in ecstasy, with radiant faces and shining eyes'.[11]

Alix was quite taken out of herself. She had not only found a community, an emotional home, she had found – or so she was convinced – an escape from the endless series of failures by which she had been plagued since she first came to Russia. She had found the divine key to success at last.

Guided by Philippe, she could accomplish what had so far eluded her. She could give the Romanov dynasty, and her husband, a son and heir. She could gain respect and authority among her in-laws, among the courtiers, among the people at large. She could overcome her social discomfort. In short, she could become the triumphant woman God surely meant her to be, having called her to her important role as empress.

'How rich life is since we know him,' Alix wrote to Nicky when he was apart from her, 'and everything seems easier to bear.' Philippe's 'thoughts and earnest prayers' followed them both constantly, Alix assured Nicky; even though he was away from them in body – he had returned to Lyon late in the summer of 1901 – his presence hovered near them, watching over them.[12]

Buoyed by this new-found belief, and surrendering to the divine force she knew resided in Philippe, Alix asked him to return from France to treat her – specifically, to use his powers to help her conceive a son.

Just what form this treatment took no one recorded. Probably it involved much prayer, Philippe's trademark magnetic manipulations, and hypnotic suggestions. By January of 1902 Alix was convinced that she was pregnant, and that her child would at last be the long hoped-for son.

Throughout the winter of 1902 her conviction strengthened. Her periods had ceased, her waist was thickening, her face growing more full and exhibiting the 'glow' of a mother-to-be. Philippe assured her that all was going well, that the child in her womb was the Romanov heir. He advised her to pray to Serafim of Sarov, an eighteenth-century holy man, who would add his wonder-working powers to the process unfolding within her. Nicky immediately ordered the church to canonize Serafim and, though there was opposition to this canonization by imperial fiat, it proceeded.

Alix was expecting her baby to be born in August, 1902, but no official announcement of the pregnancy was made.[13] In April she confided to Xenia, who was also pregnant at the time, that she was in fact expecting, and that her swelling abdomen was beginning to be 'difficult to hide'. She felt well, she told her sister-in-law. She was hopeful. Only a few more months, and everyone would be gratified.[14]

She did not consult the court accoucheur Dr Ott or the imperial surgeon Dr Girsh. Philippe advised against it and, besides, Alix had had four children; she was an old hand at pregnancy. She ordered her dressmakers to let out her gowns, she rested, she prayed in front of the wall of icons in her bedroom.

Among them was one given her by Philippe, from which hung a tiny bell. It was an icon of protection, for Alix herself and for her child. Philippe had warned her that, if the bell rang, it meant there were 'evil people all around'. But the holy image, like the Virgin of Vladimir and the Redeemer over the Spassky Gate, would ward off all harm. No evil could penetrate the sacred barrier. She was held, safely forever, behind the strong and certain shield of the divine.

15

Magnificent sunsets fanned out in fiery reds and pinks over the Gulf of Finland in the summer of 1902, their dramatic colours more intense than at any time in recent memory. Sunrises too were exceptionally vivid, and throughout the long daylight hours the air seemed to hold a pinkish cast that lent gardens, buildings, even people a healthy, faintly unreal glow.

Alix, sitting on her balcony at Peterhof, watching the gradual deepening of the intense colours in the sky over the blue waters of the gulf, waited calmly for the onset of her labour, the culmination of her hopes. The unusual beauty of the sky and the rosy light must have seemed to her a fitting backdrop for the birth of her son. She was tranquil, sanguine, serene. Nothing troubled her when she was at her most reflective, not the recent assassination of the Interior Minister Sipyagin, not the distress of the War Minister Kuropatkin over growing tensions between Russia and Japan, not the huge increase in the numbers of dissidents and demonstrators being sent into exile – not even the puzzling shape of her own body which, though swollen, had not taken on the ripe roundness of a full-term pregnancy. Despite appearances, all was well, she believed, for Philippe was always near, and he assured her that everything was working out for the best.

In August the skies darkened and a chill wind blew across the gulf. Rain splashed down in torrents day after day, making the palace fountains overflow and keeping the fretful, irritated members of the imperial family, who had gathered to await the confirmation of the empress's pregnancy by the doctors, indoors.

They conferred with one another about the assassination of Sipyagin and its aftermath of increased police activity, about the explosion of the volcano on Martinique that had sent tons of volcanic ash into the air, causing the lurid sunrises and sunsets; about the dowager empress's fury at Militsa and Stana for leading Nicky and Alix into religious extremism and a dangerous dependency on the foreign Dr Philippe.

The best informed among them spoke in serious terms about the deteriorating state of Nicky's ineffectual leadership, of feared weakness in the army and navy, of the evident lack of clear direction in the government. Others aired personal grievances. Uncle Vladimir complained that Nicky had had the audacity to tell him whom he could and could not bring into the royal box at the theatre – of course he ignored his nephew's directives. Sandro complained about the government post he had been given and insisted on a change. The usual factions that gathered around Aunt Miechen and Minnie spread gossip about each other.

But there was unusual unanimity about this very odd and un-settling matter of the empress's state of health, and its connection to the sinister Dr Philippe. Was she or wasn't she pregnant? No one knew for sure. She avoided going out, except to her clandestine meetings with the French medium, so the truth could not be discerned by the shape of her body. She had told Xenia that she was expecting, but was very secretive with Ella, who distrusted Dr Philippe and everything about him; to Ella she simply said that she had taken a remedy of some sort that had helped her conceive.[1]

Philippe had been thoroughly discredited, his police record in Paris brought to light, yet Alix continued to put her trust in him and Nicky, against all reason, punished the Russian agent who had revealed his fraud. What motive could Nicky have had for doing this? Speculation burgeoned. Philippe claimed to be able to cure syphilis; was the emperor a syphilitic? Did Philippe know some other dark secret that gave him a hold over the imperial family? What was going on?[2]

Or was there some even more sinister plot at work? It was whispered that Philippe had been brought to court in order to entice

Alix into an unhealthy reliance on him, so that she could be revealed as mentally unstable, a melancholic, and shut away in an institution.[3]

Amid the darker rumours there was also a good deal of laughter about Dr Philippe and the imperials. Nicky and Alix were seen as fools in the grip of a quack – fit subjects for caricature of the kind Alix had once drawn so unkindly. It was absurd that Nicky and Alix should imagine they could conceal their dealings with the quack, for the secret police knew everything, had spies everywhere; for all anyone knew, Philippe himself might be a spy!

Tensions rose, the rain poured down, and on the night of August 31, 1902, Alix began to feel contractions.

No one recorded exactly what took place, whether the pains went on all night or only for a short time, whether Philippe was summoned to her bedside, whether Nicky, who must have been present, was caught up in his wife's hopes or whether by this time, if not earlier, he had come to realize that there was no child in her womb.

For Alix, the terrible moment of truth must have been among the great shocks of her life. Instead of delivering a child she suddenly began to bleed, as she had not bled for nine months, and, as Xenia wrote, 'a tiny ovule came out'. Her abdomen deflated, her pains ceased. Dr Ott was at last allowed to examine her, and 'confirmed that there was no pregnancy, but that luckily everything internally was all right.'[4] He diagnosed amenorrhoea, the result of anaemia.

'At last a natural way out of this unfortunate situation has been found,' Xenia wrote. 'She is in bed – as a precaution, as there can sometimes be bleeding [haemorrhaging] in such cases. Thank God so far she is in good health.'

Xenia was sympathetic, but others were far less so. Inevitably, there was laughter – and anger, for had not the foolish empress embarrassed the entire family and the country? She was a trouble-maker, a blight on Russia. Not only was she barren of sons, but she was apparently delusional as well. And why hadn't the emperor handled the entire awkward matter more capably, so as to prevent all the confusion and embarrassment? Why hadn't he been able to control his wretchedly inconvenient wife?

Lying in her bed, emptied of all her hopes, Alix cried. Shock had given way to sorrow and bewilderment. She struggled to understand. She had been so certain that in all things she was acting under divine guidance. Was this awful emptiness too God's will? Or had she failed?

Alix 'cried terribly' when Minnie and Xenia came to her bedside and she told them what had happened. She had accepted the truth, but was sad and low.[5] The shock, the loss, the violent wrenching of all her expectations brought out the vulnerable girl in Alix, a side she almost never showed to anyone but her husband, her late friend Juju Rantzau and Martha Mouchanow. She reached out to Xenia and Minnie as she might have reached out to her own mother, had she lived. For a brief time, the brittle control she normally maintained in the presence of her in-laws cracked open, leaving her shattered emotions exposed.

But the moment passed quickly, for Minnie took advantage of the embarrassment over Alix's false pregnancy to lecture her and Nicky about how misled they were in trusting the tricks and false promises of Philippe and, as soon as she did that, Alix's wall of self-protective reserve went up once again.

Minnie confronted her son and daughter-in-law with the contents of the police report on Philippe, but Nicky's response was that 'all the rumours were very much exaggerated', and he refused to be pinned down as to how intertwined his and Alix's lives had become with their spiritual mentor.

Dr Ott issued an official announcement about Alix's indisposition. 'Thanks to a departure from the normal course,' it read, 'the interrupted pregnancy has resulted in a miscarriage.'[6] It was the least embarrassing explanation. There was no mention of anaemia.

Inwardly still in a vulnerable state, Alix was in need of reassurance, and she soon found it, once again, in Philippe and her emotional anchor, the spiritual circle. Within months, by the end of 1902, her hopes and expectations had been raised yet again, all her confusion dispelled. Philippe had convinced her that, with the aid of the holy Serafim of Sarov, she could yet triumph over all limitations, physical or spiritual, and conceive a son.

The year 1903 was the two hundredth anniversary of the founding of St Petersburg and, all over the city, preparations were under way for a variety of commemorations. The city's builder, Peter the Great, whose modest log cabin was still preserved and visited by travellers, was to be honoured with exhibits in the Yekaterinov Palace, the Technological Institute, and at the Admiralty. There were to be special observances at Palace Embankment and the Petrovsky Embankment, in the Peter and Paul Fortress, on St Isaac's Square and in the Summer Gardens. Book stalls were selling Jubilee Almanacs, and special historical publications were issued.

In keeping with the mood of recalling the past, two balls were held at court in February of 1903, historical balls, recalling not the time of Peter the Great but that of his father Tsar Alexis, whose era, the mid-seventeenth century, was of particular interest to Nicky.

Alix applied herself to preparing for the historical ball with that devotion to minutiae – akin to the cataloguing of her lace and the more recent meticulous inventorying of her children's wardrobes – that was becoming her hallmark. She consulted the director of the Hermitage Museum in the design of all the costumes, and had antique jewellery and clothing brought from the Granovitaia Palace in Moscow for use at the ball. Seamstresses prepared elaborate sarafans for her ladies-in-waiting and maids of honour and others in the imperial household.

Alix's costume was a marvel of antiquarian reconstruction, if not of comfort. Dressed as Tsar Alexis's first wife, Tsarina Maria Ilinichna, she wore a sarafan of gold brocade with a silver design inlaid with emeralds, pearls and diamonds. An antique jewelled headdress crowned her head, and from beneath it a white veil fell over her shoulders. Her long bejewelled earrings, so heavy they had to be fastened to her ears with loops of gold wire, glittered in the candle-light. The headdress immobilized her so that she had to sit down for most of the evening, and could not bend her head to eat.[7]

Nicky was equally magnificent dressed as Tsar Alexis in a rich red caftan thickly embroidered in gold thread, an authentic headdress from Alexis's time and in his hand a gold staff. Unkind critics remarked that he was too short to look dignified in his finery.

At both historical balls, the great halls and supper tables at the Hermitage and the Winter Palace were awash in velvet gowns and gleaming golden headdresses, colourful ribbons, dangling festoons and flashing sequins. The fur hats of the men, hung with jewels, their bright sashes, their gold-trimmed boots and gleaming sabres, all had the effect of creating a tapestry of the past, brought to life for a few glorious hours.

In that far-off past a respite could be found from the violent dislocations of the present, with its workers' strikes and assassinations and demonstrations, its omnipresent police, its massacres and pogroms and ominous rumblings of war and the threat of war.

For as the year 1903 opened, the tsar's government was racked by conflicts. Its strongest and most capable member, the Finance Minister Witte, despised Nicky for his dreamy impracticality and, in Witte's view, his weak grasp of foreign affairs. Diplomatic disagreements with a militarily formidable Japan, victor over China and aggressor in Korea and elsewhere, were worsening. The Japanese objected to Russian military occupation of the left bank of the Yalu River and, exasperated by the Russians' intransigence on this issue, eventually turned to England and negotiated an alliance with the government of Edward VII. Pressure was brought to bear on Russia to withdraw its troops from Manchuria, and the Russian ministry gave its guarantees that a withdrawal would be accomplished by early October of 1903.

To Witte and Kuropatkin it was nonetheless evident that the tsar, caught up in a vision of a Russian empire stretching eastwards to the Pacific, was bound to entangle the country in a war with Japan. And it was equally evident that he was bound to bring his vision of an expanded empire into actuality by dangerously unconventional means.

Convinced that he understood far better than his ministers what was best for Russia, Nicky had begun to turn to shady intriguers who convinced him that, if only he gave them enough money, they could deliver foreign territories into his hands. One such enterprising schemer was a cavalry officer named Bezobrasov, who promised to put all of Manchuria and Korea under Russian rule. Financed by two million roubles from the imperial treasury, Bezobrasov installed himself and six hundred mercenaries in the disputed Yalu River region and sent the tsar encouraging reports – reports that no doubt influenced Nicky, when he thought about the guarantees he had given to withdraw Russian troops, to ignore the diplomatic assurances and risk conflict.

Events in the international arena were put aside during the summer of 1903 while Russians celebrated the canonization of Serafim of Sarov, the monk Philippe had urged Alix to pray to for a son. The canonization had gone ahead, and in the last days of July the Diveyevo Convent near Sarov was the scene of a vast gathering of pilgrims, among them many members of the imperial family.

The days were extremely hot, the roads dry and dusty in July 1903. The few thin clouds that floated in the sky were obscured by a film of brown that rose above the roadways to a height of twenty or thirty feet, and as the slow procession of pilgrims made its way towards the monastery the sound of coughing was constant among them.

They came in a great stream, nearly all of them on foot, nearly all of them poor peasants in thick dark tunics and bast shoes, the women's faces shrouded by headscarves. They carried icons of Serafim, baskets of food, sacks with offerings to lay before the shrine. Sometimes they sang as they walked along, though in the hottest part of the day it took all their energy to keep walking, wary of the mounted Cossacks and police who rode among them, vigilant for stragglers or subversives.

Many among the pilgrims limped, some were carried on litters. Amputees swung themselves along on crutches. Mothers carried sick children in their arms, fathers supported the elderly. They had come dozens, even hundreds, of miles to kiss the relics of the holy Serafim, who had cured so many thousands both in his lifetime and after his death. They were weary, but 'full of fervour and expectation', as one of them wrote.

They knew the story of St Serafim, how he had gone as a monk to live in a cottage deep in the forest, keeping to himself and fasting, purifying himself in his solitude for fifteen years, comforted only by the wild animals who sought him out and brought him food. How he had been attacked by robbers and nearly killed, and how the Virgin Mary had come to him in a vision and healed his wounds. And how, after this signal instance of grace, Serafim had become a starets, receiving all those who came to him and healing them and advising them, giving to them freely from his own divine gifts.

Serafim's miracles were too many to count. Those who kissed his shrine, or bathed in the holy pool where he had bathed, rose up renewed. He straightened crooked limbs, restored sight, made the barren fertile and gave vigour to the old and weak. Now he had been declared a saint by order of the Holy Synod, and his remains were to be taken from his modest grave in the churchyard and interred in the new cathedral built for them. His canonization confirmed Serafim's holiness, the pilgrims believed, and redoubled his healing powers.

And so they streamed towards the monastery day after day, coming from as far away as the Caucasus and Siberia, entire families, almost entire villages, with here and there a priest, a town councillor stiff and hot in his black suit, babies crying, old men praying, hands lifted heavenwards, the entire massed community orderly in its onward march, under the fierce sun.

In the midst of the vast procession rode the troikas of the imperial family, greeted, as they passed through each village, by crowds of brightly costumed peasants crying 'Little Father!' as Nicky and Alix alighted to talk with them. The heartfelt adoration of the peasants was reassuring; they surged forwards and kissed the tsar's hands, his clothing, making of him a living icon. 'It was too moving for words,' Nicky's sister Olga wrote. 'Nicky was just batushka tsar, Little Father, to all these people.'[8]

The imperials were much sought-after, yet as they resumed their journey they melted into the sea of humanity, pilgrims among the pilgrims, seeking the blessing of Serafim like all the others. Alix had come with particular faith and devotion, intending to carry out Philippe's advice that she bathe in Serafim's pool – and perhaps also to seek a cure for the terrible headaches that had begun to afflict her, and for her sciatic pain. She was only thirty-one, but her pregnancies had taxed her body, making her thick-waisted and at times short of breath. Her fervour was as great, her attitude as humble and reverent, as those of the peasants as the vast crowd reached the pine wood at Sarov and turned into the narrow path that led to the convent.

Three days of ceremonies marked the canonization of Saint Serafim. His disinterred relics were placed in a golden coffin and borne on the shoulders of the tsar, his Uncle Serge and his cousins around the grounds of the cathedral, then brought inside to be displayed in front of the chancel in the presence of the Metropolitan Antony of Petersburg and the bishops of Kazan and Tambov and other prelates.

The hushed silence inside the immense golden-domed cathedral was full of hope as, with the utmost reverence, the sick began to come forwards to kiss the saint's relics, murmuring prayers, as the choir sang quietly in the background. The huge congregation watched, expecting miracles, whispering to one another that a cure had already been experienced, while the saint's coffin was carried around the church.

One by one the afflicted came, or were brought forward, some so feeble they could barely shuffle past the coffin, each reaching down to place a kiss on the gilded wood.

'Oh, what misery, what illnesses we saw, and what faith!' Ella wrote. 'It seemed as if we were living in Christ's time . . . Oh, how they prayed, how they cried, these poor mothers with their sick children and, thank God, how many were cured! We had the blessing of seeing a little dumb girl speak, but how her mother prayed for her!'[9]

The extraordinary spectacle went on for nearly four hours, as the congregation stood in wonder, weeping from the extreme strain and overcome with holy feeling. Madmen were led forward, shrieking and howling, some writhing so violently that it took several people to control them. When they touched the shrine, however, their inhuman cries subsided, their tortured limbs seemed to relax.[10]

Waves of awe passed through the onlookers with each cure, or perceived cure. Held in the grip of the miraculous, convinced beyond any doubt that they were witnessing marvels, the faithful prayed and continued to come forward, until at last the metropolitan brought the service to an end.

On the final evening of the ceremonies, in the gathering dusk, Nicky and Alix, Minnie, Olga, Ella and the others made their way in twos and threes down to the holy pool of Serafim and stepped into the freezing water. They were in a unique frame of mind, beyond doubt, beyond ordinary thought. They had seen with their own eyes the dumb speak and the paralyzed walk.[11] They knew, with all the fervour of belief, that St Serafim could heal them.

And Alix was certain, as she bathed in the holy waters, that her prayers for a son would be answered. She came out of the pool and knelt by the nearby shrine, thanking the saint for the baby he would give her. Then quietly, their identities cloaked by the darkness, the imperials made their way back to the convent.

'Truly,' Nicky wrote in his diary that night, 'God works miracles through his saints.[12] Great is his ineffable mercy towards dear Russia, this manifestation of the Lord's grace towards us all brings inexpressible comfort. In you we put our trust, Lord; we shall never be confounded.'

16

The first word to arrive in Petersburg about the Japanese attack on Port Arthur came from a Russian commercial agent, who sent a telegram warning the navy that the Russian squadron protecting the immense, decaying fort on the Liaodong Peninsula in north China, at the mouth of the harbour adjacent to Peking, was being decimated.

There had been no declaration of war. The Japanese fleet under Vice-Admiral Togo had sent torpedo boats to attack the Russian warships at night, severely damaging the *Tsarevich, Retvizan* and *Pallada* and leaving a number of other vessels with ruptured hulls and torn rigging.

Phones rang, telegrams went out across the continent. The news was startling. Was it possible that tiny but bellicose Japan could have the daring to take on the entire Russian empire, with its population of a hundred million and more, its million-man army and its large battle fleet? Japan of the delicate fans and fragile cherry blossoms, of the geishas in their wispy houses? The disparity between the two countries was almost too great to be comprehended – and besides, the Russians, despite the tinge of the Asiatic in their culture, belonged to Europe; they were Christian, civilized, Caucasian. They belonged to the dominant bloc, the superior force in the world. The Japanese were unchristian, to the Russians uncivilized (though their culture was, paradoxically, much admired by Europeans), non-white. For such a nation to even think of challenging a European empire was unsettling to the natural order of things – or so it seemed to Europeans in the winter of 1904.

When he heard the news of the Japanese attack the Russian Interior Minister Plehve was gratified. There was nothing like a war to stimulate patriotism, to subdue anti-government feeling and revolutionary activity. Let the conflict go forwards, he advised, but let it be brief, and overwhelmingly victorious for the tsar and his empire. That should stop the mouths of the critics for awhile.

Kuropatkin, on the other hand, was worried. He knew from secret reports that the fortress of Port Arthur was far from being the impregnable bastion Russians supposed it to be. Its garrison was weak and short of ammunition, its old walls crumbling from years of neglect. And the ships that rode at anchor in the harbour were also in disrepair, some of them too unseaworthy to risk manoeuvres, most of them under the command of mediocre officers. No wonder the Japanese had been able to cripple three of them so easily. Most of all Kuropatkin worried about supplying the army in the event of a full-scale conflict. The Trans-Siberian Railway, which when built would connect Petersburg with Vladivostok, was at least a year away from being completed; in the meantime there was no efficient way to send supplies and reinforcements to the Russian garrison.

'God be with us!' Nicky wrote in his diary on the night he heard the news of the attack. He had known that the Japanese ambassador had taken his leave of Petersburg two days earlier, after six months of unsuccessful deliberations and ten failed attempts to draft an agreement over territorial rights. He was aware, for Kuropatkin had told him, that the Japanese actually had many more fighting men in the region than the Russians had, and that their troops were better trained and better equipped. Yet he had not anticipated this sudden, treacherous attack.

More shocks arrived in the following days. Port Arthur came under bombardment. Seven more Russian ships were sunk or heavily damaged. The Japanese had mined the harbour, preventing what remained of the Russian squadron from escaping. And Japanese torpedo craft were attempting to run the gauntlet of the fortress guns and land troops ashore.

Public sentiment was aroused, there were patriotic delegations and mass demonstrations. Crowds cheered and sang 'God Save the

Tsar'. Every man who possessed one put on his military uniform, even if he had seen no active service in decades, and wore it every day, parading through the streets of Petersburg as if in anticipation of a military review. Money poured into the treasury to support the war effort, millions of rubles contributed by the nobility, wealthy industrialists, bankers and traders.

But no amount of money could suddenly awaken the dormant, under-prepared troops and crews, or make proficient the incompetent commanders. There was no forceful Russian counter-attack. Instead, the flagship, the *Petropavlovsk*, was sunk with six hundred men aboard, including Admiral Makarov, and another battleship was badly damaged. And, with the navy unable to offer much resistance, the Japanese began bringing tens of thousands of their troops ashore. Opinion in Petersburg, which had dismissed the Japanese venture as ultimately futile, now began to take the threat to Russian interests more seriously.

The empress's first response to the outbreak of conflict was to reinvigorate her charitable guild, Help Through Handwork, and to move it into larger rooms in the Winter Palace. Now instead of making clothing for the poor she and her ladies sewed bandages and warm clothes and knitted stockings for the soldiers. The workshop became a collecting point for medical supplies and other necessities to be readied for shipment eastward into Siberia. Hundreds of women volunteered to sew and knit and pack boxes, and Alix appointed her maid of honour Princess Obolensky ('Litty') to oversee the work-shop. ('She has such a clear, practical brain and good memory,' Alix wrote to her sister Victoria.)

Each morning after she had heard her children's prayers, dressed, and eaten breakfast, Alix gathered her sewing things and, preceded by an attendant, entered the workshop where she looked over what had been produced the day before, talked to the volunteers and discussed the present day's efforts with Litty and the Robes Mistress Princess Galitzine, who also had a supervisory role.

'There is no end of work to be done, but it is a great comfort to be able to help one's poor sufferers a little,' Alix wrote. 'All work hard. Litty manages it splendidly . . . We work for the army hospitals (apart

from the Red Cross) and for the well who need clothes, tobacco . . .
and then we furnish military trains."[1] Alix and her group could not
supply garments or goods to the Red Cross, for that was among
Minnie's charities, and any contribution the empress's workshop
made would have been considered a trespass on the dowager empress's prerogatives.

The work and its urgency, the daily ritual associated with it gave
Alix a welcome sense of purpose and direction, but the outbreak of
war depressed her and brought on severe migraines; though she
encouraged Nicky and reassured him that 'God and our dear Friend
[Philippe] will help us', the strain she was under showed in her pallor,
the hours she spent weeping alone in her room, her attacks of flu
and her 'air of suffering'.[2]

'She had always been very delicate,' Mouchanow wrote, 'and
developed violent nervous headaches which totally prostrated her
and confined her to her bed in a dark room, sometimes for two or
three days at a time. These attacks left her terribly weak, and she
would require care and quiet to get over them.'[3] Nothing could be
done for her when her headaches were at their worst. No one could
go near her, not even the children, for her senses were so acutely
attuned during these attacks that the slightest sound, even the sound
of a footfall in the next room, could redouble her pain.

Worst of all, there were times when one migraine had hardly passed
before another began, forcing her into another period of isolation
and suffering.

She was pregnant again. The visit to St Serafim's shrine, the bathing
in his holy pool, had had its result. But instead of bringing her joy,
this pregnancy was overshadowed by anxiety, not only because of
her physical distress and worry over the war, and Nicky's frequent
absences as a result of it, but because, according to Mouchanow,
Alix was secretly apprehensive that her child might be another girl.
She no longer enjoyed the peace that had emanated from the spiritual
circle, the confidence that had been so evident during her false
pregnancy. She still believed, she still trusted Philippe. But doubts
had invaded her serenity.

And not only doubts, but grief. In the fall of 1903, while she and Nicky were staying at the hunting lodge of Skierniewice, her young niece Elizabeth, daughter of the divorced Ernie and Ducky, fell ill of typhoid and died within days. Ernie had adored the beautiful little girl, his 'sweet little sunshine', and was overcome by his loss. Alix, exhausted from nursing her seriously ill lady-in-waiting Sonia Orbeliani, helped Ernie through the terrible first days after his daughter's death, suffering along with him and looking pale and thin.

In the first week of the Japanese war she had another shock. Her sister Irene's youngest son, four-year-old Henry, died of the 'English disease', haemophilia, after falling and injuring his head. He bled internally, the bleeding could not be stopped, and death was inevitable – as it had been for Alix's brother Frittie after his fall. (Irene had two sons with the bleeding disease, though the older one, Waldemar, continued to survive.) While mourning her sister's loss Alix must have felt increased anxiety over her own pregnancy, for if her child was a boy he would be at risk of the disease.

Was her difficult pregnancy a sign that her child would be diseased, or were her migraines and nervous tears merely the result of her concern over the war, and her long hours of work with the ladies of her guild? This question led to still more distress as the spring of 1904 advanced and the war continued to go badly for Russia. In May the forces of the mikado soundly defeated the Russian forces on the Yalu and shortly afterwards laid siege to Port Arthur. In Petersburg, the early patriotic fervour gave way to a grim realization that Japan was a powerful enemy and that the war was likely to be prolonged. Casualty lists grew longer. Now many families mourned lost sons, read the newspapers with sober faces, and prayed for peace.

And, as might have been anticipated, the prolongation of the war stirred up social turmoil. On the gates of the Summer Gardens in Petersburg a large hand-lettered sign appeared: 'Dogs, Beggars, all Lower Ranks of the Army and Navy Not Allowed.' It was an insult to the fighting men, so many of whom were crowding into the city, their conspicuous presence a constant, disturbing reminder to Petersburgers of the war. They sat in cafes, milled in shops, occupied park benches, wandered aimlessly along Nevsky Prospekt, waiting to be called to the front or sent home.

Anti-government forces were once again at work, stirring up ill feeling and spreading fear with their sudden attacks and secret plots. The Governor General of Finland was shot by a student revolutionary. Interior Minister Plehve was killed by a bomb thrown just outside the Warsaw Station in Petersburg, in a well planned attack carried out by a number of conspirators in defiance of Plehve's secret police. Mayors, regional governors, officials were assaulted or threatened with assault, and spies sent word to the ministries of plots against the life of the tsar as he travelled from Moscow to Poltava to Tula to Suvalki to Vitebsk, reviewing the troops and encouraging them as they went off to the war, icons of St Serafim held before them to protect them in their holy cause.

In the midst of all the turmoil Alix continued to do her part for the war effort, giving audiences to generals about to leave for the front, supervising her workshop, sewing and knitting. 'I like following all and not to be a mere doll,' she wrote to her sister Victoria in June of 1904. 'Yes, it is a trying time, but one must put all one's trust in God, who gives strength and courage. Unluckily I cannot get about at all and spend my days on the sofa . . . walking and standing causes me great pain.'[4] She was advised not to walk, yet she got up anyway, 'dragging herself through the park at Peterhof', as Mouchanow remembered, 'looking so ill that one wondered whether she would be able to stand the trial which was awaiting her'.

The baby was due in August, and once again the family gathered in order to be present at the baptism. There was no mystery about this pregnancy; Dr Ott had verified it, and the child appeared to be developing normally. Huge and all but immobile, Alix lay on her sofa in the final weeks, full of apprehension.

One evening as her maids were dressing her for dinner, there was a bang and a splintering of glass. 'Suddenly we heard a crash behind us, and were dismayed to see that a heavy-looking glass which hung upon the wall behind [Alix] had fallen to the floor, where it had been shattered into a thousand fragments. The Empress cried aloud in her emotion, and for one moment I believed that she was about to faint, so white did her features become.'[5]

It was an omen, she said. She would surely die in childbirth. No one could persuade her otherwise.

In this mood of doom the empress felt her labour pains begin. All her attendants were summoned, the family alerted. Nicky came from a meeting with his officers, expecting to have lunch with Alix, and instead found that the birth process was well advanced.

The baby was delivered, and Dr Ott turned to Nicky. 'I congratulate Your Majesty on the birth of a tsarevich!' he announced.

The news was stunning, unexpected, wonderful. The tsar beamed. Joyful murmurs spread through the assembled staff. The signal was sent on its way to Petersburg, where the gunners began firing their cannon. This time the citizens of the capital were gratified. Three hundred loud reports boomed across the river from the Peter and Paul Fortress. A boy! A tsarevich! Caps were tossed in the air, shouts rang out, toasts were drunk again and again. In her dark hour of war, Russia was given the boon of an heir to the throne at last.

Alix, slow to recover from the effects of chloroform, came sleepily awake. 'When she opened her eyes,' Mouchanow wrote, 'she looked so weak that no one dared to tell her the good news, but she seemed to read it in the face of her husband, because she suddenly exclaimed, "Oh, it cannot be true; it cannot be true. Is it really a boy?"'[6]

She had feared that she would die; instead she was given that which she most longed for, a son. They named him Alexei, after Nicky's favourite predecessor, the father of Peter the Great.

All the family came in to see the new baby, his sisters, aged eight to three, crowding around and Nicky's brother Michael, no longer the designated heir, announcing that he was happy to go into 'retirement'. Everyone exclaimed how large and robust the baby was, how heavy at eleven pounds, how sturdy he looked, like his grandfather Alexander III.

The family was satisfied. It had taken ten years, but Alix had finally done what she had been brought from Hesse to do.

Alexei travelled to his baptism ceremony in a gilded coach, escorted by a troop of cavalry. He was borne to the font by the Robes Mistress, Princess Galitzine, on a cushion of cloth of gold, secured to her shoulder with a broad gold band. (To prevent her from slipping on the waxed floor, she wore rubber shoes.) His tiny ermine-lined mantle was held by the Grand Marshal of the court. A long procession of grand dukes and duchesses, ambassadors, and officials attended the ceremony, dressed in their full finery to honour the tsarevich. Every soldier in the Russian army was declared to be Alexei's godparent, along with the Prince of Wales – the future George V – and the German Emperor. Ribbons and decorations were presented to the infant, and he was made honorary colonel of many regiments.

The rejoicing went on for weeks, with banquets and ceremonies held in many cities and gifts and telegrams arriving from all over the world. The 'baby tsar' was thriving, taking milk from both his mother and a wet-nurse, growing fat and healthy. He was a placid, contented child as he rode on his proud father's shoulder or was carried in his mother's arms.

'He's an amazingly hefty baby,' Xenia wrote of Alexei, 'with a chest like a barrel and generally has the air of a warrior knight.'[7] He would not be puny like his father, but tall and strong like his grandfather Alexander III, a mighty tsar, robust and fearsome.

Then one afternoon blood began to ooze from the baby's navel in a bright red trickle. There was not much blood, but enough to be worrying, for it did not clot and continued to seep out for hours, all afternoon and into the early evening.

Alexei did not appear to be disquieted or in pain. He didn't cry, but was alert and calm, though as he lost more blood he must have become pale.

When they saw that the bleeding from the tiny wound did not stop in a reasonable period of time Alix and Nicky were anxious. They knew the signs, and feared the worst. It might be the bleeding disease, the English disease, the terrible disease that had killed Irene's son Henry and that made her son Waldemar a virtual invalid much of the time.

The doctor, Korovin, and the surgeon Fedorov were summoned. They applied a bandage to the baby's navel, and watched over him as, that night, he continued to lose blood.

What conversations took place during those interminable, alarming hours cannot be known with certainty, but the emperor and empress must have questioned the doctors urgently, perhaps frantically.[8] Would there be haemorrhaging from the wound? Would the tsarevich die? Did he have the bleeding disease? What could be done to stop the flow of blood? Alix must have recalled the shattered mirror, the omen of tragedy, with a frisson of horror. She and Nicky both must have prayed fervently for the healing of their son before the crowded screen of icons in their bedroom and Alexei's. They must have petitioned God and Jesus and Mary and all the saints, and Philippe as well, in a torrent of heartfelt appeal.

The following morning the bleeding continued, finally ceasing at noon. When the bandages remained free of blood for several hours, the tension began to ease – but only slightly. The doctors, the wet-nurse and other servants, the family remained watchful, alert for a resumption of the bleeding. And watchful too for bruises or dark patches on the tiny body, evidence of internal bleeding.

A son had been born, but with his birth had come an anxiety so overwhelming as to be incalculable. For the baby's life to be preserved – and few babies with the bleeding disease survived childhood in 1904 – he would have to be guarded and protected with extravagant care. And even then there was no certainty that he would live into boyhood, much less into manhood. A fall, a jar, an accident of any kind could carry him off within hours.

What was more, Alix must have realized that if she had another child, and it was a boy, there was a strong chance that this second son too would inherit the English disease. So Alexei was to be her only hope.

Meanwhile, the court and nation, and the public outside of Russia, who were still in a celebratory mood and sending gifts and congratulations, must not find out that the heir to the throne was unhealthy. Those who knew were sworn to secrecy, and Alix and Nicky steeled themselves to hide their pain and worry.

'Oh, what anguish it was,' Alix wrote after the tsarevich's first attack of bleeding, 'and not to let others see the knife digging in one.'[9] Dissimulation was not natural to her, yet she forced herself to adopt a closed expression; neither her apprehension nor her relief must show. She continued to nurse her 'little sunbeam', and to show him off to visitors, busying herself making Christmas gifts for the soldiers and inspecting the products of her workshop before they were sent east.

For of course the demands of the war had to take precedence over all else. The soldiers suffering in Port Arthur must not suspect that their tsarevich, whose godfathers they were, and in whose birth they had rejoiced, could die at any time. They must be supported, encouraged, healed, kept alive so that they could fight on.

But as Christmas approached the soldiers were increasingly unable to fight. They had no ammunition left. They had little to eat. They froze at night and, in the daytime, sweated with typhoid fever. Day after day they waited for a relieving force to arrive by sea, but none came.

They could no longer bury the dead in the frozen ground. The bodies, naked and pale, were heaped into piles and left to the elements, until the snow made them into white mounds, featureless and stark against the grey sky.

Early in January, 1905, the Russian defenders of Port Arthur surrendered to the Japanese, and as the news spread throughout Russia there was disbelief, then lamentation, then churning resentment and a resolute cry for revenge.

17

Frost rimed the metal railings of the bridges over the frozen Neva, and the sky was low and heavy with grey clouds. Trams ran along Nevsky Prospekt, passing the vast, many-windowed Winter Palace, then crossing the river to Vassily Island and going down Eight-Line Street towards the poorer quarters of the city. The streets were quiet, few sleighs glided along the roads, bells jangling, and even fewer pedestrians were out amid the shops, their breath freezing in the harshly cold air. Only a handful of droshky drivers sat, huddled in layers of wool and fur, their beards white with frost, waiting to be hired, for most of the drivers were on strike and only the most desperate came out in the cruel chill of the midwinter morning in hopes of earning a fare.

Out on the icebound river, the marine police were patrolling in groups of two and three, examining the frozen surface for cracks and marking thin, dark patches of ice with poles topped with red flags. Near Tushkov Quay, men had been at work since dawn, cutting huge blocks of ice to be loaded onto horse-drawn sleds and sold to householders to cool their cellars.

The hush that enveloped the snowbound city was deceptive, for Petersburgers had reacted to news of the surrender of Port Arthur to the Japanese only weeks earlier with alarm and dismay, and factory workers, their determination to force change in their working conditions building over several months, were out on strike in record numbers.

The labour unrest had begun several weeks earlier, in the Putilov metals factory where railroad cars were being built. Four workers were fired, and thousands of their fellow workers came to their defence, one factory after another going on strike until nearly four hundred factories were idle, and a hundred and fifty thousand former employees had left their jobs. With no pay and nothing to eat, shivering in the bitter weather, seething with grievances, they met to plan a joint strategy. To make their demands for higher pay and an eight-hour day known, and to ask – perhaps even to insist – that they be represented in a national assembly.

But on this cold morning there were no meetings in the street or on the ice, only the sound of hammering as a wooden dais was erected on the river just below the palace, where the tsar was to stand during the ceremony of the Blessing of the Waters.

Towards mid-morning the street lights went out as a pale sun shone intermittently through the veil of cloud. More trams passed now, along with horse-drawn omnibuses, the traffic in the street increasing, the number of pedestrians growing. In Palace Square, weak sunlight gleamed on the high-piled snowdrifts, lit the roof of the army general staff headquarters, glinted on the cross atop the Alexander Column. The thousand windows of the palace came alight, the river ice sparkled blue-green and, as the dignitaries assembled on the wooden dais for the opening prayers of the ceremony, the gilded casements of the palace glowed with a warm burnish.

Many members of the imperial family were gathered to witness the ceremony, watching from behind the palace windows. They had come into Petersburg with some trepidation, for the reports from the secret police of increased revolutionary activity were unsettling and every day, it seemed, revolutionaries armed with bombs were discovered and arrested. The tsar's uncles were known to be among the plotters' primary targets. Uncle Vladimir had begun to take the precaution of never planning his route of travel beforehand, lest the route become known to a revolutionary with a bomb. Uncle Alexei, who according to the tsar was being 'tracked like a wild beast, in order to be killed', remained largely out of sight. And Serge, in Moscow, the most hated of the imperial uncles, had moved out of his Governor General's residence and slept in a different Kremlin palace every night, under heavy guard, increasingly fearful that one day his protection would fail – or that one of his protectors might become his assassin.

The tsar himself, despite the apprehensions of his relatives and his ministers, continued to maintain his dogged faith in the basic loyalty of his people. To be sure, there were abundant, even unprecedented, signs of unrest among his subjects – peasants burning crops in the fields, labourers demolishing factories, most of the workers in the capital on strike and a mounting clamour from among the educated, articulate professional classes for an end to autocracy and for a new form of government based on a constitution and popular representation. But despite all this, he believed that he himself, Tsar Nicholas, was venerated and loved. When he appeared in public, his ecstatic subjects bowed in reverence. They saw him almost as one of themselves, or so he thought; he imagined himself as the 'peasants' tsar', shunning European-style living and eating borscht and kasha, dressing in blousy peasant shirts and Turkish trousers, always happy to meet his peasant subjects in the course of his travels. He had made himself the friend of the workers too, and of the urban poor, recently building a theatre in Petersburg where for a few kopecks students and factory workers could enjoy operas and plays of high quality thanks to an ongoing government subsidy.

Nicky trusted in his subjects' loyalty – and left the rest to fate.

It was time for the blessing of the waters. The bishop of Petersburg stepped forwards onto the blue-green ice where a hole had been made to expose the dark water. He dipped his gold cross into the water, and said the words of blessing. Almost a once a sharp report rang out from the Peter and Paul Fortress on the far side of the river. The guns were firing their salute.

With a loud cry a policeman standing behind the tsar fell, wounded, his blood spreading out across the ice. Shots were fired into the palace, windows were shattered, other shots struck the Admiralty building and ricocheted off.

The fortress guns, which were supposed to shoot blanks, were shooting live charges. Revolutionaries. Assassins.

The tsar, hearing the whizz of bullets over his head and knowing they were meant for him, stood where he was, and crossed himself.

'I knew that somebody was trying to kill me,' he told his sister Olga later. 'I just crossed myself. What else could I do?'[1]

Around him, all was panic. Police and soldiers were running in all directions, shouting for help, attempting to take cover, trying to see whether the assassins had wounded the tsar. Armed guards from the palace ran out onto the ice, and from Nevsky Prospekt more police came, swarming down towards the dais where the tsar still stood.

Within seconds, the shooting ceased. Whether soldiers in the fortress overpowered the revolutionaries as they fired, or whether, having made their attempt, the would-be assassins fled, is unknown. Out on the ice, police surrounded the stunned tsar and escorted him to safety. Inside the palace, the dowager empress, her daughter Olga, and several others had been sprayed with glass when a bullet struck a window near where they were standing. Their shoes and skirts were covered with glass splinters, but they were not injured.

No more shots came. It was over. The platform on which the aborted ceremony had taken place was quickly dismantled, the bloodstains covered with snow. By late afternoon the only sign that the tsar had come near to being shot, possibly killed, was that there were more guards in evidence around the palace. The hole cut in the ice for the blessing of the Neva had quickly frozen over, and the marine police had resumed their methodical examination of the ice. As evening fell the cold deepened, mist rose above the river and the windows of the palace glowed yellow. At the headquarters of the secret police, activity quickened, and in the workers' neighbourhoods, strikers met to discuss their demands.

Frightened and worried, her worries increased by her increasing conviction that her husband's advisers lacked good judgment and were giving him bad counsel, Alix ruminated on a prophecy attributed to St Serafim.

'They will wait for a time of great hardship to afflict the Russian land,' the prophecy read, 'and on an agreed day, at the agreed hour, they will raise up a general rebellion all over the Russian land.'

Certainly it was a time of great hardship, certainly there was the threat of a great rebellion. The prophecy went on to predict that many soldiers would join the rebels, that 'much innocent blood will be spilt, it will run in rivers over the Russian land'. The empress sent to the Sarov monastery for copies of Serafim's prophecies. Deeply upsetting as the unrest was, it was reassuring to her to know that it had been predicted, that it was not merely random mayhem but part of a larger divine scheme that the saint had foreseen.

On Sunday, January 9, 1905, the prophecy appeared to be coming true.

Thousands of workers gathered in groups in different parts of the city to demonstrate, intending to converge on Palace Square to carry a petition to the tsar. They were disgruntled, angry, hungry and desperate – and yet hopeful, for the majority of them believed that Tsar Nicholas was well disposed towards them and cared for their welfare, and might respond with compassion when he heard their grievances and saw how many of them were suffering.

They had composed a petition, under the guidance of their leader and spokesman Father Gapon, founder of the Gapon Society, which called on the tsar to aid them in their extreme distress.

'We workers and residents of the city of Saint Petersburg, of various ranks and stations, our wives, children and helpless old parents, have come to Thee, Sire, to seek justice and protection.'

They had become beggars, the petitioners said. They were overworked, grossly underpaid, forced to live as slaves. They had pledged themselves to die rather than endure any longer the humiliation and wretchedness of their condition. The tsar was their last hope.

'Sire! Is this [their poverty] in accordance with God's laws, by the grace of which Thou reignest? . . . Is it better to die – for all of us, the toiling people of all Russia, to die, allowing the capitalists (the exploiters of the working class) and the bureaucrats (who rob the government and plunder the Russian people) to live and enjoy themselves?'[2]

Plaintive though the petition was, it was also, in the judgment of the imperial ministers, subversive, conducive to undermining the social order. And the demonstration the petitioners were planning to make was plainly illegal. The police and military, following the attempt on the tsar's life at the Blessing of the Waters, had issued a prohibition against all large gatherings. They were not opposed to Father Gapon, in fact they encouraged and supported him and much preferred him to either the recently formed Marxist political parties – the Mensheviks and Socialist Revolutionaries – with their campaigns of violent disruption or the Constitutional Democrats with their demands for an end to autocracy and the establishment of a constitutional monarchy. But in the volatile climate of Petersburg, with so many tens of thousands of workers idle and so much seditious rhetoric in the air, so much violence and so many incitements to violence, to permit any large crowd to gather for any purpose was to invite disaster.

Illegal though it was, the gathering proceeded, on the morning of January 9, with large groups of marchers assembling in various parts of the city. Most were labourers, both men and women, but a number of the marchers had children with them, and there were old people in the procession as well, some of them feeble.

Watchful police did nothing to break up the crowds, which swelled to many thousands. At the head of each group, held high on tall staves, were large portraits of the tsar and icons, crosses and pennons with religious symbols. Here and there a white flag was displayed, with the ominous message 'Soldiers! Do not fire on the people.'

It was nearly noon when the marchers set out for their destination, singing hymns as they went. They had not gone far when it became evident that they would not be allowed to reach the palace. Warning shouts were heard, ordering the marchers to turn back, to disperse, yet they went on, their momentum difficult to halt, their determination unwavering, their singing so loud, perhaps, that it drowned out the warnings.

Suddenly bugles sounded and the marchers were horrified to see mounted grenadiers galloping towards them, sabres raised. Behind the cavalry came infantry, rifles at the ready.

Quickly, efficiently, the soldiers went about their work, following their orders, the cavalry slashing at the unarmed marchers, the riflemen shooting them down. Disbelief soon turned to panic as, screaming in pain and terror, the petitioners scattered, many wounded, dozens lying dead. The confusion was terrible, the slaughter ghastly. To observers it appeared that a peaceful religious procession had met with an attack of calculated brutality. 'A well-behaved, dignified, unarmed crowd walking into cavalry charges and the sights of rifles – a terrible spectacle,' one of them wrote.[3]

Yet the marchers, once they came under attack, were quick to resist. Seizing pushcarts, wagons, bits of furniture, they began to erect barricades in the streets. Some climbed onto the roofs of buildings and hurled bricks on the soldiers below. Others broke into gun shops and armed themselves. Cries of 'Revolution!' were heard, impromptu speeches were made in favour of armed revolt, red flags waved high. Some Petersburgers, who earlier in the day felt sympathy for the marchers, became frightened of them after the shooting began and, barring their doors and windows, retreated into their cellars for safety.

For several hours there was chaos in the capital, with some areas disrupted by skirmishes and looting and others, such as the Alexander Gardens, remaining relatively calm, the gardens filled with casual strollers and children playing in the snow and skating on the ice. Volleys of gunfire erupted from time to time. Cossacks rode past, swords drawn, hunting for resisters. Bodies still lay in some streets, dark blood stained the snow in many places and, as the afternoon advanced, relatives of the dead brought coffins to carry them away. Eventually the clashes between military and demonstrators ceased, and the barricades were torn down by the soldiers. Yet attacks by squadrons of troops went on, the soldiers firing wildly into crowds of bystanders as if unable to stop themselves from continuing the slaughter.

No one counted the dead, but at the end of the day there may have been as many as three or four hundred, perhaps twice that many. At least a thousand more were injured, many of them seriously.[4] Apart from the actual number of injuries, what shocked Petersburgers – and soon the rest of the world, for reports went out immediately to all the foreign capitals by phone and wire – was the inhuman cruelty of the assaults: the multiple sabre cuts, the merciless rifle fire, the deliberate trampling of old people and the pitiless injuring of children.

The only possible conclusion was that the tsar, far from caring about his subjects, had ordered their massacre. This was the tsar of Khodynka Field, the tsar who had done nothing to alleviate famine, and who had let his ministers impoverish the countryside. This was the tsar who had led the Russian armies into defeat at the hands of the Japanese. Now he had shown his true nature at its most heartless.

Now truly, as St Serafim had predicted, much innocent blood had been spilt, and it ran in rivers over the Russian land.

As if to mark the significance of the bloodshed, a sign had been given, a vision in the heavens. Many people on the afternoon of January 9 had observed the apparition. Some described it as a triple sun, others as a huge red circle surrounding the sun and blotting out its rays.

It was a portent of disaster, an indication, surely, that there was worse to come.

Alix had not been in Petersburg on the day of the disturbances. At the insistence of the imperial ministers, she and Nicky and their children had taken refuge at Tsarskoe Selo, where the number of soldiers, detectives and secret police was increased. Telegrams arrived at the Alexander Palace in record numbers, sent from Europe and America, expressing outrage at the carnage and condemning the tsar for murdering his own subjects. In the eyes of much of the world Nicholas II had become a villain, and Alix felt obliged to defend him.

'Don't believe all the horrors the foreign papers say,' she wrote to her sister Victoria in England. 'They make one's hair stand on end – foul exaggeration. Yes, the troops, alas, were obliged to fire. Repeatedly the crowd was told to retreat and that Nicky was not in town (as we are living here this winter) and that one would be forced to shoot, but they would not heed and so blood was shed."[5]

The many deaths and injuries were 'ghastly', she admitted, but had the soldiers not fired and the cavalry not charged, the crowd would have grown 'colossal' and even more deaths and injuries would have resulted from the crush of bodies. In effect, the attacking military had saved the crowd from itself.

In her letter Alix blamed the Interior Minister Prince Sviatopolk-Mirsky ('all these disorders are thanks to his unpardonable folly'), the lack of good advisers available to the court, political extremists, even Petersburg itself ('a rotten town, not an atom Russian'). Casting her net wide, she blamed the late Tsar Alexander III; his policy of isolating himself and his family had depleted the number of reliable public servants, she argued, which led to a lack of what she called 'real' men – those who were neither too weak nor too liberal nor too narrow-minded to be of use to her husband.

In this, her first genuine political crisis, Alix showed her sympathies and her prejudices. She was, first and foremost, fiercely loyal and sympathetic to her husband, and firmly opposed to anyone whom she perceived as a threat to his authority. That he lacked personal vigour, conviction and effectiveness she must have seen all too clearly, for she constantly urged him to be more forceful and assertive. But she also saw that, as she put it, his 'cross was a heavy one to bear', that 'he had a bitter hard life to lead', and that he worked diligently, if largely ineffectually, to bear it. Her sympathy towards him, and her contempt for all those who did not share her feelings, and who failed to give her husband credit for his efforts, were so vast that they swamped her objectivity.

She saw that Russia was in need of reform, and believed that reforms could be made, 'gently with the greatest care and forethought'. But she misjudged the gravity and intensity of the upheaval caused by the stirring of the forces of reform: the widening disenchantment with the tsar himself and his autocracy, the harsh resentment at the harm done by ministerial economic policies, the profound thirst for change, above all the deep wellsprings of bitterness among the working poor.

If Alix could not be objective about the events of January, 1905, it was partly because she was preoccupied with her son.

Baby Alexei, a beautiful child with pale skin and dark hair, was a source both of joy and of constant distress. Boys with the English disease nearly always died very young; however watchful Alix and others were, however often she prayed to the wall of icons by her bedside, Alix knew that the constant threat of death hung over her son. When she saw him bathed or dressed, when she held him and rocked him and sang to him, she was always looking at his arms and legs, especially his elbows and knees, watching for the discoloured swellings that indicated internal bleeding.

When the dreaded swellings developed, the tiny joints grew swollen and stiff, the gathered blood pressed on the nerves, and the baby screamed with pain. There was nothing to be done. The doctors were helpless, and little Alexei's suffering went on, hour after hour, until, exhausted yet unable to sleep or eat, he lay moaning, his face white, looking as though he would die.

Each attack, Alix knew, could be his last. Many babies whose blood did not clot properly died in their first year. Watching her son through each of his crises, trusting in the protection of Philippe yet anxious and drawn, Alix suffered along with her son. It was hard for her to avoid giving in to despair.

Struggling with her own illnesses, dealing with the ongoing provocations from her antagonistic in-laws, ever more mindful of her husband's difficulties and of the threat to the entire imperial family from forces inimical to the throne, the empress had entered a dark season. Her mouth was set in a grim line, her lips pinched together tightly, her eyes sad. She was not yet thirty-three, but her expression was that of a hardened middle-aged woman, a woman beset by ill luck – a woman, as she sometimes said, who carried ill luck with her.

As she sat looking down at her son, the son St Serafim had given her after so many years of waiting and disappointment, she prayed earnestly for him to be spared. Yet her reason told her that, in human terms at least, Alexei was not likely to live very long. Unless help came from a divine source, and soon, he would surely succumb to one of the terrible attacks of bleeding, ending all her hopes and those of the Romanov dynasty.

18

Philippe Vachot was dead. The message reached the palace in late July or early August of 1905, six months after the killings in Petersburg which had come to be known as Bloody Sunday. He had died in Lyon, collapsing suddenly.

Philippe was dead, but the day of his death was significant: it was St Elijah's day, and according to the Bible Elijah had not died, but had been taken up into heaven. Philippe had told his admirers that he would not live much longer, that his mission on earth was drawing to a close. And that, once he laid aside his earthly body, his spirit would enter into another man, and live on through him.

This comforting thought – that Philippe, or his spirit, might have found another embodiment – helped to assuage the dismay Alix must have felt at the news from France. For Philippe, she believed, had protected her family from harm, and they were more in need of protection than ever.

In the previous February, assassins had thrown a bomb into Serge's carriage, blowing his body to pieces. The secret police believed that this killing was only the first in a series of planned attacks on the tsar and his relatives; the family did not dare to attend Serge's funeral because of the danger to themselves. Only weeks later a much more sinister conspiracy was uncovered. Two revolutionaries were arrested and forced to reveal that they had intended to masquerade as members of the court choir. It had been their plan to conceal bombs under their choir robes and then, at the Easter Eve mass, throw them into the midst of the tsar's family, killing them all.

The fact that the terrorists were caught only hours before the intended massacre renewed the fears of the imperials. Surrounded as they were by detectives and guards, virtually smothered by protectors, they had nonetheless come close to being annihilated.

Their daily life, in the spring and summer of 1905, had a surreal quality. Immured behind the iron gates of the Alexander Palace at Tsarskoe Selo or within the fortress of Gatchina, constantly made aware not only of their own personal danger but of crop burnings in the countryside, assassinations, strikes, mutinies, and general mayhem, they continued insofar as possible to live as they had in less troubled times. Nine-year-old Olga and eight-year-old Tatiana studied English and French, went riding, and, with their six-year-old sister Marie and little four-year-old Anastasia, accompanied their father on long walks – always under heavy guard. On fine days baby Alexei, wrapped in puffy furs, was put into a basket strapped to a donkey and led down a garden path by a top-hatted groom.

There were even family picnics, with food spread out on tables under the trees and leisurely strolls in the grounds after lunch.

It was on one such picnic, in fact, that news of the decisive sea battle of the war with Japan reached Nicky. The news could not have been worse; the Russian fleet, which he had sent from the Baltic to the Sea of Japan to defend the Russian land forces, had met with overwhelming defeat by the Japanese fleet off Tsushima Island in the Korea Strait. The fleet was annihilated, just as a great many Russian soldiers had been annihilated in March at Mukden, a battle that had cost nearly a hundred thousand Russian lives.

The tsar blanched when he read the terrible message, but said nothing. He was stoic about the course of the war, as he was about the social chaos and the threats to himself and his family. His inherent fatalism came to the fore. He smoked a cigarette, stroked his beard, and went on with the picnic.

The war was lost, the grave weaknesses in Russia's army and navy exposed. Nicky accepted the offer of the American president Theodore Roosevelt to oversee negotiations to end the conflict, and by midsummer talks were under way.

Alix, made irritable and rebellious by the constant smothering surveillance, found a way to escape the secret police. Taking the children or a single lady-in-waiting, she ordered a carriage and, dismissing the footmen who usually rode on the outside of the vehicle and the uniformed Cossack who customarily drove her coach (a conspicuous emblem of her status), she went out into the woods, ordering the driver to keep to the unfrequented roads. She stopped from time to time and got out, shepherding the children to a beauty spot overlooking lakeside or hillside, going into a shop or entering a small church to say a prayer.[1] She liked to drive slowly through the village near the palace, passing the villas and peering out of the carriage window to see what the people inside were doing.

These clandestine carriage drives, during which the empress eluded her bodyguards and the secret police, were dangerous, not only because of the very real possibility that her carriage might be blown up by a bomb but because of the risk of accidents. On at least one occasion the carriage in which she was riding overturned after colliding with a bicyclist. No one was injured, but the inconvenience was great, as there were no footmen to go for help and no soldiers to escort the empress and her companions home.

To outward appearances at least, Alix was in her prime in 1905. 'The tsarina was still a beautiful woman at that time,' wrote the grand duchesses' French tutor Pierre Gilliard. 'She was tall and slender and carried herself superbly. But all this ceased the moment one looked into her eyes – those speaking, grey-blue eyes which mirrored the emotions of a sensitive soul.'

Which emotions her eyes revealed Gilliard did not say, but sternness and anxiety and a haunted sorrow were surely among them – and the anguish of keeping secret her worry over her son. She was magnificent – but emotionally and physically overburdened, constantly disappointed in others and with a wilful side that showed itself in her occasional hectoring of her servants, her defiance of the security guards and her increasing domination of her husband. Resigned and passive as Nicky was, he became accustomed to giving in to Alix's will, in small things and large. Their bond could hardly have been deeper or more affectionate, frayed only very slightly by such minor irritations as Alix's keeping her husband awake by 'crunching her favourite English biscuits in bed'.[2] Yet an important dynamic between them was shifting; more and more, when decisions were to be made, it was Alix who made them.

Her war work went on. Though the last of the battles had been fought, and peace talks were under way, thousands of wounded men were still being sent to the capital, and the need for bandages, warm clothes and knitted stockings, medical supplies and blankets went on, and Alix described herself as 'sewing away hard'. In addition to her workshop, she opened a home for disabled sailors in the park at Tsarskoe Selo, and a School for Nurses and Housemaids, whose day-to-day operation she delegated to others.[3]

She was kept busy, with her close supervision of her children, her overseeing of their lessons, her attention to their wardrobes – on which she spent as much time as she did on her own, making lists and inventories of garments, ordering new clothing made every six months, frequently going through the nursery closets and giving away what was worn – plus her time-consuming concern for servants and household members in need or ill. Letter-writing took much time as well. But then, in the midst of all her occupation, she would feel the onset of a severe headache, and would have to lie down on the chaise longue in her mauve boudoir, a lace shawl draped over her legs, silk curtains covering the windows to prevent the light from hurting her eyes. In the view of at least one family member, Alix's health worsened after Alexei's birth and the diagnosis of haemophilia. She became 'troubled and apprehensive', her 'character underwent a change and her health, physical as well as moral, altered'.[4]

Having had to give up exercise after Alexei's birth because of recurrent leg pains and shortness of breath, Alix returned to her earlier pastimes of singing and playing the piano. Every week Professor Kuendinger came to the palace to play piano duets with her for several hours, and Madame Iretsky, her singing coach, trained her voice. Alix was a contralto, and liked to sing duets with sopranos. Sometimes well known singers from the opera would join her, or members of her retinue. Her invalid maid of honour Sonia Orbeliani, whom she had taken to live in the palace, gave musical parties in her rooms where professional pianists and singers entertained; the empress was often to be found in the small audience, but she was far too uncomfortable and withdrawn to perform herself.

When in private, she liked to play one of her many grand pianos, by herself or with Olga, who had a precocious musical gift. She would sit down at the keyboard, take off her rings, and toss them on the nearest table or sofa, then begin to play. Long afterwards, missing her rings, she would summon her maids of honour and order them to find the rings – which were very valuable, as among them was her pink diamond engagement ring. 'This sometimes caused considerable annoyance,' Martha Mouchanow wrote, 'as they could not always be found immediately, and a frantic search was made all over the palace, until at last they turned up in some impossible place or other.'[5] Eventually the maids of honour must have learned to begin their search in the immediate vicinity of all the grand pianos.

In August 1905, Nicky journeyed to Pskov by train and took Alix and his sister Olga with him. Alix wrote to the children. 'Papa and Auntie Olga have gone for a walk in the lovely woods; my old legs hurt too much to walk, so I remained at home,' she began. 'Now the train has at last stopped. We got quite soaked this morning; my new waterproof cape was wet through. We saw lots of soldiers; cavalry, infantry, and artillery. The country is very pretty.'

She described how, when they stopped at one village, many peasants crowded around them and one woman asked after the grand duchesses' health and wondered why they were not on the train. The tsar and tsarina were greeted with bread and salt and flowers picked from the small gardens behind the wooden houses.

'I wonder how you all are,' Alix went on. 'I feel so sad without my sweet little girlies. Be sure to be very good and remember, elbows off the table, sit straight and eat your meat nicely. I kiss you all very tenderly.'[6] Alexei, or 'Baby Tsar', as she called him, was teething, and had been left behind in the care of his nurses and the court doctors. 'I hope he is quite well and does not have pain,' Alix wrote. Had he had an attack, she would have been summoned.

Violent disruptions in many parts of Russia continued into the autumn of 1905, and seemed to escalate as the year wore on. In the countryside around Pskov, at the time of the imperials' visit, all was temporarily quiet, but the calm was deceptive, for in many provinces members of a recently formed Peasants' Union burned crops, murdered their landlords, and assaulted government officials. In the Caucasus there was murderous street fighting, with rebels firing at troops from the windows of their houses. Weary soldiers returning from the war against the Japanese aboard troop trains found themselves under attack as they made their way home; having survived months of artillery fire, disease, and scanty rations they faced a hostile Russian populace bent on forcing political change.

In the midst of the escalating chaos the imperial family went aboard the yacht *Polar Star* for a two-week vacation. The weather was exceptionally fair in September 1905, the Baltic blue and smooth, the clouds high and white, the breezes mild. Alix took pictures of the children with her box camera, made drawings for them with coloured pencils, and sat chatting with her favourite new lady-in-waiting Anna Vyrubov on the deck of the ship, wide straw hats protecting their faces from the strong sun. The yacht wove in among the islands off the Finnish coast, and the family went ashore to hike; Nicky hunted birds and the children swam, waded and collected bugs and fish.

Telegrams from the palace told of the rapidly deteriorating situation, with Moscow virtually shut down because of spreading strikes. Banks were not functioning, for the clerks refused to work; trains and trams were not running, no bread was baked, no newspapers published, no goods of any kind produced. There was not even any running water, because the engineers and maintenance workers had walked away from their jobs. The price of food was rising rapidly. After a few days the telegrams ceased, for the telegraph offices were deserted. Now the true seriousness of the crisis became unmistakably clear. Moscow had been all but shut down, and the massive paralysis was spreading to other cities – soon Petersburg would be without workers, without communications, without order of any kind.

This was a crisis on a scale no one in Russia had ever faced, not even in the time of Catherine the Great when the great rebel Pugachev had taken over a third of the kingdom. Now there was not one rebel leader with hundreds of thousands of followers, but millions of independent subjects, working together in a common aim – to bring the country to the brink of irreversible chaos in order to compel reform.

The *Polar Star* returned from its odyssey and the imperial family was once again immured at Tsarskoe Selo, under heavy guard.

Alix compared the tumultuous weeks of October 1905 to a very difficult labour. A new order was coming slowly and painfully to birth, forced into the light by the harsh midwife of revolution. The tsar was in an agony of indecision; should he attempt to crush the unrest by force (a doubtful proposition given the mutinous mood among the soldiers), which might at best delay the granting of civil rights and citizen representation, or should he follow the urgent advice of his principal minister Witte and submit to the revolutionaries' demands?

He felt keenly the weight of his responsibilities, the burden of carrying, in his person, the honour of the Romanov house. For centuries his ancestors had borne supreme, autocratic power; for him to suddenly break that tradition and decide to share the power of the throne, to however moderate an extent, would be, or so it seemed to him, to lose the crown itself. 'You cannot imagine the anguish this has cost me,' he wrote to his mother. Yet Witte pressed him almost hourly to see that no other course of action was feasible, that he must grant some constitutional rights, and cousin Nicholas Nicholaevich, strutting and fuming dramatically in the halls of the Alexander Palace, drew himself up to his great height in the tsar's presence and threatened to shoot himself unless the necessary changes were made – and at once.

Guests at the palace that October, unsettled and full of fears, shivered when they entered the drawing room and saw, side by side on one wall, portraits of Empress Alexandra and Marie Antoinette. With anarchy in the cities, thefts of land and murder of landowners in the country, their thoughts naturally turned to the French Revolution and the ferocity it had unleashed. Marie Antoinette and her well-meaning husband Louis XVI had gone to the guillotine as a result of their subjects' ever escalating political demands. If the tsar made concessions to his subjects, how secure would his throne be? How safe would his life be, and the lives of his family?

In such an environment, Alix's efforts to maintain a facade of serene unconcern, presiding at dinner parties, could hardly succeed. She soon abandoned her futile social endeavours, said her prayers, did her best to say to Nicky what she thought he needed to hear – and waited for him to make his decision.

With the darkness of anarchy closing in around him, and clamorous voices in his ears, ever mindful of his increasing personal danger, on October 17, 1905, Nicky called for the papers Witte had drawn up and signed his name to them. He promised to allow an elected assembly, a Duma, to meet and, in the words of the manifesto, 'to grant the people the unshakable foundations of civil liberty on the basis of true inviolability of person, freedom of conscience, speech, assembly and association'. He permitted the organization of unions and political parties.

In effect, Nicky was carrying forwards the reform begun by his grandfather Alexander when he freed the serfs and instituted the first significant body of reforms.

But like his grandfather, he instituted the changes – and then backed away from them. Within weeks of issuing his manifesto, he had authorized the military to punish revolutionaries, workers, anyone who had been vocal in his or her opposition to the government. Arrests, executions, the widespread destruction of homes and villages went on throughout the winter, along with brutal pogroms against Jews in many cities. In town after town, village after village, dragoons rode in and set fire to barns where food was stored, killed animals, burned houses. Mass executions were held, there was random slaughter and mayhem.

Thousands died in the bloodbath of reprisals – yet the revolutionaries had won. The rights had been granted. In a single year the tsar had been forced to surrender his absolute power and also to concede defeat to the Japanese, ceding to them half of Sakhalin, and to evacuate Manchuria.

The old order had collapsed. And instead of bringing calm and restoring peace, the advent of reform brought demands for further reform, and more violence.

Shut away under guard at Tsarskoe Selo, besieged by frightening rumours, never knowing from one day to the next whether conspirators armed with dynamite might find a way to steal into the Alexander Palace and blow them all up, apprehensive about the tsarevich and without the comforting protective influence of Philippe, the imperials waited for news to arrive by courier from Moscow and Petersburg as the days grew short and darkness closed in around them.

In their worry and isolation they heard, from Bishop Theophan, Alix's confessor and President of the Petersburg Theological Seminary, and from Nicky's confessor Father Alexander, of a healer from Siberia, now living in Petersburg, called Father Gregory, said to possess extraordinary gifts of prayer and curative powers and the ability to read the future. Hundreds of miraculous healings had been attributed to him. In particular he was said to be able to 'bewitch the blood', to control the flow of blood from one part of the body to another, even to stanch the bleeding of wounds.

Militsa and Stana too knew of Father Gregory and his reputation for remarkable healings, and they told Alix and Nicky about him.

The Siberian was brought to court, and ushered past the battery of watchful guards into the presence of the imperials. He stood there, in their midst, a middle-aged peasant with long reddish hair and an uncombed beard, reeking of dirt, speaking in short bursts of nearly incomprehensible Russian – the heavily accented Russian of the Tobolsk region. His face was deeply scarred and weathered, his teeth blackened and neglected, and his gleaming eyes rolled like the eyes of a madman as he talked.

But there was a warmth in his presence, a radiance that was familiar to Alix and Nicky from countless other encounters with healers and psychics, most recently Philippe Vachot. As Father Gregory talked on, jumping rapidly from topic to topic, quoting from the Bible, making pronouncements about the future, he wrapped his hearers in the mantle of his charisma. They listened contentedly, then eagerly, for his presence was powerful, and his words seemed to carry the weight of the divine.

Had not Philippe promised that his spirit would enter into another man, and live on through him? Perhaps Father Gregory was that other man, the avatar of the powerful Frenchman who had protected the family for so long. Perhaps Father Gregory was sent from God, to continue the work Philippe had begun. Alix, seeing him and hearing his words, began to feel certain of this. And the more certain she became, the more hopeful she was for the future, for if only she and her family remained within the orbit of Father Gregory's power, as they once had within that of Philippe, they might never have to worry again.

19

When Nicky's sister Olga first saw Father Gregory she was struck by how primitive he was. His guttural, uncouth voice, his uncontrolled gestures, his habit of tossing his head and rolling his eyes as he talked made him seem like something out of the Siberian forest, a man yet more than a man, more like a primal force, an eruption of nature with the raw purity of a waterfall or an avalanche.

And along with this raw natural vitality went another very arresting quality: a deep and unfeigned spiritual feeling, expressed through gentleness and piety.

'When I saw him,' Olga wrote, 'I felt that gentleness and warmth radiated from him. All the children seemed to like him. They were completely at their ease with him. I still remember their laughter as little Alexei, deciding he was a rabbit, jumped up and down the room.'[1]

As Olga watched, Father Gregory took Alexei by the hand and took him into his bedroom, and the adults followed.

'There was something like a hush as though we had found ourselves in church,' Olga remembered. 'In Alexei's bedroom no lamps were lit; the only light came from the candles burning in front of some beautiful icons.' Father Gregory bowed his head in prayer, and little Alexei, standing beside him, grew very still.

'It was all most impressive. I also knew that my little nephew had joined him in prayer. I really cannot describe it – but I was then conscious of the man's utter sincerity.'[2]

At the time he met the imperial family Father Gregory was one of a number of startsy, or stranniki, in Petersburg, many of them rough-spoken, uncultivated men who dressed in peasant garments and were coarse in their habits and tastes. Many were flagrantly dissolute, holding orgies, drinking heavily, brawling and making public nuisances of themselves; most were well known to the police. Their immorality and vulgar behaviour was part of their theology of 'salvation through sin,' which required them to sin lustily in order to attain the maximum salvatory effect.

Aristocratic ladies invited holy men to their salons, just as Militsa and Stana invited psychics and healers to theirs. The patronage of the high-born women, combined with the startsy's healings, assured them a large following and a secure livelihood. Many of them fell foul of the clergy, however, and were eventually denounced and driven out of the capital. Father Gregory was an exception in that he had the support of several prominent members of the church hierarchy and, at the time he was first invited to Tsarskoe Selo, he had been living in Petersburg for several years enjoying increasing repute for his healings.

His origins and earlier life were obscure. A few sketchy details were known: that his name was Gregory Yefimovich Novy, and that he came from the village of Pokrovsky in Tobolsk Province in Siberia, that he had a wife, two daughters and a mentally deficient son (the wife and daughters sometimes came to the capital to stay with him), and that he had acquired, early in life, the nickname 'Rasputin,' which means 'the Debauched One' or 'the Vagabond'.

A vagabond he claimed to have been. Leaving Pokrovsky, he had wandered widely, repenting of his wayward past and, dragging the iron chains of a penitent pilgrim, travelling from one monastery to another seeking alms. He said that he had gone as far afield as Jerusalem.[3] Everywhere he went he healed the sick, even sick animals, bewitched the blood, and foretold the future. His name became known. Ultimately he found his way to Petersburg, where he lodged with a priest.

After his initial visit to court it did not take long for Father Gregory's fame to spread even more widely. His apartment swarmed with people, all waiting patiently for his blessing. A visitor described the scene: 'To a stranger Rasputin's flat seemed a madhouse,' he wrote. After passing through a 'dark musty-smelling hall,' the newcomer entered a waiting room 'full of people from early morning until late at night. The whole of Russia seemed to be represented there: peasants in leather jerkins and high boots, smelling of earth and dung . . . an officer of the Guards in a splendid uniform . . . portly village priests sat monumentally immobile with beards spread over their fat chests, on which great crosses hung on massively linked chains.'[4] There were students, journalists, artists and bankers. But most of Father Gregory's devotees were women, peasant girls, noblewomen, 'elderly women full of a holy enthusiasm.'

It was a mixed group of women who surrounded the starets, titled ladies in silk and diamonds, crippled grandmothers from the provinces, middle-class matrons, all waiting for Father Gregory to extend his dirty hand for them to kiss, to offer them tea or Madeira wine. Their devotion was absolute. They came, bringing flowers and other gifts, and stayed for hours, sitting at his table with its none too clean cloth, joining in when he burst into song, eating the black rye biscuits he handed out – or wrapping them in handkerchiefs to be kept as relics. The lucky ones received Father Gregory's cast-offs – faded, reeking shirts – to be put on reverently and worn to bring good luck.

The physicians of the capital, stunned by Father Gregory's cures, tried to expose him as a greedy charlatan, but failed. Too many reliable witnesses had seen, and reported, that the healings were genuine; whether they were achieved through hypnosis, or whether, as the starets consistently claimed, the power of God came through him, made no difference to the outcome.[5] And his own belief in his abilities compelled trust and belief in others. As to the accusation of greed, this too collapsed in the face of Father Gregory's simple manner of living and his habit of giving away the money grateful clients brought him. He was not poor, and was shrewd enough to manage his financial affairs adroitly, but he had few possessions – even the furniture in his apartment was not his.[6]

To assess Father Gregory with anything like objectivity is very difficult for anyone far removed in time and culture from the Russia of 1905. The extraordinary veneration accorded to religious figures, the pervasiveness of faith, the credulous religious climate all separate the modern reader from the world in which the Debauched One flourished. Father Gregory's contemporary John of Kronstadt, a saintly healer who performed miraculous cures and gave away all that he had, devoting himself to ministering to the poor, was worshipped by a cult of women who believed him to be Jesus reincarnate. In a frenzy of adoration the women assaulted their adored Father John and tore at his flesh with their teeth until he bled.[7] At a time when such extreme religious practices as self-flagellation, self-castration and even mass suicide were part of provincial religious life – though far from its mainstream – miraculous healings seemed a relatively moderate and entirely credible phenomenon.

Certainly Father Gregory's powers gained credibility in 1907, when the tsarevich, after falling in the gardens at Tsarskoe Selo, suffered terrible pain when internal bleeding made his leg swell and his fever rise. The court doctors, who assumed that his life would be short and were surprised that he had survived into his third year, were prepared for this crisis to end in death, and were helpless and frightened. Observers saw them 'whispering among themselves' and looking resigned.[8]

With his parents by his bedside, Alexei's condition grew worse by the hour. His face was a white mask, his eyes dark-rimmed and dim. His grotesquely distorted leg stuck out at an odd angle. He cried but could not move, so great was his pain.

In the early hours of the morning Father Gregory arrived from Petersburg. He stood at the foot of the tsarevich's bed and bowed his head, and everyone in the room prayed with him.

No one recorded what took place over the next several hours, but when Alexei awoke later that morning, the change in him was little short of miraculous. He sat up in bed, his cheeks pink, his eyes bright, his leg back to its usual size and shape. When the astounded doctors came to take his temperature they found it to be normal. The attack had passed.

Sceptics told one another that it was only a coincidence that the boy's remarkable recovery should have followed the starets's visit and prayers, that the remission of bleeding in his leg and the reduction in the swelling must have occurred naturally. But the doctors insisted that there was no way the body could return to normal so rapidly. Had the internal bleeding stopped on its own, it would still have taken days for the accumulated blood to gradually work its way out of the leg and for the swelling and fever to go down.[9]

To Alix the remarkable healing was yet another sign that God was guiding her destiny and that of her family. Father Gregory was God's gift. There was a mysterious divine symmetry at work in the lives of the imperials; the tsaverich was born with a potentially fatal illness, but at nearly the same time God had provided, in the Siberian healer, the means to counteract the disease. So the balance was righted, her prayers were answered. As long as she continued to believe and to trust in God, all would be well.

She struggled, with all her considerable willpower, to cling to that belief as her thirty-fifth birthday approached. The face she showed to the world – a world now restricted, for the most part, to the grounds of Tsarskoe Selo – was dour and closed, the eyes hooded, the mouth set and downward-turned. She looked like a woman under emotional siege, embattled against life. She spoke of herself now not only as a 'bird of ill omen' but as 'a great worrier,' and she had much to worry about.[10]

It was not just that her only son was fatally ill, spared only through the mercy of God, or that continuing social unrest and harsh repression threatened the future of Russia, or even that foiled plots against the tsar's life and her own were still coming to light despite extreme police and military precautions: it was that her kind, forbearing husband was proving to be more and more ineffectual as a ruler, making it necessary for her to provide the strength and force of will that he lacked.

She saw no alternative. The new form of government brought into being in response to the ongoing social crisis was unstable, and, in her view, manned by mediocrities. The first Duma, convened in

April of 1906 and dominated politically by the inexperienced liberal delegates representing the Cadet party, was floundering and the imperial ministers were weak and vacillating. The Romanov family, now split into factions with the overbearing Aunt Miechen speaking out forcefully against Alix and lobbying to have the tsar step down in favour of his brother Michael, offered no practical advice or support, only criticism and complaints. Of Alix's own relatives, her brother Ernie does not seem to have given her any meaningful counsel – and in any case his standing in Russian eyes was low because his divorce from Ducky made it possible for Nicky's cousin Cyril to marry her, resulting in Cyril's banishment and disgrace. Alix's sisters wrote often and came to Russia from time to time, but neither the sympathetic Irene nor the more forceful and much older Victoria seems to have had any serious influence over her, and Ella, her life shattered by Serge's assassination, was in a process of personal transformation that ultimately led her further and further away from her youngest sister.[11]

Ella embraced the ascetic life, remaking her bedroom at Illinsky into a stark room like a nun's cell, stripped of furniture, the walls hung with icons. She kept the bloody clothes worn by her husband on the day he died and preserved them inside a large wooden cross hung on one wall. Ella and Alix were both finding new strength in their religious faith, but where Alix sought help through a personal connection with a starets, Ella turned to the Orthodox monastic tradition. She gave away her jewels and finery, greatly simplified her life, and began modelling herself on the sisters who had no connection to the world and devoted themselves to works of charity undertaken in the name of Jesus.

A distance was growing between Ella and Alix, and for Alix it only emphasized the fact that she was alone, or felt alone, in her responsibilities – alone, that is, save for Father Gregory. And while her faith was strong, it was not unwavering. There were moments when her certainty was shaken, especially when she felt ill; there were moments when her anxiety rose and a panicky feeling threatened.

The times were agitated, with accepted authorities toppling and established boundaries crumbling as political institutions were shifting and no steadying hand appeared to be guiding the transition to a new era. Predictions of imminent apocalypse haunted literature, the theatre, drawing room conversation; some said that the approach of Halley's comet, due to appear in 1910, was a sign of the end, others that the recent discovery of a mammoth buried in the ice in Eastern Siberia, perfectly preserved for millennia, had a deeper meaning than mere scientific interest.[12] Petersburgers, confronting the enormous shaggy beast unearthed from his resting place and installed in the newly built rotunda of the Zoological Museum, awed by his size, his huge fearsome tusks, seemed to see in him an emblem of their own transitoriness, a reminder that all human institutions, however immemorial, occupied but a fleeting moment in the long span of creation, and might well be swept away in a single awful instant of catastrophe.

In the aesthetic realm, to which Alix had always been sensitively attuned, old principles of order and meaning were being abandoned. In music and art, primal forces, even savage forces were being unleashed; cacophony and chaos reigned, outraging audiences and museum-goers (and thrilling a small but appreciative group of music lovers and art collectors). To the empress, whose taste ran to Wagnerian assertions of harmonic concord and mystical transcendence, the new directions in the arts seemed brutal and horrifying. 'Twentieth-century culture' was to her a culture of inhumanity, and she used the phrase as a term of opprobrium.[13]

In social relations the traditional proprieties were being abandoned, and nowhere more than in the imperial family itself, where the tsar's weakening authority did nothing to counteract the centrifugal effect of a prevailing current of permissiveness (the tsar called it selfishness) among the well-born. Alix observed with extreme disapproval the dissolving of marital and family ties, the increasing number of divorces among the Romanovs, the disregard for loyalty and for the integrity of the succession.

With Alexei's illness being kept a closely held secret, the expectation was that he would in time succeed his father. However, he was the only son, and an accident or an assassination (always, in these years, a genuine threat) could remove him suddenly. Those coming next in the line of succession (daughters being excluded by law from succeeding), though quick to disparage their patriarch and ignore his authority, were casual about jeopardizing their own legal standing vis-à-vis the throne. The tsar's brother Michael was in love with one of the court ladies-in-waiting, Dina Kossikovsky, and begged Nicky to let him marry Dina morganatically. Nicky's ageing, peremptory Uncle Vladimir, next in line after Michael, had brought shame on the family by debauchery abroad, while of Vladimir's sons, Cyril was in involuntary exile due to his marriage to Ducky, Boris was an irresponsible playboy and Andrew was living with Nicky's former love, the ballet dancer Matilda Kchessinsky; if he married her he too would be banished.[14]

A number of others further down the line of succession were surrounded by scandal. Vladimir's brother Alexis had had a series of disreputable relationships and was living with an actress in Paris, and his brother Paul had been banished after marrying a commoner. Sandro's older brother Michael had also married a commoner and had gone to live in England some years earlier. Stana had divorced her husband and married Nicky's cousin Grand Duke Nicholas, while Sandro and Xenia, until recently a model couple in every way, had abandoned their fidelity to one another and were both romantically entangled with others. (They eventually found their way to a comfortable reconciliation and went on with their marriage.)

The entire Romanov edifice was tottering and Alix, seeing clearly that her husband would not be capable of preventing its collapse, increasingly took on herself the uneasy task of helping to shore it up. It was not a new task; it was, in fact, an extension of the role she had undertaken when she married Nicky, to be his encouragement and support, to help him when he faltered. Only now he was faltering much more conspicuously, and her ability to act as his brace and prop, indeed to do what he could not, might make the difference between life and death.

The clear, cold waters of the Gulf of Finland were calm on the afternoon of September 11, 1907, as the yacht *Standart* cruised slowly among the rocky islands off the Finnish coast. Though it was late in the season, the air still held a faint touch of warmth, and Alix, lying on a couch on deck as she usually did, with Alexei and her companion Anna Vyrubov nearby, was alternately occupied with embroidery and sketching.[15]

It was noticed that the empress was more at ease on the yacht than almost anywhere else, perhaps because she could be certain that within its confines her family was safe from would-be attackers, more likely because the atmosphere was informal, the family having been on comfortably familiar terms with the crew members for many years.[16]

Alexei and the girls were as much at home on the immense yacht, with its comfortable state rooms, chapel, and extensive staff quarters, as they were in the Alexander Palace, running up and down the teak decks in their navy-blue sailor suits, heavy pea coats buttoned to the neck, the girls with their long hair flying out behind them. Olga, now nearly twelve, looked eagerly out over the rail, across the transparent waters towards the empty horizon. With her considerable intelligence and outgoing nature she sought fun and stimulation, unlike ten-year-old Tatiana, whose affectionate, emotional nature drew her close to her mother and made her more reserved. Marie, at eight the most active of the quartet of daughters and the one most avid for parental attention, ran and jumped with noisy abandon while six-year-old Anastasia teased the crew members and played hide and seek with her sisters. The empress watched Anastasia closely, for she had become more cherished following an accident the previous summer; she had nearly drowned when a freak high wave swept her under and pounded the air from her lungs.

The quiet of the lonely landscape was what drew Nicky and Alix to it every fall, the expanse of dark firs on the deserted islands, the silence broken only by the lapping of small waves on the pebbled shoreline and the cries of birds flying overhead. Now and then a fisherman could be glimpsed, or a small hut in among the trees, but for the most part no other humans were visible, only the wide expanse of sky and blue water, dense woodland and grey beach.

A sudden lurching of the ship startled the passengers, followed immediately by a violent shudder, a wrenching of the hull, and the terrifying sound of rock scraping against metal. The ship listed sharply leewards, throwing passengers and crew off their feet and sending them reeling, arms outstretched, to catch hold of some support.

Within seconds sirens began blaring, though there was no one for miles around to hear them. Crew members ran back and forth along the sloping deck, making their way from one handhold to another. The ship had struck a rock, the passengers were told. A large hole had been torn in its side beneath the water line. It was filling with water, and would sink.

A radio message was sent to Kronstadt, but it was only a formality; even if ships from the imperial navy were dispatched to rescue the *Standart*'s passengers, they could not possibly navigate the narrow, shallow waters between the islands, nor could they arrive in time to help, for the ship was sinking rapidly.

Nicky occupied himself, stopwatch in hand, in watching the rising water line, as crew members rushed to ready the lifeboats and supply them with water and food. He called out his observations. The *Standart* would sink, he thought, in twenty minutes or less.

Alix, by contrast, began giving orders to the crew. Grabbing Alexei, and calling her daughters, she herded them to the nearest lifeboat and gave orders that the children and the female staff members be lowered away first, keeping only Anna Vyrubov behind with her. Having watched the lowering of the first boats, she and Anna made their way into the cabins, their progress slow because of the increasingly sloping deck, the ceaseless screaming of the sirens adding to the general confusion. Alix flung the counterpanes off the beds and began emptying jewellery boxes, medicine chests and drawers onto the sheets. Icons stripped from the walls were added, along with warm coats and blankets. Tying the corners of the sheets together to form bundles, she and Anna managed to drag the bundles out on the deck and heave them into the remaining lifeboats.

It all happened quickly, too quickly for careful calculation. Alix and Anna climbed into a boat, Nicky and the rest of the crew abandoned ship as well and in less time than Nicky had calculated, everyone was safely off the sinking vessel, which lay on its side in the calm water, still buoyant but gradually dipping lower and lower under the waves.

Tragedy had been averted. Before long the crew sighted a Finnish ship, hailed her, and the passengers and crew were taken aboard and delivered safely to one of the cruisers steaming towards the area from Kronstadt.

Recalling the incident later, one of the passengers, Princess Obolensky, was struck by how 'resourceful and full of energy' the empress had been. It was she, and not her husband, who had seen to the safety of the family and staff, who had mobilized everyone's efforts, and who had managed to salvage the valuables from the cabins. Forgetting herself – she had been the last woman to leave the ship – and caught up entirely in the peril of the moment, Alix had acted as one born to command. This instinct to lead, to rescue, to take command in a crisis, would increasingly be called on in the years to come.

Alexandra as a young girl.

Young Alexandra knew her own mind, and resisted an arranged marriage.

A formal portrait of the young Alexandra and Nicholas.

The Romanovs with Queen Victoria, Alexandra's grandmother, and Prince Edward, later Edward VII.

Alexandra as a young wife.

Alexandra and the Tsarevich Alexei.

Tsarina Alexandra, melancholy and ill.

Alexandra's deep devotion to her son Alexei only increased when he survived near-fatal attacks of haemophilia.

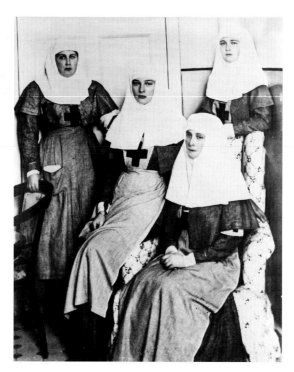

Alexandra and her daughters were trained as nurses and worked long hours in military hospitals.

Alexandra and her daughters Olga, Tatiana, Marie and Anastasia.

Incapacitated by severe pain, Alexandra often took the air in a wheelchair.

The Romanovs at Livadia in the Crimea in 1914.

20

In autumn 1907, soon after the accident aboard the *Standart*, the empress once again fell ill, and took to her bed, this time staying there for months.

Her legs and back gave her so much pain that even the smallest movement hurt her, and the doctors came daily to give her injections in alternate legs. With the pain came weakness, fatigue, fever and headache. Week after week she lay all but immobile, insisting on getting fully dressed each day as if to go out – she disliked dressing gowns, with their air of idleness and languor – and waiting impatiently to improve.

She occupied herself with her everpresent embroidery and other handcrafts, wrote letters (often at night when pain kept her from sleeping), read, prayed, fretted over her inactivity. She was accustomed to being busy, indeed to feeling hurried, there was so much to do.[1] It was not in her nature to lie back and rest, even though her weary body demanded it. 'She was convinced,' Martha Mouchanow wrote, 'that every single hour of any man's or woman's existence ought to be consecrated to duty or occupation of some kind.'[2] Obsessive occupation had always been her hallmark, and without it she felt useless.

She not only felt useless, she felt burdensome. The doctors, observing that any exertion made her tired, diagnosed heart trouble, and warned Nicky that his wife showed signs of becoming seriously ill, and this greatly increased the concern shown for her by everyone around her.[3] To her sciatic pain and migraines was now added the strain and worry of a weak heart and, although Alix never complained, and rarely admitted to suffering, it was evident to her family and even to her ladies-in-waiting that she was struggling as never before with physical illness. It vexed her that others made what she called a 'fuss' over her, that her sisters were worried about her and Irene was contemplating making a special trip to Russia to visit her.

Christmas 1907 came, and Alix was still very ill, too weak to stand beside her husband when he received the diplomatic corps, too enervated to allow a performance of KR's new play, *The Bride of Messina*, to be put on in the palace grounds.[4] She was 'being careful', he said, avoiding fatigue by resting. She made an effort to read, and tried, no doubt, to read the intellectually stimulating, challenging books she had always preferred, books on astronomy, natural history and mathematics. (History she disdained as boring, having to do with 'the sayings and doings of people long dead'.[5]) She may have tried to reread *The Origin of Species*, a book she had long admired, a copy of which she kept in her room, much to the horror of her Father Confessor who considered it dangerous. But reading made her head ache, even the light reading she normally disapproved of as frivolous; novels did not distract her or lift her spirits, and she soon wearied of the trivialities of the plots.

It did distract her, or at least it satisfied her need for orderliness, to keep a careful chronology of her days of illness, just as she kept careful track of her lace and of the garments in her own and her children's wardrobes. 'Today it is the forty-ninth day that I am ill,' she wrote to her daughter Tatiana in January of 1908. 'Tomorrow begins the eighth week.' On that forty-ninth day, she lay in the dark a long time, her head pounding, her legs aching.

Her spirits were very low. 'When one feels ill, all seems harder to bear,' she once wrote to Nicky. With illness, with weakness came a greater difficulty in 'mastering herself', she admitted. What had looked bright and hopeful now looked dim, and she became over emotional, too quick to give in to tears.[6]

She could no longer master herself. Mentally as well as physically, Alix now stood on uncertain ground.

She was depressed, 'despairing', as she wrote to her sister Victoria, about her life. Though she talked endlessly, especially to her daughters, about the power of prayer and the inevitability of miracles, about how nothing was impossible for God, her anxieties were not quieted by her faith.[7] Instead, as she approached her late thirties, Alix entered a murky cognitive realm in which reason often tottered and balance was all but lost. She had veered off the path of common sense and sound judgment, and in an effort to regain clarity and peace of mind she clung to the religious certainties impressed on her in childhood and reinforced by men such as Philippe and Father Gregory. The more she struggled for understanding, the more she insisted that God ruled all; her constant need to reiterate the primacy of her faith underscored its insecurity. The inner conflict, the tension between trust and fearful doubt, preyed on the empress's mind and increased what others perceived as her 'air of suffering'.

Alix's suffering was in fact more hidden from view than ever in 1908 and 1909, years when she spent more and more time in seclusion. She was very seldom to be seen on public occasions. She did go aboard the *Standart* – repaired and restored after the accident in Finnish waters – and made journeys to Livadia and Peterhof and even went as far away as Stockholm and Cowes for vacations and family visits. But moving from place to place was painful, so much of the time she lay on her sofa in the mauve boudoir at Tsarskoe Selo, or on the terrace at Livadia, or even on a mattress placed on the ground in the open air of the garden, wincing every time she shifted her position and gritting her teeth when the pain in her back and legs was especially severe.

The imperial doctors suggested that she go to a spa, not only to ease her physical pain but to calm her overwrought nerves, but she resisted the idea. She tried to cultivate an attitude of acceptance. 'Don't think my ill health depresses me personally,' she wrote to her sister Victoria somewhat disingenuously. 'I don't care, except to see my dear ones suffer on my account, and that I cannot fulfil my duties. But once God sends such a cross, it must be borne. Darling Mama also lost her health at an early age.'[8]

That she had, once and for all, 'lost her health' seemed clear. She did not expect to regain her full vigour. Yet there were times when she rose energetically from her bed or mattress and strode across the room or, if out of doors, climbed a hill, leaving those who watched her puzzled, and giving rise to whispers among the servants that she had never been truly incapacitated or in pain at all. Certainly she had appeared robust when giving orders and taking charge during the *Standart* disaster, and when nursing Anastasia through diphtheria, when she stayed by her daughter's bedside through most of five long nights until her fever broke. In truth Alix could nearly always be counted on to get up out of her sickbed in response to the strong pull of others' needs. All her rescuing impulses were triggered, and she responded, without hesitation, to whatever crisis arose.

But between crises, fatigue overcame her, and she succumbed to chronic pain and to the shortness of breath that indicated a weakened heart.

'My darling Mama!' Tatiana wrote to Alix early in 1909, 'I hope you won't be today very tired and that you can get up to dinner. I am always so awfully sorry when you are tired and when you can't get up. I will pray for you my darling mama in church ... Please sleep well and don't get tired.'[9]

With Alix in seclusion, resting on her couch or bed, and the children in the nursery wing of the Alexander Palace with their governess Sophie Tioutchev or their principal nurse Mary (about whom Olga complained, claiming that Mary got angry 'without reason'), notes passed back and forth between mother and children during the day. Alix often sent them instructions and exhortations, reprimanding Olga ('don't be so wild and kick about and show your legs, it is not pretty'), telling them all to be obedient to Mary and Sophie, cautioning them against becoming overly fond of clothes or jewellery (as Tatiana was inclined to do), gently but firmly reprimanding Olga for her temper and Marie for her stubbornness. She was anxious about their delicate health, and very concerned about the formation of their moral character, repeatedly reminding them of their duty to help those in want and making every effort to keep all the children from becoming arrogant or haughty.[10]

All five of the children had an abundance of animal spirits. When their Aunt Olga took them out walking in the palace park, she had trouble controlling them. Freed from their nurse's oversight they ran off in different directions, 'lively and full of energy'.[11] Alexei in particular was not only high-spirited and energetic, but undisciplined. Fearing that to curb his behaviour might cause him to have tantrums, during which he might bang his head or kick furniture, and knowing that any such violence could bring on an attack of bleeding, his parents chose to let him do as he liked, and told the household staff to do the same. As a result he was recalcitrant and ill-mannered, disruptive and thoroughly spoiled – in contrast to his sisters, who when others were present sat with their hands folded, or busy with needlework, spoke in measured tones and always remembered their table manners.

Both Alix and Nicky wanted to raise their children simply – or as simply as possible amid surroundings of great magnificence. At birth each child inherited a very large fortune, but this endowment was never brought to their attention. Instead, the girls in particular were encouraged to be thrifty, not to waste anything, never to squander the small sum given to them each month for pocket money. The girls' fine clothes, made by the Moscow couturier Lamanov, were worn for many years, Olga and Tatiana's outgrown dresses handed down to Marie and Anastasia.[12] The small silver ornaments, books and diaries they spent their money on were modest in cost and they were encouraged to save some of their monthly allowance to give to charity.[13]

With Alexei, as heir to the throne, always given pre-eminence and absorbing the majority of his parents' care and attention, a situation his illness intensified, the imperial daughters had to be emotionally self-sufficient. They looked to one another for support, and seem to have formed a bond strong enough to overcome whatever personal conflicts arose among them. Like their mother, who had learned from the stouthearted, iron-willed Baroness Grancy 'never to give in, either physically or morally', they were taught self-discipline from an early age. But they did not all respond well to this harsh tutelage, which called for a great degree of self-sacrifice. And when Alix's illness removed her for long stretches of time, at least two of the girls reacted emotionally. Tatiana wilted. In her notes to her mother there is a plangent tone, an underlying sadness. And Marie, whom her sisters called by the unkind nickname 'Fat Little Bow-Wow', became 'wild and naughty' and lashed out verbally, saying that nobody loved her, that she was only in the way, and keeping company with Xenia's daughter Irina instead of her sisters.[14]

Alix noted all this, brooded over it, and did her best to guide and comfort her children while coping with her own physical wretchedness and low spirits. 'Motherliness lay at the root of her character,' Sophie Buxhoeveden wrote of Alix.[15] But the empress's idea of motherliness was idiosyncratic; it reflected, naturally enough, her own priorities. She saw herself in her motherly role as guide and protector, leading her children away from all that she condemned as 'frivolity' and towards a high-minded vision of self-improvement and duty, within the framework of a self-denying morality. She was suspicious of pleasure, mistaking it for self-indulgence.

Fortunately for the girls, Nicky's sister Olga, who spent a good deal of time with the family during the years of Alix's illness, offered her nieces a respite from their mother's well-intentioned strictures. When the family was in residence at Tsarskoe Selo, once a week the imperial daughters spent an entire day in Petersburg with their cheerful, somewhat unconventional young aunt, lunching at the Anitchkov Palace with their grandmother Minnie (an 'irksomely formal' event, Olga recalled), then going on to Olga's townhouse for a tea dance with other young people, at which they 'all enjoyed themselves immensely'. There was much laughter and music, games and conversation, and the light-hearted presence of Olga, who seemed, in her spontaneity and jokiness, almost as young as the girls themselves.[16] 'These Sunday afternoons were great events in the girls' lives,' Sophie Buxhoeveden thought. It was always with regret that they heard a footman announce the arrival, at ten in the evening, of a carriage from the palace, waiting to take them home.

How well Alix bore her poor health and unwelcome seclusion is impossible to say. To her children she showed a stoic fortitude. 'When God thinks the time comes to make me better, He will, and not before,' she wrote to daughter Olga. 'He knows why He sent the illness, and we must be quite sure it's for some good.'[17] One thing was certain: she took great comfort from Father Gregory, whose visits to Tsarskoe Selo became more frequent in these difficult years 1908 and 1909.

Unlike Philippe Vachot, who had been the teacher and master for an entire group of devotees, Father Gregory came to offer his spiritual gifts to the imperial family alone. He was their 'dear friend'; Nicky and Alix were his 'Little Father' and 'Little Mother'. With the children he was on the most affectionate terms, Alexei trusting him and turning to him when in pain and Olga, Tatiana, Marie and Anastasia always happy to see him in the nursery and admitting him eagerly to their bedrooms – sometimes secretly, for they knew the governess Sophie Tioutchev did not approve. He sat on their beds, talking familiarly with them as a close relative might, exuding, no doubt, the gentleness and warmth Nicky's sister Olga had been aware of in him, putting the girls completely at ease. With his shaggy long hair and childlike genuineness, his simplicity and constant talk of divine love and the sweetness of the natural world, he must have seemed to the children like a creature out of a fairy tale, real yet touched with the surreal, and no doubt they were much in awe of his often demonstrated power to heal.

'My dear pearl M!' he wrote to Marie in 1908, 'tell me how you talked with the sea, with nature! I miss your simple soul. We will see each other soon! A big kiss.' His words were those of a rapturous innocent, a holy fool. 'My dear M! My little friend! May the Lord help you to carry your cross with wisdom and joy in Christ. This world is like the day, look it's already evening. So it is with the cares of the world.'[18]

This blithe, elemental lyricism was Father Gregory's trademark, an ability to dwell mentally in a realm beyond the ordinary, on a higher plane of existence where the cares of the world were overshadowed by an ecstatic joy in the knowledge of God's omni-present, benign power. Trusting in the goodness of creation, fearful of nothing, seeing the future and knowing that it too was good gave the Siberian a radiant optimism that drew the beleaguered imperials to him.

'When I can see our dear friend, I shall be very happy,' Alix told her daughter Olga.[19] In his presence her doubts receded, her faith increased. And her headaches (and Nicky's too) were cured – at least for a time. Father Gregory had only to shout, 'Be off!' and the terrible blinding pain ceased.

Beneficial as he was to the tsar and his immediate family, Father Gregory struck others as not only odd but threatening. Xenia thought him 'sinister'.[20] Ella, remembering how Alix had been led into delusion by Philippe Vachot, sent warnings to her sister cautioning her against drawing Father Gregory too deeply into her family life and relying too much on his ministrations.[21] Few among the household staff held the Siberian starets in awe, rather the reverse.[22] He continued to attract a large number of followers to his Petersburg apartment, and word of his cures was spread through the capital. But he also aroused distrust. His true nature eluded comprehension. He made people uneasy. His surreal, fey quality was taken by some to be something else entirely: the evasive cunning of the trickster. Indeed even those who admired him admitted that he was 'like a chameleon, whose words and actions changed their colour according to the varied needs of the people he met, the environment and, finally, his own moods'. And while this chameleon-like adaptability made Father Gregory a sympathetic guide and teacher, it also allowed him to slip with disarming ease into intimacy with people, intimacy that could, or so it seemed to those who were suspicious of him, prove to be dangerous.[23]

By 1909 the imperial doctors were amazed that Alexei was still alive. Chronic bleeding in his stomach threatened to turn into a fatal abscess. Pain from internal bleeding in his back made him scream, sometimes for days, his hoarse cries so piteous that the servants, hearing them as they passed along the corridor outside his room, had to cover their ears. His legs grew stiff with engorged blood, the left leg so distorted that for a long time he could not use it at all and had to be carried everywhere by his constant companion, the burly sailor Derevenko.

He could become ill very suddenly: in the midst of a family meal, while out for a drive, while reciting his lessons. Bleeding would begin, the colour would suddenly drain from his face and he would begin to cry. The sight of him in such a condition, his limbs distorted, his face 'drawn and seamed with suffering', was terrible – it made Nicky weep and take refuge in his study – and his moans and screams wrenched the hearts of his doctors, his sisters, above all his parents.

Alix had seen Alexei through many crises by the time he was five years old, but every fresh attack made her panic. White-faced and agitated, she took charge, calling in the doctors, sending to Petersburg for Father Gregory or, if he was away from the capital, sending him a telegram, praying to the saints whose icons hung around her son's bed.

'God has not abandoned us,' she repeated when Alexei's suffering was at its worst. Though at times she looked despairing, her will to believe was strong. She trusted in Father Gregory to pray for Alexei, and his prayers, she once told an officer of the *Standart*, 'have a particular force' because of his ascetic life.[24] Each time, even if it looked as though the boy would surely die, he recovered – if not immediately, then within hours or days.

For some reason Alix did not expect Father Gregory to cure her, beyond easing her migraines. Her sciatic pain had never been as acute as during the years when the Siberian was coming to the palace increasingly often. Her weak heart seemed to be growing weaker. Beyond the facile explanation that for her to be cured was outside the will of God, there was no way to account for this apparent paradox. Of course, Alexei's recurrent attacks of bleeding were potentially fatal, while Alix's chronic pain and fatigue were not. Still, she must have longed for relief and, so far as is known, the starets did not provide it.

Sometime in 1910 one of the nursery staff, a nanny named Vishniakov, asked to see Alix. The nanny was very upset, and Alix, who was accustomed to listening sympathetically to the problems of her servants and household members and to helping them whenever she could, was no doubt prepared to be understanding. But the story Nanny Vishniakov told – between sobs – brought forth another response entirely.

Vishniakov had gone with Father Gregory and others to his village of Pokrovsky in Siberia for three weeks of rest. While there, she said, he had entered her room stealthily, at night, crept into her bed and seduced her. Nor was she the only one, the nanny said; she had seen with her own eyes the starets's flagrant and indiscreet seduction of at least one other member of the household.[25]

It was not the first time the empress had heard, and rejected as slanderous, first-hand accounts of Father Gregory's seductions and debaucheries. A trusted woman of the court, sent to Pokrovsky to learn the truth about the starets, confided to Alix that Father Gregory had tried to seduce her maid. The empress's own confessor, the Archimandrite Theophan, and other important clerics had come to the palace to inform the tsar and tsarina that the man they turned to for spiritual guidance was bringing discredit on the imperial family by his immorality and the notoriety it was creating. Militsa and Stana had begun to have doubts about Father Gregory after becoming convinced that he behaved himself scandalously at times. The ladies-in-waiting, Nicky's sister Xenia, the governess Sophie Tioutchev were uncomfortable around the Siberian, gossiped about him, and made Alix aware that they disapproved of his being allowed near the four grand duchesses, especially when the girls were in their nightclothes. It was improper, unwise and reckless to put a wolf among the innocent, trusting lambs, they thought; it was inviting disaster.

Alix's immediate response to the accusations of Nanny Vishniakov was that 'she did not believe such slanders, and saw in them the work of dark forces, wishing to ruin' Father Gregory.[26] 'Saints are always calumniated,' she told Dr Botkin, who came to the palace twice each day to listen to her heart.[27] Theophan was sent away, Sophie Tioutchev and others in the household told to be silent – though they continued to shake their heads and whisper about the starets, their stories reaching the capital and being told and retold there with elaborations.

Alix knew that her guide and mentor was flawed and full of vices, but she trusted him not to harm her children and she told herself that the allegations against him were invented by her husband's enemies. To attack the starets was just one more way to attack the tsar himself, for Father Gregory had all but become a member of the imperial family. Besides, the starets himself denied everything, and she wanted to believe his denials.

The campaign to expose Father Gregory as a sordid libertine had the effect of driving the empress more deeply into isolation. Her own poor health, and the need to keep Alexei's illness a secret, meant that there were few people she could confide in. Now that small circle of intimates shrank still further.

Anna Vyrubov, Alix's young, stout, rather cloying devotee, came to the palace every day. Somewhat dim-witted but stubborn and above all loyal – not only to Alix but to Father Gregory, whose disciple she had long been – Anna was welcomed eagerly by the empress as long as she was not 'too gushing or too exacting'.[28] It was an incongruous friendship, between the tall, earnest, sad-eyed invalid empress and the short, shallow, vivacious maid of honour, but they were bound by their common faith in Father Gregory, by Anna's hero-worship of Alix, and by a mutual fondness that had begun when Anna, as a girl of sixteen, had nearly died of typhoid and Alix had come to sit by her bedside often, supporting her in her recovery.[29] Despite what others saw as her aloofness, Alix had a gift for friendship. Julia Rantzau, Marie Bariatinsky, Martha Mouchanow, her wardrobe mistress Princess Galitzine, all had, to a greater or lesser extent, been good friends of Alix's, as Lily Dehn and Sophie Buxhoeveden would become her close friends later on.

Another woman admitted to the shrinking circle of the empress's intimates was Princess Dondukov, a follower of Father Gregory whom Martha Mouchanow described as 'a physician of no mean skill' and high intellect. Aggressive and scheming, the princess was generally more feared than liked, according to Mouchanow, who may have been jealous, but Alix had confidence in her and sought her opinion on many subjects and confided in her, and may even have taken medicines she prescribed in preference to those prescribed by the court physicians.[30]

The number of those who could be trusted was growing smaller and smaller. Only Nicky and Alexei and the girls, a few stalwarts such as Anna, Princess Dondukov and the faraway Marie Bariatinsky with whom she corresponded, sister Irene and brother Ernie (not Ella, she was too opposed to Father Gregory), and Father Gregory himself could be relied upon completely. The others she could not be sure of. They might belong to the dark forces that threatened Father Gregory, and through him, the imperial family, indeed Russia itself.

And the dark forces were growing strong, or so it seemed to Alix as the second decade of what she saw as the barbaric, inhumane twentieth century advanced. They were gathering, like a towering thundercloud, over the capital.

21

A reckless hedonism reigned in Petersburg in the mild winter and warm spring of 1911. There was a mania for skating, and the indoor rinks were full of eager skaters racing, leaping and turning with perilous abandon. The gaudy red, orange and green trams that sped along the main avenues of the city ran on oblivious of obstacles in their path, knocking over carts, injuring horses and maiming pedestrians who tried to jump on and off without waiting for the conductors to bring them jerkily to a halt. For three years running cholera epidemics had carried off thousands of Petersburgers, leaving the survivors with an avid thirst for life; they sought pleasure, sensation, the thrill of risk, and they seemed to care nothing for the danger.

In the drawing rooms and ballrooms of the great palaces were to be found the ultimate risk takers, the speculators who made and lost immense fortunes on the stock exchange and in financial ventures in steel and coal, copper and oil. Deal making was the preoccupation of the hour, how to raise money and which schemes to invest it in to make it go up the fastest. And once the wealth was acquired, there was the excitement of the gambling house, where it could all be wagered and, if lost, where a bullet to the head could put an end to the whole mad spiral of chance.

The reigning hostesses of the capital, Countess Betsy Shuvalov, Grand Duchess Victoria Melita (Ducky, recently returned to Petersburg from exile with her husband Grand Duke Cyril, and the leader of the young 'smart set'), and, above all, the widowed Grand Duchess Marie Pavlovna (Aunt Miechen), took the risk of throwing

open their salons to a wide variety of guests, from the great aristocratic families – the Orlovs, Tolstoys, Dolgorukovs and Gorchakovs
– to the nouveaux riches, wealthy foreign investors, painters and
composers, and a variety of hangers-on whose manners were said
by more staid guests to be 'fast' and whose morals did not bear
scrutiny. Some said the social tone had been lowered, but there was
no turning back; old and new elites together were swept up in the
craze for loud music, strong cocktails and the newest fad, dancing
the tango until the early hours of the morning.

Nowhere was the hedonistic mood more in evidence than in the
explosive realm of the erotic. Censorship laws were repealed in the
wake of the government upheaval of 1905-06, and the result was a
wave of novels, poems and paintings that celebrated sexual expression
in all its forms. Subjects once held to be unmentionable were now a
frequent topic of conversation. People held forth on homosexuality,
voyeurism, and pederasty and were not reticent on the theme of
their own personal pleasures and gratifications. Women took 'oriental
pills' to enlarge their breasts and men sought potions to enhance
their virility. Nightlife became marked by decadence. Husbands and
wives visited brothels together in the evenings, then went on to dance
the tango at the fashionable Suicide Club. Young men from noble
families amused themselves at parties dressing in women's gowns
and long ropes of pearls, bright blue eyeshadow on their lids and
chalk-white make-up on their faces. The comet of 1910 had come
and gone without destroying the world, but the sense of approaching
doom, of the end-time, was still strong. People boasted of living for
the moment, and seemed to vie with one another in causing scandal
– though it was harder now than in the past to find someone to
shock, at least among the worldly elite of the capital.

In the countryside there was no equivalent disorder in morals,
though the combination of social unrest and financial hardship
created immense resentment and a growing longing for change. These
were the times memoirists, looking back across a decade, would call
the 'troubled years', the 'black years', for the Russian peasants, who
lived in dread of being identified as radicals or rebels and being sent

into Siberian exile, or worse. Many thousands were hanged as subversives or conspirators, their animals slaughtered and their villages burned by government agents who were even more feared than the robber bands that roamed unhindered from province to province, stealing from well-off peasants, relieving tax collectors of their sacks of gold and even purloining entire shipments of grain and oil and coal.

But if the mood of recklessness did not take hold outside Petersburg, the gossip from the capital did penetrate to the provincial cities and villages, and nearly all the gossip was centred on the man the newspapers called Rasputin, the Siberian charlatan who in the guise of a holy healer was said to have mesmerized and seduced the empress and gained control over the entire imperial family.

The sensation-loving public, avid for scandal and sexual gossip, could not get its fill of stories about the man one newspaper called 'that fornicator of human souls and bodies', Rasputin. Pressure was brought to bear on the newspaper editors by the imperial ministers, and fines were levied for every scurrilous story printed, but public demand was insatiable and the stories continued to appear.[1] Soon all Petersburg knew of Rasputin's sordid past, his inexhaustible sexual appetite, his seductions of his female followers, the boasts he made that the tsar knelt down and washed his feet, that he had slept with the empress, her daughters and other women of the court, and that he had a chest full of letters from Alix and the girls, all testifying to their love for him and his complete domination of them.

Obscene graffiti began to appear on the brick walls of palaces, crude images of the empress and her unholy paramour making love, and in the streets children sang bawdy songs about the pair. Delegates to the Duma – the third Duma, the second, convened in the spring of 1907, having been dissolved as too radical – heard speeches about how the court was being controlled by intriguers and frauds, and no one doubted that the references were to Rasputin.

The private life of the imperial family, and especially the empress, had been dragged into the mire of titillating sexual scandal. Petersburgers whispered that Alix was not only the lover of Rasputin but the lover of Anna Vyrubov as well. She had no shame, they said. She had no morals, no loyalty. She was the Niemka, the German bitch, German to the core.

Alix was once again very unwell. The least exertion exhausted her, and she was often short of breath and in pain. Now and then she would attend the theatre, or sit for a time enduring some public function, looking alternately worried and sour, but it was noticed that she was always ill at ease, and greatly relieved when the time came to leave.[2] Her private routines had altered. Her chronic shortness of breath prevented her from singing, and playing the piano overtired her. She took up painting still lifes and, as ever, occupied herself quietly with reading and handwork and writing letters.

'Dearest Madgie,' she wrote to her old governess late in the spring of 1911, 'very tenderest thanks for your dear letter. We came over here [to Peterhof] on Saturday and hope to go to sea . . . We long for that rest.' She had been sick for seven months, she told her correspondent, and Nicky had been overworking. They both needed relaxation. 'I hope to get a little better, so as not to be always lying [down].' 'The children are growing up fast. In November Olga will be sixteen, Tatiana is almost her size at fourteen – Marie will be twelve, Anastasia ten, Alexei seven.'

She told the governess that the older girls were taking her place at luncheons and receptions, military reviews, and commemorative events, learning, as Alix herself had learned at their age, how to make the rounds of a roomful of guests, pausing briefly to exchange a few words with each and then moving gracefully on to the next. All the young grand duchesses were fluent in four languages – Russian, English, German and French – and were able to mingle comfortably with diplomats, government ministers, generals and admirals, and the aristocrats of the household. 'They must get accustomed to replace me,' Alix wrote, 'as I rarely can appear anywhere and, when I do, am afterwards long laid up – over-tired muscles of the heart.'[3]

There was one place where Alix always felt better, where she could be out of doors, resting on a chaise longue or driving in her pony carriage, where her energy seemed to return and her natural urge to make improvements could find an outlet. Livadia, the Crimean villa perched high on its cliff above the blue ocean, had become her favourite place. Their movements less restricted now than in previous years, and the threat of terrorist attacks presumed to have decreased, the family visited Livadia each spring and autumn. Daily life there was much less formal than at Tsarskoe Selo, the pace more leisurely and the atmosphere unceremonious. Servants, guests, even the officers of the *Standart*, which rode at anchor in the bay, all joined the family at one table for the midday meal, and when ministers from Petersburg arrived, places were laid for them as well. There were no state carriages with outriders and liveried coachmen, no resplendent uniforms for the staff, no rigid schedule to be kept. Guests sat on the terrace or amid the rose bushes and blooming vines in the colonnaded garden, lingering over cups of tea and talking. In the evenings, the balalaika orchestra from the yacht gave concerts, or the Cossacks who guarded the family sang in chorus. There were entertainers from the local Tartar villages as well, and, on occasion, Olga and Tatiana gave readings of French plays.

According to Martha Mouchanow, the empress was 'never so happy as in the Crimea', and she contentedly joined in the social life that developed within the small colony of aristocratic villa owners. There were dances for the young people, dinners for visitors, jaunts aboard the *Standart* to the palace of Novy Sviet for banquets of roasted lamb and baked fowl, saffron rice and baklava, accompanied by wine made from grapes grown in the estate's extensive vineyards. Among Alix's favourite visitors was the Emir of Bokhara, a very grand dignitary who never travelled without an interpreter and at least two of his ministers, tall, exotic figures in robes of silver and gold whose long beards were dyed scarlet.[4] It amused Alix to converse with the emir who, though he spoke fluent Russian, thought it more in keeping with his dignity to speak in his own language; the solemnity with which he spoke, and the whole cumbersome procedure of translating their remarks back and forth, made it hard for Alix to keep her composure and gave her funny stories to tell later, after her guest had left.

However carefree the mood at Livadia, it was a place of sorrow –
and this was part of the attraction of the area for the empress – for
patients with tuberculosis came by the hundreds to Yalta and the
surrounding coastal area to seek healing in hospitals. Some recovered,
but many did not and funeral processions were a frequent sight.
Emaciated, blanket-wrapped consumptives basking in the sun were
on every terrace, or so it seemed. Alix joined the Anti-Tuberculosis
League, sold her own and her children's handcrafts in the organization's annual bazaar, and sent her daughters out to sell flowers on
Flower Day to benefit the patients. She organized the construction
of two new sanatoria, built on property owned by the imperial family
at Massandra, and visited many of the worst cases there herself,
sending Olga and Tatiana when she was too tired and ill to go. It was
good for the girls to see for themselves just how severe the illness
could be, and how much suffering it caused, she said when questions
were raised about the wisdom of exposing her daughters to the
contagious disease. 'They should realize the sadness underneath all
this beauty.'[5]

At Livadia, Alix was able to accomplish a good deal despite her
intermittent invalid state. Far from Petersburg, away from the stresses
of the court, the criticism of her in-laws and the libels of the press,
she was restored – at least some of the time. The old villa from
Alexander III's day having been torn down, she took pleasure in
furnishing the new, larger structure that was built in its place, ordering
white furniture and chintz curtains for the airy rooms, placing antique
statues in the garden, overseeing the tending of the groves of olive
and cypress trees that surrounded the house.

Nicky welcomed his wife's bursts of energy, but was confused by
them. Just when he had accustomed himself to living with an invalid,
the invalid rose from her couch and went off to the sanatorium to
visit patients or drove out in the pony carriage. He confessed to KR
that the situation was 'tiresome and depressing'.[6]

Compounding the confusion was Alix's odd manner and behaviour. She was capable of gaiety, she laughed easily, with her
children she was warm and affectionate. But she gravitated towards

illness and death, towards any circumstance in which tragedy loomed and in which she could assume the role of rescuer – a role that allowed her to step out of her everyday, troubled self and assume a simpler, less emotionally demanding identity, that of self-sacrificing caretaker.

For she was very troubled indeed. Her inner tensions had brought on not only illness but a disturbing sense that she had lost self-command, which made her fearful and worsened her symptoms of anxiety – shortness of breath, a pounding heart, sweaty palms, a sense of doom. She suffered, so Dr Botkin thought, from 'progressive hysteria', a psychological condition that had more and more severe physical manifestations.

And by 1911, in the words of the court minister Baron Fredericks, Alix 'often conducted herself strangely'.[7] Her behaviour was erratic, she did unexpected things and reacted in unexpected ways. She muttered in a very low voice, so that others had to strain to hear her. Yet they had to speak very loudly to her, for she had begun to lose her hearing.[8] Consciously or unconsciously, she used her heart condition to manipulate people and to try to control situations. Among family and uncritical staff and servants, her symptoms were quiescent. But when contradicted or frustrated, or among people she knew to be hostile to her or to hold contrary opinions to hers, she complained of chest pain and began gasping for breath. The symptoms were not feigned, but they were, in Dr Botkin's view, psychosomatic.[9]

The empress's 'strange' behaviour and the gossip about it, the emperor's passivity, the turmoil in the Duma and among the ministers following the assassination of Stolypin in September, 1911, led to renewed suspicion of Rasputin and a fresh wave of articles and rumours in Petersburg.

'Everybody already knows and talks about him, it's terrible the things they say about him, and about Alix, and everything that goes on at Tsarskoe,' Xenia wrote in her diary early in 1912. 'How will it all end? It's terrible.'[10]

As to the government's attitude towards the Siberian, conflicting views were aired. Some said the police were protecting Rasputin, and that a book exposing his crimes and sordid habits had been confiscated and burned by police officials.[11] Others whispered that the police were watching Rasputin and keeping a record of all that he did. Cynics argued that both could be true, for it was well known that the police could not be trusted and that they represented conflicting interests.

Police agents were in fact following Rasputin when he was in the capital, gathering detailed evidence of where he went and with whom, what women he slept with, what others he accosted. It was quite a full dossier, giving times and places and names, recording drunken brawls, visits to prostitutes, assignations at bath houses and violent incidents in the course of which offended women threatened Rasputin or spat on him.[12] Nor was this the only record of the starets's lewd behaviour. Iliodor and Mitya Kozelsky, a strannik who had at one time been in favour at the palace, prepared a written record of what Rasputin had said and done that reflected badly on the imperial family – his boasts of his sexual prowess and long list of lovers, his seduction of at least one nun, his claims of intimacy with the empress and her daughters.

In the Duma, Alexander Guchkov, leader of the influential Octobrist party, had copies made of several letters the empress was said to have written to Rasputin and distributed them widely.[13]

'My Beloved, unforgettable teacher, redeemer and mentor,' one letter began, 'how tiresome it is without you. My soul is quiet and I relax only when you, my teacher, are sitting beside me.' 'I kiss your hands and lean my head on your blessed shoulders. Oh, how light do I feel then! I only wish one thing: to fall asleep, forever on your shoulders and in your arms.'[14]

The furore in the Duma grew more heated, the gossip in the capital more salacious. Vladimir Kokovtsov, who had replaced Stolypin as principal minister, was visited by Rasputin and was repelled by him. They had met before; in the previous year Rasputin had come to Kokovtsov and, 'on orders from Tsarskoe Selo', offered him the post of Minister of the Interior. Now, however, with all the damaging reports and stories that had come to light, Kokovtsov saw the Siberian not as a messenger from the palace but as a maleficent, half-mad character, a grotesque from a melodrama.

'I was shocked by the repulsive expression of his eyes,' Kokovtsov wrote years later in his memoirs, 'deep-set and close to each other, small, grey in colour.' Rasputin stared at the minister for a long time with his 'cold, piercing little eyes', as if intending to hypnotize him. 'Next he threw his head sharply back and studied the ceiling; then he lowered his head and stared at the floor; all this in silence.'[15]

When Kokovtsov advised the starets to leave Petersburg, the latter not only refused but protested at the top of his voice that he was innocent of any intrigue or wrongdoing. He never went to the palace without being ordered there, he shouted. 'They summon me!' The minister was unimpressed, sent Rasputin away and told the tsar about their conversation. He told Minnie about it too, and Minnie, who for years had kept her distance, for the most part, from all that went on in the imperial family, decided that the time had come to intervene.

Minnie went to tea at the Alexander Palace in February of 1912. She was nearly sixty-five years old, but retained her bustling air and much of her charm. She knew that her daughter-in-law was often unwell, and that her chest pains and breathlessness had once again been severe the previous month. She had only limited sympathy for Alix, however, dismissing her constant ill health as the result of living in draughty rooms and throwing open her windows to the frigid air. Minnie blamed Alix entirely for 'ruining both the dynasty and herself' by her ill-advised favouritism for Rasputin.[16] Alix did not see the harm she was doing, but she must be made to see it, Minnie had confided to Kokovtsov. Someone had to bring both the tsar and his wife to their senses.

It must have been a long, tense afternoon. Minnie laid out the case against Rasputin – his well-documented debaucheries, his damaging and indiscreet boasts and loose talk, the angry speeches being made by deputies, the crude stories and jokes repeated at dinner tables and in ballrooms. The dignity and authority of the throne were being undermined. Unless Rasputin was sent away, immediately, and never again allowed near the palace, the future of the dynasty was in peril.

Nicky said little, other than to observe that he didn't see how he could send Father Gregory away.[17] The year before, under pressure from his critics, the starets had gone on a pilgrimage to Jerusalem and Athens, then had spent the summer away from the capital. In all he had been gone for the better part of the year. But his absence had not led to any lessening of the furore over his presumed intimacy with the tsarina, and Minnie was well aware of this.

It was Alix who spoke up in response to her mother-in-law's accusations. Her voice no doubt taut with strain, red blotches appearing on her cheeks as she became impassioned in her defence of Father Gregory, Alix began by excoriating 'dirty-minded gossips' for inventing all the slander. Sophie Tioutchev had started it all, the empress said; the governess had lied, turning a beautiful, innocent and holy relationship into something ugly. And when the lies began to spread, the imperial ministers, 'all cowards', had failed to stand up and defend the family's honour. The truth was that Father Gregory was 'an exceptional man', whom Minnie should spend time with before she passed judgment on him. He sought neither influence nor wealth, Alix insisted. She herself had never given him anything valuable, only a few hand-embroidered shirts and handkerchiefs, and inexpensive icons and amulets. He had sent her in return Eastern cakes he had blessed, and prayers and cards he had written.[18]

Minnie listened as Alix went on, noting with increasing resignation that she, and not Nicky, was speaking for the throne and the family. Most of what Alix said was beside the point, Minnie told Xenia afterwards. She did not grasp the deep political issues involved, the true severity of the damage. Alix was blind, Nicky passive: such was the dowager empress's assessment. There was nothing more she or anyone else could do. 'We are powerless to ward off the misfortune which is sure to come,' she told Kokovtsov.[19]

Send him away! The suggestion must have rankled with Alix after her mother-in-law had gone. How could they possibly send Father Gregory away? They needed him, each of them. He had become their assurance, their succour, their lifeline, as Philippe had once been. Far from destroying the dynasty, Father Gregory was the one on whom the entire Romanov future rested, for without his prayers the heir to the throne would surely be dead. Russia owed much to him.

Alix kept nearby the tokens Father Gregory had given her, icons, painted Easter eggs, telegrams. The previous winter, when she had been so ill, he had written in one of her notebooks, 'Here is my peace, source of glory on earth, a present for my warm-hearted Mama.'[20] She treasured his message. She needed his peace. Why couldn't the world understand how much she needed it, how, without it, she feared that she could not go on?

22

A few weeks after the uncomfortable conversation with Minnie, in March of 1912, Alix came to an important decision. It was time to reveal, at least to the most trusted family members, the true nature of Alexei's disease. Once they knew that he had the bleeding disease, and that Father Gregory was able to keep him alive despite even the most severe attacks, they would be sympathetic and supportive.

She sat down with Nicky's sister Olga and told her the truth about Alexei. He was fatally ill, yet he had not died because Father Gregory had only to pray for him whenever he bled uncontrollably and he recovered. It was miraculous, the empress told her sister-in-law. Alexei had only to be in Father Gregory's vicinity, and immediately he felt better.[1] She could not praise the starets highly enough. 'He always senses when I need him,' she said, her usually dour expression brightening at the thought. 'How can I not believe in him?' Alix went on to confide to Olga, who then confided it to Xenia, that her own illness was caused by her worry about her son. She was quite ill, and did not expect to recover.

The year 1912 was an important commemorative year, with celebrations in Moscow marking the hundredth anniversary of Napoleon's invasion of Russia and monuments erected at historically significant sites. The tsar and his family were present for the dedication in Moscow of a statue of Alexander III. There were luncheons and teas and receptions, military parades and gatherings of diplomats. Alix could not attend them all, but did her best to go to as many of these events as possible, sending Olga and Tatiana when too fatigued or in pain to go herself. It was all 'terribly tiring', as she told one of her correspondents. After the celebrations were over, she was 'for a very long time quite done up'.[2] Her fatigue was evident to all in the summer, when even a refreshing cruise aboard the *Standart* could not revive her. The French foreign minister Raymond Poincaré, who visited the tsar and tsarina at Peterhof that hot summer, was struck by her evident pain and discomfort.

'The empress remained motionless like a statue,' Poincaré recalled. 'But after a few minutes she took part [in the conversation] by moving her head to accentuate the remarks of the emperor and she put in a few discreet remarks of her own.' Nicky, the minister thought, looked well, his skin bronzed by the sun. But Alix, suffering in the heat and encased in a dark dress, a bothersome black hat trimmed with ostrich feathers and lace weighing down her head, was decidedly ill at ease. 'From time to time a red flush spread suddenly over her face and it looked as if she felt a pain stab at her heart, or had difficulty to breathe.'[3]

She was worried about Alexei. The doctors were unanimous in advising that he have a hernia operation, but were gravely concerned that any surgery could cause a haemorrhage. Father Gregory had been sent to Siberia and, though Alix believed that he would know, through his psychic abilities, if he was needed, she worried none-theless. Could Father Gregory's prayers overcome the consequences of surgery? Alexei had never before had an operation, so no test of Father Gregory's prayers under those extreme circumstances had ever been made. No postponement of the surgery was possible. It had to be done in the summer, to allow time for the patient to recuperate sufficiently to undertake all the travelling the family was obliged to do in the autumn – trips to the Borodino battlefield and to Moscow for more commemorative ceremonies, a visit to Poland for the shooting season, then back to Petersburg for the winter. But what if the worst happened, and neither the doctors nor Father Gregory were able to save the child? His death could hardly come at a worse time, with the monarchy in disgrace and talk of European war and the tsar himself the subject of renewed gossip. (It was said that he drank too much, and was becoming lax and negligent.)

A decision had to be made. The surgery was performed, no haemorrhage resulted. Enormously relieved, in September the family set out for Moscow.

Alexei seemed to be recovering well. He stood proudly beside his father at the Borodino battlefield, in uniform, his bearing erect and a look of authority in his dark blue eyes, while the soldiers passed in review. He was charming, good-looking, said to be intelligent though relatively untutored. He had more promise than his father had possessed at the age of eight. It was now known within the Romanov family, thanks to Alix's revelations during the previous winter, that the heir to the throne had the bleeding disease, but it was also noticed that in the past year he seemed to be in better health than in the past. His crises came less frequently, his episodes of bleeding were fewer. There was some hope that Alexei might belong to that very small minority of haemophiliacs who, like his cousin Waldemar and his great-uncle Leopold, lived into adulthood.[4]

This hope began to wane, however, when Alexei bruised his thigh while the family was in residence at the hunting lodge of Bielovezh and his groin and left leg began to swell with engorged blood. After weeks of rest the swelling went down, and the tsarevich, immobile for three weeks, began to try to stand up on his own. The family had moved on to the hunting lodge of Spala, deep in the forest, at a site so remote that there was not even a village for many miles around. Here, on the night of October 15, another haemorrhage began, much more serious than the first.

Alexei's screams woke his mother, who came at once to sit by his bedside. By morning the boy was in terrible pain, his lower back and hip bulging, the skin stretched taut, his eyes bright with fever. He could not bear to be touched.

The paediatrician in attendance, Dr Ostrogorsky, recommended that specialists be brought in and so messages were sent to Dr Fedorov, who had been treating Alexei for a long time, and to the Royal Paediatrician Dr Raukhfus, telling them to come to Spala at once. Meanwhile the tsarevich's fever continued to rise and his leg and back to swell, and he cried and moaned piteously.

Spala in hunting season was a gathering point for Polish nobles, who came to join the tsar in organized hunts for elk and stag, bison and wild boar. Nicky was inordinately proud of his skill with a gun, and boasted of the large numbers of beasts he brought down every autumn.[5] Each evening, the dead animals taken that day were laid out on the ground for the guests to admire by torchlight – a macabre spectacle and a depressing one, given Alexei's worsening condition.

Death was everywhere at Spala, in the rows of animal corpses, in the daily business of slaughter, in the discussions of guns and trophies that went on during and after dinner. Visitors to the hunting lodge were not informed of the crisis in the family, and so they continued to enjoy the tsar and tsarina's hospitality, their pleasure unshadowed by concern over the little tsarevich's condition. Each day they woke very early and assembled at the sound of the hunting horn for the ride through the forest; each evening they feasted and drank in the dining room, becoming boisterous at times, their high spirits a jarring contrast to the apprehension in the nursery.

Alix spent less and less time with her guests as her son's fever rose and his hoarse screams became more shrill. She sat beside him all night, sleeping hardly at all herself, watching as he became delirious. Dr Fedorov arrived on October 17 and the following day the patient seemed to improve slightly. But on the nineteenth he was much worse, his face white and thin, his body contorted. He could neither sleep nor eat. Even to cry brought him added pain. He repeated, 'Lord have mercy,' again and again, wailing and crying out, 'Mama, help me!' He allowed no one near him besides his mother and father and Derevenko, his sailor attendant, who carried the wailing boy in his arms for hours.

Dr Fedorov drew Nicky and Alix aside and told them that Alexei's stomach had begun to haemorrhage, and that he was at risk of blood poisoning and peritonitis. He told them to prepare themselves for the possibility that their son would die, and soon.

In the dim corridors of the lodge, so dim that electric lights had to be kept burning both day and night, the servants and staff went about their tasks with sombre expressions. No official word had been given out about Alexei's condition, but everyone knew he was in grave danger of death. He had never before suffered so acutely, or for so long. Those who had occasion to enter his room were shocked at the pallor of his face, the fragility of his thin small body. It was as if he had already passed from life into another realm at the threshold of death, his body already corpselike in its whiteness, his breath already beginning to cease as, lacking the energy to scream or cry, he murmured his prayer for divine mercy and whispered his mother's name.

Alix had not slept for five nights. She began to nap, briefly, from sheer exhaustion, but she could not allow herself to sleep for any length of time lest she be needed. She barely kept herself groomed, napping in her day-clothes, washing hastily, sitting while her maid dressed her hair simply and rapidly. Her hair had grown dull and lustreless. Grey streaks appeared within its dark gold mass, signs of her anxious state. Weakened and confused from lack of sleep, she could hardly take in Dr Fedorov's pronouncements and cautions, but she realized that Alexei might well die. In his worst moments he cried out for death, begging for the pain to stop, asking to be buried, as he said, 'in the light', out of doors with the sky over his head, not in a dark damp mausoleum with his Romanov ancestors.

With infinite weariness Alix forced herself to preside at the dinner table, to keep up a pretence of lightheartedness in front of her guests. She heard them talking about the latest invention of sensation-seeking journalists in Petersburg. The Russian newspapers were full of stories about political extremists who managed to get aboard the imperial yacht and attack Alexei. The supposed attack was said to have been made during the summer, leaving the boy alive but weak. The reports caused a stir, and though there were no journalists at Spala – thankfully – questions were once again being raised about the succession.

Alix listened to it all, letting the talk wash over her in her weariness, glad that her sister Irene was there to help her do all that was expected of her. She often had to get up from the table, or leave the sitting room, to go to Alexei's bedside, and Irene, with her pleasant, relaxed manner, took over as hostess. Irene delivered her sister's messages and instructions to the staff, dealt with the papers that were brought from Petersburg, helped to keep order and stability in the household.

Alexei continued to cling to life, but his heartbeat was feeble when Dr Fedorov listened to it, and his fever had risen to a dangerously high 105 degrees. He could not live much longer, his heart was giving out.

Now the crisis had become a matter of state. The heir to the throne was about to expire, and protocol had to be followed. Lest the tsar's subjects be taken by surprise by the inevitable sorrowful news to come, they had to be warned. On the night of October 21, a medical bulletin was issued. Now the vigil beside Alexei's bed became a death-watch.

The guests dispersed. In the outdoor chapel, the servants said their prayers and villagers from the district began to gather out of reverence, knowing that the tsarevich's life was ebbing. A package was delivered from Petersburg, containing herbs to be infused and given to the patient to reduce fever and calm the stomach. They were sent by the Tibetan healer Bachmanov, whose skill Alix trusted. Whether or not she tried to administer the infusions is unknown, but on the following day, October 22, the tsarevich lay very still, and Alix was convinced that he could not last more than a few hours. The priest came, another medical bulletin was prepared. Irene asked that, out of respect, the members of the household would retire to their rooms to await further news.

There was nothing to do now but wait, and pray.

Why Alix waited until her son was dying to send word to Father Gregory in Siberia can only be guessed. Perhaps she assumed that he was unreachable. Perhaps, despite her staunch defence of him to Minnie, she was concerned that any contact she had with him would cause renewed scandal. Or perhaps, as she often said, she trusted that the starets would sense, without being told, that she needed him, and felt that no message was necessary. Whatever the reason, she at last sent a telegram, asking for his help.

Hour by hour, the vigil around the boy's bed went on, lasting throughout the night. There was no change in his condition. Morning came, then afternoon. Still no change. That he had survived this long surprised the doctors, who had said that hope was futile.

Father Gregory's telegram was brought to Alix that evening. 'Fear nothing,' it read. 'The malady is not so dangerous as it seems to be. Do not let the doctors bother him too much.'[6]

To the utter amazement of the family, the doctors, the entire staff, Alexei began to improve within hours of the receipt of Father Gregory's reassuring message. His heartbeat was stronger, his pain and swelling beginning to subside. He still had a high fever, but it was dropping, and when Dr Fedorov and Dr Raukhfus came in to examine him, he actually let them touch him for the first time.

Word of the seemingly miraculous change in the tsarevich's condition spread quickly, and a service of thanksgiving in the chapel drew a large crowd. A positive medical bulletin was prepared, to be sent out to the court and to the country at large.

Alix had the gratifying experience of responding to telegrams of sympathy with the good news of her son's recovery. Father Gregory had cured him, from far-off Siberia. He had brought him back from the very brink of death.

It was nearly a month before the patient was recovered sufficiently to make the journey to Petersburg. He put on weight, colour returned to his cheeks and he was able to go out riding in the pony cart, although the groom who led the cart had to be careful to avoid bumps in the road. His left leg was still bent, and he still had some pain in his right knee which made walking difficult. But he was his cheerful self again.

All Petersburg knew that the tsarevich had recovered and, for a few weeks, all Petersburg rejoiced. The dynasty, the long line of Romanovs that stretched back into the early seventeenth century, would go on, no matter how disappointing the current occupant of the throne might be. No matter that the succession had been disturbed and altered yet again by the recent marriage of the tsar's brother Michael to his commoner mistress – an act of rebellion, indeed of betrayal, in the tsar's view. What mattered was that his-torical tradition be maintained, that the house of Romanov survive.

The three hundred years of Romanov rule were much on the minds of citizens of the capital as the new year 1913 began. It was the tercentenary year, and the shops were full of commemorative objects – scarves with the images of Nicholas and the first Romanov, Tsar Michael, miniature crowns and sceptres, candies in the shape of medallions, with the tsar's face stamped on them, mugs and plates with the imperial profiles. New commemorative postage stamps were put into circulation. Special flags flew from public buildings, special gifts from the imperial bounty were provided to the poor, who lined up at hospitals and shelters to receive their bundles of food and trinkets. Beggars were given a hot meal and a new suit of clothes.

In preparation for the ceremonies to be held early in March, choirs met to rehearse their litanies; workmen in thick gloves and warm hats and coats painted and repaired the fronts of mansions and churches. Both banks of the Neva were decorated with gigantic letters painted in red and purple and gold, spelling out 'God Save the Tsar', and on the Nicholas Bridge, crimson and violet lights cast eerie reflections on the river ice at night. A huge scrim hung down from the roof of the Academy of Sciences, bearing the painted form of Peter the Great, dressed as a workman in peasant blouse and trousers, a hammer in his outsize hand.

The full majesty of Russia's past, or, at least, a simulacrum of it, was made to loom up over the pygmy present, lending an ennobling glow to the city. Strollers along Nevsky Prospekt, socialites on their way to balls and parties, even the jaded habitués of night clubs and brothels could not help but be caught up in the gaudy glamour of the lights, the colour and the flashy tinsel, the party-like atmosphere. Throughout the holiday season and on into the deep cold of February, a superficial air of gaiety prevailed, underscored, as always, with some sour notes of gossip and ongoing scandal.[7]

Alix's pleasure at her son's recovery, though profound, was to be brief, for his health continued to be fragile and his recovery slow. She discovered that her candour in revealing the true nature of his illness to trusted family members had been a terrible miscalculation. Far from eliciting sympathy and understanding, it led to deeper hostility towards her. She was now blamed for having, as one of the grand duchesses said, 'contaminated the Romanovs with the diseases of her own race'.[8] Nicky was pitied for having a crippled son, and a wife who had caused his disability.

'A sense of endless despair filled the tsarina's soul,' the children's Swiss tutor Pierre Gilliard wrote. 'The last hope had failed.' She felt, Gilliard thought, as if 'the whole world were deserting her'. The hostility of her in-laws had deepened, her few friendships were dwindling. Even her new wardrobe mistress, Madame Naryshkin, reserved, respectable, and judgmental, conveyed her disapproval and the two women often clashed; Madame Naryshkin was Minnie's close friend and, through her, Minnie's attitudes were brought into the palace and, as it were, installed there.[9]

Stana, the Montenegrin grand duchess, did not share the general view in the family that Alix was blameworthy. But Alix sent Stana away, telling her 'it was useless to be empress of Russia if one could not do what one liked, and that all she craved was the privilege to be left alone and allowed to enjoy, unrestrained, her taste for solitude'.

Many days, solitude was what she claimed. She stayed alone in her boudoir, her head throbbing, worrying over Alexei and no doubt dreading the forthcoming festivities, where she would be required to appear. Her teeth ached, she suffered from neuralgia in her face and from the usual intermittent chest pains.

She had once referred to herself as the Pechvogel, the bird of ill omen, which brought bad luck and catastrophe. Now nearly everyone saw her that way, as the carrier of misfortune into the Romanov family. She shrank from the caustic tongues of Aunt Miechen and the others, from her mother-in-law's criticism and advice and her wardrobe mistress's disapproving glances. Alone with her thoughts, often in pain, she rested, prayed and brooded, dreading the days to come.

23

Alix stood, her husband beside her, in the gold-curtained imperial box in the Mariinsky Theatre, listening to the orchestra play 'God Save the Tsar'. Everyone in the vast theatre was standing, singing along with the musicians, their attention on the tsar and tsarina. Her face was expressionless; her eyes, grave and thoughtful, gave nothing away, though the tribute of the crowd was moving and the singing robust and thrilling. She was pale, her hands, clutching her fan of white eagle's feathers, trembled and her cheeks, which had been pale, began to flush. She tried to master her mounting discomfort, to mentally remove herself from the crowded theatre and from the people who stared at her while they sang. But her breath became shallow, and the bodice of her white velvet gown began to rise and fall rapidly, the diamonds sprinkled across its surface twinkling and flashing.

At last the anthem was over. The crowd applauded and cheered and the empress nodded her head briefly before sitting in her gold-upholstered armchair. The tribute was ended, but the stares and whispers of those in the audience went on. Alix knew what they were saying, how they were judging her and blaming her, holding her accountable for her son's illness, accusing her of controlling her husband and forcing him to govern according to her views, influencing him to favour Germany and all things German because she did. She knew what they were saying about how she had contaminated the Romanov succession, and about her unholy relationship with Father Gregory. She knew that they condemned her and sneered at her behind her back.

She bit her lip and clutched her fan more tightly, her hand trembling convulsively, her chest heaving. She was feeling faint. She couldn't stand the stares, the whispers any longer. She leaned over and said a few words to her husband, then got up and went to the rear of the box, where she could not be seen by the audience.

Her move was noticed. 'A little wave of resentment rippled over the theatre,' Meriel Buchanan, daughter of the British ambassador, recalled. 'Women glanced at each other and raised their shoulders expressively, men muttered despairingly below their breath.' They told each other that, after all, the empress hated the capital, had always rejected and scorned it. Even on this important day she could not manage to take her proper place beside her husband, to put her feelings aside and do her duty for his sake. She created a 'disagreeable impression', as usual. But her panic was real, as Meriel, who was in the adjacent box, could clearly see. She was in a torment of distress and anguish.

It was the same on the night of the ball given by the nobility for the tsar and tsarina. Alix made her entrance on her husband's arm, and danced the opening polonaise with him, but her face was grave and taut with strain, the expression of her mouth 'most tragic'. The splendour of her white and silver satin gown, the magnificent diamond necklace at her throat that had once been worn by Catherine the Great, the flashing diamond tiara all gave the appearance of regal serenity. But however splendid her garb, her fatigue and discomfort were evident and she looked, Martha Mouchanow thought, like a 'middle-aged, haggard woman, racked with cares and anxieties'.[1]

The noise, the crowd, the icy politeness and hostile stares directed towards her assaulted her nerves and made her long for escape. Her breathing became shallow, and she felt so ill, she confided afterwards to Sophie Buxhoeveden, that she could 'scarcely keep her feet'. Afraid she might faint, she soldiered on, suffering 'tortures' from dizziness. Had she fainted, there would have been no end of fuss and talk. She had to stay alert. Finally she managed to catch her husband's eye and he came over to her, 'just in time to lead her away and prevent her from fainting in public'.[2] She left the ball early.

One cause of Alix's apprehension was her bright-eyed, eager daughter Olga, who with her sister Tatiana had been allowed to attend the ball and who was happily dancing every dance. Olga was seventeen, fresh and attractive in her simple pale pink chiffon dancing gown, and her cousins were eager to dance with her – sometimes three of them asking for the same dance. Alix disapproved, wanting no inconvenient infatuation to arise between Olga and any of her more knowing cousins, whom she considered to be 'unwholesomely precocious'; like her sisters, Olga had always been sheltered and, apart from innocent crushes on Guards officers and *Standart* crew members, she had never had a romance. A change was bound to come, indeed many at court were saying that it was time Olga was engaged. But her mother, who knew from her own experience how strong and enduring youthful attachments could be, was made uneasy at the thought of Olga's forming a romantic bond with any young man, and Olga's delighted participation in the dancing was yet one more source of strain for Alix. She dreaded that her girls might leave the high-minded path she had tried to keep them on, and give in to frivolity and even to sensuality. Like her other fears, this fear ate away at her and clouded her perception of Olga and her carefree evening.

The elaborate tercentenary celebrations were dampened, literally, by constant rain. The expensive pageantry, the ceremonies, receptions and banquets passed in a blur of downpours, and even the triumphal imperial tour of historic sites associated with the first Romanov was marred by a constant freezing wind that curtailed the tsar's itinerary and disappointed the waiting crowds.

It was a flawed observance, the cheering throngs sparse at times, drawn more, one observer thought, by 'shallow curiosity' than devotion to the ruling house. There was no question but that the name of Romanov had been tarnished and, while some of the tsar's subjects fell on their knees and kissed his shadow as he passed, many others simply took the festivities in their stride, sceptical of all government and, though outwardly deferential, were inwardly indifferent to the official goings-on in Petersburg and Moscow.[3] The attention of the public was drawn elsewhere in that spring of 1913, to the orgies at the Villa Black Swan, the palace of an erotomanic millionaire, the craze for bridge-playing and cocaine, the escalating numbers of suicides and the details of a series of sensational criminal trials.

One thing the Russian public was not indifferent to: the threat of war. Self-regarding celebrations by the Romanov ruling house might be considered of little consequence, but the bellicose talk and the build-up of weaponry in neighbouring Germany was a continual threat, to be taken seriously. Emperor William, with his swaggering, bullying oratory, his pompous vanity and evident craving for domination, was an alarming figure on the European stage, his wild eccentricities exaggerated by the sensationalizing press. With his secretary of state for naval affairs, Admiral von Tirpitz, the emperor had expanded the German navy by building a number of immense swift battleships – dreadnoughts – equipped with heavy long-range guns, in competition with British battleships of equal size and firepower. Clearly the German aim was pre-eminence at sea; as for pre-eminence on land, though the Russian armies were much larger than the German, they were ill equipped, and guided by an inexperienced, woolly-headed War Minister, General Sukhomlinov. In any test of arms, the German forces were bound to prevail.

But the tsar's private opinion was that there would be no test of arms. Willy, though a 'bore and an exhibitionist', was not likely to start a war, Nicky thought. He had had several opportunities, when Germany's ally Austria clashed with Russian interests in the Balkans. Had he truly wanted war, he could have backed Austria in aggression against Russia's Slavic allies. But he had chosen to take no action. In recent months, in fact, the German Emperor had actually cut back his ship-building programme, causing cautious relief in Britain, and had met with General Sukhomlinov, a successful meeting that left the emperor with a favourable impression of the general as 'very nice and interesting.'

Willy's personal messages to Nicky were warmly familial. 'I sincerely hope and believe that 1913 will flow peacefully as you telegraphed me on New Year's day,' he wrote in early January. 'I

think that we can both look on the future quietly.'⁴ To encourage
the peaceful flow of events, Willy invited many of his relatives,
including Nicky and George V, to Berlin to celebrate the wedding
of his daughter Victoria Louise, known in the family as Sissy.

They came to the German capital at the end of May, dozens of
relatives converging, meeting at the train station, embracing and
kissing and chattering much as they had nearly twenty years earlier,
when they had come together in Coburg for Ernie and Ducky's
wedding. Then Queen Victoria had been the matriarch of the clan.
Now there was no matriarch, no single personality to whom all
deferred. But the sense of a family bond was still strong. Alix was
reunited with her sisters Victoria and Irene, Minnie with her sister
Alexandra, dowager queen of England. Nicky, Willy and George
met as cousinly equals, not as rivals; that the sovereigns of Russia
and Great Britain were diplomatically allied in opposition to the
German Emperor was easily overlooked as they toasted one another
and the bride and groom, wore the uniforms of one another's military
services out of courtesy, and acted like the wedding guests they were.

If Alix was uncomfortable and anxious at the banquet in the
imperial palace, amid a crowd of two hundred and fifty people, no
one noted it. She was among friends and supporters and, though she
disliked and distrusted Willy, there were many in the crowd whom
she loved and looked forward to seeing. Just being away from
claustrophobic Petersburg, with its vicious newspaper reports and
mocking gossip, must have felt to her like a reprieve.

But the reprieve was to be brief. Soon enough the family was back
at Tsarskoe Selo, and Alix was once again immersed in family affairs
– the worrisome attachment of Xenia and Sandro's daughter Irina to
the dissolute, immensely rich young aristocrat Felix Yusupov ('I
would never let a daughter of mine marry him'), daughter Anastasia's
inconvenient and irritating efforts to 'breed worms', the worsening
illness and invalidism of Alix's long-time friend and maid of honour
Sonia Orbeliani, who continued to live at the palace, quarrels with
the ungrateful Anna Vyrubov ('Here we gave our hearts our home
to her, our private life even – and this is what we have gained! It is

difficult not to become bitter'), Nicky's sister Olga's divorce, and
the self-destructive deterioration of Father Gregory, whose lechery
(he even pawed the startled divorcée Olga), brawling and heavy
drinking expanded.[5]

'My heart is heavy and sore,' Alix wrote. She continued to stand
by her spiritual mentor, denying what was being said about him,
and denying to herself the evident worsening of the danger of war in
the autumn of 1913.

Reports reached Nicky's desk that the Austrian army was
concentrating its forces on the Russian frontier in Galicia as a
consequence of Bulgarian attacks on Serbia. Despite diplomatic
efforts, it looked as though the fragile truce in the Balkans might
give way to further aggression at any time. Meanwhile the newspapers
were full of editorials about the suffering Serbs and the menacing
Austrians, rousing the patriotic ire of the public. And the Duma
leader Rodzianko was urging the tsar to take advantage of the weakness of Turkey to send Russian troops to conquer Constantinople,
an imperial enterprise well suited to the celebration of the three-
hundredth Romanov year.

Sore-hearted, Alix wanted nothing more than to be left in peace,
yet peace, it seemed, was always denied her – except during the
family's excursions to Livadia in autumn and spring. Back in Tsarskoe
Selo during the winter social season, as the new year of 1914 opened,
she kept to her practice of avoiding the numerous parties and balls,
uncomfortably aware that the best dinners and dances that year were
said to be given at the stark new mansion of Count Pourtalès, the
elderly German ambassador.

The only ball she attended was the one Minnie gave at the
Anitchkov Palace for the four imperial grand duchesses, Olga,
Tatiana, Marie and Anastasia. The girls were lovely, especially the
slender, enchanting Tatiana. But their mother, though ill and middle-
aged, eclipsed them. One observer thought that Alix 'was the very
picture of beauty' with her stately posture, fine features and delicate
manners. 'There was something sad in her smile,' he wrote, but that
note of wistfulness only added to her charm. (Clearly the 'haggard,

middle-aged' empress Martha Mouchanow had perceived was not evident to everyone.)⁶ Though the ball went on until four-thirty in the morning, Alix left at midnight, quite worn out.

A mild winter and sodden spring gave way to an unusually fair, cloudless summer. New leaves on the trees in the park grew dusty in the heat, peonies wilted in the flowerbeds and along the pavements of the capital, a fine yellow dirt accumulated, blown into piles by occasional gusts of warm air off the dark blue river.

Petersburgers shed their coats and scarves and basked in the fine weather, eating ice cream, staying out late in the light evenings, worrying that the heat might bring an epidemic, as it often did. The air stank of smoke from country fires, tinting the silvery light of early summer with a brown cast.

Those who could afford to left the city for their rural estates, or for resorts in Finland, not only to escape the heat but to escape the prospect of a worsening labour protest. Already by mid-June over a hundred thousand workers in the capital had gone on strike, and more were walking out of the factories daily.

They drifted through the city in groups, gathering at street corners in dozens, then hundreds, herded by police and patrols of mounted Cossacks armed with sabres. Many in the city remembered Bloody Sunday, nine years earlier, when the soldiers had been ordered to fire on the crowds and dozens had died in the snow. And they recalled hearing of a more recent, more terrible massacre in the Lena goldfields, when soldiers had fired on striking workers, killing hundreds.

The workers of Petersburg began building barricades, claiming portions of the streets as their own. As their numbers grew, their confidence expanded. They recruited others to their ranks. Hundreds of factories emptied. Before long, people said, half the workers in the country would be on strike.

In the midst of the heatwave, a series of thunderstorms broke over Petersburg. Sudden showers drenched streets and drowned gardens in full bloom. Wet through, the workers abandoned their half-built barricades and took shelter in halls and warehouses, watching as bolts of coloured lightning shot across the sky, burning like meteors, or struck spires and stone turrets. Thunder boomed out across the Neva, louder than any artillery in the tsar's armies, loud enough to be heard at Peterhof, where the tsar and his family were staying in preparation for the arrival of an important visitor, President Poincaré of France.

It promised to be a significant visit, one that would strengthen Russia's diplomatic ties with her French ally and further a settlement – without the direct military involvement of Russia – in the increasingly tangled and ominous crisis in the Balkans.

Towards the end of June an act of terrorism had entangled the situation further. A Serbian assassin had killed the heir to the Austrian throne, Franz Ferdinand, and his wife as they rode in a carriage through the streets of Sarajevo. The diplomatic after-effects were serious, and urgent; every foreign ministry in Europe was obliged to react, telegrams and telephone messages went back and forth, crucial decisions were being debated.

The tsar continued to feel, despite the mounting exigency of the situation, that peace would be maintained, and he told Poincaré so when they met. He could not believe that the Germans would start a war, that Emperor William would 'launch his country on some wild adventure'. Nor would the bereaved, elderly Emperor Franz Josef of Austria be drawn into a massive conflict – for war, if it came, would surely involve all of Europe.

Poincaré disagreed. He gauged the mood of the other states of Europe more realistically than his host could. War seemed to him inevitable. The ubiquitous military culture demanded it. The massive build-up of weaponry, the immense navies, the diplomatic configuration that made it virtually impossible for any of the major states to act alone, the millions of men under arms, poised to take their places once battle lines were drawn, all pointed to conflict – and a conflict, he thought, that could not long be postponed.

During the French president's visit two splendid military displays were carried out at Krasnoe Selo.[7] Rank on rank of uniformed men marched past the reviewing stand, the dust raised by their marching feet rising in the warm air to make a golden halo around them. Flags waved, bands played stirring patriotic marches, from time to time the watching crowd burst into song. High in the cloudless sky an airplane buzzed, circling the reviewing field again and again.

The pageantry, the feelings of loyalty stirred by the massed troops, the sight of magnificent young officers and valiant, limping old generals, veterans of long-ago wars, walking along between the lines of soldiers moved many in the crowd to tears.

And then, as the guests of honour watched, the tsar, riding on a white horse, rode past, looking tall and soldierly, no longer a man but a mythic leader of men, a symbol of power and greatness. The crowd cheered and cheered, as the imperial uncles and cousins rode along behind the sovereign, a parade of resplendent, stalwart figures, followed in their turn by the imperial family in open carriages, escorted by outriders in scarlet and gold.

A band began to play the Evening Hymn, and almost at once, an observer wrote, 'from across the entire wide, vast plain the men's voices joined in, taking up the melody', as the sky was filled with a blaze of sunset light. No theatrical spectacle could have been more majestic.

It was poignant, it was glorious. And it augured war.

Alix rode in one of the carriages, her immaculate white gown covered in dust, which made her cough. Her daughters rode beside her, all of them in large flower-trimmed hats to shade them from the sun. The empress had been present at the diplomatic dinners, the palace entertainments presented in the French president's honour, forcing herself to play her appropriate role. She knew that much was at stake. But throughout the eventful days her thoughts were elsewhere.

Within hours of the assassination of the Austrian archduke, Father Gregory had also been attacked, in Pokrovsky, by a follower of his enemy, the monk Iliodor. Though his wounds were nearly fatal, a doctor from Tiumen had saved his life – Alix had sent the doctor a gold watch and a fervent letter of thanks – and he was recuperating.

The assault on Father Gregory, and the sudden turmoil over the Balkan situation, broke in upon what had promised to be a quiet

summer for the imperial family, filled with picnics and games of
tennis, long walks in the woods and yachting trips along the Finnish
coast. Alix had been planning the next visit to Livadia, sending out
letters to Ernie, Irene and Victoria, and to her old friend Marie
Bariatinsky, instructing the staff to prepare the guest rooms and stock
the larder. She had been looking forward to the warm autumn days
in the Crimea, to visiting her gardens and sitting on the broad terraces
overlooking the ocean, to visiting her sanatoria and helping out with
the charity bazaars.

The commotion of recent days had interrupted all those plans.
Too much was happening too quickly. Making plans had become
impossible. The most she could do was take her place beside Nicky,
and do her best to help while he coped with the difficulties.

By the final evening of the French president's visit, after hours of
dining followed by long speeches, she was worn out. She invited the
French ambassador Maurice Paléologue to sit beside her, to keep
her company as the evening drew to a close.

'With a forced smile,' Paléologue recalled, 'she said in a tired tone:
"I'm glad I came tonight . . . I was afraid there would be a storm."'
She chatted about trivial things, the decorations for the dinner, the
good weather to be expected for the president's return voyage.
Though making light conversation was always an effort to her, she
made the effort, though Paléologue knew how hard it was. He had
watched her for the past four days, and observed her discomfort,
how in the midst of a crowd her smile would become set and the
veins in her cheeks would stand out. How she bit her lip with tension,
her breathing shallow, her eyes restless and on the edge of panic. He
thought, at times, she was 'obviously struggling with hysteria', and
she relaxed only when her husband was nearby, or when she could
fix her attention entirely on him.[8]

As Alix chatted with the ambassador, the musicians suddenly began
playing a loud, fast passage, complete with blaring brass and throbbing
kettledrums. She winced, and put her hands up to cover her ears. 'With
a pained and pleading glance,' Paléologue remembered, she timidly
pointed to the band, and murmured, 'Couldn't you? . . . '

It was all too much, the jarring noise, the din of voices, the exhausting socializing, the intrusion of disturbing events and the threat of still more disturbing events to come. Like a violent summer squall rising up to buffet the land, whirling all into chaos and confusion, the events of the past weeks had arisen out of nowhere to create mayhem and confuse her plans, leaving her once again on edge and lost, abandoned to chance, as weightless as the yellow dust of the fields blown about by the winds of chance.

24

O n the night of August 1, 1914, the empress's lady-in-waiting
Sophie Buxhoeveden received a phone call from her mistress.
'War is declared,' Alix said, her voice hoarse with suppressed sobs.
'Good heavens!' Sophie said. 'So Austria has done it!'

'No, no. Germany. It is ghastly, terrible – but God will help and
will save Russia.'

It was after ten o'clock, but Alix was alert and active, telling Sophie
that 'we must work,' and instructing her to begin at once to open
the sewing workshop at the Hermitage.[1] She had prepared a list of
things for Sophie to undertake, despite the lateness of the hour,
secretaries and staff members to contact, notes to write, telephone
calls to make. As she read Sophie her instructions she grew calmer,
her voice resuming its normal timbre.

During the year she had occupied the office of lady-in-waiting,
Sophie had come to know the empress well. She had become
accustomed to her high-strung temperament, her eccentricities – her
obsessive list-making and itemizing, her occasional sharpness and
imperiousness with servants, her preference for white lilacs and
orchids, her liking for cold rooms and her poor appetite and
vegetarianism. She had grown accustomed to Alix's craving for
solitude and distrust of strangers, her headaches and fatigue and
frequent attacks of anxiety and her fatalism about what she referred
to as her loss of health.

The lady-in-waiting learned that her imperial mistress was sensitive
on the subject of her ill health, that she became angry when people
said she suffered from 'nerves,' and insisted that her nerves 'were as

strong as ever,' and that it was only her 'over-tired heart' that gave her trouble.[2]

Sophie was well aware, as were others in the empress's household, that her illness was more than physical, more than a perpetual over-anxiousness that brought on severe physical symptoms in the presence of crowds or strangers. That her mental compass was awry. As Nicky's cousin Maria, daughter of his uncle Paul, put it, Alix had 'lost . . . her mental equilibrium' and showed an 'increasing inner rigidity' and a 'fading sense of proportion.'[3] She clung to those she perceived to be her friends and allies with an excessive loyalty. ('When the empress thought well of a person,' Sophie wrote, 'in politics as in friendship, he had to reveal himself almost as a criminal before she would give him up.'[4]) Towards those whom she distrusted she became vindictive, and no one could persuade her – indeed, it would seem that few, other than Minnie, ever tried – that her judgment was askew and her knowledge of the world too narrow to lead her to sound opinions.

The deterioration was unmistakable. As Alix's maid Madeleine Zanotti, who had served her since 1892, would later say of her, 'in the last years she was not the same as she had been earlier,' convinced that bad luck pursued her, and that 'in the eyes of Russia' she could 'never do right.'[5] Beneath her constantly reiterated assertions of trust and faith in a miracle-working God she was deeply distrustful, fearful of catastrophe, desperately unhappy.

Only in incessant activity could she find relief from the troubling thoughts that plagued her, and her preferred activity was rescuing and nurturing those in need.

'It is my daily prayer,' Alix affirmed, 'that God should just send me the sorrowing.' 'After all, it is life's greatest consolation to feel that the sorrowing need one, and it has been my daily prayer, for years that God should just send me the sorrowing, and give me the possibility to be a help to them, through His infinite mercy.'[6]

The outbreak of war was certain to increase the numbers of the sorrowing, and the empress meant to take her place on the battle lines as a fighter in the war against sorrow and pain.

The sheer scale of the effort was certain to be overwhelming, for within a few weeks of the declaration of war the head of the zemstvo Red Cross calculated that Russia would need hospital space for a million wounded, and the hospital trains were bringing thousands of wounded men to Petersburg – now rechristened Petrograd, to avoid the former German-sounding name – and its surroundings each day. Minnie was the patron of the Red Cross, but Minnie was in England; she appointed Alix to take her place temporarily, and nothing could have pleased the empress more, until she began to encounter opposition and hostility from various officials in the organization.[7] The improvements she suggested were criticized, the instructions she gave ignored; she was assumed to be pro-German, and to lack compassion for the Russian soldiers.

The opposition and accusation of being pro-German stung, for Alix had always disliked her cousin Willy and in her twenty years in Russia had become an ardent Russian patriot.

From the time, in the 1880s, when the youthful Willy had courted Ella and shocked the entire family of Grand Duke Louis by his arrogance and presumption, Alix had disliked him. 'He thinks he is a superman,' she once said, 'and he's really nothing but a clown. He has no real worth. His only virtues are his strict morals and his conjugal fidelity.'[8] She called him the 'monstrous Kaiser' and was, as all her relatives observed, 'passionately anti-German.'[9] Her father, who had fought against Prussia in his youth, had raised her to hate all things Prussian, and the kaiser was Prussian to the core.

Alix worried that Willy would send her brother Ernie to the Russian front, and was greatly relieved to learn, in the early months of the war, that the armies of Hesse-Darmstadt were not engaged against Russian troops. Sister Irene's 'very amiable' husband Henry was an admiral in the German navy, and sister Victoria's husband Louis was a high-ranking British admiralty official. She was concerned about them too, and indeed about all those placed in harm's way by the war.

'One's heart bleeds, thinking of all the misery everywhere and what will be afterwards!' she wrote to Victoria in November, 1914.

She wept for the loneliness of Ernie and all others far from home, for the pain and wretchedness of those in combat, for the fear suffered by those taken prisoner. She had seen that fear at first hand, when German prisoners were brought to her hospitals. They had been terrified at first that the Russians would shoot them, or cut off their noses and ears; she had seen the look of amazement on their faces when, instead of being brutalized, they were well treated and fed.

Before long Minnie returned to Russia and resumed her patronage of the Red Cross. Alix relinquished her temporary headship with relief, and concentrated on the larger issues of setting up hospitals and trying to fill the huge gaps in supplies for the wounded.

Royal palaces, with their hundreds of rooms, vast kitchens and larders, their garages and stables and staffs of servants, made ideal hospitals. Alix went to work making the arrangements for converting dozens of royal and aristocratic palaces, and other mansions and large public buildings, into military hospitals. Within the first four months of the war, eighty-five such hospitals were operating in and around Petrograd, all under her patronage. In Moscow, the Petrovsky Palace had begun taking in wounded and the Nicholas Palace, which had been Ella's home before she founded her monastery, became a workshop where blankets were made and warm socks, mittens and hats knitted for the soldiers.

The vast blue and white Catherine Palace at Tsarskoe Selo was made into a hospital for officers, its beautiful amber-, lapis-and malachite-decorated reception rooms filled with beds, its ornate ballroom converted to an operating theatre. Alix had never liked the grandiose palace. Now, however, she had found the perfect use for it, and went there nearly every day to supervise its operations.

The Russian troops had gone bravely into battle, pushing westwards in numbers nearly half a million strong into the marshy wastes of East Prussia in the last days of August. But the Germans had surrounded them, trapping them in the treacherous swamps near the village of Tannenberg. Bogged down, sometimes swallowed by quicksand, men and horses, artillery and equipment sank into the morass, helpless against the German guns. The Chevaliers Gardes, the Red Hussars, the Preobrazhensky regiment, the Tirailleurs de la Garde – all perished, or were forced to surrender. Some ninety thousand troops were taken prisoner. The Russian general Samsonov, overwhelmed by dishonour, killed himself.

The citizens of Petrograd, reading of the battle in special editions of the evening papers, could not believe at first that their mighty military forces had suffered so sudden and so decisive a defeat. Unlike the tsar's ministers, they were not aware of the vulnerability of the enormous Russian armies, their shortages of equipment and inept leadership. They had assumed that German and Austrian arms would not be able to hold out long against their own armies and those of the French, that the war would be over quickly and that they would win it. That the 'Russian Steam Roller,' as the press called the army, would flatten the enemy, that there would be Cossacks riding into Berlin by Christmas.[10] Instead, they read of massive casualties, they saw the trains crowded with the wounded coming into the Petrograd stations, and they heard rumours, terrible rumours, of treachery and betrayal.

It was being said that Samsonov and his army had been deliberately abandoned, delivered into the hands of the enemy for slaughter, by General Rennenkampf – a Russian general with a suspiciously German-sounding name. General Rennenkampf's own subsequent defeat at German hands did nothing to stifle these accusations. They heard whispers that Warsaw had fallen and that very soon all of Poland would belong to the Germans and Austrians, that instead of Cossacks in Berlin there would be elite German troops in Petrograd, pillaging houses and desecrating churches, befouling the Neva and marching up and down Nevsky Prospekt. The smell of smoke that had lingered in the air since early summer was now said to be due to German subversion; it was whispered that the Germans had set the peat bogs near Petrograd on fire, and were burning down the trackless forests of Siberia.

Fear and suspicion replaced the patriotic fervour that had prevailed in the days following the outbreak of war. Many in the streets wore black armbands or black gowns, the looks on their faces blank or apprehensive. Troops marched past in large numbers, on their way to the front, but they no longer marched to spirited tunes or roused the bystanders to loud cheering. The autumn days were growing short, snow had begun to fall, and the citizens of Petrograd had begun to count their losses and look for scapegoats. There was revived talk of the tsar's German wife, that unfeeling woman who had danced on the night of the Khodynka massacre and whose immoral relations with the infamous Rasputin had shamed the imperial family and made foreigners laugh at Russia.

If indeed there was treachery in the air, then the German bitch was sure to be guilty of it.

But Alix, far from betraying Russia to her German relatives, was attending lectures on anatomy, internal medicine and surgical nursing, with her daughters and several dozen other women, all working towards receiving their certification as Red Cross nurses. It was not enough for her to supervise the running of hospitals, she felt the need to be physically present at the bedsides of the wounded, offering trained assistance.

'To some it may seem unnecessary my doing this,' she said, 'but help is much needed and my hand is useful.'[11] By the first week of November, 1914, Alix and her older daughters had completed a full surgical course, with supplemental lectures, and were planning to attend still more lectures. The training courses were held at night. In the morning the empress and her daughters, along with Anna Vyrubov, assisted at operations, cleaned bed-sores, changed dressings and offered what comfort they could to the wounded who crowded the hospitals.

It was dirty, tiring, emotionally draining work. Operations went on for hours, and often the empress was called upon to attend two or three operations in a row. She dripped ether onto masks, passed instruments to the surgeons, swabbed blood, handled amputated legs, arms and fingers. 'I washed and cleaned, and painted with iodine and smeared with vaseline and tied them up and bandaged all up,' she wrote to Nicky in November of 1914. 'My nose is full of hideous smells from those blood-poisoning wounds.'[12] Attending the men in the wards meant hearing their screaming and swearing, their delirious ravings and groans. Some moaned in agony and called for death. Many did die, despite the efforts of the nurses and doctors, and Alix was there, by their bedsides or beside the operating table, doing her best to comfort them and afterwards weeping in sorrow.

For those that lived, the pain and wretchedness were extreme. Amputations were all too often performed without anaesthetics; post-operative wounds became gangrenous because there were not enough disinfectants. The overworked doctors and nurses made mistakes, grew short-tempered, went to sleep on their feet. There was never enough medicine, or enough bed linen, soon not enough beds. The men were crowded together cheek by jowl, severe cases next to curable ones, with no ability to isolate men who carried infectious diseases. Crisis conditions prevailed.

But Alix, who had always been at her best in a crisis, and who had been yearning to prove herself to her husband's subjects for twenty years, seemed at first to thrive. She rejoiced when she graduated from the nurses' training programme, and wore the Red Cross patch on her apron with great pride. Going to her hospitals gave her a fresh sense of worth; devoting herself with ardour to the taxing labour of nursing made her burn with purpose and commitment. She could forget herself, immerse herself in sacrifice.

Wearing the robe and wimple of a nursing sister – a uniform that disguised her high rank and lent her a measure of anonymity, reducing her shyness and discomfort – she walked the overcrowded wards, becoming familiar with the men, stopping often to greet and talk with those she came to know. She liked to call herself a 'sister of charity,' and when one hospital official referred to her as 'mother of mercy,' she recorded the incident with pleasure. 'It's shy work,' she told her sister Victoria in a letter, 'but the sisters' dresses help one.' 'Every hand is useful.'[13]

From the outset of the war Alix took special interest in the welfare of her own regiment of Lancers, and in a Siberian rifle regiment of which she was patroness. She said goodbye to all the officers and many of the men in person when they left for the front, and followed closely the movements and actions of the regiments and their vicissitudes. After every battle she wrote individual letters to the families of the men who died, and invited the wives and daughters of those who were wounded to stay in the palace, near their husbands and sons, while the injured men were treated; she made sure that when they arrived, she greeted them herself, telling her ladies-in-waiting to suspend the usual protocol of formal welcome.[14]

The empress's concern for the suffering was universal. She was often to be found at the bedsides of German prisoners of war, and worried over the anxiety of their loved ones. When the 'monstrous' cousin Willy's son was captured by Russian troops, she knew that Willy and his wife Dona would be desperate for news of him, and sent a personal message to Dona via the neutral Swedish court to let her know that her son was safe and well. 'Only a mother pitying another mother,' she wrote to Nicky when she told him what she had done.[15]

Alix was not the only member of the imperial family to dedicate herself to war work – Aunt Miechen headed a Red Cross effort to collect and distribute medical supplies, Ducky and Ella travelled, visiting hospitals, Nicky's sister Olga and Grand Duke Paul's daughter Marie became nurses, as did several of their cousins – but Alix was perhaps the most earnest, and the least appreciated. For to most soldiers she was the German Whore, suspected of colluding with the enemy, her nursing and war efforts nothing more than a smokescreen to disguise her treachery. For every soldier who was comforted by her presence or appreciated the goods her workshops provided there were thousands of others who abhorred her, some who even called out insults to her when she tried to attend to their needs. Once when she was inspecting a field ambulance she heard a voice call out 'German bitch!' and she burst into tears.[16]

'Oh, this miserable war!' she wrote to Nicky, who was away from Tsarskoe Selo visiting troops, early in November. 'At moments we cannot bear it anymore, the misery and bloodshed break one's heart.'[17] The imperial family had recently buried its first casualty, Grand Duke Constantine's son Oleg, who had been wounded with the First Army in East Prussia and had slowly wasted away in a hospital in Vilna. 'Life is difficult to understand,' Alix wrote, putting into simple words her mental turmoil.

Her mind already overtired and her thinking distorted by her fears and mental instability, Alix was exhausting herself trying to puzzle out what course needed to be taken to rescue, not only the ailing soldiers, but Russia itself from its evident peril.

'My brain is cretinized,' she wrote to Nicky. 'My brain is tired and heavy.' 'Anything only not to think . . .'[18] She smoked, she had been fasting since the beginning of the war. Worst of all, she had become an insomniac, lying awake until three or four in the morning, turning over and over in her mind all that needed to be done. 'The brain seems to be working all the time and never wanting to rest . . . Hundreds of ideas and combinations come bothering one.'[19]

'During the sleepless nights which had become her portion she fancied all kinds of evils,' Martha Mouchanow wrote, and then she would call headquarters and ask the aide-de-camp on duty for news of Nicky.[20] He had been away so much since the war began in August, gone for weeks at a time, his absence increasing her anxieties and making her insomnia much worse. More even than her religious faith, her love for her husband was the solid granite on which her life rested. Without him nearby, she was edgy and restless, her thoughts awash in worries. The frightened child in her came to the fore, especially in the long watches of her sleepless nights.

Yet at the same time she knew, with the certainty of a perceptive adult, that the husband she relied on emotionally was himself far too vacillating, too easily influenced by others, too weak to confront the supreme test with which he was now faced. It was up to her to stiffen his backbone, just as it had been up to her to make him face his responsibilities when his father died. She alone was his disinterested, loving friend and helpmeet, the only one he trusted completely. She dared not let him down.

Caught between her fears and her obligations, she tossed and turned, searching for answers. The problems were clear enough: inept generals, soldiers fighting barefooted in the snow, ten men sharing a single rifle with only a few cartridges between them, casualties mounting, the Germans sweeping through Poland and a new enemy, Turkey, announcing its entry into the war.

She knew instinctively that unless she took action to avert it, disaster would surely arrive, and soon.

It was as if she were back on the *Standart* on its ill-fated cruise off the Finnish coast seven years earlier. With the yacht rapidly sinking, Nicky had stood back from the panic on the deck, consulting his stopwatch and calculating the time they had left; she, on the other hand, had hurried the women and children off the boat and gathered up all the valuables. She had rescued all, saved all, and the yacht had not sunk.

Now she had to step in, while her husband stood back, unsure how to proceed, and save and rescue Russia. She had to take charge. He needed her to do so. It had always been the essence of their partnership. She would do as much as she could, game to the end as ever, to the limit of her strength.

25

She would work to the limit of her strength – but her strength was limited. Her nursing, her visits to all the Petrograd hospitals, her train trips to hospitals in Moscow and other distant towns, her battles with the Munitions Committee and the Red Cross and evasive local officials who tried to keep her from scrutinizing their operations, her reading of petitions people handed her on her trips, her collecting of cribs for the Society for Mothers and Babies ('every baby must be cared for, as the losses are so heavy at the war'), her supervision of her workshops, of her school for nurses and house-maids, of her home for disabled sailors left her 'dead tired,' her chest aching and her breath coming in short nervous gasps.

'Only sheer willpower kept her going during the first five months of the war,' Sophie Buxhoeveden wrote of Alix. By December of 1914 she was seriously ill, and in danger of collapse.[1] Nursing had to be put aside, though the invalid Alix insisted, during her months of convalescence, on knitting garments for the soldiers and preparing icons and images of her husband to be distributed to each regiment.

She insisted too on writing long, urgent, pleading letters to the usually absent Nicky, assuring him of her deep love and support, reaffirming her indissoluble loyalty to him and obsessive concern for him, letters in which, while retaining a certain tentativeness of tone, she nonetheless steered him towards the course she saw that he needed to take. He was the faltering helmsman, she the strong hand at the tiller.

'I bless and love you, as man was [sic] rarely been loved before,' she told him. 'I long to lessen your weight, to help you carry it – to stroke your brow, press you to myself . . . I long often to hold you tight in my arms and let you rest your weary head upon my old breast. We have lived through so much together in these twenty years – and without words understand each other.'[2] She called him by pet names, Lovebird, Huzy, Sunshine, the intimate 'Agooweeone' – a name she sometimes applied to Alexei, sometimes to Nicky. She perfumed her letters and sometimes enclosed sprigs of lilac in them; he sent her jasmine flowers in return. Everything she wrote, even when she was at her most decisive and categorical, was couched in loving, tender phrases, and the tsar received her letters as a thirsty man in a desert receives cool water. ('I drink them and savour every word you write, and often bury my nose and press my lips to the paper you have touched.')

He basked in her ardour, her nurture. She was gratified by being a much-needed unlimited font of reassurance and advice. Such was their exchange. There was never a cold or critical word, never a note of domineering wife and subservient husband. Only love, flowing back and forth between them as it always had, and unquestioned understanding.

Embodied in Alix's long letters were certain fixed principles: that Nicky needed to be much stronger in exerting his authority, and to protect himself from bad counsel; that there were 'always liars, enemies' around him – and her – and that these liars and enemies needed to be identified; that interfering relatives and a group she referred to as Ella's 'bad Moscow set' were to be shunned; and that Grand Duke Nicholas – 'Nikolasha' – was not sufficiently loyal and was doing an unsatisfactory job in commanding the military.

Alix tried to keep herself informed about all that was going on, in the war, within the ministries, and in the country at large, but her sources of information were severely limited. She read the newspapers, and Nicky's letters, but she talked to only a small circle of people, chiefly Anna Vyrubov (who was carrying on an unpleasant petty feud against her in the first year of the war, though their friend- ship continued), and the members of her household staff.[3] Rumours from Petrograd reached her via chance conversations with wounded soldiers, doctors and nurses. Through Anna, an invalid after early 1915 but still able to get about a good deal, Alix learned what was being said at Anna's father's house, among his social circle which included officials, artists and aristocrats, and also at the salon of Princess Paley, Grand Duke Paul's wife, who kept open house at her mansion in the capital. Most of what Alix heard or was told by others was partial or biased or tainted either by flattery or criticism. And none of it changed her opinions, or softened her rigid judgments.

Instead of information, she relied on her instincts; she prayed in her own chapel in the cavelike crypt of the cathedral at Tsarskoe Selo for divine guidance, she listened for the tinkling of the little bell attached to the icon Monsieur Philippe had given her years earlier, to warn her when evil threatened, and she turned, as ever, to Father Gregory.

She had always needed help from the occult, the divine, the Beyond. Now she needed it more than ever. Who better to give it to her than Father Gregory? But he had changed, and she saw that he had. He had grown fat, his previously gaunt face puffy, his nose the inflamed red of the alcoholic. The years of dissolute living were evident in his face, and he had long since exchanged the coarse cloth garb of a peasant for silken shirts and velvet breeches. He drank steadily, deeply, often uncontrollably. He staggered along the streets of Petrograd at midnight, calling out loudly to prostitutes, stopping to urinate against the side wall of a church or unbuttoning his trousers in public places and waving his penis at shocked onlookers, always drinking, ultimately passing out.[4]

He had always been indifferent to wealth, but in 1915 he was surrounded by money, gambling with it until the police closed the gambling house down, involved with lending it (or involved with those who were involved), flinging twenty-five-and fifty-rouble notes into the air and passing them out with abandon to casual acquaintances he met in night clubs. If not exactly venal, Father Gregory had become at least entrepreneurial; he obtained lucrative army supply contracts for friends, he arranged deferments from army service, he used his influence to obtain desirable billets for those who bribed him.[5]

Though supplicants and sycophants continued to crowd his apartment, and though he still performed remarkable healings, most notably saving Anna Vyrubov's life after her near-fatal accident early in 1915, Father Gregory gave less attention to spiritual pursuits. Having given in to temptation and cynicism, he became self-destructive, and having survived two assassination attempts, the one in Pokrovsky in the summer of 1914 and the other in January of 1915, when assassins from Tsaritsyn tried to run him over with a troika, he became daring, even foolhardy. Perhaps he thought himself immortal. Perhaps he foresaw inevitable catastrophe, both for Russia and for himself, and no longer took care to avoid it.

Whatever Father Gregory had become, the empress continued to defend him when confronted with proof of his profligacy, and continued to be soothed and comforted by his blessings and reassurances. Because Alexei had no major attacks of bleeding, there was no need for her to send for Father Gregory as often as in the past, but the operators at the palace switchboard were ordered to put his calls through at once whenever he made them, and Alix knew that whenever she summoned him, if he was in Petrograd, he would come.

In March, 1915, she was 'horribly weak' once again, forced to curtail her personal visits to hospitals. She had only just recovered from the severe symptoms she had experienced the previous winter, and this new assault was dispiriting. She obeyed her doctors and went to bed, 'heart a good deal enlarged', suffering from a racking chest cough, unable to put on her clothes or put up her hair. But even in bed she kept herself occupied. Easter was coming, and she hoped for an Easter truce. Alix packed special parcels to be sent to the troops, boxes stuffed with decorated eggs and Easter bread, writing paper, tobacco, candles, clean linen, and a small icon to be hung around the neck.

She could not do her nursing, or say her formal goodbyes to those who were leaving the hospitals for the front, but she could still write long letters, and look through the papers her secretary sent to her, and meet with her household staff and her ladies-in-waiting who attended to her personal affairs.

Not until late April did she begin to return to her usual routine, and even then she was still taking 'lots of iron and arsenic and heart drops [Veronal]' to build up her strength, and suffering from sharp pains in her lower back, which she attributed to kidney trouble.[6]

She had received a 'long, dear letter' from Ernie in Germany – an important letter, in that it seemed to hold the promise of a possible end to the war. Ernie wrote that he felt certain Nicky understood him and that he had Alix's empathy, that despite the enmity between their two nations, their personal feelings for each other were unchanged. 'He longs for a way out of this dilemma,' Alix told Nicky, 'that someone ought to begin to make a bridge for discussion.'[7] There were no formal peace talks under way, but Ernie proposed sending a secret envoy to Stockholm who could begin private talks between the belligerents. If only Nicky would send an envoy of his own, the secret communication could begin.

Whether or not Alix was naive enough to believe that Ernie was writing entirely on his own is unknown, but she thought enough of his letter to pass on the suggestion to her husband. She sent Ernie a reply – indirectly, through family channels – to say that Nicky was away from the court and would not be able to send anyone to Stockholm soon.

She did not consult the war minister, or the interior minister, or, as far as is known, anyone else in the government about her brother's letter. She mistrusted them; they were among the liars and enemies to be avoided. And besides, they were preoccupied with the new German offensive which coincided with Ernie's letter, a sustained push eastwards that resulted in a series of major defeats for the Russian armies.

There was no resisting the German advance that spring. The heavy German guns shelled the Russian trenches with more than a thousand high-explosive shells a minute, 'churning into gruel', as one contemporary wrote, the waiting Russians, most of them unarmed, unprotected by helmets. Corps after corps were decimated, entire regiments swept away, or nearly so, by the relentless guns.[8] In the air, the Russian pilots had no machine-guns, and were reduced to trying to ram the enemy at the cost of their own lives and planes. Reinforcements were sent to the ever-receding front, most of them unarmed raw recruits, destined for slaughter. Transport and supply lines reached new levels of inefficiency, and even the telephones failed to work when the exchange stations, located deep in the Polish forests, were demolished by wild boars.

Throughout the wet spring of 1915, as the Neva ice broke up and constant rain fell on Petrograd, a steady stream of refugees from the fighting sought shelter in the capital. They arrived at the Warsaw Station, hundreds of tattered families in dire need of food and rest, lining up at hastily organized feeding stations for rations of black bread and hot soup. There were not enough barracks to house them all, and so they lived under bridges, in abandoned warehouses, in sheds, any dry place they could find. Petrograd's European community rallied to help the refugees, and Alix, once she began to resume some activity in late April, went to see for herself what was being done, inspecting the food distribution centre, the maternity home set up by the wife of the British ambassador, the stores of clothing and blankets and small coffins for the many infants and children too weak to survive their ordeal.[9]

It was said that for every homeless family in Petrograd, there were ten on the way, clogging the roads, crowding the soldiers going back and forth from the front. 'One ought really to do something more for the refugees,' Alix wrote to Nicky, 'more food stations and flying hospitals – masses of children are homeless on the high road and others die – all returning from the war – one says it is bitterly painful to see.'[10]

The endless procession of refugees was disturbing to the citizens of Petrograd, not only because of their evident suffering but because they were an indicator of worse to come, harbingers of an ultimate German onslaught that might well reach the Russian capital itself. Only Warsaw stood between the Germans and Petrograd, and it was greatly feared that Warsaw would soon be in enemy hands. Was it time, people asked one another, to hide their valuables? To send precious things out of the country, or at least into the hinterlands of

Russia, perhaps to Siberia, where they could be kept safe until the war ended?

The war had moved onto Russian soil, a large part of Russian territory was now occupied by the central powers. One high-ranking official openly made it known that, in his view, only Russia's enormous spaces and the difficulty of moving troops along roads turned to thick, clinging mud by spring rains could save the country from foreign occupation within a very short time.

In her ill, insomniac, fearful state, her brain 'cretinized', as she often said, Alix saw herself to be at the centre of the crisis. She was the hub around which all revolved, she needed to be the still centre at the heart of the chaos. It was up to her to act, to make the important decisions, and to urge her husband to follow them. Relying on divine inspiration, and perceiving that inspiration to come through Father Gregory – as in the past it had come through Monsieur Philippe and others – she listened to what Father Gregory told her, though his words were often cryptic and his advice came in spurts. She sought his advice, she listened, and she clung to her principles.

She fought to retain her emotional equilibrium, but felt it slip away, under assault from the irritations of daily living – the 'odious humour' of Anna Vyrubov, the close surveillance of the Alexander palace by her critics who harangued the servants and reported every minute detail of the imperial family's life to the newspapers – her worries over daughter Olga, who was becoming overtired and thin from her war work, and over daughter Tatiana, who was so 'awfully sad' and feeling neglected, worries over Nicky's heart, which 'did not feel right', and over the armies, now in full retreat.

'I had been praying and crying and feeling wretched,' she told Nicky in June of 1915. 'You don't know how hard it is being without you and how terribly I always miss you.'[11] She felt 'very low', hearing of 'nothing but deaths', soldiers dying, children and elderly people dying, death everywhere. Late at night, for consolation, she took out Nicky's old letters, some written before they were engaged, and sought to 'warm up her aching heart' by rereading them.

Again and again, one solution to the military crisis, the threat of further invasion, all the heartache of loss and confusion presented itself: the tsar must rule alone, governing not only the country but the military. After all, he alone was master and sovereign of Russia, he had been set at the pinnacle of power by God himself. He alone was the font of wisdom, steadfastness, courage and strength. Now all that force needed to be exerted to reinvigorate the routed armies.

'Nobody knows who is the emperor now,' Alix wrote to Nicky, and it was all because of Nikolasha's command – and his meddling, his 'false position'. He hectored the ministers with his loud voice, he blundered into bad decisions, being 'far from clever, obstinate and led by others'.[12] He was nothing but a stumbling block, and a stumbling block that had to be removed.

Nikolasha had to go.

When she met with the British ambassador George Buchanan, Alix confided to him that in her view, her husband should have taken command of the armies from the start of the war – as in fact he had wanted to do. She knew that the ministers had been opposed to this, but she had no patience with ministers who tried to 'prevent him doing his duty'. 'The Emperor unfortunately is weak,' she told Buchanan, 'but I am not, and I intend to be firm.'

The ambassador saw from the set of her features that the empress would not listen to any contrary arguments.[13] That she had not fully weighed the consequences of the proposed shift in command, consequences endlessly discussed by the governments of Britain and France as well as by the tsar's own ministers. She had not considered, or adequately considered, the effect it would have if the tsar, as military commander, lost a major battle, or several major battles. His political authority would plummet as his military reputation declined. She had not given enough consideration to the sheer workload of keeping up with both political and military responsibilities – a workload no single man could reasonably carry, in Buchanan's view, and do it well. She had forgotten to consider that, only ten years earlier, there had been a revolution in Russia, and revolutionary extremists still awaited their opportunity to take over the government.

Worst of all, in Buchanan's view, was the consequence he dared not speak of to her, the one most often whispered about and hinted at by everyone else concerned: the dread that, with the tsar away from Petrograd, preoccupied with military affairs, the empress would in effect be regent.

And if the empress were to become regent, so it was supposed, then Rasputin would rule all. For it was assumed that the empress was nothing in herself, or nothing more than a cardboard figure, haughty in appearance but, beneath her frosty carapace, a quivering mass of insecurities, incapable of purpose or direction. Her strength of character, her intelligence, her resilience were all discounted; she was only a woman, a disagreeable German woman at that, and in 1915 everyone knew that women were innately childlike, overemotional, easily dominated, prone to hysteria. The rumours about Rasputin's strong influence over the empress were so deeply entrenched in the public mind as to be taken as fact. The presumption of her incapacity, coupled with the presumption of her subordination to the Siber.... starets, made it all but impossible for her true role to be accurately gauged.

In actuality, Buchanan was incorrect in believing that Alix had not thought through what would happen if Nicky took over as commander in chief. She had given it much thought – and prayer – and she believed she had been guided to the right decision.

In her view, the benefits of having her husband replace Nikolasha as commander in chief far outweighed the disadvantages, though the benefits were as yet visible to only a few people – herself and Father Gregory and those to whom God had revealed the splendid future.

'It is the beginning of the glory of your reign,' Alix told Nicky. 'He [Father Gregory] said so and I absolutely believe it. Your sun is rising.'[14] She had become convinced that there was a divine purpose behind all the ugliness and suffering of the war. She called it a 'cleansing of minds and souls', a sweeping away of old ideas, old misplaced loyalties, so that 'a new beginning' could emerge.[15] With the new beginning would come new paths of thought, so that the misguided minds and souls could be 'led aright and guided straight'.[16]

Her words were vague and her meaning obscure, but she felt that she had been given confirmation that the cleansing was under way and that the new day would soon dawn. A miraculous vision had been witnessed by many people on the feast day of St Tikhon the Miracle Worker, in the village of Barabinsk in Siberia, as the saint's relics were being carried in procession around the church.[17] A cross appeared in the sky, and remained there for fifteen minutes. Bishop Varnava of Tobolsk had sent word of the apparition directly to the palace.

Alix knew that crosses were not always good signs, that a cross could indicate disaster as well as blessing. But coming as it did, at this important juncture in the war, with the Russian armies retreating amid such upheaval, the vision was surely a positive sign. God was sending her a message that St Tikhon the Miracle Worker was about to save Russia from the hands of its enemies. Eleven years earlier, God had worked through St Serafim to give her a son. Now St Tikhon was to be the means of Russia's deliverance. And the first step in that deliverance would be her husband's transformation from an amiable cipher into a magnificent battlefield commander, a great and glorious leader of men.

26

Alix sat in her accustomed place next to the hearth in the salon of the Alexander Palace, listening to the melancholy, plangent music of Goulesco's Rumanian orchestra. She loved the wild gypsy music, full of heart-rending tremolos and sombre minor chords, the slow introspective passages giving way from time to time to pulse-racing explosions of rapid dance music. The ululant violins, plaintive harmonies and impassioned rhythms suited her own quicksilver moods, and she had begun to invite the orchestra to play at the palace every Thursday night for a roomful of guests.

When the guests arrived – the latecomers welcomed by the empress 'with a gesture and a sweet smile' – they found their hostess installed in her usual chair, wearing black as had become her custom by the autumn of 1915, a sapphire cross around her neck and a ring set with an immense pearl on her finger. Her hair was always dressed simply in those wartime days, and the nails of her soft hands were never painted, because her husband disliked women who painted their nails and even when he was away, she respected his preference.[1] Her one indulgence was Atkinson's White Rose perfume, which she wore to mask the clinging smell of her cigarettes; the scent of roses and of her verbena toilet water filled the air around her.

While she listened to the music, she knitted or sewed, making winter masks for the soldiers or stitching cushions – she had set herself the task of completing a cushion or a pillow cover each day to sell in her bazaar. The work quietened her, even as the gypsy violins stirred her emotions, moving her to tears. Her emotions were very near the surface, for her insomnia had become chronic and she took

Veronal, a barbiturate, in a vain attempt to rest, and the barbiturate depressed her.[2]

Her eyes were kind, but at the same time 'infinitely tragic', her friend and lady-in-waiting Lili Dehn thought, sitting nearby on those Thursday nights. The tsarina was sorrowful about so many things, about the ugly Petrograd gossip that claimed that Anna Vyrubov was the tsar's mistress and that the tsar was a drunkard and had the evil eye, about the rioters in Moscow who shouted for the tsar to abdicate in favour of Nikolasha and for herself to be shut away in a convent, about the rumours that Ella was hiding Ernie and that Ernie was intriguing with the court, on behalf of the German government, to make a dishonourable peace.[3]

It saddened Alix that the citizens of Moscow and Petrograd, who had shown themselves to be fiercely patriotic and loyal to her husband at the outset of the war, had now turned cynical. They suspected that German spies were everywhere, and spread rumours that spies lurked in the ministries, among the members of the palace staff, even in the imperial family itself. The city-dwellers trusted no one, their loyalty had been corroded, they were hardened and disillusioned. But Alix took some comfort from her certainty that the real Russians, the millions who lived in villages, retained their faith in their rulers. She often reminded Lili of a trip they had taken together not long before to a small village near Peterhof, and of how, when she got out of the car, she had been surrounded by peasants who knelt down before her, saying prayers for her well-being, tears standing in their eyes.[4] She had been praised, idolized, mobbed by the crowd; she had barely been able to make her way back to her car. No one in that village had called her the German Whore, or had hurled scandalous accusations at her.

The memory of the visit was a consolation, and the empress sought consolation often, finding it when with her children, when visiting the wounded – her illness prevented her from doing any real nursing any more – and when praying before an icon of Christ in the small dark chapel adjacent to her bedroom.

'Faith, love and hope are all that matter,' she was fond of saying. These were what sustained her, along with her Veronal and her iron self-discipline. She knew where her duty lay, and she was doing it, day after wearying day. She knew that she had to 'take things personally in hand', as she wrote to her sister Victoria. That she had to continue to write to her husband, upholding him and advising him, so that he could do the work God had called him to undertake.

For, after much persuasion, he had at last taken on himself the command of the armed forces, relieving the 'traitor' Nikolasha of his responsibilities. It had taken her nearly two months, from June to August 1915, to convince Nicky to do this, months of strain during which, to add force to her arguments, she had summoned Father Gregory from Pokrovsky to talk to Nicky.

It had been an uphill battle, for everyone had opposed the prospective shift in command. There had been a terrible scene between Nicky and his mother in the garden of the Anitchkov Palace, with Olga, Tatiana, Marie and Anastasia present. For over two hours Minnie had argued with her son, trying to persuade him that if he took command, it would be assumed that Father Gregory had forced the decision on him – which would so outrage all Russia that the monarchy would come under fatal attack. He had faltered under his mother's barrage of argument, he had blushed and stammered, and had emerged shaken, but in the end he had held firm. The fall of Warsaw to the Germans had helped to stiffen his resolve.

She herself had made him see how important it was that he take command, though she knew that he was ill and frightened, not of battle – for he was a staunch and courageous soldier – but of the responsibility itself, and the mental labour it was certain to impose. He had never been a man to think things through, to analyze a situation creatively and find solutions to problems. He had always turned away from complexity; it bewildered him and left him mentally prostrated.

But of course, as she told him, there was no need to exhaust himself in thought. All he had to do was listen to her advice, and Father Gregory's divinely inspired wisdom, and all would be well. He had to listen, and then he had to be forceful, decisive, and fearsome. He had to be angry, even violent, thumping his fist on the table, swearing and making threats. He had to be formidable, as his immense, commanding father had been, the father whose messages from the other world were brought to her by Father Gregory.[5]

She had convinced her wavering husband that he was not alone, that he could call on irresistible psychic forces whenever he needed them. He carried an icon of St Nicholas blessed by Father Gregory, a magic stick from Mount Athos also blessed by the starets, a talisman once touched by Monsieur Philippe, and a special little comb with which to comb his hair before all important meetings and decisions, which would make him strong and ensure that his will would prevail. He was surrounded by divine magic. He could not fail.

Sitting by the warm hearth listening to the gypsy orchestra on that autumn night, her face pale against the harsh black of her gown, Alix had the severity of an ascetic. She had reached a point in her life where she was living her principles, fully and without compromise. Insofar as she could, she had left behind the trivia and dross of daily existence, to expend her energy in pursuit of a noble purpose. She was completely dedicated, completely engaged. Melancholy, depressed, weary and ill she might be, but she was fulfilled.

When in the autumn of 1915 Nicky assumed command of the armed forces from the newly designated command headquarters in the small town of Mogilev on the hills above the Dnieper River, the Russian army was in full retreat. German forces were advancing along the coast of the Baltic Sea, moving without resistance through Lithuania, intent on capturing Riga. Once they took Riga, they would be only three hundred miles from Petrograd.

The Russian forces were in disarray, severely beaten, demoralized, still some six million strong but no longer an army of young, vital soldiers; many of the men were middle-aged, others raw and frightened young conscripts – among them Father Gregory's simpleton son Dimitri – led by mediocre and inexperienced officers. Even six million were not enough men, for Serbia was being overrun as well as Lithuania, and the Russians, perpetually short of weaponry, were reduced to fighting with sticks and stones, and with their fists. Casualties continued to be very high.

The War Minister Sukhomlinov, tainted by scandal, had been dismissed in June and his successor was inept. No one was attending to the desperate need for efficient transport and adequate food supplies; even though it was harvest season, men and horses alike were growing thin from deprivation, the men tempted to eat the horses' greatly reduced rations of oats and hay. No one, least of all the tsar who believed that the peasants were loyal and patriotic, was forcing peasant speculators to disgorge the crops they withheld from the market in hopes of driving up food prices.

The army needed a strong leader, just as Alix said. But Nicky, however sincere in his dedication, was not that man.

'In the moment of danger the duty of a sovereign is to be with his army,' he said, 'and if need be perish with it.'[6] No one doubted his sincerity, but the senior officers, knowing him as they did, and aware that he had no experience of large-scale command and no knowledge of strategy or weaponry, had no faith in him. They knew that he was an essentially passive, weak-willed man, lacking in initiative, resigned rather than defiant or aggressive. With the soldiers, one of his generals wrote, 'he did not know what to say, where to go, or what to do'. The men felt his awkwardness. Far from heartening them, filling them with courage and hope for victory, he filled them with dismay.

The strains of recent years had coarsened the emperor physically, and made him mentally rigid, preoccupied with his health. He deliberately locked himself into comforting routines that took up much of his time and shut out unpleasant interruptions.

'Today I was able to take a close look at him,' an observer wrote in October of 1915. 'The tsar is not handsome, the colour of his beard and moustache is tobacco-yellow, peasant-like, his nose is fat, his eyes stony.'[7] Others saw in his eyes a unique blend of melancholy, sweetness, resignation and tragedy, and noted that in conversing he was alternately vague and evasive, never looking anyone directly in the eye for very long. Instead he gazed out of the window, or into the distance – anywhere but at the person he was speaking to. Father Gregory told his friend the moneylender Simanovich that the tsar was 'afraid of everyone'. 'When he talks to me in his study,' the starets said, 'he looks around to see if anyone is eavesdropping.'[8]

Despite the escalating dangers and urgent exigencies of the war, Nicky settled into the governor's mansion at Mogilev as if into a safe oasis, a retreat from burdens and tensions. He felt calm, never read the newspaper or saw any war footage in newsreels. He set up fresh routines for himself, taking long afternoon drives in his Rolls-Royce or walks in the woods with his English setters, his aides trailing along behind, unable to keep up with his vigorous stride.

He rose late, listened to the reports from the front, attended briefings for officers, gave out medals, and read his wife's long letters – letters which, with their abundance of chatty, homely anecdotes, their passionate declarations of undying love, made his eyes fill with tears.[9] In the evenings, after dining with his officers, he watched American movies and played cards and dice and dominoes.

He liked the rustic quiet of Mogilev, the picturesque groves of beech and chestnut, the orchards and meadows where cows and sheep grazed, the flowing river and sleepy small town. He brought Alexei to live with him there, in his spartan rooms in the governor's mansion. Together they reviewed troops, went to church, watched films, said their prayers before lying down next to one another in narrow camp beds. Alexei played sentinel, in much the same way as he and his friends played war with toy guns at the Alexander Palace. Amid the serenity of the forest, the tranquil meadows, the real war seemed remote indeed.

And in fact, shortly after Nicky took command, the intensity of the German push eastwards diminished. Activity shifted to the western front; the eastern front became a rearguard. Nicky had stumbled into a period of relative quiescence; from the autumn of 1915 on, Russian assaults resulted in large-scale casualties for the Russian army, but there were no German assaults, nothing on the scale of the previous spring's advance.

Alix redoubled her letter-writing efforts when Nicky moved to Mogilev. 'My pen flies like mad over the paper and the thoughts tear through my head,' she told him. 'I long to poke my nose into everything (Ella does it with success) – to wake up people, put order into all and unite all forces.'[10] The elderly premier Goremykin called the empress 'Madame Energy' as she dashed off letter after letter, throwing herself with relish into the attempt to harden her husband's resolve and make him a stern ruler.

'You are master and sovereign of Russia,' she wrote him. 'Almighty God set you in place, and they should all bow down before your wisdom and steadfastness.' If only Nicky would model himself on his mighty predecessors. 'Be Peter the Great, Ivan the Terrible, Emperor Paul – crush them all.'[11] She complimented him on 'showing his mastery, proving himself the Autocrat without whom Russia cannot exist', but in reality, as she said, it was she herself who 'wore the trousers' and longed to 'show her immortal trousers to those poltroons' in the ministry of defence and at staff headquarters.[12] Alix liked to say that she had the heart of a soldier's daughter and a soldier's wife. She liked to think herself formidable; it amused her that Prince Orlov ('Fat Orlov', she called him), head of the military chancery, was so ill at ease at the thought of meeting with her that he had to take large doses of valerian drops in order to steady his nerves before coming to see her. He always 'reeked of valerian', she told Lili Dehn.[13]

Alix was beginning to nourish a dangerous delusion: the delusion that, if necessary, she could rule effectively. That she had the will, the courage, the discernment to decide and carry out policy, while standing up to the ministers and others in the government – men she considered to be, most of them, either stupid, treasonous or both. Encouraged in her conviction by the increasingly wayward Father Gregory, who did not want power for himself, but feared prosecution for a range of misdeeds from assault to bribery, Alix imagined herself on a path to greater and greater authority.

She imagined that she saw clearly what needed to be done, guided by her narrow view and her confidence that God was speaking to her through Father Gregory. She was even confident that, should the starets be removed from the scene entirely, another divine spokesman would appear, for had it not been so when Monsieur Philippe died?

Lili Dehn noticed that Alix, who was 'greatly addicted' to card games, 'never liked to lose'.[14] She not only disliked losing, she expected to win, in whatever situation she found herself. She was coming to see herself as locked in an increasingly sinister contest with those in her husband's government, and was becoming contemptuous of her opponents' power, which she consistently underestimated. When, the day after the tsar took command of the military, eight of the thirteen cabinet ministers signed a joint letter of resignation, she was undismayed. Let them make disloyal gestures – it only proved what she had always said, that it was all but impossible to find truly capable men.

She was feeling her power, yet exhaustion nagged at her, for the struggle drained her and left her weak. In the long autumn evenings, she lay on her couch, surrounded by her daughters. Olga played the piano, the others took turns reading aloud. Anna Vyrubov (whom Alix in her letters referred to as 'The Cow'), alternately clinging, critical, and sulky, occupied a chair, a perennial guest. On Thursdays the Rumanian orchestra played; once in a while a concert was given at the hospital. On other evenings, the family played cards, put puzzles together. Alix knitted and embroidered.

Olga was doing too much, and was looking 'nervous and anaemic'. She had had to stop nursing, and could only supervise the work in the wards. Tatiana, thin and fragile-looking, was sturdier. She continued to work in the hospital, and to meet with her relief committees. She imitated her mother's austerity; she sold the pearl necklace her father had given her on her eighteenth birthday and gave the money to the relief fund. Marie and Anastasia, now sixteen and fourteen, kept up their nursing work and, with the older girls, took their mother's place at hospital openings and charitable bazaars.

They brought their mother news from Petrograd, which, that autumn, had become a city of grey uniforms and black mourning gowns. Under dark skies full of rain-laden clouds, anxious pedestrians walked up and down Nevsky Prospekt, looking for the telegrams posted in the shop windows, telegrams with news from the front and lists of casualties. There were soldiers everywhere, young boys on their way to the war, truckloads of wounded being taken to hospitals, amputees begging in the streets. Nurses hurrying to work, red crosses on their white aprons, Duma deputies driven past in cars, workers on strike milling in dozens in the wide squares, shoppers in the markets dismayed at the high prices of bread, meat and fuel: such was Petrograd in the late months of 1915.

Although society congregated in the capital and entertainments were offered, the socializing was subdued. There were no balls, no lavish parties. Gowns from Paris, delicacies and fine wines – apart from those already in the cellars of the elite – were hard to come by; imported flowers and greenery from the south of France for decorating the grand rooms of mansions were not to be had at all. Besides, so many of the guests were in mourning that they lacked the zest to enjoy themselves. They were apprehensive. Like the other citizens of the capital they gathered in nervous groups, exchanging war news, the latest rumours about German spies. There was said to be a spy at Mogilev, one of the generals. The emperor and empress were both suspected of carrying on secret peace discussions with the Germans. And Rasputin, as always the favourite topic of gossip, was said to be the most notorious spy of all, passing on the secrets he heard at court to his paymasters in Berlin.

The news was bleak, and beyond all her other concerns Alix was faced, in November, with a personal sorrow. Her long-time friend and former maid of honour Sonia Orbeliani, for years an invalid living in the palace, was dying. Sonia had been courageous, fighting her disabilities and remaining as active as possible despite being unable to walk. She was a political creature, the niece of a former liberal prime minister, and she had been blunt in her assessments of the various Russian regimes – indeed in all her opinions. Sonia had told Alix what she thought of the current state of affairs and, though they often differed, Alix had listened to her views, admiring the spirit Sonia displayed as an 'undaunted Georgian' who never gave up. At Sonia's request, Alix remained with her in her last days and, when the end came, Sonia died in her friend's arms.

'One more true heart gone to the unknown land!' Alix wrote to Nicky afterwards.[15] She arranged the funeral, took it on herself to carry out Sonia's last wishes, and wrote to all the Orbeliani relatives – in itself a sizable task. When she went to the memorial service, she did not go dressed as the empress, but in her plain nursing gown. 'I hate the idea of going into black for her this evening,' Alix told Sophie Buxhoeveden, 'and feel somehow nearer to her like this, like an aunt, more human, less empress.'[16] Later on, after the long service had ended, she lingered near the coffin, sitting down beside it and stroking Sonia's hair, as she might have stroked the hair of a sleeping child. She wept for the loss of her friend and 'true heart', for the honest voice that had been stilled.

But there was no time to indulge her grief, for a worrying crisis was at hand. On the very day of Sonia's funeral, Alexei was brought home from Mogilev, his lower face swathed in bloody bandages. His nose had been bleeding without stopping for two days. The doctors had cauterized the nostril repeatedly but the bleeding would not cease, and the boy had lost so much blood that his skin was dead white.

'Above the blood-soaked bandages his large blue eyes gazed at us with pathos unspeakable,' Anna Vyrubov remembered. The doctors continued to cauterize him – a painful process – but he was growing very weak, and could hardly talk.

Alix watched in agony as her son reclined against his pillows, unable to lie flat lest the blood flow increase. Sophie Buxhoeveden noticed that she was, as usual, 'calm on the surface', but knew that she was remembering the terrible attack of bleeding Alexei had endured three years earlier at Spala, when it had seemed certain that he would die.[17] Then Alix had waited for days before contacting Father Gregory. Now, however, she was prompt to send for him.

She put in a call to Petrograd, and sent a car to Father Gregory's apartment.

He came into the sickroom, his long hair lank above his silk peasant blouse, a gold cross that the empress had given him around his neck. As usual, he was assured. If he stank of Madeira, none present recorded it.

He walked to Alexei's bed and looked down into his chalky face. He made the sign of the cross over the bed, and reached down and touched the boy's face briefly.

'Don't be alarmed,' he told Alix and Nicky, who were kneeling beside the bed. 'Nothing will happen.' He left as quickly as he had come.

Almost as soon as he had gone, those nearest the bed realized that the bandages on the tsarevich's face were remaining white. The blood had ceased to flow.[18] Once again, as even the most sceptical in the room had to acknowledge, the starets had bewitched the boy's blood. When the doctors advanced a medical explanation for the sudden cessation of bleeding, it was not believed. The doctors had failed; Father Gregory had succeeded. Alexei recovered.

Nicky returned to Mogilev, to his quiet life and long afternoon walks. Alix ordered a stone for Sonia Orbeliani's grave and began sending Christmas letters to the families of the men in her Siberian rifle regiment, many of whom had been severely injured by poison gas. On Thursday nights, however, she interrupted whatever occupied her to sit by the fire and listen to the sad, plaintive music of the gypsies, letting it calm and nourish her, and bring her the catharsis of tears.

'I prayed last night till I thought my soul would burst, and cried my eyes out,' Alix wrote to Nicky as the year 1915 ended. 'I cannot bear to think of all you have to carry.'[19] Her mood was 'of the saddest'; she had taken Veronal and it made her stomach hurt, so she took opium to soothe it. Sedated and depressed, she had lost her brave assurance that a turning point had been reached, that a new era of Russia's glory had arrived. All that had arrived was the threshold of a new year, a year that was sure to be filled with deprivation, sorrow and crisis. She would face the new year as bravely as she could, with prayer and tears, until the deliverance she ardently wished for was at hand.

27

Father Gregory was losing his powers. He had managed to stop the tsarevich's bleeding, but he felt a distinct waning of his abilities. When asked to help the sick he demurred, apologizing. 'I cannot do it,' he said bluntly. 'The Lord has taken my power from me.'

Certainly his drinking increased, as did his frequent visits to the notorious Villa Rode, a nightclub in a Petrograd suburb, where the owner had added on a special room that he kept ready for the starets's use. There amid his entourage of admirers and hangers-on, lost in an alcoholic haze, the Siberian danced clumsily to gypsy music, twirling and kicking with frenzied abandon. Most nights he did not cause scandal – the members of his secret police escort kept him restrained and, when they could not restrain him, bribed any witnesses to his excesses to remain silent – but from time to time incidents occurred that became notorious.

One night early in 1916, as Father Gregory was cavorting in the night club, he was confronted by several young men in uniform, one of whom had taken out his revolver. They faced each other, the drunken peasant and the steely-eyed young officers, and before long the men flinched, turning aside.

'You want to kill me!' Rasputin shouted. 'There is no power left which can direct you against me. Go home. I want to stay with my party here and relax.'

The young men left – but everyone in the room had felt their menace, and experienced a shiver of fear. Rasputin had won the confrontation, for the moment, but the menace remained. For weeks the episode was talked about, analyzed. Was it proof that the Siberian was indeed powerfully protected? Or was it a harbinger of disaster to come?

The starets was receiving obscene phone calls; people insulted him to his face. Hundreds of admirers and petitioners still came to his apartment each day, asking for help and favours, for money, for healing. Women sent him flowers ('Silly creatures, these women,' Rasputin told Felix Yusupov, 'silly creatures who spoil me'); Simanovich brought him large sums of money from grateful petitioners on whose behalf he had contacted ministers or other officials.[1] He was at the height of his worldly power – he who had never sought power, but by 1916 had become edgily, uncomfortably accustomed to wielding it.

Yet the very root of that power lay in his ability to heal, and he felt he had lost it.

But if he could no longer heal anyone, he could still help them. Drawing on the large subsidy of five thousand roubles a month he was receiving from the interior ministry, and the bribes brought in by Simanovich, Father Gregory handed out money to nearly everyone who came to him. Widows, schoolgirls, impoverished veterans, peasants who had lost their lands, refugees, invalids, the wretched of the streets who found their way to him: he gave freely to them all, while taking with equal freedom from dishonest officials, businessmen, lawyers, politicians. He rewarded himself generously, with cases of wine, expensive sturgeon and imported delicacies, nightly banquets and debauches, expensive prostitutes. He sent money to his wife in Siberia and enrolled his daughters in costly private schools.

Demoralized, bombarded with sensation, trapped by his protectors who both shielded him and gathered damning information about him, Rasputin floundered, yet he managed to be available when called to the palace. And he continued to advance his influence, keeping up his close ties to the journalist and informer Manuilov, socializing with his secret police handlers, recommending candidates for high office and afterwards cultivating them. He was the spider at the centre of a vast web of contacts, adept at putting people in touch with others who could help them or conspire with them. He seemed to know everyone, to be able to find out about everyone. No one in Petrograd was more feared, more sought out, or more reviled.

In the spring of 1916 the imperial train moved slowly southwards from Petrograd, carrying the tsar, the tsarina and their children towards the Rumanian frontier. Nicky was on his way to review troops, Alix to visit hospitals and workshops, so the journey had a serious purpose. But it had the air of a family holiday and, as they went farther south, and the land grew greener and the temperature milder, the holiday feeling increased.

Alix had declared that they could not go to Livadia, that would be 'too great a treat to indulge in during the war'. But after stopping at Vinnitza and Bendery they went to Sebastopol, and to Eupatia, where she had set up several sanatoria, and to Odessa, where she inspected the iodine factory, and in each place there was a little time for relaxing and lying in the hot sun. Everywhere flowers bloomed in the sunshine, growing against whitewashed walls, along stone paths, in stone urns on broad terraces and in enclosed gardens where fountains splashed and birds sang. There were orchards scented with pink blossom, and fields where white oxen pulled ploughs turning the earth for spring planting.

Reminders of the war were everywhere. Recuperating soldiers sat amid the blossoms in the gardens, ambulances and military trucks rumbled along the narrow streets and funeral processions congested the roads. At night, on the train, it was necessary to draw heavy black curtains across the windows because of the danger of bombardment by German planes, launched from cruisers in the Black Sea.

Still, with the coming of spring, hopes temporarily rose. The Germans had not, after all, marched towards Petrograd. Russian armies were receiving materials and supplies from abroad, and an offensive was about to be launched. Apart from chronic pallor and abdominal swelling and some internal bleeding in both his arms, Alexei had been holding his own since December. He was nearly twelve years old, tall and thin and good-looking. Father Gregory had said that, if he lived to be seventeen, he would be completely cured.[2] In her most buoyant moments, Alix looked forward with optimism to his seventeenth birthday, just as she looked forward to the beneficial results of the most recent changes in the government – changes she felt sure would be for Russia's good.

At the end of January 1916, the prime minister, the antique Goremykin, had been replaced by a man Alix believed to be 'excellent and honest', a crony of Rasputin's, Boris Stürmer. On Alix's advice and against the objections of every responsible, thoughtful voice he heard, Nicky appointed Stürmer, possibly to placate his wife, possibly because he simply did not know what else to do.

The appointment was disastrous, and was soon followed by further ill-advised changes. The able war minister Polivanov was dismissed, and Stürmer took his place. In June, 1916, the foreign minister Sazonov was dismissed – again to be replaced by Stürmer, who also took over the interior ministry for a time.

The pre-eminence of Stürmer was a telling symptom of the tsar's incapacity. He vacillated, alternately acting with fitful resoluteness and withdrawing into glassy-eyed inactivity. He mistrusted strong, capable leaders; he could not bring himself to delegate authority to able men, lest they rob him of his own powers. He trusted only his wife, as he told Sandro, and she had little more than her devotion to recommend her. What trust he had placed in Father Gregory was being eroded for, by the spring of 1916, after years of denial and inaction, he was at last becoming convinced that the starets was unredeemably corrupt.

The extent of Father Gregory's unholy activities – his influence peddling at the highest reaches of government, his brokering of army contracts, his indiscreet revelations of military secrets to his wide circle of contacts, plus his long history of priapism and his outrageous vulgarity, his general hatefulness in the eyes of educated Russians – was made clear by, among others, G. I. Shavelsky, arch-priest of the Russian army and fleet. Shavelsky's aim was to persuade the tsar that what confidence the soldiers and sailors still retained in the monarch and his government was rapidly being destroyed by the stories circulating about Father Gregory – stories that were, in many instances, true. The most notorious tale, that the Siberian was the empress's lover and controlled everything she did and said, was not true, but it was believed anyway. And even if they were not lovers, Shavelsky said, the empress relied on her spiritual adviser to far too great an extent. She was naive, she trusted Father Gregory too much and was unable to see that his advice was merely self-serving, not oracular or divinely inspired. It was up to the tsar to intervene immediately, lest the situation worsen.

Shavelsky's message underscored what Nicky had been told the previous year by the interior minister, Shcherbatov, by his relatives, and by many others. All the advice, all the investigations and reports, pointed in the same direction: the rot beneath the fabric of Russian governmental life went very deep, and Father Gregory was an integral part of that rapidly spreading rot. Because of Alix's reliance on him, his subversive influence was increasing.

But what could Nicky do? Just as Alix relied on her starets, so he, Nicky, relied on her. He leaned on her, needed her. He had begun to wear her portrait on his person day and night.[3] He called her his 'heart, brain and soul'. He missed her terribly, especially when he felt ill, as he often did. The cocaine that he took to revive him and ease his heart trouble was ageing him, clouding his mind and sapping his strength.

Though he was only in his forty-ninth year, Nicky had begun to look, many observers thought, like an old man. The change was startling. His face had become thin and hollow and was covered with innumerable small wrinkles. His eyes were sunken and darkly shadowed, the pupils faded, like the lifeless eyes of an ageing invalid. His face wore a helpless expression; his lips were fixed in an odd little smile, humourless and unsettling.[4] As Father Gregory had noted, he had developed an obsessive wariness, and was forever looking around him.

He looked, and felt, helpless. He had taken on the persona of Job. The strain of psychological martyrdom the tsar had always displayed now came to the fore in him. He had always felt doomed; now his country too seemed to him doomed, the recent slight upturn in her fortunes to the contrary.

'Perhaps a sacrificial victim is needed to save Russia,' he had declared in the summer of 1915. 'I will be that victim.'⁵

By the autumn of 1916 it had become evident that no amount of self-sacrifice could save the Russian monarchy from being swept under by a tidal wave of popular unrest. The immense losses in the war (the Russian campaign launched earlier in the year had led to nothing but more dead and wounded), the rumours about the empress and Rasputin, and about her maintaining secret communications with the German enemy, the cynicism about the tsar and his government, the increasing hardships of daily life caused indirectly by the war were pushing even the staunchest patriots to the breaking point and beyond.

Newspaper headlines warned of German influence at court, of 'dark powers behind the throne,' and newspaper editors, no longer controlled by the government, printed fabricated stories about the empress. People spoke of both the emperor and empress with 'open animosity and contempt,' and sang derisive songs about Alix and Rasputin. The word 'revolution' was heard often, and not only whispered but spoken aloud, as if in defiance of the secret police.

Dim lights shone on the unswept streets of Petrograd in October and November, 1916. Uncollected garbage piled up, clogging the roadways, and snowdrifts accumulated for want of workers to clean the streets. Deaths in the large homeless refugee population began to accelerate, with typhus carrying off many.

Unusually harsh frosts warned of the onset of a severe winter, and the secret police, who watched and listened in every street in an effort to gauge the mood of the city, notified the tsar that the labouring poor were 'on the verge of despair'.

Among those who could afford to escape the rigours of the capital, there was an exodus that autumn; people crowded the ticket windows to buy tickets to Finland via Haparanda, or to travel south to the Crimea or the Caucasus where food was sure to be available in the local markets and where the winter would not be so cold. Rationing had begun, and among unrationed goods prices had risen so high that meat now cost more than treble what it had in 1914, and butter and flour had more than doubled. Rents in the city too had risen a great deal, fuel was scarce and exorbitant. People stood in lines stretching down many streets to buy oil for their lamps and vegetables for their supper. In front of the Society for Fighting High Prices, crowds formed very early in the morning, waiting for foodstuffs that, most of the time, did not arrive at all.

For the trains carrying food and other necessities no longer pulled into the Petrograd stations in large enough numbers to supply the city adequately. There were not enough locomotives, there were not enough workers, even when prisoners of war and workers imported from Persia and China were brought in, to operate the trains. Soldiers deserting from the army had begun drifting into the capital, but they were not put to work; some had shot off their feet and were incapacitated, some were in hiding, and all were hostile to authority and unwilling to collude in the perpetuation of the regime by which they felt betrayed.

As the autumn wore on, and the lines for food and fuel grew longer and those who waited in them colder, more and more soldiers poured into Petrograd. There were thirteen million men on the army rolls, and most of them, it seemed, were coming to Petrograd. Their disruptiveness, their hostility, the stories they carried with them from the front – stories about Rasputin and the empress carrying on nightly conversations with the Kaiser in Berlin, about Grand Duke Nicholas, their beloved former commander, who was said to be plotting to overthrow the tsar, about the tsar himself and his ministers, said to be so fearful of the peasants that the Germans had been paid to exterminate them all – added to the already overstrained atmosphere and led to fresh secret police alarms.

The Third Duma opened in November, and its irate members seemed to give vent to all the pent-up resentment in the country. In a 'thunderous voice' the ultraconservative delegate Vladimir Purishkevich denounced the tsar's ministers who, he said, had been turned into puppets – puppets whose strings were held by the empress and Rasputin. The leader of the moderate Cadet party, Paul Miliukov, exposed Stürmer for stealing from the treasury and accused the empress and Rasputin of wielding power illegally and of betraying Russia. 'Treason!' shouted the delegates when Miliukov challenged them.

Miliukov's speech, millions of copies of which were printed illegally and distributed throughout the country, stirred yet more disaffection. Warned not only by his own most perceptive advisers but by agents of the British Secret Service in London that a revolution would surely come 'in the very near future' unless he acted decisively, the tsar dismissed Stürmer and replaced him with the transport minister Alexander Trepov.

Trepov's appointment was significant, not only politically, but as a signal of a major turning point in the relations between Nicky and Alix. In appointing Trepov, Nicky had ignored his wife's advice. And Alix, who had been feeling invincible, 'not the least bit afraid of the ministers any more', as she wrote to Nicky, was immediately aware of the change.

It was a crack in her armour, a rift in her self-esteem. Her letters to her husband became more frantic, more urgent. For the first time in their correspondence, she implored him to listen only to Father Gregory, not to the generals or ministers.

But Father Gregory had never held a central role in either her decision-making or Nicky's. Her pleading was gently ignored. She knew, with a deep intuitive knowledge that made her shiver inwardly, that her power was gone.

She had known for some time that the imperial family was united in its purpose to marginalize her by any means available. They wanted her influence suppressed.[6] They were convinced that she and Father Gregory were planning to take over the government entirely. She, in turn, suspected that her mother-in-law and others were planning to remove Nicky from the throne and to establish a regency until Alexei came of age to rule.[7]

Her power was gone, and she feared that she would never regain it.

Just before Christmas 1916, Alix went to Novgorod to visit hospitals for the wounded. She took her children with her and Sophie Buxhoeveden and others of her retinue, and was met at the station by the provincial governor, who escorted the entire party on their tour.

Novgorod was an ancient town, set in the midst of apple orchards, the trees bare and all but lifeless in winter, their trunks black against the snow. Alix was presented with apples from the previous harvest, kept preserved in cool cellars, and met with a large crowd of townspeople who, if not entirely enthusiastic, did not show her any disloyalty – perhaps because they had been carefully chosen by the governor.[8]

She passed through the hospital wards, viewed the town monuments and attended a service in the cathedral, her attention drawn to the dozens of very old icons being restored there. The local nobility held a tea in her honour, and the members of Alix's retinue felt a marked coldness in the reception given her, though Alix herself seemed unaware of it.[9]

She had heard of a celebrated starets living at the Dessiatin monastery, a holy woman, Maria Michaelovna, said to be one hundred and seven years old, and wanted to meet her and receive her blessing. She turned her visit into a pilgrimage, walking on foot through the wet snow to the small hermitage where the old woman lived.

The afternoon was cold, the sun had long since set as the empress trudged through the snow in the dark. The interior of the hut was dim, and only when a candle was brought was Alix able to make out the small, frail body of the starets, lying on her bed. She went nearer, and saw the old woman's face surrounded by an aureole of scraggly grey hair, 'a sweet fine, oval face with lovely young, shining eyes and sweet smile'.

The starets held out her thin hand in blessing. 'Be joyous, uncrowned bride,' she said softly. 'Here is the martyr Empress Alexandra.'

28

Alix was still feeling the comfort and consolation that followed her visit to the elderly starets Mother Maria when she learned, on December 30, 1916, that Father Gregory was missing.

And not only that he was missing, but that he might be dead, for there were rumours in Petrograd of gunshots fired in the middle of the night at the Yusupov mansion and it was known that Father Gregory had said that he intended going there the previous night.

'I cannot and won't believe he has been killed,' Alix wrote to Nicky. 'I still trust in God's mercy that one has only driven him off somewhere.'[1]

Her heart was bothering her again and Dr Botkin had given her an exceptionally large dose of Veronal, which had made her sleep longer than usual the night before. Drowsy, lulled by the drug, she could not bring herself to believe that the rumours were true.

She was still basking in her memories of her encounter with Mother Maria, 'so lovely and restful, warming to the soul'. In the old woman's presence she had felt blessed and consoled, hearing Mother Maria say that the war would soon be over, that she need not worry about the children, that they would marry, that she should not 'fear the heavy cross'. This Mother Maria had repeated several times, that Alix should not fear the heavy cross.

'I thank God for having let us see her,' Alix told her husband. She was sending Mother Maria a gift, three small lamps to light her dim hut, along with an icon. She much preferred to think about Mother Maria's shining eyes and sweet smile than to confront the rumours from the capital.

But it soon became apparent that they were more than mere rumours, and again her intuition told her that something was terribly wrong. She had known that there were plots to kill the starets, and had given orders to Interior Minister Protopopov to make certain that Father Gregory's guards did not allow him to go out at night.[2] She had known that Felix Yusupov had been spending time with Father Gregory, and that Felix's mother Zinaida Yusupov was among the starets's most vehement adversaries.[3]

Bewildered, then frightened by the message from Father Gregory's daughter, Alix did her best to compose herself and continued to receive her callers.[4] But the news grew worse throughout the day.

By mid-afternoon the police investigators had discovered reddish-brown stains on the Great Petrovsky Bridge over the Malaya Nevka river, at a place where the river ice was thin and disposal of a body was possible. A brown boot was also found there, and when the boot was shown to Father Gregory's daughters they said that it belonged to their father.[5]

To the elite of Petrograd, gathered at the Yacht Club to exchange information, these discoveries seemed to prove beyond doubt that the infamous Rasputin had at last been eliminated. Nothing else was talked of, the news was passed around with excitement and relish. By late afternoon congratulatory phone calls were being made and telegrams sent off saying that it was now certain that the Siberian was dead; and adding that Felix Yusupov and Grand Duke Dimitri Pavlovich had killed him.[6]

Alix sat, 'very despondent', with Anna Vyrubov, doing her best to calm Anna, and not to give up hope herself while waiting for definitive news from the police investigation.

'We are sitting together – can [*sic*] imagine our feelings – thoughts – our friend has disappeared,' she wrote to Nicky.[7] 'Such utter anguish (am calm and can't believe it),' she added. Her body languid, her mind agitated, she sent several telegrams as well as writing Nicky a long letter.

Every bit of news passed on to her seemed to confirm the fatal rumours. Grand Duke Dimitri, seen at the Yacht Club, had looked 'pale as death'. Felix Yusupov was fervently denying any involvement in the alleged crime – an incriminating denial, sent in writing to the palace when Alix refused to allow him to come to her in person. She knew that he had been seeing a good deal of Father Gregory recently, that a connection between them had been established. Now it seemed that the purpose of that connection might have been murder.

Alix tried not to give up hope – but at the same time she took practical steps to protect herself and those she loved, for her common sense told her that the disappearance of Father Gregory might be only the first stage in a coup whose ultimate aim would be to eliminate her and replace the tsar with a regency. She protected Anna by moving her into the palace and securing her rooms with new locks. ('They will get at her next,' she told Nicky.) She ordered the guards to prohibit any of the young grand dukes from entering the palace. What precautions she took to protect herself and her children her letters do not reveal, nor do they reveal what she told her daughters about Father Gregory's mysterious disappearance.

Nicky had told her that he planned to return to Tsarskoe Selo soon. ('Oh, the joy, the consolation of having you home again,' she wrote to him.) Until he arrived, she would do her best to hold on to her hopes and say her prayers. She ordered an all-night mass to be held in the palace chapel. She would insist that the entire household attend and pray for the safety of the starets.

'We women are all alone with our weak heads,' she told her husband, and her 'weak head' was spinning with questions. What had gone wrong? Why hadn't Protopopov succeeded in protecting Father Gregory? Could it be that Protopopov himself was no longer to be trusted? And if so, was any safety possible for the family?

The same questions continued to disturb her on the following day, December 31, as word of the notorious Siberian's presumed death spread throughout the capital and outward into the country-side. The police continued their interrogations, Alix continued to refuse to speak to Felix Yusupov, now universally presumed to be the principal conspirator and murderer. She clung to the hope that 'God would spare her her comforter and only friend', but the chances of his survival were diminishing, and she knew it.[8]

Early on the morning of January 1 Father Gregory's body, frozen and mutilated, was found in the ice of the Malaya Nevka below the bridge at Krestovsky Island. The palace was informed.

The suspense was over; now her suffering began.

She mourned him. She mourned him, with all the force and depth of her Wagnerian soul. That he was gone seemed to her far more than an ordinary human loss, that he had been murdered was far more than a mere human crime. It was a catastrophe, a ruinous denouement, a deathblow for her and for Russia.

With Father Gregory gone, who would say prayers over Alexei when he was ill? To whom could she turn in a crisis?

She slumped under the weight of her sorrow, suddenly feeling old. She wrote letters, and signed them 'An Old Woman'.[9] She took more heart drops, which deadened her and enabled her to sleep. In her waking hours, she sent telegrams to Nicky at Mogilev, told her children that their friend Father Gregory had died, and, ever analytical, tearfully pondered the meaning of Father Gregory's murder.

What had happened was grievous, yet even in her worst moments she could not bring herself to believe that it was final. Had not Father Gregory been sent to her to replace Monsieur Philippe? And had not another messenger from the divine been sent to her only recently, just before Father Gregory's death? Surely her encounter with Mother Maria was not merely fortuitous, but divinely ordained. The continuity of divine help was assured.

What was more, just as she had never felt that Monsieur Philippe was entirely gone, so now she sensed that Father Gregory was still with her. She still felt protected by Monsieur Philippe's icon with its little bell, the warning bell that rang when danger was near. Father Gregory's relics too would protect and warn her. Nicky had Father Gregory's comb, and his stick from Mount Athos. She had his letters. She sent word to the police to send her everything removed from his body – his blood-stained shirt, a platinum bracelet he wore with the imperial monogram, the small gold cross inscribed with the words 'save and protect' which he wore around his neck.[10]

She had his relics, and she believed that his spirit lived on, and that she could contact it.

'My dear martyr,' she wrote in a note placed in Father Gregory's coffin, 'give me thy blessing, that it may follow me always on the sad and dreary path I have yet to traverse here below. And remember us from on high in your holy prayers!'[11]

The note was slipped into the coffin by Sister Akulina, one of Father Gregory's admirers and his sometime mistress, who laid the body out, with the aid of a hospital orderly, after the autopsy was performed. Alix did not see the corpse. It was not important. The body was only a hollow shell, something he had laid aside. But she gave orders that no one else was to see the body, besides Sister Akulina, the orderly, and the officials who performed the autopsy. None of Father Gregory's relatives, nor any of his many followers, were allowed to pay their respects before the coffin was closed.

The simple funeral, held early in the morning at the graveside, was brief. Alix had chosen the site, on land where Anna Vyrubov planned to build a church, for its accessibility to the palace and because it was easy to guard. Desecration of Father Gregory's body was likely; the secret police were ordered to spread false rumours that it had been taken by train to his Siberian village or to a monastery in the Ural Mountains.

It was a bitter morning, the morning of January 3, 1917. Frost rimed the grass in the palace park, fog swirled around the trees and obscured the ice-covered lake. Alix, Nicky (who had returned from Mogilev the day before) and the children arrived by car and walked to the grave, looking down on the coffin, which had already been lowered into the earth. No choir sang, only a priest from the cathedral. The imperial confessor and a monk from Anna Vyrubov's infirmary said the prayers and celebrated the requiem mass.

All was done in quietness, in haste. Secret police kept watch from a distance, ready to rush in should any disturbance arise. They were prepared for anything – a coup, an assassination attempt, an effort to kidnap the tsar and his immediate family. For it was now certain that Father Gregory's murder had been a family undertaking, and the tsar's relations formed a united bloc in asking, indeed demanding, that he show leniency in his treatment of the two young men upon whom suspicion fell.

A fresh wave of threatening letters had been arriving at the palace in the aftermath of the murder. Alix had received many.[12] No one in the immediate family was safe.

The funeral passed without incident, and the tsar, having noted in his diary that the family had seen the coffin 'with the body of unforgettable Grigory, who was killed by some scum', went for a walk with the children.

Alix had her obligations, and busied herself fulfilling them. There were the servants' Christmas trees to decorate, gifts to prepare for the staff and for the wounded in her hospitals. Activity was a palliative for grief. She worked on, until interrupted by Protopopov, who came to inform her of yet another plot to murder her. She received the information coolly, Sophie Buxhoeveden noticed.[13] She did not flinch, or grow faint, or even turn pale. She took the news in her stride, and then returned to her tasks, outwardly calm but feeling inwardly like an old woman, her grief like a heavy stone weighing down her heart.

29

The news of Rasputin's death loosed an immense wave of popular rejoicing. People shouted aloud for joy, strangers embraced one another in the streets.

'The Nameless One! The Unmentionable! He is dead!' they told one another, clapping and laughing.

It was as irresistible, as unstoppable a force as the spring thaw, this effusion of public jubilation, which went on for days and seemed to ignite a conflagration of excitement.

To the excitement were added other provocations in the early days of the new year 1917 – strikes, demonstrations by hundreds of thousands of protesters, commemorations of Bloody Sunday and a huge rally to greet the opening of the Duma – plus the ever-present incitements of severe cold, lack of food and extremely high prices for what little bread and milk, what few eggs and sausages were available. It was rumoured that prices would double or treble before spring came. Meanwhile many people were existing on soup and mouldy crusts, and shivering in their damp, icy rooms for want of firewood.

When the weather turned milder early in March the numbers of strikers and demonstrators increased, and their daring expanded. Now the Cossacks that patrolled the streets on horseback, whips in hand and sharp sabres hanging from their belts, were cursed and assaulted by volleys of stones. Vocal crowds shouted 'Down with the monarchy!' 'Bread for the Workers!' and, on International Women's Day, March 8, 'Equality for Women!'

There was an exhilarating air of power amid the tumult. Hostile messages written on frozen walls were wiped away, only to reappear again almost immediately, and covering more walls than before. Hostile crowds, threatened by police and armed troops, dispersed only to form again enlarged in size. Workers carrying red flags, singing the 'Marseillaise', the triumphant song of the French revolutionaries of 1789, paraded around squares and along canals, skirmishing with police when the latter attempted to put a halt to their marches. Groups of insurgents overturned cars and smashed the windows of trams. Shop windows were broken, looting began.

On the following day, March 9, it was as if the entire population of Petrograd took to the streets, a vast tide of humanity flooding every avenue, lane and alley. To some two hundred thousand striking workers were added tens of thousands of former soldiers, students, government workers, ordinary citizens from a variety of social ranks. Drawing strength from one another, feeling more forceful the larger their numbers grew, the crowds invaded the bakeries, confronted the police (who backed down) and called out to the soldiers – who, until that evening, were under orders not to fire – to join them.

There was a sense of elation, of relief as more and more people joined the chanting, cheering crowds. Orators harangued the demonstrators, stirring up their fears, their hatred of privilege, above all their sense of empowerment. At last all the corruption, the poor governance, the political puppets could be swept away, the speakers shouted. The people had only to seize power – it was within their grasp.

And indeed it seemed to be within their grasp, as on March 11 anarchy was unleashed in the city. Warnings had been posted by the military commander General Khabalov that demonstrators would be fired upon, but the warning posters were torn down and trampled underfoot as, once again, people poured into the streets and squares, forming living tides that ebbed and flowed around buildings and monuments. From every section of the capital they surged towards the centre of the city, ignoring the guards stationed on the bridges and the armed troops brought in to replace the ineffectual police. Though the secret police had been out in force before dawn, arresting hundreds of the previous day's insurgents, the arrests seemed to have no effect, for the crowds were even more dense, more determined to bring all business to a halt in Petrograd.

Gunfire could be heard throughout the day, the steady sputter of machine guns, bursts of rifle fire and the crack of pistols. Along the margins of the crowds, men ran here and there, rifles strapped to their backs, swords at their waists. Small groups of soldiers, police, ordinary citizens armed with revolvers or grenades encountered one another, skirmished, and ran off, leaving bleeding bodies on the paving-stones.

Troops fired on demonstrators in Znamenskaya Square, and along Nevsky Prospekt. Units of the Preobrazhensky regiment mowed down many in the crowd that had gathered near Kazan Cathedral, leaving hundreds dead and dying in the square.

But still the crowds did not disperse; the momentum that had brought people out in such numbers did not dissipate, but rather seemed to grow. The sun shone brightly down, the air was cool and brisk but not harsh. And as they milled in the streets and kept watch from their windows, the citizens of Petrograd observed that something remarkable was beginning to happen.

Soldiers and police began firing on each other.

In the Pavlovsky regiment, soldiers turned against their officers and, refusing to fire on the insurgents, joined with them. In the Preobrazhensky regiment, men shot their own officers rather than obey orders and shoot more civilians. Other regiments joined the trend, fearing to become the targets of the rebellious soldiery. What had begun as an intermittent clash between demonstrators and the military became an ongoing battle between renegade soldiers and the dwindling number of police units that remained loyal to the titular authorities.

Word swept through the city: there was mutiny in the forces of the tsar! There was no longer anything to fear; the military was on the side of the citizens.

Now the police came under attack, individual officers murdered, thrown onto the river ice, shot down as they tried to reach safety – even burned alive on bonfires while jubilant crowds collected to watch.

Seizing the initiative, on the following day, March 12, workers and soldiers captured the Military Arsenal and looted it, arming themselves for further acts of daring. They burst into the Central Office of the secret police and ransacked it, burned the Law Courts with their records of property and privilege, and broke into the city's largest prisons, setting all the prisoners free. Finally the soldiers manning the capital's principal bastion, the Fortress of Peter and Paul, yielded to the superior armed force of the revolutionaries – for that is what they had become – and gave up their arms.

It was over, or nearly over. A few troops continued to defend the Winter Palace and the Admiralty against the victorious insurgents, a few more fired down into the crowds from isolated rooftops. But long before midnight, the city was in rebel hands.

The noise and confusion went on all night, sounds of gunfire and shouting, cars and trucks roaring up and down the street, as here and there a skirmish broke out or a band of soldiers, drunk on wine and victory, slouched along the broad quays. When the sun rose the next morning, March 13, Petrograd no longer belonged to the tsar.

Rodzianko, president of the Duma, sent a telegram to Nicky: 'Situation grave. Anarchy in capital. Government paralyzed. Transport . . . has reached complete breakdown. Public discontent growing. Disorderly shooting occurring on the streets. Military units are firing on each other. Vital to call on a figure trusted by the country to form a new government. No time to lose. Any delay is as good as death. I pray God that in this hour the blame will not fall on him who wears the crown.'[1]

But the tsar, contemptuous of Rodzianko and assured by his commanders in Mogilev that the Duma president was exaggerating the crisis, ignored the telegram and did not send a reply. He did, however, dissolve the Duma, leaving the country without any governing authority save his own – backed by those troops that remained loyal to him.

The gravity of the situation eluded him, but to others it was only too clear. In the space of a few days, the imperial government, faced with an unprecedented upwelling of popular resistance, had all but melted away.

Fourteen battalions of the guard, seven thousand police and mounted Cossacks, several hundred thousand armed troops stationed in the city and just outside it: of these defenders, only a token force remained. And the capital had fallen.[2]

Word had reached the Alexander Palace at nine o'clock on the morning of March 12 that the regiments had mutinied. Sophie Buxhoeveden, the empress's lady-in-waiting, took the message to her mistress, who was still in bed.

'I told her everything,' Sophie wrote. 'She listened with perfect self-possession, only remarking that, if the troops had mutinied, "it was all up."'

While she dressed Alix sent for the Acting Commander of the Palace guard, who assured her that the garrison in Tsarskoe Selo was still loyal and would defend the palace should revolutionaries from Petrograd attack it. As for the situation in the capital, more troops were being sent in. The rebellion would soon be crushed.[3]

All that day, Alix did what she could to preserve order among the staff and discourage panic. All the children but Marie were ill with severe measles, and she was preoccupied with nursing them, keeping vigil by their bedsides. Their fevers were rising – Alexei had a fever of 104 degrees – and complications had begun to set in, with Tatiana developing abscesses in her ears and Olga showing symptoms of pericarditis.[4]

Preoccupied as she was with worry about Alexei and her daughters, and expecting Nicky to return the following day from Mogilev, Alix could not at first spare much energy for confronting the crisis in Petrograd.

'In the palace we had lulled ourselves into believing that no serious rising would take place during the war,' Sophie Buxhoeveden recalled in her memoirs. No matter how grave discontent might grow, no matter what political extreme might be reached, Russians would be loyal and patriotic, as long as there was a threat from a foreign enemy to be faced.

And the strength of the alliance against the German enemy had only recently been demonstrated, at least formally, when Alix received the members of the diplomatic corps at the palace. For two days, while rioters (she called them 'hooligans') were marching through the streets of Petrograd, she had greeted all the ministers and secretaries of foreign missions who had never before met her in person, holding out her hand to be kissed as each elaborately uniformed dignitary approached in turn.[5] It was a spectacle reminiscent of her grandmother's court, a parade of supernumeraries worthy of an Italian opera – elaborately costumed masters of ceremonies, lackeys in tall hats with sweeping plumes, liveried servants gleaming with gold lace, velvet knee-breeches and buckled shoes.

The receptions symbolized stability and order. Yet, less than forty-eight hours later, it was clear that disorder was in the ascendant, and stability had become an illusion.

On the morning of March 13, Alix called her lady-in-waiting and told her to quietly pack her bags, taking as little as possible to avoid alarming the other servants. It might be necessary for the family to leave the palace at short notice, and Alix wanted Sophie to be ready to go with them.

The Grand Marshal of the court, the elderly Count Paul Benckendorff, and the acting guard commander Grooten had been discussing whether or not the empress and her children ought to leave Tsarskoe Selo for a safer place. Alix was against it, both because the children were so unwell and because for her to flee the palace would look like cowardice. But the question seemed to be academic, at least for the moment; it was doubtful whether the imperial train would be allowed to come to Tsarskoe Selo, and the train lines were sure to be in rebel hands.

But if they could not leave by train, some other way out might have to be found. Knowing this, Alix passed on the caution to Sophie, and quietly began to collect a few things of her own, relying on Lili Dehn to take over the task of nursing the children.

'She could scarcely master her anxiety,' Sophie wrote, remembering her mistress's state of mind that morning. Nicky had not come

from Mogilev as promised. Alix had sent telegrams to him there, but
had received no reply – an ominous sign, for in the past he had always
replied quickly. Perhaps the revolutionaries had seized him, or were
besieging the army headquarters. Count Apraxin, newly arrived from
Petrograd, brought word that no relieving force had reached the
city, and that the government, such as it was, had taken refuge in the
Admiralty, protected by a tiny force of loyal troops. The Duma had
taken over – illegally, as the tsar had disbanded it – and was attempting
to run the country.

Among the palace servants, trepidation began to spread. Many left.
Though none dared say it aloud, everyone whispered that the
Alexander Palace would be the next likely target of attack by the
revolutionaries. If they could capture the heir to the throne they would
strengthen their position many times over. And if they could capture
the empress, that hated symbol of moral evil and corruption, they
could take vengeance on her as Grand Duke Dimitri and Felix Yusupov
had taken vengeance on Rasputin, endearing themselves to all Russia.

Shortly after midday on March 13, water ceased to flow from the
taps in the palace. The rebels had cut off the water supply. Soon the
electricity too was cut off. Candles and lanterns were collected, and
water brought from the lake, but the lack of electricity and pure water
caused the remaining servants to became even more fearful. What if
all food supplies were cut off as well? Would they be left to starve?

There were more desertions towards evening, more of the household staff melting away into the village or disappearing into the palace
park. Then, at about eight in the evening, thousands of soldiers of
the Tsarskoe Selo garrison left their barracks and began a mini-
revolution of their own.[6] They fired their rifles into the air and shot
out windows in nearby houses. Storming the small prison, they
liberated the inmates and, smashing the windows of wine shops,
drank their fill before starting to make their way slowly towards the
palace.

That their mood was murderous no one doubted. At the very
least, if the most rational among them succeeded in restraining the
most violent, the empress and Alexei would be kidnapped and taken

to Petrograd where they would be imprisoned. But to judge from the shouted threats of the men and their continual rifle fire, their wild bawling of revolutionary songs and their obscene name-calling, rational voices were not likely to prevail. Made brutal by drink and with no one in authority to restrain them, the soldiers seemed likely to overwhelm the palace defenders, kill the empress and rape her daughters in an orgy of bloodshed and looting.

The palace guard proved loyal. Assembling in the wide courtyard of the palace were three battalions of guardsmen, two squadrons of Cossacks, a company of railway soldiers and a single heavy field battery, its guns pointing outwards into the empty blackness beyond the tall iron gates.

The defenders knelt in a long line in the snow, another line standing behind them, reserves in the rear. There was no moon, only the faint glow thrown up by the snow and the looming whiteness of the palace itself, its windows flickering yellow with candlelight. The temperature had dropped sharply; the men's breath froze in the air as they waited for the mutineers to come closer.

Though the strain on her heart was great, Alix had managed, with the aid of Lili Dehn, who pushed her from behind, to climb the stairs to the second floor of the palace where the children's sickrooms were. It was there that she was informed of the mutiny of the garrison.

When the initial shock had passed, she went to Olga, Tatiana, Anastasia and Alexei and told each of them, keeping her voice as calm as she could, that there would soon be firing very close to the palace and that they were not to be frightened; the guard would protect them. This done, and without changing out of her white nurse's uniform, she threw a black cloak over her gown and went out into the courtyard, accompanied by Count Benckendorff and her daughter Marie.

Alix knew, and the soldiers knew as well, that they were in the minority. Fidelity to the tsar was diminishing; the men were under pressure to join the revolutionaries. They and their families might well suffer severe punishment for what they now did in defending the palace and its occupants.

Still, Alix trusted in their constancy, and she told them so, walking up and down the long defensive lines with Marie beside her. She trusted in their devotion to the tsar, she said. She knew that they would not hesitate to defend the tsarevich. She hoped that they would not have to fire their weapons, that a show of force would be enough to turn back the mutineers.

Meanwhile the disloyal troops of the garrison were coming through the palace parks, weaving in and out among the statuary and pergolas, the grottoes and antique pavilions that ornamented the gardens. They churned the snow to slush, flattened the bushes and kept up their bursts of gunfire.

But, having spent themselves in mayhem, they were beginning to falter. It was after midnight, too dark for them to see across the broad lawns, formal gardens and lakes that separated them from the Alexander Palace, but they had heard that the palace courtyard was full of soldiers, in numbers greater than their own, and that there were gunners on the roof waiting to mow them down as soon as they came within range. Having come as far as the cluster of houses and pavilions known as the Chinese Village, they halted; they would wait until morning before deciding whether or not to proceed.

They had decided to wait, but no one in the Alexander Palace knew this, and the soldiers, staff and family spent the entirety of that long, bitterly cold night expecting an assault. Believing the empress to be the principal target, the few remaining household members slept on sofas outside her bedroom, along with two of the tsar's aides who had managed, despite considerable danger and mostly on foot, to make their way to Tsarskoe Selo from Petrograd.

Alix herself hardly slept that night, shuttling between the sickrooms and the sitting room, her footsteps echoing in the empty dark rooms in between. The palace felt all but deserted, save for the soldiers who came and went from the guardroom and the few remaining gentlemen of the staff who patrolled the corridors.

At last morning came, and the threat of immediate assault abated. The mutinous troops from the Tsarskoe Selo garrison were no longer poised to attack the palace; instead they joined with revolutionary forces from Petrograd which had been brought in by train during the night in great numbers. Now a much enlarged body of troops siding with the revolutionaries surrounded the palace, held in check for the time being but able, at any time, to overwhelm its defenders.

That day and the next, March 14 and 15, no one within the Alexander Palace knew what to expect. Fragments of news, much of it unreliable, reached them but there was still no word from Nicky, and Alix's worry about him increased.

She continued to nurse her children, who were growing more and more ill. Tatiana could not hear at all out of her abscessed ears, Anastasia too was developing abscesses and Marie, who had come down with double pneumonia, had such a high fever that Dr Botkin thought she might die.[7]

Alix smoked, prayed, looked after her sick daughters and son, and now and then snatched an hour or two of sleep. Her face took on a haggard look; she could no longer disguise her weariness.

Day by day, her worries were expanding. Her husband's silence (Was he safe? Had he been imprisoned or even killed by the revolutionaries?), her children's increasing debility, with Marie desperately, perhaps fatally ill, the capital in rebel hands and the government in complete disarray, her own life under threat: she was close to complete exhaustion.

Then, on March 16, came the most shocking news of all.

Leaflets distributed in Petrograd and brought to Tsarskoe Selo by the few servants who returned to their posts announced the abdication of the tsar.

He had signed the instrument of abdication at Pskov, while aboard the imperial train, the leaflets said. He was tsar no longer.

When Count Benckendorff came to Alix to confirm this painful news, she could not at first believe it. 'She could not imagine he had taken such a step so hurriedly,' the count wrote, 'especially since he knew Alexei was so ill.'

But Alexei's illness no longer mattered, dynastically, for the tsar had abdicated not only on behalf of himself but on behalf of his son. He had given up the throne so that his brother Michael could rule, and so that Russia, governed by a firmer hand, could rally and win the war.

But the swift rush of events had not ended there. When Michael was told of his brother's abdication, and informed that he was now tsar, he was deeply troubled. His accession had been brought about under duress; it was the revolutionaries, and not his subjects, who had made him tsar. He saw the virtue of serving as a figurehead, a force for stability. Yet if the people did not want him – and the people, at least those in the capital, seemed to be against the monarchy – then his accession might lead to renewed violence, increased instability. He and other family members might well be killed. He decided to abdicate in his turn.[8]

Three hundred years of Romanov rule had come to an end. Loyalties maintained over centuries now had no clearly defined focus. Though often criticized and belittled, the tsar had been loved. He had been, to a degree realized only after his abdication, a sacred figure, venerated not so much for himself but for the tradition, the patriotic feelings, of which he was the natural focus. And now the throne was empty.

Officers of the palace guard wept openly as the news of the abdication spread. 'Consternation was general,' Count Benckendorff wrote.[9] The tsar had been their anchor. Protecting him and his family had been their mission in life. Knowing that he was now just an ordinary man, at the head of an ordinary family, they felt lost, adrift, and inconsolably sad.

Members of the household came forwards to assure Alix that, even though she was no longer empress, they were and would remain loyal to her.

They found her in her daughters' schoolroom, where she had taken refuge in solitude. 'She was deadly pale and supported herself with one hand on the schoolroom table.' When Sophie came up to her, the two women embraced, Sophie 'murmuring some broken words of affection', Alix kissing her lady-in-waiting. Count Benckendorff took Alix's hand, 'tears running down his usually immobile face'.

'It is for the best,' Alix said, speaking in French for Benckendorff's benefit. 'It is God's will. May God grant that this saves Russia. That's all that matters.'[10]

The marshal and the lady-in-waiting left her there in the schoolroom, collapsing into a chair, crying and covering her face with her hands.

Like the soldiers of the guard, she too was adrift. The purpose that had sustained her during the war years, to serve as her husband's prop and support in the work of ruling, to bolster his will with hers, had fallen away. She had given her all to the enormous task of being his strength: her failing health, what remained of her vigour, her staunch faith. Now that task was at an end.

The task, the ruler, the throne itself had been swept away, swiftly and finally, and an important part of her had been swept away with them, leaving only confusion, bewilderment and a crushing sense of loss.

30

The provisional government, created by the Duma deputies who continued to meet, though the Duma itself had been dissolved, was now the ruling authority in Russia – ruling by virtue of its own self-declared sovereignty, in the absence of a tsar.

Under the presidency of Prince Lvov, who also took on the duties of Interior Minister, the new council established itself, with the liberal deputy Alexander Guchkov (Alix's bête noire) becoming Minister of War, Paul Miliukov, leader of the moderate Cadet (Constitutional Democratic) party becoming Minister of Foreign Affairs, M. I. Tereshchenko Minister of Finance and the fiery young lawyer Alexander Kerensky Minister of Justice. These specific titles and responsibilities were due to prove fluid, changing suddenly and often in the coming months, and the Provisional Government was to prove fragile.

Not so the other leading political body formed in the immediate aftermath of the tsar's abdication: the Petrograd Soviet of Workers and Soldiers Deputies. The Soviet, composed of union leaders, leading figures from the leftist parties and intellectuals who had long been opposed to imperial rule, met in the Tauride Palace where the Duma also sat, and were led by an Executive Committee which had no official role.

The Soviet functioned as a second governing body, its views much more radical than those of the various Duma delegates, its influence strong yet its precise relationship to the Duma ill-defined – and evolving. But since everyone expected that the current political arrangements were only temporary, to be in force only until elections to a Constituent Assembly could be held, the imprecise nature of the Soviet's position was tolerated.

Everywhere committees sprang up, township committees, factory committees, committees of soldiers and workers. The thirst for democratization, for abandonment of all hierarchies of authority, spread quickly, and with it came a thirst for revenge against the rulers, the owners, the bosses, anyone who had held authority in the past. The rights of each individual, and of the people collectively, were exalted above all; any title or office or institution that appeared to diminish those rights was challenged, and threatened with destruction.

Such was the mood in the capital where, in response to news of the tsar's abdication, another wave of violent upheaval had begun to build up. Police were shot and ambushed, police stations burned, along with the law courts with all their records. Mansions were looted and set on fire. Prisoners had been liberated from the jails, and they roved through the city, taking vengeance, along with throngs of soldiers who had thrown off their allegiance to their officers and milled about in a disorderly way, answerable to no one and spoiling for a fight. It was unclear whether the Provisional Government would be able to restore order.

Nearly all of the telephones at the Alexander Palace at Tsarskoe Selo had been cut off, but the private line to the Winter Palace in Petrograd still functioned and, by means of this private line, word came that the capital was in chaos, and that the chaos was spreading.

Meanwhile at Tsarskoe Selo the members of the Palace Guard, dejected after hearing that the tsar had abdicated, obeyed the orders they received to return to Petrograd.[1] The palace was defenceless, and Petrograd, with its tens of thousands of striking labourers, roaming soldiers and liberated convicts, was only a few miles away.

No one in the palace slept, Sophie Buxhoeveden wrote, remembering the first days following the abdication. Meals were forgotten, routines abandoned. The temperature was well below freezing, and the soldiers had used up nearly all the firewood. Supplies of food were very low as well. Alix continued to watch over her daughters and son, wearing her white nurse's uniform over her black gown, staying occupied.

On March 18, late at night, a cordon of trucks pulled up in front of the locked gates of the palace, and a large contingent of men spilled out. Alexander Guchkov, the new Minister of War, along with General Kornilov had arrived with his escort. 'His thugs were everywhere,' Sophie wrote, 'abusing the servants for working for the oppressors and reviling the "bloodsuckers" who were members of the imperial suite.'

Alix sent a hasty message to Grand Duke Paul, asking him to come to the palace to be with her when she met the envoys of the Provisional Government. With Paul beside her she received the minister and the general, not knowing what they might want of her, or indeed whether they had come to take her away. She had, finally, after days of uncertainty, received a phone call from Nicky; she knew that he was still alive. But she could not be sure that he was safe.

It was nearly midnight when Guchkov and Kornilov were ushered into a room where Alix waited. They asked her whether she had everything she wanted. She said that, as far as she and the children were concerned, she needed nothing more for the moment, but asked that her military hospitals be maintained and supplied. Guchkov put a contingent of soldiers in place as guards, with an officer who was to serve as a go-between to keep him informed of conditions at the palace. It was to be a temporary arrangement, he said. Nothing permanent had yet been decided.

The discussion was brief. Guchkov and Kornilov left, without arresting Alix or mentioning anything about her future or Nicky's. But the rough, foul-mouthed revolutionary soldiers stayed behind, keeping up their shower of abuse and acting, Sophie thought, less like guards and protectors than jailers.

All the palace doors were locked and sealed up. Apart from representatives of the new government, no one was allowed in or out except through a door in the kitchen, where a soldier stood guard. A very limited number of deliveries were allowed. Only one phone, in the orderly room, was kept operational, and when anyone spoke on that line, they had to speak in Russian – no English or French – and with an officer and soldier listening in.

Kornilov told Alix and Marshal Benckendorff that these measures were essential, for the time being, but that soon the former tsar would arrive and the entire family would be sent by special train to Murmansk, where they would board a ship for England.

The Provisional Government was in fact negotiating with the British government to allow the tsar and his family to emigrate. Foreign Minister Miliukov had sent a message to the British Prime Minister Lloyd George asking for asylum on behalf of the Romanovs and, despite the prime minister's initial reluctance, they had come to an agreement.

It was with this expectation in her mind that Alix met with General Kornilov again on March 21.[2] She was waiting for him in the green drawing room, wearing her white apron with its red cross, the starkness of her simple uniform incongruous against the backdrop of the enormous, elegantly appointed room with its gilded walls and ornate carved chairs and sofas, costly pictures and objets d'art.

The general delivered his message. He had come, he said, to put her, Alexandra Romanov, officially under arrest, by order of the Provisional Government. The former tsar had also been arrested, at Mogilev, having returned there following his abdication.

Alix, calm and gracious, told the general that she was glad he had been the one to arrest her, since he knew what it felt like to be a prisoner, having himself been a prisoner of war in Austria. She knew he could empathize with her situation.

Her manner was no longer grand or distant, but she had acquired, Count Benckendorff thought, a wonderful dignity. The count watched as she carried on her dialogue with Kornilov, asking nothing for herself, only that her hospitals and ambulance trains be maintained, so that no matter what happened to her the wounded would continue to be looked after. She asked that the servants in the nursery might be permitted to stay on, for the girls and Alexei were still recovering.

She asked for leniency. 'I am only a mother looking after my sick children,' she told Kornilov.

He responded that the servants and staff would be allowed to remain, but those who did would be arrested; all who wanted to avoid arrest would have to leave the palace. Among those who made the decision to stay were Marshal Benckendorff and his wife, the wardrobe mistress Madame Narishkin, Alix's reader and companion Mademoiselle Schneider, who had been with her since the early days of her engagement, Alexei's tutor Pierre Gilliard, and the two ladies-in-waiting Sophie Buxhoeveden and Anastasia Henrikov.

Kornilov stressed that the arrests were only 'a precautionary measure', and that soon the family would be in Murmansk, on their way to a new life in England. And, as Alix knew, there was plenty of money to fund that new life. Her husband had nearly half a million roubles in cash, plus nearly two million roubles in securities, not counting the value of all his estates and palaces with their valuable furnishings. Alix herself owned a priceless jewellery collection. In exile, their every need would be supplied.

Benckendorff advised Alix to begin packing, and the servants began filling trunks and suitcases. But Alix was very reluctant to leave, not only because the children were still recuperating but because, as she told Sophie Buxhoeveden, 'it was such a nightmare to her that she prayed daily against it'. If they had to be 'dragged' out of Russia, she said, she preferred not to go to England, but to Norway, which had a climate that would suit Alexei, and where the family could live quietly and not be subjected to the stares of the curious.[3] Nicky could be a farmer – his lifelong dream – and she could live the retired life she had always craved.[4]

There were other possibilities. Grand Duke Paul offered his house at Boulogne. Minnie's relatives in Denmark would probably take the family in. After the war was over, Alix's brother Ernie would be certain to make the Romanovs welcome, or her sister Irene. There were also relatives in Greece.

But she did not want to go, not even when Madame Narishkin came to her with a very practical plan. Alix and Nicky should go on ahead to England, as quickly as possible, the wardrobe mistress advised. She and Count Benckendorff would look after the children.

When they were completely well, the count and Sophie would bring them to England, or to wherever the parents had gone.

Preparations for departure were being made, but in actuality the door to emigration was rapidly closing. Unknown to Alix or Nicky, the Soviet of Workers and Soldiers Deputies was determined not to let the former tsar leave Russia. In their view, his tyranny, his years of heartless exploitation of the poor, his harsh economic policies and personal greed all deserved punishment. Memories of the Khodynka massacre, of the millions of Russian deaths from famine and disease for which the policies of the tsar's ministers were blamed, of the tens of millions of war dead were evoked to justify bringing the man now known simply as Nicholas Romanov to justice. Besides, if he were allowed to go into exile, he would be certain to raise a foreign army and return to crush the revolution. He was very rich, after all, and had powerful relatives. Once he was allowed outside Russia, he would pose an immense threat.

The Soviet sent a large group of soldiers armed with machine guns to the Alexander Palace on March 22 to take the former emperor prisoner and bring him back to Petrograd to be confined in the Peter and Paul Fortress until his inevitable execution. They came up against the guardsmen supplied by the Provisional Government, who had orders to keep watch over the Romanov prisoners in the palace, and had not been told to release any of them. To prevent a clash, the Soviet contingent agreed not to take the former tsar away, but they became belligerent, waving their guns and bullying the other company of guards.[5] They refused to leave until they were shown the security arrangements within the palace, and shown Nicky himself, who was forced to walk past them all, a prisoner on parade.

To make certain there were no dangerous emigrations within the Romanov family, the soviet ordered the railroad workers to prevent any train from reaching Murmansk. It was a needless gesture for, despite General Kornilov's assurances to Alix, no British cruiser was waiting at Murmansk to provide a way of escape. The British government had changed its position, on orders from George V. The Romanovs were not to be allowed to enter England, lest their presence trigger a leftist rising there.[6] The goodwill of Nicky's and Alix's cousin King George did not extend to granting them asylum. 'It would not be reasonable,' he told Foreign Minister Miliukov, 'for the imperial family to be settled in our country.'

Neither Alix nor Nicky knew of this decision, nor were they told of the similar conclusion reached by the government of Denmark. They continued to believe that, before long, arrangements would be made under which they would leave Russia – or that they would be sent to Livadia for a long stay.[7]

In the meantime, they were prisoners, their every move watched, their every conversation overheard. Their lives had ceased to be their own.

Slowly a routine evolved. Alix and Nicky took their meals with their children, and spent most of the day in their rooms, except for the daily walk Nicky was allowed to take for half an hour with his aide-de-camp Prince Dolgorukov. While the soldiers stood by, rifles at the ready and with fixed bayonets, he and the prince shovelled snow. Alix too went out, but in her wheelchair. She had not been able to take walks in a long time, though she could still move very quickly if she had to; her elderly page Wolkov told Sophie Buxhoeveden that when Nicky's first phone call came through following the abdication, Alix 'ran down the stairs like a girl' to answer it.[8] She spent time with the children, worked at her sewing or knitting, said her prayers, and read the many letters that came to the palace – each one having already been opened and read by an officer.

In the evening Alix and Nicky went to sit by Anna Vyrubov's bedside. Relations between Anna and Alix had been strained for several years, but long habit and an underlying affection still bound them together, and Alix still felt loyal to Anna and responsible for her, all the more so since her crippling accident. Alix had moved her friend out of her house in Tsarskoe Selo and into the palace after the soldiers, who hated Anna for her years of association with Rasputin, had threatened her life.

'Those evenings were unspeakably sad,' Sophie thought. 'The empress [so Sophie continued to call her] was growing thinner and thinner, and was terribly aged in appearance. She sat almost in silence.'⁹ There was nothing to talk about; every topic raised painful emotions. And besides, they couldn't speak freely. The guards were listening.

They said little, sitting there beside Anna's bed, but each could imagine the others' thoughts: of the war, and how the Russian armies were faring, of the wounded in the hospital nearby, of the stories brought from Petrograd of soldiers murdering their officers and of the noisy clamour of the palace guardsmen demanding that Nicky be tried and sent to Kronstadt to await execution.

Alix confided to Sophie that one thought often preoccupied her. If, as she believed, the Russian people were still faithful to the tsar, then how long would it be before they rose up and overthrew the Provisional Government and the Soviet, demanding his return to power? And when would foreign rulers take action against the revolution, as they had against the revolutionaries in France in the time of Louis XVI? She waited for the revolution to falter, for the counter-revolution to begin. She trusted in a 'sudden miraculous change' that would sweep away the nightmare of the abdication and its aftermath, and restore her husband to the throne.¹⁰

She took heart from the few letters of consolation and encouragement she received. When an unknown lady sent Nicky a small icon, along with a prayer, Alix was 'cheerful for a whole day'. The handful of letters that came from friends were cherished, and a warm letter from Nicky's sister Xenia – the only letter from a family member that the soldiers did not confiscate – was comforting, as were the phone calls from Petrograd with messages of sympathy, and the flowers and notes sent to Alix by Queen Olga of Greece.¹¹

But for every comforting letter there were hundreds of insulting ones, accusing Nicky of treason, accusing Alix of everything from adultery to cruelty to sacrilege and crimes against nature. The hatred in these venomous letters was extreme, the appetite for revenge chilling. Alix had not suspected that such deep reservoirs of hatred existed, and she was very troubled by the letters.¹²

Each day Alix had further searing proof of the current upwelling of resentment and contempt. The soldiers who guarded her, loud, ill-mannered, rowdy, truculent men, openly and incessantly hostile, harassed her and tried to unnerve her by telling coarse jokes in her presence and blowing the smoke from their cigarettes in her face.[13] They singled her out as the special focus of their animosity, calling her 'the tyrant's wife' and scrawling obscene graffiti on walls and on the benches in the garden where she would be certain to see them. They called out rude insults when she passed in her wheelchair, and threatened the servant who pushed the chair, swearing to kill him if he continued to serve his vile mistress.

From morning to night, Alix was under siege from her jailers. When she dressed in the morning, a sentry was watching through the window; to preserve what modesty she could, she put on her clothes in a corner of the room, facing the wall, still in full view of him. When she went to mass, soldiers stood behind the altar screen, observing her. When she walked along the palace corridors, the guards shouted out rude greetings or snickered. She could never count on being alone, not in her private sitting room, her bedroom, even her bathroom. For the soldiers roamed at will through the palace, bursting into any room they liked, on any pretext, knocking over tables and lounging on sofas in their dirty boots, shouting to one another and haranguing the servants. At night she went to sleep with the sound of their raucous noise in her ears, knowing that even her sleep would be watched.

The constant malevolence of the guards wore Alix down, as did their petty meanness to her husband and children. Shouts of 'Tyrant!' or 'Traitor!' met Nicky wherever he went (along with a few murmurs of 'Good day, Colonel'). Though he tried to ignore the insults, he could not ignore outright attacks, as when, riding on his bicycle in the park, a soldier stuck his bayonet through the spokes, making the bicycle swerve dangerously and nearly causing an accident. Such incidents, and the loud laughter of the soldiers who were looking on, were maddeningly provocative.[14]

But it was the soldiers' treatment of her daughters that angered Alix most. She had kept them sheltered, away from men. They had worked as nurses among soldiers, and had flirted with the officers of the imperial yacht, but the men had always been polite. The girls had never been subjected to anything like the barrage of leering, suggestive comments they now heard every hour. Their innocence was outraged by the sight of the soldiers, stripping naked to bathe in the ice-cold ponds, knowing that they would be seen by the girls and anticipating their well-bred confusion.

Alix was angry, watching such incidents, but she was more fearful than angry, for there was always the chance that the lurid remarks, the sly looks and smirks might lead to kisses or rough fondling, and ultimately to rape. The girls' very innocence was a provocation to men bent on revenge, men whose edgy meanness was barely kept contained by their officers. Often the guards were bored and restless: they marched around in groups, singing the 'Marseillaise', they picked fights with the palace servants, they shot the tame deer and swans in the palace park for target practice. Their pent-up aggression could not be controlled forever and, as the weeks passed, it seemed to be getting stronger.

Late one afternoon Alix was in the garden, sitting in her wheelchair under a tree, doing needlework. A soldier, a deputy from the Soviet, came and sat in a chair close beside her. Sophie Buxhoeveden, who was nearby, began to protest – for none of the soldiers had come so close to Alix before – but Alix gestured to Sophie to be silent, fearing that the slightest fuss could provoke the guards to order the entire family back indoors, and the girls and Alexei were enjoying their brief hour of fresh air.[15] Sophie went off to find an officer.

Alix began to engage the soldier in conversation. He took the opportunity to accuse her, boldly and directly, of despising the Russian people. The fact that she had not travelled widely in her adopted country (which was in fact untrue) proved that she hated the Russians, he said, and that she cared nothing about getting to know the country.

Without allowing her questioner to provoke her to contradiction, Alix calmly explained that there were reasons why she had not travelled more. In her youth she had had to look after her five children, each of whom she had nursed personally, and this had limited her ability to travel. Later on, her health had been too poor to allow her to make many journeys.

As he listened to her, the deputy became less accusatory. He began asking her about her life, her children, her attitudes. He was particularly interested in knowing her attitude towards Germany, since it was so widely believed that her sympathies were all with the Germans. She told him, speaking simply and straightforwardly, that although she had been raised in Darmstadt among Germans, and was a German herself by birth, whatever feelings she had once had belonged to the distant past. The people she loved best, her husband and her children, were Russians, and she had become a Russian too, 'with all her heart'.

The conversation went on, eventually turning from politics to religion. At this point Sophie returned, having found an officer and bringing him with her. The deputy rose as they came nearer and took Alix's hand, saying, 'Do you know, Alexandra Feodorovna, I had quite a different idea of you? I was mistaken about you.'

From then on, he was polite – no matter what his fellow guards said or did.

But one man's politeness was an oasis of civility in a waste of vulgar taunting and overt hostility. She had won over one man, yet there were a hundred who detested her and menaced her and her family. Meanwhile she heard nothing further about the family's being sent out of Russia to safety. No one brought news, official or otherwise, from Petrograd. There were only whispers and rumours, nearly all of them alarming, and more guards being brought to watch their every move.

Kornilov had told her that the present arrangements were only temporary. But as the weeks passed and the first green of spring appeared in the park, she began to wonder if that were true. When would they receive their orders to leave? Would they ever again find themselves among family and friends, free of surveillance and deprivation? When would the sudden miraculous change come about, the providential transformation that would bring their deliverance?

31

Family photographs from an album of Anastasia's, taken in the spring and summer of 1917, show not a harsh captivity but a rustic idyll.

Olga and Tatiana stand in the sun in a flower garden, wearing white dresses and white hats. Alexei sits on a stone jetty above the lake, his tutor beside him. Nicky poses beside the broad stump of a tree he has just felled, his arm resting possessively on its raw surface. Alix sits in a wooden chair opposite Nicky, holding a silk parasol, her face shaded by a wide-brimmed straw hat.

Images of summer, of idleness and pleasure.

Yet in actuality the family was far from idle in its captivity. As the spring advanced and the ground thawed, their captors allowed them to spend more hours outdoors, and they used the time to dig an extensive vegetable garden. Everyone but Alix took part, sometimes spending three hours at a time clearing away bushes and rocks, turning the earth with shovels and digging deep straight furrows for the young plants. After weeks of labour, the vegetable patch was finished. In the lengthening daylight the plants took root quickly, and flourished. Beans, turnips, lettuce, squash, cabbage – especially cabbage, five hundred plants – lifted their leaves to the sun and intermittent rain.

And when the garden was finished, they began a second vegetable patch for the servants, everyone joining in, digging enthusiastically 'with great energy and even enjoyment', as Nicky wrote in his journal.[1] Having received permission from the guards, the former emperor devoted himself to felling the dead trees in the park, lopping off the branches and cutting them into lengths for firewood, then loading the chopped wood onto carts to be stored in the palace basement. He threw himself into the work with zest, losing his sallowness and his melancholy and emerging from the wood at the end of the afternoon, pink-cheeked and bright-eyed, a happy man.

Thanks to the family's efforts, there would be plenty of wood for the fire and plenty of food to sustain them in the coming winter – if indeed they were to be in Tsarskoe Selo that long.

Alix watched the exertions of her husband and children from a shaded bench near the lake, looking up from her embroidery to see her son swimming or playing on the 'children's island'. She worried about Alexei. He continued to suffer periodic haemorrhages in his abdomen, his skin turning yellow and his appetite diminishing; when the attacks came she sat beside him, holding his sore legs and saying her prayers.

No doubt she thought often of Father Gregory at such times, how he had always been able not only to alleviate Alexei's pain but to predict the outcome of each attack. Father Gregory had known the future. And he had often said, echoing the words of Christ, 'where I go, you shall go also'. He had known that his fate would be a harbinger of the fate of the Romanovs. He was a martyr; would they be martyred too?

The elderly Mother Maria had called Alix 'the martyr Alexandra'. Was this too prophetic? Or was the martyrdom to be metaphorical, the psychological martyrdom of deprivation, mental suffering, strict captivity?

Crucial to these ruminations was Alix's absorbing interest in the course of political events. By May newspapers were being delivered to Tsarskoe Selo from Petrograd, and Alix and Nicky both read them avidly, well aware that the information they contained was heavily biased and controlled by the Duma yet valuing what news they provided.

It was clear from the papers that the Duma was finding itself enmired in a quicksand of indecision, pressured by an increasingly pacifist public to end the war yet committed to prosecuting it, in conflict with the Soviet over the distribution of land to the peasants (who had begun to seize land on their own), and unable to keep order in Petrograd.

The turmoil that had begun in the winter was increasing, with acts of violence, demonstrations and protests continuing. Meanwhile the German armies were close at hand, and might at any time take advantage of all the tumult to march on Petrograd.

Again and again Alix turned recent events over in her mind, confiding to Sophie Buxhoeveden that in retrospect she realized that before the revolution Nicky, with her encouragement, had trusted the wrong people, ministers who had 'mismanaged affairs'.[2] It had not been this mismanagement that caused the revolution; the revolution had come about, she was convinced, as the result of the strident rhetoric of extremists. But she came to believe that there was another force at work, a powerful historical justice which demanded that her husband be made a scapegoat for all the errors and misjudgments of his imperial predecessors. For three hundred years the Romanov tsars had lived in great wealth and luxury, often ruling heedlessly, without taking sufficient thought for their people. Now a karmic retribution was under way.[3]

But that time of retribution, as she envisioned it, would be relatively brief. When it was over, when the tsar and his family had suffered sufficiently, then the monarchy would be restored, and Alexei would become tsar.

'She was ready to bear everything in order that [Alexei] might come into his inheritance,' Sophie wrote. 'His reign should be glorious; he should institute the reforms for which his parents would slowly prepare.'[4]

Alix was confident of this future triumph, yet in the interim there were more humiliations to be faced.

In the first week of April the Justice Minister Kerensky had come to the Alexander Palace accompanied by an ill-assorted suite of deputies and delegates – 'a mixed and ill-favoured crowd,' Sophie remembered, 'some dressed like well-to-do workmen in black shirts, with sheepskin caps pulled well back on their heads, and some soldiers and sailors, the latter with hand grenades, daggers and revolvers disposed all over their persons.'[5]

The minister was 'abrupt and nervous', Benckendorff thought. With the others at his heels he walked quickly through all the many rooms of the palace, including the basement, talking very loudly and giving orders. He and his entourage searched most of the rooms in the palace thoroughly, looking in every corner, lifting up furniture and looking underneath, opening every drawer and cupboard.[6] When they broke into Anya Vyrubov's rooms, they found her burning her letters and other papers. She was arrested and taken away.

The family waited nervously for the searching to be over. At last Kerensky summoned them into the schoolroom, where he addressed them, calling the former tsar 'Nicholas Alexandrovich' and Alix 'Alexandra Feodorovna'.

'I am the Procurator-General, Kerensky,' he said, shaking hands. 'The queen of England asks for news of the ex-tsarina.'[7]

At the words 'ex-tsarina', Alix's cheeks grew red. She had not been addressed that way before. She told Kerensky that her heart was troubling her as usual.

He explained that he had come to the palace in order to see for himself how the family was living, 'to verify everything', so that he could make his report to his colleagues in Petrograd. 'It will be better for you,' he said. He then took Nicky aside and into another room. The others, waiting, became more nervous, assuming that the Justice Minister was delivering bad news. In fact he was telling Nicky that he still expected to be able to make arrangements for them to leave Russia, though he could not say when.

Before Kerensky left he took his entourage into Alix's apartments, intending to search them, but then thought better of it, and decided not to go in after all. Turning abruptly around and barking orders to the others, he left the palace.

Had the Justice Minister entered Alix's rooms, he would not have found anything he could use to discredit her, for she had burned all her private correspondence except her husband's letters. Her diaries, her letters from her father and her grandmother, Nicky's letters written when they were first engaged, and especially every scrap of writing about Father Gregory: everything had gone into the fire.[8]

Alix knew that in Petrograd it was being said that she was instigating a counter-revolution. Kerensky came again to the palace, this time specifically to question her about any political activities she was suspected of engaging in, and she answered his every question, her precision and straightforwardness impressing him. Kerensky's tone was restrained, not hectoring. Nicky, pacing up and down in the next room, listening for raised voices and fearing that any heated argument would lead to Alix's imprisonment, was greatly relieved when Kerensky emerged and told him, 'Your wife does not lie.'[9]

She had been in great danger, and she knew it. Had Kerensky concluded that she was communicating with outside governments, or with right-wing factions within Russia, he would surely have taken her away to be tried – as many others that spring were being tried – and executed as an enemy of the revolution. Had she faltered in response to his questions, or been evasive, or panicked – as many in her position would have panicked, facing Kerensky's forceful, focused interrogation and high intelligence – she would have been lost. But she came through the ordeal courageously, and survived.

It had been a time of testing. Yet in her own view, the time of testing came, not from the revolutionaries, but from God. 'Once He sent us such trials, evidently He thinks we are sufficiently prepared for it,' she wrote to Lili Dehn. 'It is a sort of examination – it is necessary to prove that we did not go through it in vain. One can find in everything something good and useful.'[10] She continued to believe in 'better times' to come, that 'the bad will pass and there will be clear and cloudless sky'.

Alix's letter to her friend was smuggled out of the palace. No letters were being allowed in, and the guards searched every package that was delivered to make certain it contained nothing written. When Alix's dressmaker sent her a blouse, the officers insisted that the lining be opened at the seam to reveal any hidden message. Chocolates were bitten into to expose their centres, yogurt was stirred with a finger to make sure there were no lumps which might turn out to contain carefully wrapped notes or valuables.

The scrutiny grew more intense as the political situation in Petrograd deteriorated. The arrival in Petrograd in April, 1917, of Vladimir Ilyich Lenin, who for years had led the radical Bolshevik party from exile, aroused fresh conflict for, unlike the moderates in the Provisional Government, Lenin advocated immediate action to end the war, distribute land to the peasants, end food shortages and bring all factories and farms under direct control of the workers and peasants.

Lenin's Bolsheviks were few in number – perhaps twenty thousand in Petrograd and Moscow, and a similar number in the countryside. But their message soon spread. The populace had lost confidence in the Provisional Government, and were weary of the strikes and the constant hunger and the armed clashes in the streets. Lenin seemed to offer a clear and attractive alternative. He was blunt and decisive, his message simple and powerful. 'All Power to the Soviets,' the Bolshevik banners proclaimed. 'Peace, Land and Bread.' The radical-ization of the revolution was under way.

In June and July, 1917, the Bolsheviks continued to advocate an end to the Provisional Government, amid scenes of upheaval and violence. Troops loyal to the government fired on rioting crowds, which gathered to protest against mounting inflation, severe food shortages and the collapse of the army. Kerensky succeeded Lvov as prime minister of a reorganized coalition cabinet, but his hold on authority was tenuous, and the downwards slide into chaos seemed irreversible.

Kerensky came to Tsarskoe Selo in the last week of July and told Nicky that he was in great danger. 'The Bolsheviks are after me,' the prime minister said, 'and then will be after you.'[11] The family was too close to Petrograd, they needed to go far away, where they would be out of reach.

They would go to Livadia, to the warm south. They would live in their beautiful white villa on the cliff, walk in their flower-filled gardens amid the scent of ripening fruit from the orchards nearby. The Bolsheviks had not overrun Livadia. They would be safe there.

But by mid-August all had changed. It would not be Livadia, after all. They would be going east, not south, to a remote town in the Urals, or even further. They were not told exactly where, but were cautioned to take their fur coats. It would be a cold place.

Alix, who had been longing for the warmth and peace of Livadia, was discouraged.[12] With an effort she gathered herself together and began to supervise the packing.

Her wardrobes and chests were full of gowns, splendid satin court gowns, light summer gowns in fine white lawn, the black gowns she had worn since the outbreak of the war. But none of them fitted her any more. She had grown gaunt in the five months since the revolution began. All her dresses hung limply on her thin frame, the long skirts sweeping the ground. She ordered the chambermaids to bundle up most of the gowns, along with her many dozens of hats and pairs of gloves and silk stockings, and sent them – once they had been inspected by the soldiers – to Polish refugees living in the village of Tsarskoe Selo and to friends in need.[13]

So many of the accoutrements of her former life seemed gratuitous now, the cabinets of fine lace that she had so carefully catalogued, the crystal bottles of Atkinson's White Rose perfume and verbena toilet water, the creams that had kept her face smooth, the lotions that had softened her limbs. She needed none of these things, only what was most precious to her: her sapphire cross, the icons and keepsakes she had from Father Gregory, mementos of her father, her brother and sisters and of Sonia Orbeliani, the pictures of Windsor from her childhood, the grey dress she had worn the day she and Nicky became engaged, photographs and drawings by the children. All else she could dispense with.

It was part of the divine test, this discarding of what was unnecessary; part of her purging in the refiner's fire, so that she could be cleansed and purified of all that was dross.

To be sure, she did take a quantity of jewels, not for adornment but to be used as currency if needed, or to be sold to fund a new life abroad should they find themselves in England or elsewhere in Europe. She had to be practical, to think ahead. There was no telling what they would find when they arrived at their new quarters. She ordered the maids to pack sheets, pillows and feather beds, dishes, pans, table linen and storage jars. Chest after chest of household goods were filled, all the packing done quietly, out of sight of the guards whenever possible, for Kerensky had not told the soldiers (or his colleagues in the government) that the family was leaving, and they knew that if the jailers found out, there would be an uproar.

Finally on the night of August 13, everything was ready for the departure. All the chests and boxes were assembled, all the staff and servants who were to accompany the family were packed and ready to go. It was a large party. Besides General Ilya Tatishchev, who was taking over as marshal of the court, and Prince Dolgorukov, there were the two doctors, Botkin and Derevenko, and Dr Botkin's two children, the tutor Pierre Gilliard, Mademoiselle Schneider and Anastasia Hendrikov, and a staff of chambermaids, footmen, valets, kitchen boys, and other servants – nearly three dozen in all. The elderly Count Benckendorff was to stay behind, as was Sophie Buxhoeveden, who had been ill and who was about to undergo an operation.

From late in the evening the family and staff sat waiting for the cars that would take them to the train. Kerensky had said they would leave at around midnight, but one o'clock came and still the cars had not arrived. Alexei sat on a box, 'green with fatigue', Sophie Buxhoeveden thought, holding his spaniel Joy. Nicky chatted with General Tatishchev and Prince Dolgorukov and the doctors. He was allowed a brief, upsetting visit with his brother Michael, who was not permitted to see anyone else in the family.

Every half-hour or so the cars were announced, but did not arrive, though the chests and boxes and luggage were taken away, one by one. As the hours passed the continual delay was nerveracking. Tired and sad, Alix wrote a sombre farewell note to Sophie. 'What shall the future bring to my poor children?' she wrote. 'My heart breaks thinking of them.'[14]

In actuality the delay was an indication of danger. The soldiers had discovered that Kerensky was ordering the transport of the Romanovs to safety in an eastern Russian location, and they immediately called a meeting in the barracks. In keeping with the prevailing climate of decision-making by committee, they debated whether or not the family ought to be permitted to leave the palace. It was a tug-of-war between Kerensky's authority and the collectivist mentality of the men, and it took all of the prime minister's persuasiveness to restrain the soldiers from taking matters into their own hands.

For five hours, until nearly six o'clock in the morning, the arguments went back and forth, with Kerensky's harangues eventually wearing down the resistance.[15] During that time, Sophie thought, Alix 'had seen her life at Tsarskoe [Selo] passing before her', and she had given way to tears.

'The Empress's face was ashy white as she went out of the door of her home for the last time,' Sophie wrote. 'Count Benckendorff and I were left alone on the steps to see them drive away.' Alix wrote to Sophie later that, seeing her two friends standing there on the palace steps, leaning against the wall for support, she felt their desolation, and no doubt it increased her own.

The sight of the two faithful members of her household, her staunch lady-in-waiting and the frail old marshal who had stood by her so loyally in recent months, moved her to tears. As the car moved forwards, taking her away from the palace, she felt fresh sorrow, knowing that she might never see any of those she was leaving behind, or her home, ever again.

32

The train chugged its way through birch forests, past reddish-brown marshlands and across wide meadows where the grain had been harvested and tall haystacks stood pale yellow in the autumn sunshine. Clover and daisies bloomed amid the green flax; ripe apples and pears hung on the branches and in the birch groves; peasants in bright clothes with baskets hung on their arms went in search of mushrooms.

It was the season of abundance, mellow and rich, but Alix, who in other circumstances would have savoured the view out of the train window, the villages with their blue-domed churches, the country houses and fertile fields, now turned her face away from the lush country scenes and lay all day on her bed, heartsick and worn out.

On they travelled, eastwards past lakes and hills and across broad rivers, as the countryside unfolded itself in endless amplitude, the wide horizons ever receding. By the third day Petrograd had been left far behind, and the train began to climb into the foothills of the Urals. Yet even here, deep in the rural landscape, the scars of revolution were evident: manor houses burned, fields torched, barns reduced to heaps of blackened timber. Kitchen gardens uprooted and destroyed. And there was evidence too of the war, village cemeteries full of new graves, crude monuments erected in town squares, only young boys and old men in the fields, all the mature men having left long ago for the front.

All this Alix might have seen, had she managed to lift herself out of her exhaustion.[1] On the fourth day the family left the train and boarded a steamer at Tiumen for the journey up river to Tobolsk, their destination. The steamer was much less comfortable than the train, the cabins small and cramped, the toilet facilities inadequate. Alexei and Marie caught cold, boils erupted on the arms and legs of the tutor Pierre Gilliard, who had to suffer in his bunk. Alix roused herself sufficiently to go to the rail when the steamer passed Pokrovsky, Father Gregory's village, but no one recorded her reaction.

A mansion, formerly the governor's residence, had been set aside in Tobolsk for the use of the Romanovs, but no one had cleaned it or prepared it to be lived in. When they arrived in the town and were escorted to the the residence on Freedom Street, they found the house in a shambles. The windows were boarded up, the floors dirty, the rooms dank with mould and the plumbing badly in need of repair. For many months soldiers had camped out there, staining the flooring, ruining the furniture and peeling the wallpaper off the walls. It took a week to restore the mansion to a habitable condition, which for the Romanovs meant another week of living on the cramped steamer, with Alexei, whose arm was bleeding internally, keeping the others awake at night with his crying.[2]

At last the house was clean, freshly painted and papered, the dilapidated furnishings augmented with plush upholstered chairs, tables and lamps and the floors covered with Persian carpets brought from the steamer. Pictures from the family rooms at Tsarskoe Selo were hung on the walls, and there were new curtains at the windows. Alix had her own cushioned sofa in the drawing room where she could recline, with a blanket over her feet and legs, while sewing or reading. The family settled in, Alix and Nicky in their own bedroom, Alexei in his, and Olga, Tatiana, Marie and Anastasia sharing a bedroom. Besides the drawing room, there was a room for Alexei's servant Nagorny, a study for Nicky, a sitting room for Alix, and attic rooms for the servants. Across the street, in a smaller mansion, members of the household staff were accommodated.

It was a setting of bourgeois comfort, a 'country palace', complete with potted palms and aspidistras, antimacassars and lace doilies.[3] And because the family moved in in the last days of August, when the weather was warm, the house's major flaw – an unworkable heating system – was not yet apparent.[4]

The defects in plumbing, however, were still in evidence. The toilets overflowed, the bath drains overflowed, and the septic pits were full to the brim, with no one willing to clean them. When the commissar from the Provisional Government, Vassily Pankratov, came to inspect the Romanovs' living conditions, he was 'quite appalled', Nicky wrote in his diary.

The quaint, old-fashioned town of Tobolsk in the autumn of 1917 had not yet been affected by the revolution. Newspapers from Petrograd took six days to reach the town, no trains ran nearby and the river steamers from Tiumen only came during the summer months. The harsh rhetoric of the Bolsheviks had not yet penetrated to this corner of rural Siberia; the townspeople, considering it an honour to have the former tsar and his family living among them, stopped to cross themselves when passing the mansion on Freedom Street, the men taking off their hats as a sign of respect.[5] Merchants sent food to the house, farmers sent vegetables, and hunters, fresh game for the larder. The nuns of the nearby Ivanovsky convent made regular gifts of food.

Alix, sitting out on the balcony in the September sunshine or watching from her window, took some comfort from the acknowledgments made by passers-by, as she took comfort from the sound of the bells of the town's many churches (one of which was only a short walk away from the house) and from the presence of the miracle-working relics of the saint of Tobolsk, John Maximovich, which lay in the cathedral on the hill.

Weary and often ill though she was, she had not lost hope. She was well aware that the Provisional Government had moved the family to Tobolsk in order to protect them, that their captivity was a way of keeping them from falling into the hands of the Soviet. And she kept ever in mind what Kerensky had told Count Benckendorff – that in November, only two months away, there would be elections to the Constituent Assembly, following which a new government would liberate them.

With her faith in the inherent goodness of the Russian people, despite what she saw as their immaturity (they were like 'big children', she once said, uncultured and wild, but ultimately good-hearted), she believed that eventually the Russians would come to their senses and realize that they had been deceived by those who had led them into revolution.

'Many already recognize that it [the revolution] was all – a utopia, a chimera,' she wrote to a friend, Madame Syroboyarsky, the mother of a wounded officer she had once nursed. 'Their ideals are shattered, covered with dirt and shame, they didn't achieve a single good thing for Russia.' Before long even more of her husband's former subjects would 'awake, the lie will be revealed, all the falsity, for not all the people have been spoiled, they were tempted, led astray.'[6]

What had been done politically could be reversed. The revolution did not have to be permanent.

September gave way to October, and the autumn rains began, turning the small kitchen garden of the house into a muddy bog.[7] Alix slept late, and stayed in her room most of the day, occupying herself with reading, embroidery, and her current preoccupation, learning the long, intricate choral chants to be sung in church. She gave German lessons to Tatiana and taught Alexei his catechism. And in the afternoons, she sat at the piano, playing from memory the songs and classical compositions she had learned as a girl.

Unsettled by what she did not know – for few letters arrived, and reliable sources of information were even fewer – Alix waited for November, for word that the elections had been held. She did know that the Russian army had retreated yet again before the advancing Germans, abandoning Riga and yielding more territory. There was a chance that the Germans would overrun Petrograd, unseat the Provisional Government and install a regime of their own. They might reinstate Nicky as tsar, after forcing him to sign a peace treaty. Even if the German advance could be halted, Kerensky and his cabinet were surely in a more precarious position than ever. And with the coming of winter, with its inevitable hardships and the resulting popular unrest, Petrograd might well go through another violent political upheaval.

Towards the end of October Alexei's tutor Charles Gibbs arrived in Tobolsk and was allowed to join the Romanov household staff. He brought news from Petrograd, where the turmoil and conflict between the Provisional Government and its Bolshevik rivals had worsened, though most of the Bolshevik leaders were either in prison or, like Lenin, in exile. So many workers were on strike that virtually all production had stopped, Gibbs said; the railway workers refused to operate the trains, and once again the citizens of the capital faced severe inflation and the prospect of famine. The Congress of Soviets was about to open and Kerensky, still struggling to hold the Provisional Government together, could no longer keep order. Vigilantes patrolled the streets of Petrograd, attacking violent strikers, looters, and bands of drunken soldiers.

It was 'the end of everything', as Alix wrote to Madame Syroboyarsky. Russia was descending into chaos yet, in the midst of the chaos, God stood ready to help. 'He is all-powerful and can do anything. In the end He will hear the prayers of those who suffer, and will forgive and save.' She deplored the 'spineless' men, 'devoid of character, devoid of love for their country' who were letting it happen.[8] 'We must have unshakeable faith.' She concluded, that in the long run, all would be well.

But in November 1917, everything got much worse.

The Bolsheviks, who had grown in number to fifty thousand or more, and were organized around a Military Revolutionary Committee that supplied arms and ammunition, began taking over key Petrograd installations – the post office, the telephone exchange and telegraph office. Having won many of the capital's soldiers to their cause, they soon took over the Winter Palace where the Provisional Government had its headquarters and arrested most of the ministers. Kerensky fled. Virtually unopposed, the Bolsheviks had seized governing authority; they would rule, they announced, in the name of the soviets, forming a temporary Workers' and Peasants' Government.

News of the Bolshevik coup reached Tobolsk on November 15, and in the following days the unfolding story became known. Incredulous at first, then in sadness and anger, Alix and Nicky learned what had happened, how the takeover had occurred quietly, with no gunfire, no bloodshed. How no troops loyal to the Provisional Government had been brought into the capital because the Bolsheviks had seized the railway stations. Above all, how the grand regiments of Petrograd – the Preobrazhensky, the Izmailovsky, the Semeonov – did not take part in the transfer of power, but remained neutral.

The coup itself had been virtually undetectable to the citizens of the capital, but its aftermath scarred them indelibly. A small military force rallied by Kerensky failed in its brief effort to unseat the new government. Lenin, having returned from exile in the days before the takeover, declared all private property abolished, virtually inviting the propertyless of Petrograd to confiscate mansions, shops, warehouses, churches, with everything they contained. Robbery was not robbery, under the new Bolshevik decree, but a patriotic expropriation of goods for the benefit of the people; therefore the expropriation went forward with a vengeance.

And in order to safeguard the newly constituted Bolshevik state, the killings began. All those opposed to the party in power – members of the rival political parties, some union members, the remnant of monarchists, soldiers and cadets loyal to the Provisional Government – came under suspicion. Many hundreds were murdered in the days following the takeover. And Petrograd, suddenly, was awash in liquor. The vast wine cellars of the Winter Palace were plundered, wine barrels in the vaults and warehouses of merchants were seized, tapped and their contents consumed. Wine flowed everywhere. 'The air was saturated with vinous vapours,' a contemporary wrote. 'The whole population came at a run and . . . gathered into pails the snow saturated with wine, drew with cups the flowing rivulets, or drank lying flat on the ground and pressing their lips to the snow. Everybody was drunk.'[9]

As the murders and thefts continued, the 'wine riots' went on unchecked, people wandered in a fog of intoxication, brawling, vomiting, lying dead drunk in the snow. Petrograd was the scene of a monumental crime spree and a monumental debauch – the latter a conspicuous symbol, to those critical of the new government, of the depths to which the revolution had sunk.

So long did the orgy of inebriation last that the Bolshevik officials began to suspect a plot on the part of their political enemies to befuddle the brains of the citizens, making them incapable of coherent thought and reducing them to the level of animals – a plummeting into sordidness that would be blamed on the new regime. Troops were ordered in to destroy the stocks of liquor, but instead of smashing the barrels and breaking the bottles they too became drunk, perpetuating the weeks of inebriation.

'I can imagine what a terrible time you lived through,' Alix wrote to Madame Syroboyarsky about the events of November and early December. 'Incredibly painful, sad, offensive, shameful . . . We must bear all these vile, horrible acts and humiliations with meekness (for there is nothing we can do to help). And He will save us . . .'[10]

'He will save us.' It was Alix's litany, her shield and defence against the shocks and sorrows of all that was happening. But in advocating an attitude of meekness, and in reiterating, as she did in her letters to Madame Syroboyarsky and others, that 'there is nothing we can do to help', Alix was being disingenuous. For, prayerful though she was, she was far from meek, and she was counting on the success of a rescue effort.

Boris Soloviev, Father Gregory's son-in-law, was pledged to free the Romanovs from their captivity.

Father Gregory was long dead, his corpse disinterred and burned to ashes by revolutionaries and his tomb desecrated. But his spirit lived on, Alix believed. She felt him close to her.[11] In the actions of his son-in-law Boris he was still working for the good of the entire family.

An organization had been established, the Brotherhood of St John of Tobolsk, to raise money and plan and coordinate the deliverance of the Romanovs from their captors. A banker in Petrograd had collected nearly two hundred thousand roubles from supporters, and more money had been raised from the sale of Alix's jewels, which she smuggled past the guards at Tobolsk, carried by one of her maids. Soloviev had quietly convinced most of the garrison at Tiumen to support the rescue effort – or so he claimed. Communication went on between Alix and Soloviev, perhaps in code – how much communication will never be known, as the notes were passed in the utmost secrecy and destroyed once they were read. Prearranged signals were worked out.[12]

All this activity went on in the deepest secrecy, leaving little or no trace behind. How often messages were smuggled into the house by visitors – Alix's oculist, her dentist, Dr Derevenko's son Kolia, various tradesmen – or delivered in packages of food or clothing (Alexei once smuggled out a small note in a bunch of radishes), or were concealed and carried in and out by servants, or hidden in gifts, or in the soiled clothes that were sent out to be laundered, can never be known.

Correspondence was thus of two types: the official letters, scrutinized by guards and authorized (and therefore virtually empty of meaningful content), and the private letters and notes, which came and went by unauthorized channels, many of which can no longer be read.

Of the second type were the messages from Boris Soloviev and others in the Brotherhood of St John of Tobolsk, and also the letter Alix's brother Ernie sent via a former cavalry officer, Serge Vladimirovich Markov. In this letter Ernie offered help to organize a rescue effort, but Nicky and Alix both sent a negative response. The Germans were the enemy, and no help from the enemy would be accepted.[13]

The arrival in Tobolsk of a young friend of Olga's, Marguerita Hitrovo, aroused the guards' suspicion. They knew, or supposed, that rescue efforts were under way, and were particularly suspicious of Marguerita, possibly because she had written 'imprudently worded' postcards to her family. When she delivered some letters for the Romanovs to Anastasia Hendrikov, she was arrested and taken to Moscow.[14] Countess Hendrikov was arrested and questioned, and kept shut in her room alone. Eventually Marguerita was released, but the incident marked a turning point in the Romanovs' captivity; the soldiers redoubled their watchfulness and became more harsh in their attitude.

Winter closed in like a long pale shroud. The family was used to cold, but this was the cold of Siberia, which froze the river to a great depth and enclosed the town in its icebound grip. Howling winds arose to blow snow in all directions, cutting the faces of people in the street like needles, and preventing all but the hardiest from going outside for weeks at a time. The temperature dropped to fifty, sixty, seventy degrees below zero, with the nights even colder. When the dim sun rose in the late morning, it revealed a dull white landscape, trees, roofs, fences lilac-white with hoar frost, cottages drowned in high-piled white snowdrifts, a white fog hanging low over everything.

Nicky spent his days wrapped in a warm Circassian infantry coat lined with shearling. The temperature in his study was barely 50 degrees, in Alix's drawing room even lower. Icy draughts blew in through cracks in the window-frames. There was too little fuel available to operate the heating system in the house, so the only heat came from inadequate wood stoves. The family stayed near these stoves, doing their best to stuff rags and paper into the cracks in the walls.

'We shiver in the rooms,' Alix wrote to Anna Vyrubov shortly before Christmas, 'and there is always a strong draught from the windows. Your pretty jacket is useful. We all have chilblains on our fingers.'

She described their daily life. 'I am writing this while resting before dinner. Little Jimmy [Tatiana's black and ginger Pekinese] lies near me while his mistress plays the piano.' She described their quiet evenings, Nicky reading aloud to the family and staff, her dull days painting ribbons for book markers, making Christmas cards, embroidering with her stiff cold chilblained fingers.

'Alexei, Marie and Gelik [Gilliard] acted a little play for us. The others are committing to memory scenes from French plays. Excellent distraction and good for the memory.'[15] 'I have not been out in the fresh air for four weeks,' Alix added. 'I can't go out in such bitter weather because of my heart. Nevertheless church draws me almost irresistibly.'

Such was the content of her letter that went by official post. In the same week as this letter was written, she asked Charles Gibbs to write a secret letter to her former governess in England, Margaret Hardcastle Jackson, describing in detail the floor plan of the governor's mansion and giving the times they were allowed out in the yard, when they went to church services and how many guards went with them, and other information vital to any would-be rescuers. The letter, Alix told Gibbs, was intended for George V and his ministers; she was sure that her old governess would forward it to the British government. What became of it is not recorded.[16]

'It is bright sunshine and everything glitters with hoar frost,' Alix wrote to Anna again in the last days of 1917. 'There are such moonlight nights, it must be ideal on the hills.' The sentiment was poetic, but behind it, no doubt, was a hint to Anna, and through her to Boris Soloviev, that a moonlit night would offer a good opportunity for a small band of soldiers from the Brotherhood of St John of Tobolsk to find their way to the governor's house, overwhelm the sleepy guards, and take the family out to safety.

33

Among Alix's Christmas gifts in 1917, along with dressing gowns, slippers, a silver dish, spoons and several icons, was a home-made diary. Tatiana had sewn it herself, taking one of her exercise books and making a cover for it of pinkish cloth lined with white silk.

Inside, the diary was inscribed, 'To my sweet darling Mama dear with my best wishes for a happy new year. May God's blessings be upon you and guard you for ever. Your own loving girl, Tatiana.'

Alix began writing in it on New Year's Day, noting that it was the church feast of the Circumcision of the Lord and that the morning temperature was 39 degrees and that Olga and Tatiana were in bed with elevated temperatures and symptoms of German measles.[1] The weather was clear and sunny, and there was no wind; she had lunch with her two sick daughters and then sat on the balcony in the sunshine for half an hour. In the evening, she noted, both girls' temperatures had risen. She rested until eight, 'reading and writing', then had dinner with Olga and Tatiana in the room all four of her daughters shared, then played bezique, a card game, with Nicky. The remainder of the evening was spent with the gathered household, Anastasia Hendrikov (whose isolation from the family following the incident with the letters had been brief), Fräulein Schneider, General Tatishchev, the aide-de-coup Valia Dolgorukov, the tutors Gilliard and Gibbs, and the doctors Botkin and Derevenko.

Nicky read to them all, from Turgenev's novel *Nest of the Gentry*, while Alix knitted and the fire popped and crackled in the stove.

Knowing that her diary would be read by the soldiers guarding her, Alix was careful to write nothing in it that would alert them to her hopes and plans, her inmost thoughts. It was only a bare record of her activities, of the comings and goings of those around her, of the health of her family and of the weather. She also noted the letters she wrote to be sent by official post.

The diary was as revealing for what it did not record as for what it did; Alix did not note down her variations in mood, or the waxing and waning of her hopes, or her irritations or her moments of quiet exaltation. She made no record of the secret messages she sent and received, of the whispered conversations – too low for the guards to hear – in which news and rumours were passed among the family and household. Nor did she write anything of the behaviour of her captors, or of the overriding preoccupation of everyone living in the governor's mansion and everyone guarding its occupants: that the rescue effort, and no one doubted that a rescue effort – possibly more than one – would be made, would come with the spring thaw.

The most immediate concern of the captives in January of 1918 was money. There was not enough of it and, with the fall of the Provisional Government, no more was sent from Petrograd. Alexandra had her jewels, some of which she had sent to Boris Soloviev, and there were still some funds left from what the family had brought from Tsarskoe Selo. But there was not enough cash to pay the Tobolsk merchants, who stopped advancing credit, nor enough to pay the servants, nor enough to buy food for everyone. Alix, Valia Dolgorukov and Gilliard undertook to make a budget. Some servants were sent back to Petrograd with small allowances and, while those that remained were willing to work without salaries, Alix could not bring herself to accept their offer; instead she reduced all the salaries, so that no one would go without.

Keeping the kitchen supplied with food was now difficult, and the staff offered to help pay the cost. The midday meal was reduced to soup, one dish of meat or fish, and stewed fruit. Supper was light, macaroni or rice or pancakes and a dish of vegetables. No one had more than one helping.[2] There was no butter, and very little sugar –

three lumps a day for each person. The donations of produce and game that had augmented the family's diet in September and October came rarely now and, when they did, Alix rejoiced in them as 'gifts from heaven'. Once in a while a merchant sent some caviar or fish, but such luxuries were very rare.

The captives did not know it, but Tobolsk was an oasis of plenty in that bleak January. Petrograd starved; peasants in many country villages survived by eating straw and moss and the bark of trees. The Bolsheviks were blamed for what rapidly became a widespread famine, and crowds of rioters, weak from hunger, murdered food commissars and burned the headquarters of the local soviets. The violence made no difference; the terrible scarcity continued, and many corpses were buried under the high-piled winter snows.

The family knew little, but heard rumours of overtures being made to Germany for the negotiation of a separate peace, and vaguer reports of Russian regions declaring themselves independent from the government, a fragmentation of the empire that threatened stability and promised to create further economic disruption. Official news had once again become infrequent and unreliable, and heavy snowfalls all but cut Tobolsk off from the outside world.[3] Travellers came and went in horse-drawn sledges, or followed the riverbanks along paths hewn through the snowdrifts. After each fresh fall of snow the streets of Tobolsk were impassable for days, blocked by tall mounds of new snow sparkling and glittering in the sunlight.

Alix sat with Anastasia and supervised her history lessons (the fall of the Roman Empire), taught Alexei the meaning of the Filioque Controversy (did the Holy Spirit proceed from God the Father alone, or from both God and Jesus?) in the history of the eastern and western branches of Christianity, and corrected Tatiana's German grammar. While the weather worsened ('snowstorm, terrible wind,' she noted on January 21), she read the Gospel of Mark with Alexei, thankful that by the end of the day the temperature had risen slightly and the wind was less severe.

She worried about the weather, for Boris Soloviev was due to reach Tobolsk any day and bad weather was likely to delay his journey.

Fortunately he arrived the day before the worst snowstorm. Through intermediaries he sent money, letters and goods into the governor's mansion, and was given many letters Alix had written to take back to Petrograd. The family glimpsed him from the windows of the house when he walked in the street below.

'Let me know what you think of our situation,' Alix wrote in a secret message in the first week of February, probably to Soloviev.[4] 'Our common wish is to achieve the possibility of living tranquilly, like an ordinary family, outside politics, struggle and intrigue. Write frankly, for I will accept your letter with faith in your sincerity.'

Soloviev replied the following day. 'Deeply grateful for the feelings and trust expressed,' he wrote. 'The situation is on the whole very serious and could become critical, and I am certain that it will take the help of devoted friends, or a miracle, for everything to turn out all right, and for you to get your wish for a tranquil life.' He signed the note, 'Your sincerely devoted Boris.'

Alix sent a response. 'You've confirmed my fears,' she told Soloviev. 'Friends are either in uncertain absence or else we simply have none, and I pray tirelessly to the Lord and place all my hope in Him alone.' She was discouraged, but still hopeful. 'You speak of a miracle, but isn't it already a miracle that the Lord has sent you to us here? God keep you. Grateful Alexandra.'[5]

In February, on orders from Moscow, a soviet was elected in Tobolsk, and the town was brought within the Bolshevik orbit. New soldiers from Tsarskoe Selo arrived to guard the Romanovs, 'black-guardly-looking young men', Gilliard thought, and a new commander was appointed.[6] The soviet imposed rationing, and the Tobolsk City Food Committee issued ration card number fifty-four to 'Nicholas Alexandrovich Romanov, Ex-Emperor, residing on Freedom Street, with six dependents'. It entitled him to receive, when presented in the cooperative shop called 'Self-Conscience,' 190 pounds of flour, seven pounds of butter, and half a pound of sugar – when these things were available. With the reduction in food came a reduction in the monthly stipend allotted to each of the captives, and Alix had to dismiss ten more servants.

Tobolsk was no longer a safe enclave, an obscure corner of the old Russia. It had become a battleground of sorts, where the Bolshevik government was seeking to impose new ways of thinking and living on a conservative population. There was resistance to these new ways in the town – and in Siberia generally, where political opposition to the government was strong. Special paramilitary groups called Red Guards were being formed to crush the counter-revolutionary forces. An armed clash was likely and, when it came, the Romanovs would be at risk.

'Their Majesties still cherish hope that among their loyal friends some may be found to attempt their release,' Gilliard wrote in mid-March.[7] The new guards were insolent and hostile, but their commander, Colonel Kobylinsky, was, Gilliard thought, 'on our side'. The arrogant guards were strict in their rules, but often careless; it would be relatively easy for a few resolute men, well organized and with a sound plan, to contrive an escape.

It was carnival season, and Tobolsk was full of revelry. Bells pealed, people sang and played mouth-organs and balalaikas, there were jugglers and clowns, mimes and comics. Disguised by their costumes and masks, the ordinarily staid citizens of the town plunged into merriment, drinking and flirting without inhibition. Sleighs decorated with ribbons and banners flew along the snowy streets, bells jangling. Work was forgotten, business set aside, politics ignored. The only imperative was enjoyment and, to heighten the enjoyment, there were plates of blinis and gingerbread and nuts and candy, washed down with glass after glass of pepper vodka, lemon vodka, black-currant vodka, vodka in seemingly infinite variety.

'Never was the situation more favourable for escape,' Gilliard thought. Not only was the Brotherhood of St John of Tobolsk active, but another monarchist organization was at work, and at the beginning of Lent, this group sent 250,000 roubles to the family.[8] Couriers brought letters from friends pledging assistance, and Alix managed to smuggle out more of her valuables to be sold to raise funds.[9]

Unknown to the Romanovs, the British Foreign Office was attempting a rescue plan of its own. A Norwegian steamship operator,

Jonas Lied, was recruited to coordinate the rescue and to provide a boat. Once the ice broke on the Irtysh River, it would be possible to take the family up river via the Irtysh and the Ob and then overland to the Kara Sea, where a torpedo boat from the British Navy would be waiting. King George was in favour of this effort, which reached the office of the director of British naval intelligence.[10] But it was abandoned – possibly because by the time the rivers were free of ice, the Romanovs were no longer in Tobolsk.

The merriment of carnival came to an abrupt end, and Lent began, the season of deprivation, purgation, cleansing. Stories swept through Tobolsk of bands of renegade sailors who were roaming at will through Tiumen, terrorizing the populace, stealing and shooting. Late in March some Red Guards from Omsk arrived in Tobolsk and installed themselves in a makeshift barracks in the town. No one knew whether they had been sent by some provincial authority or whether they had come on their own, to steal and kill and cause disruption.

Soon another group of Red Guards came, this time from Ekaterinburg, a leftist stronghold. This group, made up largely of workmen turned soldier, most of them Latvian, put up posters in the streets announcing that all gold and silver and valuables must be turned over to them on pain of death.[11] They went from house to house, seizing money, jewellery, and other goods, arresting the wealthy merchants and holding them for ransom.

Conflict between the Omsk and Ekaterinburg gangs – they were little more than that – erupted, and the soldiers guarding the Governor's House were caught in the middle. Their obligation was to protect the Romanovs, but the prime imperative was not to let the family fall into other hands. 'The guard announced,' Sophie Buxhoeveden wrote, 'that if anyone tried to take their prisoners, they would kill the entire imperial family themselves before they gave them up.'[12]

Confusion escalated. Groups of renegades came and went, skirmishing among themselves, fighting for turf. At any moment they might begin to fight over the Governor's Mansion, with its valuable hostages. And the defenders of the mansion, not knowing what else to do amid the chaos, were sworn to eliminate their captives.

Amid this extremely tense situation, Alexei, who had caught whooping cough from his playmate Kolia Derevenko, began to haemorrhage.

'Bright sunshine,' Alix wrote in her diary for April 12. 'Baby [Alexei] stays in bed as from coughing so hard has a slight haemorrhage in the abdomen.' Later in the day she added 'Dined with Baby. Pains strong.'[13]

The haemorrhage grew worse; the pain spread to Alexei's groin and legs. Hour by hour the swelling increased and the pain became greater. 'Baby slept badly from pain and was four times sick,' Alix wrote on the following day. 'A little better for two hours in the evening and then worse again.'[14]

It soon became evident that this was a severe attack, the most severe Alexei had undergone in years. His fever rose and he moaned and screamed in pain, his body grotesquely swollen, his skin stretched tight. He ate nothing, and the pain kept him from sleeping. With his fever rising and the risk of a fatal internal infection high, Dr Derevenko cautioned Alix and Nicky that Alexei was close to death.

Icons hung around Alexei's bed, some of them gifts from Father Gregory, and Alix must have invoked Father Gregory's healing powers many times as hour by hour she watched by her son's bedside. This was what she had been dreading ever since the starets's death sixteen months earlier: that one day Alexei would become dangerously ill, and that Father Gregory would not be available to heal him.

'Sat whole day with him,' she wrote in her diary, 'every half-hour very strong cramp-like pains for three minutes. Towards the evening better.'[15]

Suddenly, after several days of agony, he was better. Unable to find any medicines in Tobolsk, Dr Derevenko 'tried a new remedy', according to Sophie Buxhoeveden. Whatever the new remedy was, it brought relief. The bleeding ceased, though Alexei's fever was still high and he remained very weak.[16] By April 19 Alix was able to write in a letter to Anna Vyrubov that, though Alexei still had pains in his back and leg, he was eating a little and his fever was no longer consistently high, though he was still 'terribly pale and thin' and the doctor was concerned that he might start to bleed again.

Throughout the days and nights of Alexei's illness, Alix had watched by his bedside as she always did, relieved for an hour or two by Tatiana so that she could rest. She had become 'like his shadow', she told Anna in a letter, sitting there with him, holding his leg, talking to him, watching him in his fitful sleep. She was as thin, as pale as a shadow, her grey hair drawn back carelessly off her lined face, her frayed, patched gown loose at waist and wrists.

She was worried about Alexei. He had been so robust over the winter, flinging himself down the ice mountain Nicky and Gilliard had erected in the yard (and the soldiers had torn down), piling up the wood his father cut with such vigour that he tore his gloves, playing energetically with Kolia. She had hoped that his robustness was a good sign. Now that hope had proved illusory.

She still clung to her other hope – the hope of rescue – but worried that that too might prove illusory. Early in April she learned that Boris Soloviev had been arrested. In prison, under torture, he might reveal the names of the others who were working for the family's relief. She trusted that there were many others still actively making plans and arrangements on their behalf, but so far none had done more than send money and encouraging messages. She had been told that, among the soldiers from Omsk, and others from Tiumen, there were hundreds of former officers, devoted monarchists, who had enlisted in the ranks in order to be in a position to come to the family's aid when the right moment came.[17] Surely, now that spring was on its way, all the plans that had been made over the winter would come to fruition.

Meanwhile she devoted herself to watching Alexei's gradual recovery, worn out by her vigil and her anxiety.

'I worry so much. My God! How Russia suffers,' she wrote to Anna. 'You know that I love it even more than you do, miserable country, demolished from within, and by the Germans from without.' Russia was 'disintegrating into bits', she wrote. 'I cannot think calmly about it. Such hideous pain in heart and soul.'[18]

The burden of the hideous pain made her irascible. She snapped at the servants. ('My greatest sin is my irritability ... You know how hot-tempered I am.') She could endure the cold, the privation, the humiliations of captivity and the dread of harm, even the terrible apprehension that Alexei might die. But the small, everyday strains provoked her to angry outbursts – when a maid lied, or 'sermonized like a preacher.'

'I want to be a better woman, and I try,' she wrote. 'For long periods I am really patient, and then breaks out again my bad temper.' She knew that she had grown cold towards the servants and staff, and she felt guilty about it.[19]

Alix's accustomed self-scrutiny and scrupulosity of conscience were intact, as was her faith. 'We live here on earth but we are already half gone to the next world,' she wrote. 'We see with different eyes.' She looked around her, and saw not the chaos of armed bands clashing in confused struggle, not her tense, anxious husband and children and the apprehensive staff, not nervous guards ready, if need be, to kill them all, but the benign, protective presence of the divine.

'It's all right,' she told Anna Vyurubov after Boris Soloviev's arrest. 'Don't worry. The Lord is everywhere and will work a miracle.'

34

Long before dawn on the morning of April 26, 1918, four wooden carts stood in Freedom Street, in front of the Governor's Mansion. A cold wind was blowing, and there was snow on the ground. The door of the house opened, and a cluster of people began to file out, wrapped tightly in layers of garments against the morning chill.

The commissar from Moscow, Vassily Yakovlev, stood to attention as the former tsar came out, wearing his Circassian coat, and the sentry presented arms. Yakovlev remarked to Nicky that he ought to take an extra coat.

Eight others followed: Alix and Marie, Valia Dolgorukov, Dr Botkin, an officer of the Tobolsk guard, Matveev, and three servants, Alix's maid Anna Demidov, Nicky's valet Chemodurov and the kitchen boy Leonid Sednev.

Alix was lifted into one of the carts, the only one with a hood covering it. Dr Botkin saw that there were no seats, only the bare wooden floor, and protested to Yakovlev. His patient, he said, was not well enough to travel in such a crude conveyance; she would injure herself.

There was a delay while straw was found in a pigsty, and sprinkled over the wooden planks. A mattress, rugs and blankets were spread over the straw, and then Alix, wearing a thin coat of Persian lamb, was lifted in. Marie climbed in beside her.

Alix had few possessions with her, but one of them was her diary, in which she wrote, later that day, that she was suffering from pain in her chest. She was miserable. She hadn't slept the night before, worried over the decision she had been forced to make, whether to accompany Nicky on this journey or to stay in Tobolsk with her children.

It had been a terrible decision, the most terrible she had ever faced, as she confided to her maid Maria Toutelberg.[1] When told that she had to make up her mind, she paced up and down for hours, unable to choose.

'It is the hardest moment of my life,' she told her maid. 'You know what my son is to me, and I must choose between him and my husband.'

Her daughters helped her to decide. They assured her that, if she left, Olga would run the household, Tatiana would nurse Alexei, and Marie would go with her, to comfort her. Anastasia too would do what she could to help.

At last she came to a decision. 'I must be firm,' she told Toutelberg. 'I must leave my child and share my husband's life or death.'

She was leaving, not knowing whether she would ever see her children again. She and Nicky had said their formal goodbyes to the servants and staff, embracing each one in turn as they stood in the large hall of the Governor's Mansion, nearly all of them in tears. That had been difficult enough. But saying goodbye to Alexei and her daughters was a starker anguish.

That she had Marie with her now helped a little, for Marie, at nearly nineteen, was the sturdiest of her daughters and the one from whom she could draw the most strength. And Yakovlev had given his word that the others would join Alix and Nicky at their new destination in about three weeks – assuming Alexei was well enough to travel.

The convoy set out, escorted by eight sentries and ten Red Guards. The carts bumped and creaked, pitching and tossing like ships in a gale when their wheels sank into deep ruts or struck hard lumps of ice. The travellers' hands and faces soon were red with cold, stung by the relentless wind. The cold dawn came with grey skies, the sharp wind continuing. They came to the edge of the frozen river Irtysh, where the ice, groaning and straining in the first throes of the spring thaw, was too unstable to hold the weight of the laden carts.

They got out, and Nicky, taking Alix in his arms, carried her across, walking on broad planks laid down across the heaving ice veined with black cracks. Near the bank the ice had melted, and he was obliged to wade knee-deep in the near-freezing river water for the last few yards.

In the course of the long day they stopped often, to change horses and to repair the harnesses and the carts, which, jolted severely as they were, lost wheels and linchpins. At each stop they ate from a store of provisions they brought, first rubbing their numbed fingers until the circulation returned.

'Road perfectly atrocious,' Alix wrote, 'frozen ground[,] wind, snow, water up to the horses' stomachs, fearfully shaken, pain all over.'[2] She wrote a note to the children, which one of the drivers promised to deliver for her.

Finally at eight o'clock at night they came to the town of Ievlevo where they were allowed to spend the night in a small unheated house, formerly the village shop. The men slept on the floor, Alix on her mattress and blankets from the cart. 'Got to bed at ten, dead tired and ached all over.'

They surmised that they were going to Tiumen, but where they were to be taken after that was a mystery. They thought it would be Moscow, which the Bolsheviks had made the new capital of Russia – and where, most likely, Nicky would be tried and imprisoned.

The following morning they were again awakened long before dawn, and set off in the carts at five. Again they crossed the river on planks, Nicky carrying Alix, and at another point took a ferry. The weather had turned warm, and the road was somewhat easier, though there were still many deep ruts and long stretches of muddy track where the carts bogged down. Towards evening the moon rose, and the carts 'tore along at a wild rate' by moonlight. Approaching Tiumen, they were met by a group of horsemen who escorted them to the train station through the dark town. At midnight they boarded a train, exhausted, and fell into bed in their dusty clothes.[3]

Though the Romanovs did not know it, they had become the subject of intense debate. The governing soviets of the two principal Siberian cities, Omsk and Ekaterinburg, were vying to possess the most celebrated prisoner in Russia, the former tsar. Yakovlev had been sent by Moscow to forestall this rivalry and bring the prisoner and his family to the capital. Out of consideration for Alexei's weak condition, he had decided to bring only the ex-tsar and his wife and daughter, with the others to follow later.

Yakovlev's orders were clear, and his plans logical – but planning and logic were rapidly being subverted by events. On the journey to Tiumen Alix noted that Yakovlev, who appeared nervous, was 'fidgety, running about, telegraphing'.[4] He had heard that the Ural Regional Soviet Executive Committee in Ekaterinburg might try to kidnap Nicky en route to Moscow, and was sending telegrams to two members of the committee, warning them against making any such attempt or there would be bloodshed.

The train set off for Omsk but, when it arrived, representatives of the Omsk Soviet were waiting, and refused to let the prisoners continue on, fearing that Yakovlev, who had been branded a 'traitor to the revolution,' would not take them on to Moscow but further east, to Japanese-held Vladivostok, from which they could get safely out of Russia.

Yakovlev contacted Moscow, and was ordered to turn back, towards Ekaterinburg, despite the threat of Nicky's capture. On Tuesday, April 30, their fifth day of travel, the Romanovs approached Ekaterinburg. A band of soldiers surrounded the train. 'Yakovlev had to give us over to the Ural Region Soviet,' Alix wrote in her diary. 'Their chief took us three in an open motor, a truck with soldiers armed to their [*sic*] teeth followed us. Drove through by-streets till reached a small house, around which high wooden palings have been placed.'[5]

The 'small house' was in fact a large two-storey residence, not as grand as the Governor's House in Tobolsk but impressive none-theless. It belonged to an engineer named Ipatiev, who had been ordered to leave, with his family, a few days before the Romanovs' arrival. The new occupants were given three rooms, a bedroom for Alix, Nicky and Marie, a sitting room where Dr Botkin and the male servants slept, and a small dressing room for Anna Demidov. There was no view from the windows; only the boards of the high fence that ringed the house could be seen, and later, a gold cross surmounting a church. As at the Tobolsk house, the plumbing was at first inoperative; chamber pots were provided.

From the first the guards were rough and insolent. Nicky's valet Chemodurov recalled later that as soon as the family arrived at the house they were made to undergo a 'thorough and humiliating search'. One of the soldiers snatched Alix's grey suede handbag out of her hand and turned out its contents – which consisted of her supply of Veronal, a handkerchief, and smelling salts. Nicky protested. 'Until now I have been dealing with decent and honest people,' he said sharply.

'Do not forget that you are under investigation and arrest,' was the reply from the commissar Didkovsky, equally sharp. 'We are the masters now! We will do as we please.'[6] Alix had to restrain Nicky from lunging at the man, his anger flared so explosively.

But he mastered his anger, and indeed, according to Chemodurov, both he and Alix bore the harsh treatment they received and the guards' ceaseless humiliations and insults 'with apparent calm'. For the most part, they 'appeared not to notice either the people around them or what they were doing'.

For Alix to maintain her self-control, given her tendency towards irritability, was a challenge, and she did not always meet the challenge successfully. When Avdeev ordered that the Romanovs be addressed, not by their titles, but merely as 'Nicholas Alexandrovich', 'Alexandra Feodorovna' and 'Maria Nicolaevna', Alix bristled.

'And why has no one dispensed with addressing one by title before this?' she demanded of the commander. He retorted that now, at Ekaterinburg, they were in the hands of genuine revolutionaries.[7]

Petty humiliations made her indignant, but they also wore her down, there were so many of them: the lack of cleanliness and privacy, the coarse food (Alix could barely eat it, and subsisted on vermicelli which Leonid the kitchen boy prepared for her), the 'roll call' at eight each morning, reminiscent of prison life, the soldiers who entered the family's doorless rooms without warning, at all times of the day and night, the necessity of asking permission before using the toilet, once it was made workable, and the presence of a sentry at the opening where once there had been a lavatory door, the constant vulgar, offensive remarks.

These assaults on her sensibilities, combined with her worry over Alexei and her daughters, gave Alix headaches and heart pains, and during the first three weeks of the family's captivity in Ekaterinburg she often lay on her bed, her aching eyes shut, too dizzy and ill to sit up, read, or write letters. She slept badly many nights, kept awake by the pacing of the guards and their loud voices, the commander's inebriated loutishness, and her own restless musings. Marie and the maid Anna did what they could for her, Anna washing her long hair and Marie brushing it and dressing it. Anna sewed and mended, and perhaps washed the clothes as well – with much inconvenience, as in the first month at least there was no running water in the house.

Strict though the family's captivity was in the Ipatiev house, Alix continued to hope for rescue, and to write letters to their would-be rescuers. She drew a detailed plan of the house, and sent it out, presumably with Dr Derevenko when he came to see Alix, or with one of the nuns from the Novotikhvinsky Convent who came to deliver fresh eggs and milk. But the commander managed to discover the drawing, and took it to Nicky and showed it to him. According to Avdeev, he stammered out a lie about not realizing that it was forbidden to send sketches out of the house.

On May 23 Alix recorded in her diary that 'towards eleven the girls suddenly turned up with Alexei – thank God – such joy to have them again.'[8] Their arrival soothed her worries temporarily, but that same night Alexei, who had been unwell and was alarmingly thin, slipped and hurt his knee getting into bed, and woke up every hour complaining of pain.[9] In the following days he 'suffered very much' with strong pains, was unable to sleep and continued to lose weight and colour until he looked, according to a priest who came to say mass at the house, 'transparent'.[10]

For Alix, her son's renewed attack of illness meant still more nights of lost sleep, more anxiety, added to the mounting anxiety of the family's imprisonment. Twin emotions peaked and ebbed within her, the hope of rescue and the fear of her husband's execution, followed by an unknown but terrible fate for herself and her children.

That something extraordinary was happening in Ekaterinburg was clear. Even though very little news reached the family (sometimes they were allowed to read newspapers, often out of date, sometimes they were denied any newspapers for days at a time), they could tell, from the increased nervousness of their guards, from the shouting in the streets around the house and the frequent tramping of boots – a sound they associated with movements of large groups of soldiers – from the flashes of fire or light in the sky, and the loud reports of distant gunfire, that more turmoil had broken out.

In actuality, in the first week of June the authorities in Ekaterinburg faced the most serious threat they had yet encountered, and were attempting to crush uprisings in the city by making mass arrests.

Opposition to the Bolshevik government had been growing rapidly until, by May, the country was in a state of civil war. In particular, Siberia was under threat of anarchy as anti-Bolshevik forces gathered strength. Political moderates opposed to the rulers in Moscow set up a Siberian Regional Council at Omsk. Armies of patriots and monarchists ('Whites' in contrast to the Bolshevik 'Reds') were gaining strength, and one of these armies, the Czech Legion, with some forty thousand trained troops, had seized the city of Samara on the Volga and was threatening to link up with the Omsk rebels and with other discontented groups – ethnic minorities, anarchists, peasant insurgents – to conquer the Urals. Already the telephone lines between Ekaterinburg and Moscow were cut, the Trans-Siberian Railway was in the hands of the Whites and boats on the Volga were being captured.

The Bolshevik nightmare, Lenin's nightmare, was that all of Siberia would soon be under monarchist control, the Red Army would be driven out and the former tsar, from his captivity in Ekaterinburg, would be proclaimed head of a re-established empire. The revolution would be reversed.

The guards at the Ipatiev House were alarmed and frightened. They avoided talking with their prisoners, and confined their communication to announcing that they could not walk in the yard, or that there would be no supper. On June 13 Avdeev appeared and ordered the family to pack; an uprising by anarchists was feared, and the Romanovs might have to be taken to Moscow on very short notice. They packed, and waited for further word. Then at eleven o'clock at night Avdeev came again to say that they would stay in the house for another few days. The leader of the anarchists had been arrested, and the threat of an uprising had diminished.[11]

The immediate threat had diminished, but the nightly noise and disturbances continued, as more Red Guard soldiers assembled in Ekaterinburg and men and equipment were moved into position to withstand the expected assault from the Whites.

For the Whites were surely coming – and, for Alix and the others, the Whites meant rescue.

A letter was brought to them by a soldier in the last ten days of June. 'The friends sleep no longer,' it began cryptically, 'and hope the hour so long awaited has arrived. The revolt of the Czechoslovaks menaces the Bolsheviks more and more seriously. Samara, Cheliabinsk and the whole of Siberia, eastern and western, are under the control of the provincial national government [the White government]. The army of the Slavic friends is eighty kilometres from Ekaterinburg.'[12]

With what mingled joy and apprehension this secret message was received can only be imagined. Naturally, Alix wrote nothing of it in her diary. But Avdeev and the guards, shrewdly watchful, no doubt saw fleeting smiles on the faces of their captives in the days following receipt of the message.

'Be ready all the time, day and night,' the letter instructed them. 'Make a sketch of your two rooms, the places of the furniture, of the beds. Write exactly when you all go to bed. One of you should not sleep between two and three o'clock all the following nights.' The letter was signed simply, 'One who is ready to die for you – An Officer of the Russian Army.'

From then on, the family's routine changed. They continued to observe the schedule the guards imposed, but they added to it a regimen of their own, in which one of their number stayed awake each night from two to three and all of them were prepared to dress rapidly and pack simply and in haste when the signal for rescue was given.

A second letter came soon after the first, giving more explicit instructions.[13] The signal would be a whistle. When they heard it, they were to barricade the doorway to their rooms with furniture, then go out of the window, down a rope. Their friends would be waiting below.

'The means for getting away are not lacking and the escape is surer than ever,' the writer said. Nicky and Alix must come down the rope first, then Alexei, then Olga, Tatiana, Marie and Anastasia, and finally Dr Botkin. They were to make the rope themselves, quickly. Then they were to wait for the whistle in the middle of the night.

June 27, Marie's nineteenth birthday, was a day of sweltering heat. The guards had relented and allowed a single window to be opened, which let in a light breeze and the scent of flowers from the town gardens. But still there was no real ventilation, the air did not circulate freely, and Alix wrote in her diary, 'Heat intense.'

The rescue signal was expected, and each of the family members had surreptitiously laid out his or her clothes and belongings, ready to leave, to go out of the window, as soon as the signal was heard. It was hardly necessary to delegate someone to stay awake after midnight, they would all be awake, listening. There would be the usual shouts and gunshots and sounds of marching in the street, but there would also, or so they had been assured, be the whistle. Then they would swiftly get up and move the furniture in front of the doorways – hoping that the guards would not succeed in blocking their efforts – and move to the open window.

'Escape is surer than ever,' the last secret letter had said, but the family must have worried nonetheless. How would the rescuers disarm the sentries, overwhelm the guards, seize the machine-guns on the roof and on the first floor, and hold off the rest of the soldiers, those who were off duty, who would be roused from their sleep at the first sign of a disturbance? How could they prevent Avdeev or one of his assistants from calling for reinforcements? Or would they cut the telephone line from the house in time to prevent any call being made?

As they went about their daily activities, their minds must have been full of questions, hopes, prayers for divine protection. Alix spent the day 'arranging things', doing needlework, and visiting Dr Botkin, who had been bedridden with severe kidney pains. Olga sat with her in the sweltering afternoon; together they watched while two officials from the soviet inspected their rooms, and refused to open another window to provide relief from the heat.

'The waiting and the uncertainty were torture,' Nicky wrote in his diary. The day must have seemed endless.

After supper they went to bed, and lay awake, 'fully dressed', listening for a whistle in the street. It was hot even at night, and they lay in the dark, sweating in their clothes, no doubt worrying that the guards might decide to make an unannounced inspection and become suspicious on seeing them clothed for flight.[14]

Hours passed. Between two and three o'clock in the morning, they must have listened with greater focus, straining to pick up every sound, annoyed when the sentries under the windows called to each other, or when carriages passed in the street. No doubt they longed to be able to look outside, to watch for a party of armed men, hundreds of them, marching down Voznesensky Avenue, terrifying all opposition, coming their way.

Three o'clock came and went, and then four o'clock, and there was no whistle. The sky began to lighten. The opportunity for rescue had passed.

'Nothing happened,' Nicky wrote in his diary. But the waiting, the terribly uncertainty, had been 'almost impossible to bear!'

The next night the sentries received orders to increase their vigilance.

35

Mid-July came, and the family still waited for rescue, amid increasing signs that Ekaterinburg was becoming a war zone. Artillery rolled up and down Voznesensky Avenue; troops of infantry marched and at times cavalry as well. It was easy for the Romanovs to identify the troops, they only had to listen to the anthems the bands played. They were able to surmise that Austrians, former prisoners of war, had been drafted into the Red Guard to fight the Czech Legion. Ambulances passed the house, bringing the wounded to the town. Each day the ambulances passed more frequently, indicating that more wounded were in need of aid, and that the fighting was intensifying.

At night, the booming of artillery and the crackle of pistol fire troubled their sleep, as did the urgency of their ongoing vigil, their awareness that, at any time, they might be called upon to flee quickly, should their liberators arrive. The nearness of the fighting exhilarated and frightened them: would help come? Would the White Army seize the house and release them? Or would they be moved again, to Moscow this time, and put into harsher captivity there?

Surely something would happen soon. One of the secret letters had said that the White Army was only eighty kilometres from Ekaterinburg. It was coming closer by the day; they could tell that without a newspaper or an informant.

On July 5 another secret message had arrived, buoying their hopes. But the former tsar had sent a message back cautioning their deliverers not to expect them to climb down a rope out of the window. They needed a ladder. 'Give up the idea of carrying us off,' he wrote. 'If you are guarding over us, you may always come and save us in the case of imminent and real danger . . . Above all, in the name of God, avoid bloodshed.'[1] The somewhat enigmatic message was sent – and received by the Cheka at their headquarters in the Hotel America in Ekaterinburg, where it was filed away as further evidence of the ex-tsar's treasonous activity.

The Cheka had taken over guardianship of the prisoners, sending Avdeev and his men away. A new Cheka commander, Jacob Yurovsky, was in charge.

'[The commandant] made us show all our jewels we had on, and the young one [Yurovsky's assistant] wrote them all down in detail and then they were taken from us (where to, for how long, why?? don't know),' Alix wrote in her diary. 'Only left me my two bracelets of U[ncle] Leo's which I can't take off, and the children one bracelet each which we gave and can't be removed, neither Nicholas's engagement [ring?] could he get off.'[2] The inventory was superfluous, as the Romanovs' most valuable jewels had been concealed while they were at Tobolsk, put in small boxes sewn into pillows, individual gems hidden in covered buttons, belt linings, hat linings, stiff-boned corsets.[3] Alix, her daughters and her maids had quietly undertaken the work of concealment, making it look, to their guards, as though they were darning and mending.

It had been necessary to hide the jewels, for the guards had stolen many of the family's possessions, looting their boxes and trunks and making off with their gold watches and silver pins and necklaces, the gold and silver on the former tsar's military decorations, even the gold chains from which their icons hung, along with their china, linen, and stored clothing. Anything saleable.

Yurovsky put an end to the thievery. He sealed up the few pieces of jewellery he had inventoried and left them with the family.

Yurovsky was scrupulous, and very correct. But he was chillingly detached. Avdeev had been spiteful, his soldiers mean – but all had been human. Yurovsky played his role on a plane outside the human, a plane of high-minded dedication to his superiors in Moscow and to the Cheka. All considerations of humanity, it seemed, were put aside.

He went about his task with efficiency and rigour. He ordered the nuns from the convent to deliver only milk from now on, nothing more – nothing in which a message could be concealed. He increased the number of guard posts, and ordered a second machine-gun placed in the attic of the house and an additional sentry positioned in the back yard. He ordered iron bars installed in front of the window that had been opened for ventilation, an ominous change, since the Romanovs had been expecting to leave the house by that window.[4]

With the change in commander came a change in the atmosphere at the Ipatiev house. A priest and a deacon who came to say mass on July 14 observed it, though they could not define its nature.

Father Storozhev had come to the house before, six weeks earlier, and had taken note then of Alexei's extreme pallor and Alix's taut face and evident struggle for composure. Now, in mid-July, Alexei seemed healthier and Alix too appeared to be in a better state.

'Do you know,' the deacon remarked after the mass, 'something has happened to them in there.' The family appeared 'somehow different'. For one thing, they hadn't joined in the liturgical singing, as they had before.

Whatever the difference was, and it was indefinable, something had changed. Yurovsky had changed it and, just possibly, the chaotic situation in Ekaterinburg, and the exhilaration and fear to which it gave rise, were a factor too. All might go badly for the family yet, this they knew. But perhaps, just perhaps, they were on the threshold of liberation at last. No matter that there were now bars on the open window. There were thousands of monarchist troops fighting the Red Guards, beating them back (for there was no other explanation of the increasingly loud battle sounds), coming to save the tsar and his family.

On the morning after Father Storozhev's visit, four women came to the house to clean the floors. The Romanovs were playing cards when the women arrived, and Yurovsky was courteously asking Alexei how he was feeling – he was developing a cold. Yurovsky 'didn't allow us to talk with the imperial family', the women said later, 'who were all in a good mood; the duchesses [Olga, Tatiana,

Marie and Anastasia] were laughing, and there was no sadness about them.'[5]

Alix had spent that morning lying down, while Tatiana read to her from a devotional book, *Spiritual Readings*. She was doing her best to observe the fast of Saints Peter and Paul, and to examine her conscience as was the practice during fasts. Her daughters were taking turns reading to her from a book of homilies. But once again her physical complaints were distracting her. Her eyes ached. She was dosing herself with arsenic in hope of alleviating what she noted in her diary as 'very strong' pains in her back and legs, pains that had continued for at least a week and were making it hard for her to rest.[6]

She was still endeavouring to be a better woman, to conquer her impatience. But from time to time she lost her temper at the cook, the maid, probably even her family. She could not help feeling the effect of all the nervous strain. One of the guards described her as 'severe-looking', with 'the appearance and ways of a haughty, grave woman'.[7] He thought that, with her grey hair and very thin frame, she looked much older than Nicky, though he had turned fifty in May and she was only forty-six.

Despite her long hours of enforced rest, Alix still endeavoured to be usefully occupied when possible. On July 16 she noted in her diary that she and Olga continued secretly to sew gems into their corsets, corsets that they intended to be wearing when they were freed.

She continued to do all she could, but she had put her fate in God's hands. Some months earlier she had written, in a letter to Anna Vyrubov, 'Though we know that the storm is coming nearer, our souls are at peace. Whatever happens will be through God's will.'[8] The storm had come, and was reaching the climax of its force.

The White Army, with two Czech divisions at its core, was encircling Ekaterinburg and would soon have the city under siege. The Red Guard, dismayed and overcome, had begun falling back, retreating in disarray. It was impossible to keep order among the men. Anything could happen, including mass desertions of Bolshevik soldiers to the other side. Loyalties broke down when men panicked.

It was not entirely inconceivable that Yurovsky's men, fearing the wrath of the Czechs, might try to save themselves by freeing the former tsar and turning him over to the Whites.

The Soviet leadership, meeting on July 14 in the Hotel America, had to consider all these things when deciding, as artillery blasts shook the walls, what to do about the Romanovs. The city could not hold out for more than a few days. British, French, even Japanese reinforcements might come to strengthen the White Army and seize the former tsar. Much was at stake in the decision the local leaders had to make, not merely the future of Ekaterinburg – that was certain, the city could not hold out – but the future of Russia.

On no account could the former tsar, or his heir, or any conceivable future heirs, be allowed to return to power. That must be made impossible. Such was the view of the authorities in Moscow, carried back to Ekaterinburg by Chaya Goloshchokin, regional commissar for war. The former tsar must be eliminated, along with his family, and with haste. The Ekaterinburg leaders decided to implement Moscow's order.

On the following day, July 15, Yurovsky had his instructions. He was to carry out the decision. He was to execute the entire Romanov family, and the others who were living with them.

Yurovsky made his preparations methodically, choosing trusted men, bringing them together and addressing them as a group, telling them what had to be done, then replacing two of them when they indicated a reluctance to shoot the captives in cold blood.[9] Once he was assured that his soldiers were resolute, and would do as they were told, he began to plan how and where the task would be carried out, and what would be done with the bodies afterwards.

He went on with his planning the next day, the sixteenth, aware that time was growing short. A dozen revolvers were cleaned and loaded and handed out to the men, together with specific instructions as to which soldier would shoot which victim.[10] Then, apparently, he thought better of his original plan and decided that there would be only eleven victims, not twelve. The fourteen-year-old kitchen boy Leonid Sednev was sent out of the house, with the excuse that he was to see his uncle. He would be spared. The others would die that evening.

Neither Yurovsky nor any of his men betrayed, by their demeanour, what they intended to do. As a result the Romanovs, on their final day, were in no greater state of stress than they usually were, Nicky and the children walking in the garden for exercise, Alix reading from the Old Testament with Tatiana, the books of the prophets Amos and Obadiah ('And it shall come to pass in that day, saith the Lord God, that I will cause the sun to go down at noon, and I will darken the earth in the clear day: And I will turn your feasts into mourning, and all your songs into lamentation . . . and I will make it as the mourning of an only son, and the end thereof as a bitter day.'). Later, Alix and Olga sewed their corsets, and Alix was relieved to find out that Yurovsky had once again ordered the nuns from the convent to bring eggs for Alexei, along with milk.

So intense was the fighting on July 16 that an early curfew was ordered, and apart from the calling of the sentries and the rattle of rifle fire and the ever-present blasting of the heavy guns, no sounds came from the street. Traffic had been halted.

After supper Alix and Nicky played bezique, as they customarily did, until ten-thirty when they went to bed, half-alert, as they always were, for the whistle that would tell them their friends had come at last to save them.

But it was not a whistle that awakened them after midnight, it was Dr Botkin, who had been alerted to the state of danger in the town and instructed to wake the others.[11] The entire town was in turmoil, he was told. The family and household members had to be moved to the lower floor for their safety.

Alix woke, put on her heavy corset with its weight of hidden jewels, and made certain her daughters put on theirs. What was happening was without precedent. Never before had they been roused from sleep to go to a safer part of the house. Perhaps they were to be taken out of the city entirely. Or possibly rescue was at hand, and the guards knew it, and were attempting to thwart the rescue effort.

It made sense: the early curfew, the incessant firing and shouting, the activity of the guards. It might be the liberators, come at last.

Yurovsky came to escort the group of captives as one by one they made their way to the lower floor of the house, first Nicky carrying Alexei, then Alix, then their four daughters, Tatiana carrying her Pekinese dog, then Dr Botkin, Nicky's valet Alexei Trupp, Alix's maid Anna Demidov and the cook Ivan Kharitonov.[12]

Alix followed her husband, wincing from the pain in her leg, taking note, when they went out into the courtyard, that the sky was bright with flares and rockets. They were led into a small empty room on one corner of the house, with a single high barred window.

'Aren't there even any chairs?' Alix asked. 'Can we not sit down?'

Two chairs were brought. Nicky put Alexei down on one, and Alix sat on the other. Then Yurovsky did something puzzling. He asked the nine who were still standing to arrange themselves in line behind the chairs. He needed a photograph, he said. To prove that they had not been kidnapped by the Whites.

Alix sat up in her chair, assuming the regal posture she invariably presented to the camera. But there was no camera. Instead, Yurovsky gave an order and a group of soldiers came in, staying by the door, facing the captives. Yurovsky was saying something. That 'in view of the fact that their relatives in Europe were continuing to attack Soviet Russia, the Ural Executive Committee had ordered them to be shot.'

The startling words hung in the air, there was an instant of bewilderment. Nicky turned to look at the children, then addressed Yurovsky. 'What?' he said. 'What?'

Yurovsky repeated his sentence, then gave an order to the men, who took out their revolvers and took aim.

There was no time to react, only a confusion of sounds, cries of surprise, the gunning of an engine in the courtyard outside, a series of metallic clicks. Alix took a breath, murmured 'Our Father – ' and raised her hand to cross herself. Then the sound of firing, a sharp tap on the forehead as the bullet struck. She fell to the floor, aware of nothing more.

Epilogue

The solemn chants and eloquent words of the Panikhida, the Orthodox Requiem for the dead, filled St Catherine's Chapel in the Peter and Paul Fortress on the afternoon Alexandra of Russia was laid to rest. The date was July 17, 1998, eighty years after her death, and a respectful congregation had gathered to commemorate her life and the lives of those who died with her.

Her wooden coffin, draped with the yellow flag of the Romanovs, lay beside that of her husband. Three coffins, those of Olga, Tatiana and Anastasia, had been placed nearby. There were no coffins for Marie or Alexei, for their bodies have not been recovered. And there were some at the funeral mass who doubted that the bones in the coffins belonged to the former imperial family, despite the rigorous and conclusive scientific testing that had been carried out to identify them.

'Give rest, O God, unto your servant, and appoint for her a place in paradise,' the priest intoned, 'where the choirs of the saints, O Lord, and the just will shine forth like stars.' As the world watched via satellite, the coffins were lowered into the crypt, the fortress guns firing a salute of honour.

Revered as she never was in life, Alexandra was revered now, with the others in her family, as a national symbol, an icon of suffering. Her relics – her rosary of cypress wood, her crystal bottles of eau de cologne, her wheelchair, her flasks of English perfume, her gowns, became venerable objects, to be put on display for viewing by a reverent, or at least a regardful, world – a world that has largely forgotten how Alexandra, as empress, was vilified.

In death Alexandra has at last found honour, yet her stark, romantic and cross-grained nature continues to elude description. Something of her strength of will, her openness of heart, her sensitivity, always struggling towards refinement, lives on in the memoirs of those who loved her, but her deepest self remains concealed, buried with her in the dim candlelit crypt, as the solemn chants rise heavenwards and the faces in the gilded icons gaze down in infinite tenderness upon her.

Notes

Note on Dates and the Transliteration of Russian Names:

Since Alexandra spent nearly half her life in Europe, where the Gregorian calendar was in general use, Gregorian dates have been used throughout the book. Russia did not adopt Gregorian usage until February 1918, which meant that the Russian calendar date was, until 1900, twelve days behind that of Europe; from 1900 on it was thirteen days behind.

Russian first names are Anglicized (Alexander not Aleksandr, Eugene not Yevgeny), patronymics and family names are transliterated according to a modified version of the Library of Congress system. The soft sign ['] is omitted.

Chapter 1
[1.] Georgina Battiscombe, *Queen Alexandra* (London, 1969), p. 117.
[2.] *Advice to a Granddaughter: Letters from Queen Victoria to Princess Victoria of Hesse* (London, 1975), p. 9.

Chapter 2
[1.] *Letters of Queen Victoria from the Archives of the House of Brandenburg-Prussia*, ed. Hector Bolitho (New Haven, 1938), p. 231.
[2.] Baroness Sophie Buxhoeveden, *The Life and Tragedy of Alexandra Feodorovna, Empress of Russia. A Biography* (London and Toronto, 1928), p. 15.
[3.] *Ibid.*, pp. 16–7.
[4.] *Letters of Queen Victoria*, ed. Bolitho, p. 249. Victoria defended her granddaughter's choice against the rather arch negative reaction of her friend Empress Augusta of Germany.

5. Poor Princess Maximiliane Wilhelmine seems to have spent her life under a cloud. Gossip attached to her the stigma of illegitimacy; after her marriage to Alexander II she grew sickly (worn out, no doubt, by her eight pregnancies) and during most of her life in Russia she was displaced, quite literally, by her husband's mistresses, consigned to a life of obscure seclusion in a remote corner of the enormous Winter Palace in St Petersburg. A photograph of the tsarina taken in the late 1860s shows a prematurely aged, matronly woman with a sad face.

6. In her memoirs Nicholas II's sister Olga recalled that Queen Victoria was always contemptuous of the Russian ruling family. 'She [Victoria] said that we possessed a "bourgeoiserie", as she called it, which she disliked intensely . . . My father [Alexander III] could not stand her. He said that she was a pampered, sentimental, selfish old woman.' Olga thought that Victoria 'wasn't really fond of anyone except her German relations.' Ian Vorres, *The Last Grand Duchess* (New York, 1965), p. 40.

7. Buxhoeveden, pp. 18–9.

8. *Ibid.*, p. 18. Alexandra's principal maid Martha Mouchanow, *My Empress: Twenty-Three Years of Intimate Life with the Empress of all the Russias from her Marriage to the Day of her Exile* (New York, 1918), p. 80, gives an impression of Ella that is at variance with that of most other contemporary memoirists. Mouchanow described how, after her marriage to Nicholas, Alexandra was 'set trembling' whenever Ella 'swept down upon her with a complaint or in an excitement of some kind or another.' This would imply a degree of domination as well as a strong sisterly bond.

9. Nicholas's diary entry for May 31, 1884 (O.S.), cited in *Nicholas and Alexandra: The Last Imperial Family of Tsarist Russia* (New York, 1998), p. 269.

Chapter 3

1. Bernard Pares, *My Russian Memoirs* (London, 1931), p. 460. Pares thought this legend represented 'the way in which the soldiers regarded Nicholas – a not unkind contempt.'

2. Quoted in Peter Kurth, *The Lost World of Nicholas and Alexandra* (Boston, 1995), p. 31. Careless researchers occasionally write that Nicholas had brown eyes. His cousin Marie, *Education of a Princess*

(New York, 1931), pp. 194–5, wrote that Nicholas had 'grey and luminous' eyes that 'radiated life and warmth.'

3. *Nicholas and Alexandra: The Last Imperial Family*, p. 256, citing Nicholas's unpublished diary. On March 1, 1914 (O.S.), Nicky wrote in his diary, 'The thirty-third anniversary of Anpapa's excruciating death. To this day I can still hear those two terrible explosions.'

4. Alexander Michaelovich, *Once a Grand Duke* (New York, 1932), p. 57; *Last Grand Duchess*, p. 7. Alexander resented having to take refuge at Gatchina. 'To think that after having faced the guns of the Turks I must retreat now before these skunks,' Grand Duke Sandro recalled hearing him say. *Once a Grand Duke*, p. 65.

5. *Last Grand Duchess*, pp. 38, 18–9.

6. *Once a Grand Duke*, p. 166.

7. In 1916, looking back over the course of their love, Alix wrote to Nicky that she had loved him for thirty-one years. According to her own memory, then, she had first fallen in love with him in 1885, at the age of thirteen.

8. Buxhoeveden, p. 8.

9. Ella wrote to her brother Ernie that Nicky was always writing to her, asking her for news 'and feeling very lovesick and lost and having nobody except Serge and me with whom to talk.' The news he sought was, presumably, about Alix. Edith von Almedingen, *An Unbroken Unity: A Memoir of the Grand Duchess Serge of Russia* (London, 1964), p. 35.

10. Cited in Edith von Almedingen, *The Empress Alexandra* (London, 1961), p. 13.

11. Cited in Mikhail Iroshnikov, *The Sunset of the Romanov Dynasty* (Moscow, 1992), p. 122.

12. Buxhoeveden, p. 22.

13. Apparently Queen Victoria was under the mistaken impression that Alix was eighteen in 1889, when in fact she was seventeen. In her letter of March 31, 1889 to Alix's sister Victoria she wrote, 'She [Alix] is not yet nineteen . . . ' the implication being that she was eighteen. *Queen Victoria in Her Letters and Journals: A Selection* by Christopher Hibbert (New York, 1985), p. 315.

14. *Ibid.*, p. 317.

15. Bertie told his mother Queen Victoria that 'he knows Ella will move heaven and earth to get her [Alix] to marry a Grand Duke.' And Ella

wrote to Ernie, referring to a future marriage between Alix and Nicky, 'God grant this marriage will come true.' *Advice to a Granddaughter*, p. 108; von Almedingen, *An Unbroken Unity*, p. 35.

Ella's motives are a mystery. She claimed to be vastly content in Russia but, according to Kurth, *Lost World*, p. 66, her marriage to Serge was unconsummated because of Serge's 'curious tastes'. So Ella may have been lonely, and wanted Alix for company. Or, having rebelled against her grandmother's marital plans for her, she may simply have wanted Alix to find the courage to follow her heart and defy their grandmother as well.

16. Nicholas's diary entries for January to March, 1890 (O.S.), give a detailed description of his and others' activities during the social season. Iroshnikov, pp. 119ff.

17. In 1894, Nicholas wrote that he had loved Alix 'for a long time' but that he had loved her 'more strongly and tenderly since 1889, when she stayed six weeks at Petersburg.' Vladimir Poliakov, *The Tragic Bride: The Story of the Empress Alexandra* (New York, 1927), p. 13. In April 1892 Nicholas wrote in his diary 'I have loved Alix H[esse] for three years already.' *Nicholas and Alexandra: The Last Imperial Family*, p. 270.

18. Buxhoeveden, p. 23.

Chapter 4

1. James Pope-Hennessy, *Queen Mary* (New York, 1960), p. 183.

2. *Ibid.*, p. 183.

3. Madame von Kolemine pestered Louis incessantly and may have threatened to blackmail him. The fact that she had his love letters in her possession made Queen Victoria anxious; she worried that there might be further legal complications or scandal. The queen recommended that Louis get as far away from Europe as possible – India was her suggestion. *Advice to a Granddaughter*, pp. 68–9.

4. Poliakov, p. 11.

5. Iroshnikov, p. 125.

6. *Nicholas and Alexandra: The Last Imperial Family*, pp. 270–1.

7. Nicholas confessed in his diary to 'very nearly falling asleep from tiredness'. Iroshnikov, p. 118. One afternoon in March of 1890 he wrote that he 'looked at Nevsky Prospekt through the railings for something to do'.

8. In winter 1891, Nicholas wrote that he was 'madly in love with Olga

Dolgorukaya'. *Nicholas and Alexandra: The Last Imperial Family*, p. 270.

9. *Once a Grand Duke*, p. 140.

10. *Once a Grand Duke*, p. 140; *Education of a Princess*, pp. 17–8. Nicky's cousin Sandro wrote of Serge, 'Try as I might, I simply cannot find one redeeming feature in his character . . . Stubborn, rude, and unpleasant, he defied his own shortcomings, throwing complaints from anyone back in their faces, and thereby providing rich fodder for slander and calumny.' *Nicholas and Alexandra: The Last Imperial Family*, p. 245.

11. Nicholas's diary, in *Nicholas and Alexandra: The Last Imperial Family*, pp. 264–8, and Iroshnikov, p. 120.

12. Kurth, p. 40.

13. *Nicholas and Alexandra: The Last Imperial Family*, p. 268.

14. Serge Sazonov, *Fateful Years* (New York, 1928), p. 110.

15. Buxhoeveden, p. 33. Alix referred to the years between 1889 and 1894 as 'five sad years' in a 1894 letter to her governess Madgie.

16. Iroshnikov, p. 125.

Chapter 5

1. Alix confided to her lady-in-waiting Sophie Buxhoeveden that her earliest recollections were of romping with her father. Buxhoeveden, p. 6.

2. Andrei Maylunas and Sergei Mironenko, eds., *A Lifelong Passion: Nicholas and Alexandra: Their Own Story* (New York, 1997), p. 15.

3. *Ibid.*, p. 26.

4. Alix prided herself on her sexual sophistication. As she wrote to Nicky in 1894, she sometimes felt 'very old knowing things others don't know until they are married'. 'As a child I knew things others don't till they are grown up and married,' she wrote. 'I don't know how it came!' *Lifelong Passion*, p. 86.

5. Buxhoeveden, p. 31.

6. *Nicholas and Alexandra: The Last Imperial Family*, p. 271. This diary entry was written several weeks after Nicholas had been given permission to propose to Alix. A younger contemporary of Matilda recalled seeing the ballerina enter a drawing room in St Petersburg, 'an elegant woman in deep rose velvet and a picture hat with pale ostrich feathers'. She looked, the younger woman thought, like an 'exotic bird'. Edith von Almedingen, *I Remember St Petersburg* (London, 1969), p. 30.

7. *Lifelong Passion*, pp. 32–3.
8. *Ibid.*, p. 33.
9. *Nicholas and Alexandra: The Last Imperial Family*, p. 272.
10. *Lifelong Passion*, p. 33.
11. *Ibid.*, pp. 30–1.
12. *Ibid.*, p. 34.
13. These internal preoccupations are recorded in Alix's letters. *Lifelong Passion*, p. 67. It is worth noting that in all her reminiscences Alix did not mention her late mother.

Chapter 6
1. *Lifelong Passion*, p. 45.
2. *Ibid.*, p. 48.
3. *Ibid.*, pp. 48–9. Exactly what the compromise was that permitted Alix to retain, in her conscience at least, her fealty to Lutheranism is only hinted at in the surviving printed sources. After Nicholas left Coburg, he wrote to Alix from Gatchina, 'Of course I told them [his parents] all of what you wanted me to say and they gave in at once and said you would not have to renounce the old belief, but that it would be like with Ella.' *Ibid.*, p. 60.
4. *Ibid.*, pp. 48–9.
5. Victoria wrote to her namesake, Alix's sister Victoria, on May 25, 1894, 'Still the feeling that I had laboured so hard to prevent it [an engagement] and that I felt at last there was no longer any danger and all in one night – everything was changed.' *Advice to a Granddaughter*, p. 124. A few weeks after leaving Coburg, Victoria quizzed Alix unmercifully about her change of heart about marrying Nicky. Alix told Nicky how 'she [Queen Victoria] began by asking me so many questions, when, how, and where, and what made me change my decision and so on, till I no longer knew what to say.' *Lifelong Passion*, p. 60.
6. *Ibid.*, p. 49.
7. Poliakov, pp. 26–7.
8. *Lifelong Passion*, pp. 52, 55.
9. Buxhoeveden, p. 34.
10. Poliakov, p. 27; *Lifelong Passion*, p. 61.
11. Buxhoeveden, pp. 35–6.
12. *Lifelong Passion*, p. 67.
13. *Ibid.*, p. 67.

14. *Ibid.*, p. 83.
15. Poliakov, pp. 42, 46, 48, 49.
16. *Ibid.*, pp. 50ff.
17. *Ibid.*, p. 47.
18. *Lifelong Passion*, p. 72.
19. *Ibid.*, p. 80.

Chapter 7
1. Nicky referred to his becoming tsar as 'the worst . . . that which I feared all my life!' *Lifelong Passion*, p. 118.
2. *Last Grand Duchess*, pp. 9–10, 38; *Once a Grand Duke*, p. 69.
3. *Lifelong Passion*, p. 86.
4. Nicky's sister Olga, in *Last Grand Duchess*, p. 55, erroneously states that Alix arrived in Livadia two days after Alexander III's death, having made the journey in the company of Bertie. Other sources make it clear that Alix did not travel with Bertie, but with her sister Victoria and others, that Ella met them en route, and that Nicky was waiting for them all at Simferopol. Bertie arrived two days after the death.
5. Iroshnikov, p. 19.
6. Poliakov, p. 60.
7. *Once a Grand Duke*, p. 168.
8. *Lifelong Passion*, p. 99.
9. *Ibid.*, p. 100.
10. *Ibid.*, p. 87.
11. *Last Grand Duchess*, p. 55.

Chapter 8
1. Mouchanow, pp. 15–6.
2. *Ibid.*, p. 117.
3. Buxhoeveden, p. 44.
4. *Lifelong Passion*, pp. 110–1.
5. Cited in *Nicholas and Alexandra: The Last Imperial Family*, pp. 280–1.
6. *Ibid.*, p. 279.

Chapter 9
1. *The Empress Frederick Writes to Sophie: Letters 1889–1901*, ed. Arthur Gould Lee (London, 1955), p. 281.

2. Cited in Suzanne Massie, *Land of the Firebird: The Beauty of Old Russia* (New York, 1980), p. 277.
3. Iroshnikov, p. 132.
4. *Ibid.*, p. 132.
5. Alexander Mossolov, *At the Court of the Last Tsar* (London, 1935), p. 72.
6. Mouchanow, pp. 21, 23, 131.
7. *Ibid.*, p. 24.
8. *Ibid.*, pp. 25, 28.
9. *Ibid.*, p. 22.
10. *Ibid.*, p. 22.
11. Harrison Salisbury, *Black Night, White Snow: Russia's Revolutions 1905–1917* (New York, 1978), p. 62; Iroshnikov, p. 131.

Chapter 10
1. Mouchanow, pp. 50–1.
2. *Last Grand Duchess*, p. 61.
3. Mouchanow, pp. 87–8.
4. Iroshnikov, p. 138.
5. *Nicholas and Alexandra: The Last Imperial Family*, p. 18.
6. Iroshnikov, p. 123.
7. *Nicholas and Alexandra: The Last Imperial Family*, p. 250.
8. Mouchanow, p. 34.
9. Buxhoeveden, p. 58.
10. *Ibid.*, p. 58.
11. Mouchanow, pp. 43–4.
12. Buxhoeveden, pp. 166–7.
13. *Ibid.*, 166. In this preoccupation Alix was joined by her dear friend Juju Rantzau in Germany who, Alix wrote, 'understood the difficulties of this world, and the different temptations, and always encouraged one in the right, and helped one to fight one's weaknesses'. Alix and Juju exchanged weekly letters which either have been lost or, if still in existence, have not been published. Buxhoeveden, p. 167. What a treasure these letters would be to a biographer!
14. Mouchanow, pp. 39, 141. Alix embroidered beautifully; Mouchanow thought that cloths she decorated for use in church 'would easily have won a prize at any exhibition'. Mouchanow, p. 143.
15. *Lifelong Passion*, p. 131.
16. *Ibid.*, p. 130.

Chapter 11

1. Mouchanow, p. 68.
2. Mouchanow, p. 68, refers to 'some hopes of maternity she [Alix] was nursing' at the time of the coronation. Later on, after she miscarried the child, 'her doctor said that the expected child would, in all probability, have been a boy'.
3. *Lifelong Passion*, p. 133.
4. Iroshnikov, p. 306.
5. Bernard Pares, *The Fall of the Russian Monarchy* (New York, 1961), p. 131.
6. 'The unpopularity of the young sovereign [Alix] was already an established fact when the coronation took place,' Mouchanow wrote. 'It appeared quite plainly on the day when she made her public entry into the ancient city, when the crowds greeted her with absolute silence, whilst they vociferously cheered the Dowager Empress . . . When she was alone in her rooms she wept profusely over this manifestation of the displeasure of the nation in regard to her person.' Mouchanow, pp. 51–2.
7. This account of the events at Khodynka Meadow is taken from the eyewitness narrative of the reporter Vladimir Giliarovsky, cited in Iroshnikov, pp. 30–1, the diary of Nicholas II in *Nicholas and Alexandra: The Last Imperial Family*, p. 286, Poliakov, pp. 107–11, and *Last Grand Duchess*, pp. 66ff. The value of the pink enamel mugs to the Muscovites of 1896 was far greater than can be imagined by the modern reader. To them, an unbreakable cup that would last forever was an unheard-of marvel.
8. The official death toll, given in a statement released on the evening of the catastrophe, was 1389, with 2690 wounded. Actual numbers were far higher.
9. *Nicholas and Alexandra: The Last Imperial Family*, p. 286.
10. Buxhoeveden, p. 69, and Mouchanow, pp. 54–5, record the efforts the empress was making to disguise, in public, her tearful private feelings.
11. *Last Grand Duchess*, p. 68.
12. Mouchanow, p. 68, wrote that 'owing to over-fatigue', the empress 'had an accident which destroyed some hopes of maternity she was nursing'. The doctor who treated her was in no doubt that she had been pregnant, and probably with a son. Though no announcement was made, it was rumoured that the empress had had a miscarriage, 'and, with the usual wickedness of humanity, it was rumoured that the sovereign had had

reasons to hide the condition she found herself in, and that the accident in itself had been brought on more voluntarily than accidentally.'

Mouchanow was questioned about the empress's health and whether or not she had miscarried. Though Alix had tried to keep her pregnancy a secret, the press had speculated that she might be expecting, and Queen Victoria, writing to Alix's sister Victoria on June 1, 1896, noted that the papers were 'hinting' that another baby was on the way. *Advice to a Granddaughter*, p. 136.

Chapter 12
1. Buxhoeveden, p. 79; Mouchanow, p. 55.
2. Mouchanow, p. 55.
3. *Ibid.*, p. 69. 'The sayings,' Mouchanow wrote, 'circulated freely in Petersburg.'
4. *Ibid.*, pp. 118–9.
5. *Ibid.*, pp. 118–9.
6. *Ibid.*, pp. 61–2.
7. *Ibid.*, p. 61.
8. *Ibid.*, p. 64; Poliakov, p. 123; Nina Epton, *Victoria and Her Daughters* (New York, 1971), pp. 210–1.
9. Mouchanow, pp. 65–6.
10. *Ibid.*, pp. 65–6; Buxhoeveden, p. 75.
11. Mouchanow, p. 91, wrote that the empress was worried about the sex of the child she was carrying 'until at last the thought of it had become quite an obsession', doing harm to her nerves.
12. *Lifelong Passion*, p. 163.

Chapter 13
1. Alix's increasing preoccupation with orderliness, her supervision of the household and her obsessive concern with time management are described in Mouchanow, pp. 147, 150–1.
2. *Ibid.*, p. 29.
3. According to Mouchanow, Alix possessed 'one of the most remarkable collections of precious stones in Europe', and Bolin and Fabergé brought to Tsarskoe Selo every fine piece of jewellery they acquired, offering it to the emperor before allowing any of their other customers to see it. Mouchanow, p. 28.
4. *Ibid.*, p. 68.

5. *Ibid.*, p. 89.
6. *Ibid.*, p. 90.
7. *Lifelong Passion*, pp. 173–4.
8. Buxhoeveden, p. 84.

Chapter 14
1. Mouchanow, p. 85.
2. Anastasia, or Stana, divorced Duke George and in May, 1907, married
    Nicholas Nicholaevich, or Nikolasha. Stana's second husband
    Nikolasha was 6´6´´, gruff, and commanding. Militsa's husband Peter,
    on the other hand, was diffident and of indifferent health, having
    suffered from tuberculosis which led him to flee the damp and cold of
    Petersburg and spend years in Egypt seeking a cure.
3. Alix wrote to her close friend Juju Rantzau, 'I worry myself and cry
    for days on end.' She was upset that Nicky was not being well served
    or respected – in part because of the succession issue. As long as she
    had no son, the courtiers looked to Michael and accorded him the
    authority due to Nicky. Anna Vyrubov, *Souvenirs de ma Vie* (Paris,
    1927), p. 20. In published photographs of Alix taken in 1900–1 she
    looks sad, anxious, sorrowful or serious – never happy or lighthearted.
4. Buxhoeveden, p. 167.
5. *Ibid.*, p. 90.
6. *Lifelong Passion*, p. 204.
7. *Ibid.*, p. 204.
8. *Ibid.*, p. 206.
9. Descriptions of Philippe Vachot, and of his proceedings when meeting
    with the devotees in Paris and in Russia are in *Lifelong Passion*,
    pp. 206–8, 219, and *Once a Grand Duke*, p. 181. Paris police reports
    include eyewitness notes on what was actually said at his gatherings.
10. *Lifelong Passion*, p. 207.
11. *Ibid.*, p. 219.
12. *Ibid.*, p. 208.
13. Sandro, *Once a Grand Duke*, p. 181, wrote that the European news-
    papers reported that 'an important event in the family of the Czar of
    Russia' was expected.
14. *Lifelong Passion*, p. 214. 'So it is true and you are sure about yourself,'
    Alix wrote, 'so now I must confess the same thing. I know by your
    looks you have been thinking it was so, but I on purpose did not tell

you, so as that when others asked, you can honestly say that you did not know. Now it begins to be difficult to hide . . . My broad waist all winter must have struck you.'

Chapter 15

1. Early in August, 1902, Alix wrote to Nicky saying that Ella 'assailed me about our Friend [Philippe]. I remained very quiet and gave dull answers . . . I stuck to the story of the remedy.' *Lifelong Passion*, pp. 216–7.
2. *Ibid.*, pp. 217–8.
3. Mouchanow, pp. 125–6.
4. *Lifelong Passion*, p. 217.
5. Xenia wrote that she and Minnie 'found her [Alix] in a very sad mood, although she talks about it [the false pregnancy] with great acceptance'. *Lifelong Passion*, p. 217.
6. *Ibid.*, p. 219. Apparently the story of a miscarriage became the standard one in diplomatic circles. Maurice Paléologue, *An Ambassador's Memoirs* (New York, 1924–5), I, pp. 203–10.
7. Buxhoeveden, p. 98.
8. *Last Grand Duchess*, pp. 117–8.
9. Buxhoeveden, p. 93. Nicky recorded in his diary, 'We have heard of many people being cured today and yesterday. Another cure took place in the cathedral while the holy relics were being carried around the cathedral.' *Nicholas and Alexandra: The Last Imperial Family*, p. 292.
10. Felix Yusupov, *Lost Splendor* (New York, 1953), pp. 144–5. Yusupov related in detail another ceremony of glorification of the relics, along with a procession of the sick and mad seeking cures.
11. *Last Grand Duchess*, pp. 117–8. While at Sarov, Olga witnessed a peasant woman carrying her entirely paralyzed little daughter into the river. Later the girl walked in the meadow, and doctors who were present certified that the child had indeed been paralyzed, and that her paralysis had disappeared. Ella wrote that while at Sarov 'we had the blessing of seeing a little dumb girl speak'. Buxhoeveden, p. 93. Whether through mass hypnosis or by some other psychological means, the thousands who came to Sarov, including the imperial family, were convinced beyond any doubt that miraculous cures were being effected.
12. *Nicholas and Alexandra: The Last Imperial Family,* p. 292.

Chapter 16

1. Buxhoeveden, pp. 102–3.
2. Mouchanow, pp. 101, 152–4; *Lifelong Passion*, pp. 232, 238. Olga noted in her autobiography that Alix was hardly ever in good health at this time. *Last Grand Duchess*, p. 96.
3. Mouchanow, p. 101.
4. Buxhoeveden, pp. 102–3.
5. Mouchanow, pp. 160–1.
6. *Ibid.*, pp. 154–5.
7. *Lifelong Passion*, p. 245.
8. 'Alix and I were very alarmed by the bleeding of young Alexei that came at intervals from his umbilical cord until evening,' Nicky wrote in his diary. 'How painful it is to experience such anxieties!' Cited in *Nicholas and Alexandra: The Last Imperial Family*, p. 237.
9. *Lifelong Passion*, p. 249.

Chapter 17

1. This account of the Epiphany assassination attempt is based on *Last Grand Duchess*, pp. 113–4. Sophie Buxhoeveden was present in the palace on the day of the attack. Buxhoeveden, p. 113.
2. Salisbury, pp. 119–20.
3. Iroshnikov, p. 158.
4. Official government figures listed 96 dead, 333 wounded, but journalists who were present put the number much higher, at over 4000 injured. Newspaper reports published in foreign capitals inflated the numbers still further. Salisbury, p. 125 note, summarizes the various estimates.
5. Alix's letter is in Buxhoeveden, pp. 108–10.

Chapter 18

1. Alix's unescorted carriage rides are described in Buxhoeveden, pp. 115ff.
2. *Last Grand Duchess*, p. 123.
3. Buxhoeveden, pp. 105, 164, 218.
4. *Education of a Princess*, p. 61. Nearly all the contemporary memoirists note the strain caused by the empress's having to conceal Alexei's illness from even her closest personal servants.
5. Mouchanow, p. 48. According to Mouchanow, the empress was careless with the rings, throwing them down anywhere; she did the

same thing when writing letters, tossing finished sheets carelessly in a heap on a desk as she wrote them, and later on sorting them by recipient, sometimes mixing them up so that they were sent to the wrong person.

6. *Lifelong Passion*, p. 278.

Chapter 19

1. *Last Grand Duchess*, p. 134.
2. *Ibid.*, p. 134.
3. Buxhoeveden, p. 136.
4. This account of Father Gregory's private apartment is drawn from Poliakov, pp. 161–4, which gives much colourful detail.
5. Olga was in 'no doubt' that Father Gregory possessed the healing gift. 'I saw those miraculous effects with my own eyes,' she wrote, 'and that more than once. I also know that the most prominent doctors of the day had to admit it. Professor Fedorov, who stood at the very peak of the profession, and whose patient Alexei was, told me so on more than one occasion; all the doctors disliked Rasputin intensely.' *Last Grand Duchess*, pp. 138–9.

   Poliakov, pp. 171–2, cites another instance of Rasputin's healing gift. One Madame Djanumov had a niece near death from scarlet fever complicated by pneumonia. The doctors had said she was beyond hope, but the aunt sought Rasputin. According to Madame Djanumov's own account, Rasputin took the girl's hand, 'his face became different; it was like that of a dead man – yellow, waxlike and immobile: terrible. The eyeballs rolled upwards so that only the whites were to be seen.' He said, 'She shall not die, she shall not die . . . ' That evening the girl's fever broke and she began her recovery. It may have been a coincidence, but Rasputin's contemporaries observed too many such 'coincidences' over too many years to remain sceptical.
6. Nicky's sister Olga attested to Rasputin's sparse number of personal possessions, and the rented or loaned furniture. *Last Grand Duchess*, p. 133. Whether he sent money home to Siberia at this period is unknown.
7. Yusupov, pp. 131–2. Like Rasputin, Father John was sought out by hundreds of would-be clients. And, like Rasputin, he was said to have a particularly 'penetrating gaze'.
8. *Last Grand Duchess*, pp. 135–9, describes Alexei's grave attack.
9. *Ibid.*, pp. 135–9. The remarkable swiftness with which Alexei's attacks

10. Buxhoeveden, p. 144.

11. Victoria visited Alix in the summer of 1906 for two weeks. *Lifelong Passion*, p. 296. Irene too came to visit from time to time. During Irene's visits Alix must have discussed with her Alexei's condition, but whether she drew hope from the fact that Irene's surviving haemophiliac son was continuing to thrive is unknown.

12. An increase in apocalyptic literature was evident throughout Europe in the early years of the twentieth century, but was at its peak in Russia. Educated Russians saw omens of world destruction everywhere. James Billington, *The Icon and the Axe* (New York, 1966), p. 514. On the electrifying discovery of the woolly mammoth, which was the talk of Petersburg in 1905–6, see von Almedingen, *I Remember*, pp. 154–5.

13. Buxhoeveden, p. 190.

14. It was a measure of Nicky's increasingly weak position – and of the severity of Alexei's illness – that in July 1907 Cyril's marriage was officially recognized, restoring his succession rights. In November of 1908, following the death of Vladimir's brother Alexis, Cyril was permitted to return to Russia to attend the late grand duke's funeral.

    Cyril's choice of Ducky had put his claims at risk on several grounds. The Orthodox church forbade marriage between first cousins (though Nicky's cousin Sandro and his sister Xenia had married despite this prohibition), as a divorcée Ducky was ineligible to marry any member of the imperial family, and finally, she was not a baptized member of the Orthodox church.

15. This account of the *Standart* accident comes from Buxhoeveden, p. 114. Princess Obolensky, an eyewitness, told the story to Buxhoeveden in great detail. Alix, the princess said, was 'always resourceful and full of energy'. Some years earlier Alix had described herself, when accompanying Nicky on one of his autumn hunting trips, as 'game to the end', though limping on her sore leg as she did her best to keep up with his swift stride.

16. Mossolov, pp. 173–4.

Chapter 20

1. Buxhoeveden, p. 161. 'She always felt in a hurry.'

2. Mouchanow, pp. 85–6. Alix's habit of always having some piece of 'fancy

work' – embroidery, tatting, needlepoint – in her hand was, according to Buxhoeveden, a habit acquired in childhood under Queen Victoria's influence. Buxhoeveden, p. 161.

3. Buxhoeveden, p. 126.

4. Nicky told KR that Alix was 'very unwilling to receive, and is fearful of people, especially in crowds'. *Lifelong Passion*, p. 318.

5. Mouchanow, p. 143.

6. Alix's comments on illness and depression were in a letter of October, 1909, but apply to her long illness in 1908 as well. *Lifelong Passion*, pp. 322–3.

7. Count Kokovtsov, *Out of My Past* (London and Stanford, California, 1935), p. 449. Countess Hendrikov, Alix's lady-in-waiting, talked to Kokovtsov about her mistress's 'almost mystic moods'. Alix's favourite subject for discussion with her daughters, the countess said, was the efficacy of prayer and mankind's ongoing relationship to the divine. 'The Empress believed that one's whole life should be based upon complete faith in the Almighty and obedience to His will,' the countess recalled her saying. 'Nothing was impossible for God, she believed. He would hearken to every prayer of the pure in heart; faith in Him would overcome all obstacles.' Miracles, she said, were to be accepted 'with meekness and humility'.

8. Buxhoeveden, p. 126.

9. *Lifelong Passion*, p. 320.

10. Mouchanow noted that the 'extreme delicacy of the children was a source of perpetual anxiety to the tsarina'.

11. *Last Grand Duchess*, p. 100.

12. Buxhoeveden, pp. 157–8.

13. *Last Grand Duchess*, pp. 102–3. Nicky's sister Olga kept until the end of her life keepsakes that had belonged to Anastasia: a tiny silver pencil on a thin silver chain, a small scent bottle and a hatpin surrounded by a large amethyst. Olga developed so pronounced a habit of charitable generosity that when she inherited her full fortune at age twenty, her first act was to ask Alix to allow her to pay the costs of a sanatorium stay for a disabled child whose parents could not afford treatment. Buxhoeveden, p. 159.

14. *Lifelong Passion*, p. 330.

15. Buxhoeveden, p. 166.

16. *Ibid.*, p. 156; *Last Grand Duchess*, p. 105.

17. *Lifelong Passion*, p. 320.
18. *Ibid.*, p. 314.
19. *Ibid.*, p. 320.
20. *Ibid.*, p. 331.
21. *Education of a Princess*, pp. 279–80.
22. Buxhoeveden, p. 144.
23. Olga in *Last Grand Duchess*, p. 129, called Father Gregory a chameleon. It is impossible to reconstruct the true nature of the elusive Rasputin, for nearly all the surviving written records about him either come from hostile sources or attempt to exculpate him. According to Olga, 'most of what was written about him by contemporaries was hearsay', gossip from grand ducal courts and drawing-room chatter. The French ambassador Maurice Paléologue's recorded views of Father Gregory merely repeated the stories Paléologue heard at Aunt Miechen's dinner parties.

    That Rasputin was an enthusiastic debauchee and a seducer is well established; that he recognized no restraining moral code seems very likely. But his flagrant transgressions did not define him, nor did they tarnish his authenticity as a source of inspiration and healing and, despite all, his indefinable holiness.
24. *Lifelong Passion*, pp. 314–5.
25. *Ibid.*, p. 331.
26. *Ibid.*, p. 331.
27. Gleb Botkin, *The Real Romanovs* (New York, 1931), p. 123.
28. Buxhoeveden, p. 172. Mouchanow, p. 185, claimed that Anna was the only one around Alix strong enough to stand up to the 'bossing' of Alix's sister Ella.
29. *Ibid.*, pp. 170–2.
30. Mouchanow, pp. 188–90. According to Mouchanow, Dondukov may have given Alix drugs which made her nervous condition worse. But Mouchanow was hostile to the princess and her suggestion was tinged with malice.

Chapter 21
1. According to Kokovtsov, the tsar demanded that 'firm measures' be taken 'to bring the press to order' and to prohibit any reporting about Rasputin, while acknowledging that no law existed to bring the press under government censorship. Nicholas accused Stolypin of 'weakness'

in regard to the press but in the end, convinced otherwise by Stolypin's arguments, the tsar backed down. Kokovtsov, pp. 291–2.

2. Pares, p. 236.
3. Buxhoeveden, pp. 128–9.
4. *Ibid.*, p. 179.
5. *Ibid.*, p. 180.
6. *Lifelong Passion*, p. 343. In May of 1911 Nicky wrote that Alix was 'still unwell, sometimes better, then worse again'.
7. Kokovtsov, p. 312.
8. Mouchanow, p. 146.
9. *The Last Diary of Tsaritsa Alexandra*, ed. Vladimir A. Kozlov and Vladimir M. Khrustalëv (New Haven and London, 1997), pp. xv–xvi.
10. *Lifelong Passion*, p. 350.
11. Kokovtsov, p. 293, note.
12. *Lifelong Passion*, p. 373.
13. Kokovtsov, p. 290.
14. Greg King, *The Last Empress: The Life and Times of Alexandra* (New York, 1994), pp. 187–8.
15. Kokovtsov, pp. 296–7.
16. *Ibid.*, p. 296.
17. *Lifelong Passion*, p. 351. Xenia's diary records what Minnie told her of the conversation.
18. *Ibid.*; *Nicholas and Alexandra: The Last Imperial Family*, p. 327.
19. Kokovtsov, p. 296; *Lifelong Passion*, p. 351.
20. *Nicholas and Alexandra: The Last Imperial Family*, p. 327.

Chapter 22
1. *Lifelong Passion*, p. 351.
2. Buxhoeveden, p. 129.
3. Cited in Poliakov, pp. 152–3.
4. Maria Rasputin, *My Father*, Reprint edition (New Hyde Park, New York, 1970), p. 70. In 1912 Maria wrote, 'the heir seemed to be in better health, his crises of illness became less frequent and he had fewer haemorrhages, so that my father went less often to the palace.'
5. George Buchanan, British ambassador to Russia, wrote in his memoirs that when he first met the tsar, they talked about hunting, and Nicholas bragged that on his best day's pheasant shooting he had brought down 1400 birds. Such inflated claims were characteristic of him. Buchanan,

My Mission to Russia and Other Diplomatic Memoirs (Boston, 1923), I, p. 168.

6. Maria Rasputin, p. 72 gives a different chronology from other sources for the exchange of telegrams. According to her recollection, the empress's telegram from Spala was received on October 26, while her father was at dinner. His return telegram arrived at Spala October 27.

7. Petersburg in winter 1913 is described from memory in von Almedingen, *I Remember*, p. 161.

8. Mouchanow, p. 158.

9. *Ibid.*, pp. 108–9.

10. *Ibid.*, p. 123.

Chapter 23

1. Mouchanow, p. 181.

2. Buxhoeveden, p. 175.

3. *Last Grand Duchess*, p. 130; Kokovtsov, p. 361.

4. Salisbury, p. 233.

5. *Lifelong Passion*, pp. 377, 383, 392, 394.

6. Grand Duke Gavril Konstantinovich, *In the Marble Palace* (St Petersburg, 1993), p. 142.

7. The military review is described in detail in Meriel Buchanan, *Dissolution of an Empire* (London, 1932), pp. 77–8.

8. Paléologue, I, pp. 14, 24–5.

Chapter 24

1. Buxhoeveden, p. 187. Beginning in 1913, Sophie Buxhoeveden's biography of Alexandra became a record of her personal experience at the court. Before 1913 she relied on information she was given by earlier ladies-in-waiting Elizabeth Obolensky and Marie Bariatinsky. The latter was among Alix's closest friends; after Marie left the court, she continued to correspond regularly with the empress and to visit her at Livadia. Although Sophie was loyal and admiring, she was not an uncritical biographer, and she was an intelligent and shrewd observer. Her loyalty and admiration for the empress are evident throughout her long and detailed account.

2. 'If people speak to you about my "nerves" please strongly contradict it,' Alix wrote to Marie Bariatinsky in the fall of 1910. 'They are as strong as ever, it's the "over-tired heart" and nerves of the body and

nerves of the heart besides, but the other nerves are very sound.' Cited in King, pp. 176–7.

3. *Education of a Princess*, pp. 196–7.
4. Buxhoeveden, p. 232.
5. Iroshnikov, p. 140; Buxhoeveden, pp. 126, 293.
6. Buxhoeveden, p. 173.
7. Mouchanow, pp. 201–2.
8. Yusupov, p. 161.
9. Cited in Pares, p. 355. Marie Pavlovna the younger speaking to Paléologue. Nicky's cousin Sandro wrote that Alix was 'raised by her father . . . to hate the Kaiser,' and that she had looked forward all her life to seeing Germany's arrogance humbled in a war. 'For me, for my uncles and cousins, for anyone who ever met or talked to Alix,' Sandro wrote, 'the very suggestion of her "German sympathies" sounded monstrous and ridiculous.' *Once a Grand Duke*, p. 271.
10. Meriel Buchanan, *Dissolution*, p. 96.
11. Alexandra, *Last Diary*, p. xvii.
12. *The Letters of the Tsaritsa to the Tsar* (London, 1923; Reprint edition Stanford, California, 1973), p. 26.
13. Buxhoeveden, p. 192. Though Alix and her daughters usually wore nurses' uniforms, some hospital visits were made in more conspicuous attire. Meriel Buchanan, who disliked the empress, wrote that early in 1915 Alix and two of her daughters came to visit the military hospital on Vassily Island where Meriel herself was working, all wearing red velvet gowns. Meriel Buchanan, *Dissolution*, p. 125.

In her memoirs Marie Pavlovna, a critic of Alix, recalled that when the empress visited military hospitals, 'there was something in her, eluding definition, that prevented her from communicating her own genuine feelings and from comforting the person she addressed.' Marie thought that the men didn't understand Alix – who often mumbled – or when they did understand her words, her meaning was obscure.

Marie noted how when Alix came to the field hospital where she herself worked, the soldiers watched her with 'anxious, frightened eyes', whereas the tsar, when he visited the same men, 'uplifted' them and made them rapt with contentment. 'In spite of his small stature,' Marie wrote, 'he always seemed taller than anyone else in the room, and moved from bed to bed with an extraordinary dignity.' *Education of a Princess*, p. 194.

14. Buxhoeveden, p. 174.
15. *Letters of the Tsaritsa*, p. 27.
16. Mouchanow, p. 171.
17. *Letters of the Tsaritsa*, p. 20.
18. *Ibid.*, pp. 6, 14, 24.
19. *Ibid.*, p. 8.
20. Mouchanow, p. 209.

Chapter 25
1. Buxhoeveden, p. 197 and note.
2. *Letters of the Tsaritsa*, p. 3.
3. Others in Alix's confidence were Countess Fredericks, Lili Dehn and Countess Rehbinder. Sophie Buxhoeveden, Elizabeth Schneider, Martha Mouchanow and Baron Fredericks were trusted staff members. In 1914 and 1915 Grand Duke Paul came to the palace, and Alix was for a time on good terms with him, though how much actual information he brought her is hard to judge.
4. *Lifelong Passion*, pp. 373–4 citing police reports; Salisbury, p. 263; Brian Moynahan, *Rasputin: The Saint Who Sinned* (New York, 1997), pp. 215–6. The police called him 'sexually psychopathic'.
5. Moynahan, p. 212.
6. *Letters of the Tsaritsa*, pp. 82, 84.
7. *Ibid.*, p. 75.
8. Pares, p. 335, thought that in the first ten months of the war nearly four million Russian soldiers were killed, wounded and missing – a number larger than the entire British expeditionary force. Hélène Carrère d'Encausse, *Nicholas II: The Interrupted Transition*, trans. George Holoch (New York and London, 2000), estimates that by early in 1915, 1.2 million troops had been killed, wounded or were missing or taken prisoner. Seven hundred thousand new recruits were raised. d'Encausse, p. 174.
9. Meriel Buchanan, *Dissolution*, p. 112; Buxhoeveden, p. 210.
10. *Letters of the Tsaritsa*, p. 128.
11. *Ibid.*, pp. 86–7.
12. *Ibid.*, pp. 91, 100.
13. Meriel Buchanan, *Dissolution*, pp. 127–9.
14. *Letters of the Tsaritsa*, p. 114.
15. *Ibid.*, p. 68.

16. *Ibid.*, p. 68.
17. *Ibid.*, p. 104.

Chapter 26

1. Lili Dehn, *The Real Tsaritsa* (London, 1922; Reprint by Royalty Digest, 1995), pp. 68–9, 136–7.

2. *Ibid.*, p. 138. Alix told Lili Dehn that she was 'saturated with Veronal'. 'Veronal is keeping me up,' she said, meaning that it was buoying up her energy. 'I'm literally saturated with it.'

The consequences of this 'saturation' can easily be imagined. Lewis Thomas wrote in *Notes of a Medicine Watcher* that, around 1910, many middle-aged and elderly women were hopelessly addicted to the barbiturate compounds widely prescribed for 'nerves' at that time.

3. Rumours that Ernie was in Russia, being kept hidden by Alix or Ella, were widespread. Sophie Buxhoeveden recalled that in 1916 she was asked 'in all seriousness whether the Grand Duke of Hesse was not hidden in the cellars of the palace'. Buxhoeveden, pp. 224–5.

4. Dehn, p. 142. The incident with the villagers, which Dehn describes, took place early in 1915.

5. Alexandra's letters to Nicky reassured him that 'for sure your dear Father quite particularly prays for you'. Just as Nicky had attempted to contact his father in seances held soon after his accession, and would again believe, in 1916, that occult messages from his father were being relayed to him via Protopopov, so in 1915 he was probably seeking to contact Alexander III as he made up his mind to take command of the armed forces.

6. Meriel Buchanan, *Dissolution*, p. 129.

7. Iroshnikov, pp. 144–5.

8. Moynahan, p. 261.

9. Alexandra's printed letters to her husband for the years 1914–16 consist mostly of daily happenings, news of herself and the children, and warm reassurances of her devotion. The amount of space taken up by political and military matters is small, the references to Rasputin even fewer.

Though urgent in tone and sketchy in composition – she wrote in extreme haste, which was not surprising, given her extraordinarily full days – the letters were far from incoherent or 'hysterical' – the word used most often to describe both the empress and her written messages.

Her overemotional, overanxious state is evident, but the letters are far from being the work of a hysteric or a madwoman.

10. *Letters of the Tsaritsa*, p. 153.
11. Iroshnikov, p. 131.
12. *Letters of the Tsaritsa*, pp. 118, 122.
13. Dehn, p. 107.
14. *Ibid.*, p. 51.
15. *Letters of the Tsaritsa*, p. 232.
16. Buxhoeveden, pp. 214–5.
17. *Ibid.*, p. 215.
18. *Ibid.*, p. 215.
19. *Letters of the Tsaritsa*, p. 246.

Chapter 27

1. Yusupov, p. 213.
2. *Nicholas and Alexandra: The Last Imperial Family*, p. 355.
3. *Letters of the Tsaritsa*, p. 316.
4. Kokovtsov, pp. 478–80. Kokovtsov thought that the tsar was 'on the verge of some mental disturbance' if not 'already in its power'. He appeared to be nervously ill, and 'hardly knew what was happening to him'.
5. d'Encausse, p. 198.
6. It was common drawing room conversation in 1916 that the empress ought to be banished and that the emperor ought to be forced to send her to the Crimea. *Education of a Princess*, p. 265. Yusupov was told that hatred of Alix had reached such an extreme that her life was in danger.
7. d'Encausse, pp. 208–9.
8. *Letters of the Tsaritsa*, p. 451, describes Alix's visit to Novgorod, including the encounter with the aged starets. Clearly the governor controlled every aspect of the visit, and may well have controlled the crowd that he 'let come near' the imperial party.
9. Buxhoeveden, p. 223.

Chapter 28

1. *Letters of the Tsaritsa*, p. 462.
2. Moynahan, p. 321. Rasputin's crony, the moneylender Aaron Simanovich, told Alix about Purishkevich's boast that Rasputin would

soon be eliminated, giving the date of December 16 (December 29 in the Gregorian calendar).

3. In actuality Zinaida Yusupov had backed and encouraged another conspiracy in the fall of 1916 and most likely encouraged her son and Grand Duke Dimitri in their plan to kill Rasputin. Edvard Radzinsky, *The Rasputin File*, trans. Judson Rosengrant (New York, 2000), p. 425.

Zinaida Yusupov's close ties to Alix's sister Ella, Ella's apparent foreknowledge of the plot to kill Rasputin on the night of December 16/29, and Ella's congratulatory telegram to Dimitri after the crime was committed lend weight to the supposition that Ella was among those who sanctioned and approved of the event. It is conceivable that Zinaida Yusupov and Ella were the primary conspirators, urging the young men to undertake the murder of the starets. But in this they were hardly unique; most of the imperials were discussing, and many were plotting, the elimination of Rasputin in 1916.

4. Buxhoeveden, p. 243.
5. Radzinsky, p. 459.
6. *Ibid.*, pp. 454–5.
7. *Letters of the Tsaritsa*, pp. 461–2.
8. *Lifelong Passion*, p. 508.
9. Buxhoeveden, p. 244. Buxhoeveden wrote that the news of Rasputin's murder was a 'shattering blow' to the empress.
10. *Lifelong Passion*, p. 512; Moynahan, p. 333.
11. *Lifelong Passion*, p. 509.
12. Buxhoeveden, p. 244.
13. *Ibid.*, p. 243.

Chapter 29

1. Iroshnikov, pp. 185–6.
2. It should be noted that the regiments of Petrograd had for many months been alerted to the probability of a coup, and their loyalty had been compromised. Officers and men alike had been overheard talking of 'changing tsars'. Nicholas had been cautioned by the British ambassador and other Allied ambassadors, and by his own foreign minister Pokrovsky, but he took no action.

Conspirators within the imperial family contacted regimental officers in secret to ensure their cooperation in a palace revolution. Indeed, high-ranking officers knew of so many plots that they were unsure which coup to support. d'Encausse, p. 216.

Both Rodzianko and his brother Michael had been urging Nicholas for months to avert catastrophe by exiling himself to Livadia, and especially removing Alix from the capital so that she would have no further influence on the government.

3. Buxhoeveden, pp. 249–50. Buxhoeveden herself was alarmed, having been cautioned in January by General Ressine, in command of the regiment that mounted guard inside the palace, that morale among the men was low as 'revolutionary propaganda had been active among them'. Ressine added that the police had given him 'serious warnings' about the unreliability of his men.

4. Buxhoeveden, p. 251.

5. *Ibid*., p. 247.

6. The following account is based on Buxhoeveden, pp. 252ff.

7. *Ibid*., pp. 263–4.

8. d'Encausse, pp. 229–30, gives a concise summary of Michael's difficult decision and the forces influencing it.

9. Paul Benckendorff, *Last Days at Tsarskoe Selo*, trans. Maurice Baring (London, 1927), p. 16.

10. Buxhoeveden, pp. 261–2.

Chapter 30

1. Buxhoeveden, pp. 264–70, gives many details of the conditions in Tsarskoe Selo during the days following the tsar's abdication.

2. *Ibid*., p. 269, dates Alix's arrest March 21. In his memoirs Benckendorff gives March 20 as the date.

3. Buxhoeveden, pp. 275–6.

4. Immediately after the abdication, Nicholas told Count Grabbe that he could now follow his lifelong dream of being a working farmer, perhaps on a farm somewhere in England. Kurth, p. 147.

5. Buxhoeveden, pp. 277–8. The attitude of the soldiers sent by the Soviet, Buxhoeveden wrote, 'became threatening, and they were ready to use their machine-guns'.

6. d'Encausse, p. 233.

7. *Lifelong Passion*, p. 579.

8. Buxhoeveden, p. 264.

9. *Ibid*., p. 277.

10. *Ibid.*, p. 275.
11. *Ibid.*, p. 268.
12. *Ibid.*, p. 288–90.
13. Details of the guards and their hostile behaviour are in Buxhoeveden, pp. 283–4, 294–5, 298–9, 301–2; Benckendorff, pp. 37–8, and *Education of a Princess*, p. 310.
14. Buxhoeveden, p. 299.
15. This encounter between Alix and the soldier is described in Buxhoeveden, pp. 300–1.

Chapter 31
1. *Nicholas and Alexandra: The Last Imperial Family*, p. 361.
2. Buxhoeveden, p. 293.
3. *Ibid.*, p. 293.
4. *Ibid.*, p. 293.
5. *Ibid.*, pp. 278–9.
6. Benckendorff, pp. 54–5. Kerensky's visit is described in Buxhoeveden, pp. 278–9.
7. Poliakov, pp. 262–3. The record of what was said at Kerensky's interview came from Alexei, who recounted what he remembered of it to his tutor Gilliard.
8. Although in January, 1916, Alix had asked her husband to burn her letters 'so that they should never fall into anybody's hands', he preserved them; they were found at Ekaterinburg in a black box, along with his diaries and correspondence. *Letters of the Tsaritsa*, p. 255.
9. Buxhoeveden, pp. 281–2.
10. *Ibid.*, pp. 291–2.
11. *Lifelong Passion*, p. 578.
12. Buxhoeveden, pp. 303–4.
13. *Ibid.*, pp. 303–4.
14. *Ibid.*, pp. 306–7.
15. *Ibid.*, pp. 305–6.

Chapter 32
1. Buxhoeveden, p. 308. Alexandra, Sophie Buxhoeveden wrote, was 'utterly exhausted in both body and mind' on the journey, and lay all day in her carriage.
2. *Lifelong Passion*, p. 583.

3. Two photos of the interior of the governor's mansion in Tobolsk are in Buxhoeveden, facing p. 322. Dr Botkin's daughter wrote that the Ipatiev house in Ekaterinburg was 'totally unlike the governor's house in Tobolsk, where the large rooms and hall were more like a country palace'. *Nicholas and Alexandra: The Last Imperial Family*, p. 372. Nicholas wrote in his diary 'the house is good and clean'.

4. Buxhoeveden, p. 312.

5. *Ibid.*, p. 313.

6. *Lifelong Passion*, pp. 591–2.

7. Buxhoeveden, p. 311.

8. *Lifelong Passion*, p. 587.

9. *Education of a Princess*, p. 341.

10. *Lifelong Passion*, p. 591.

11. 'He is still close to us,' she wrote after Father Gregory's death. Moynahan, p. 346.

12. The rescue effort is discussed in Paul Bulygin, 'The Sorrowful Quest,' in *The Murder of the Romanovs* (London, 1935), pp. 198–9, 216, and Paul Bykov, *The Last Days of Tsardom* (London, 1934), p. 57.

    Alix had a code book with her at Tobolsk, and later took it with her to Ekaterinburg, where it was found after her death. It was the key to a cypher she and Nicky had used in 1894, when they were sending telegrams to each other.

    Soloviev was accused of being a Bolshevik whose aim was not to rescue the Romanovs but to block any possible rescue plans made by members of the former imperial family, or by friends. He was arrested when the Romanovs were sent to Ekaterinburg.

13. The letter Markov carried back to Germany from Tobolsk was seen by witnesses who claimed to recognize Alix's handwriting. King, p. 333.

14. Buxhoeveden, p. 314.

15. *Lifelong Passion*, p. 593.

16. King, pp. 330–1.

Chapter 33

1. Alix began her diary on New Year's Day according to the Julian calendar, which was still officially in use in Russia until February 1/14, 1918, when the Gregorian calendar was adopted by the Bolshevik government. By January 3/16, Alix was assigning a double date to each entry, noting both the Julian and Gregorian dates, which were thirteen days apart. The diary

was written primarily in English, with occasional Russian words or phrases. It has been published as *The Last Diary of Tsaritsa Alexandra*, ed. Vladimir A. Kozlov and Vladimir M. Khrustalëv (New Haven, 1997).

2. Buxhoeveden, pp. 322–3.

3. Nicky wrote to Xenia late in January, 1918, that newspapers were not on sale in the town every day, and that when they did come, they contained nothing but 'new horrors, being perpetrated on our poor Russia'.

4. Alexandra, *Last Diary*, p. 30 note. Soloviev made encoded copies of Alix's letters and notes and burned the originals.

5. *Ibid.*, p. 32 note.

6. *Lifelong Passion*, p. 607.

7. *Ibid.*, p. 607.

8. Alexandra, *Last Diary*, p. 77 note.

9. *Ibid.*, p. 77. On March 25, 1918, Alix passed a large cigarette-holder, some other items and a note to Sergei Markov who walked past the governor's mansion and saw the family watching from the windows. Alix 'nodded to him cautiously.'

10. King, p. 331, citing Foreign Office transcripts. The opposition of Lloyd George was no doubt a factor in the abandonment of the rescue effort.

11. Buxhoeveden, pp. 325–6, describes the mayhem caused by the Red Guards. Sophie Buxhoeveden was living in a rented house in Tobolsk at the time, having been refused permission to join the household in the governor's mansion.

12. *Ibid.*, p. 326.

13. Alexandra, *Last Diary*, p. 95. The course of Alexei's attack in April, 1918, is charted in Buxhoeveden, p. 327, *Last Diary*, pp. 95ff, and *Lifelong Passion*, pp. 610ff, where the dates given differ from those in Alix's diary.

14. Alexandra, *Last Diary*, p. 96.

15. *Ibid.*, p. 97.

16. Buxhoeveden, p. 327.

17. Alexandra, *Last Diary*, p. 79. Alix believed that there were three hundred officers at Tiumen pledged to take part in a rescue effort. Boris Soloviev and his wife Maria managed to escape Russia via Vladivostok and lived, impoverished, in Europe, where Boris worked as a car washer and night porter. After Boris's death in 1926, Maria worked as a dancer in Montmartre to support her two daughters.

18. *Lifelong Passion*, p. 606.

19. 'I long to warm and comfort others,' Alix wrote to Anna Vyrubov, 'but alas, I do not feel drawn to those around me here. I am cold towards them and this, too, is wrong of me.' *Lifelong Passion*, p. 606.

Chapter 34

1. Maria Toutelberg described the crisis in testimony to Judge Sokolov during his official investigation. Buxhoeveden, p. 329, note.
2. Alexandra, *Last Diary*, p. 109.
3. *Ibid.*, p. 112. Alix wrote that they got to the train at midnight; Nicky put the time at ten o'clock. *Lifelong Passion*, p. 616.
4. Alexandra, *Last Diary*, p. 112.
5. *Ibid.*, p. 117.
6. *Ibid.*, p. 117 note and Buxhoeveden, pp. 333–4. Buxhoeveden's source of information was Chemodurov, who was taken from the Ipatiev house on May 24, 1918, and imprisoned but afterwards liberated by the White Army. Buxhoeveden herself eventually managed to escape to safety via Japan. In her biography of Alexandra she gives a slightly different version of this exchange between Nicky and the commissar.
7. *Ibid.*, p. 121, note.
8. *Ibid.*, p. 144.
9. *Ibid.*, p. 144.
10. Buxhoeveden, p. 341.
11. Alexandra, *Last Diary*, pp. 166 and 165, note.
12. Isaac Don Levine, *Eyewitness to History* (New York, 1973), p. 138. This letter and the others that reached the Romanovs in the last days of June, 1918, were written by Cheka officials, most likely by Peter Voikov and Alexander Beloborodov, chairman of the Ural Regional Soviet, in order to elicit responses that could then be used to prove that the family was engaged in a conspiracy with would-be rescuers. The letters and responses were seen as justification for eliminating the family.
13. Levine, p. 139. The editors of *The Last Diary of Tsaritsa Alexandra*, p. 176, note, estimate that this letter arrived between June 21 and 25.
14. Although the leading officials in the Cheka were aware of the false information being given to the Romanovs, it is not certain whether the Ipatiev guards had been alerted to what the family was being told, and to their expectation of imminent rescue.

Chapter 35

1. Levine, p. 139.
2. Alexandra, *Last Diary*, p. 186. Yurovsky noted in his memoirs that he allowed Alexei to keep his watch.
3. The tutor Gibbs estimated that this jewellery was worth a hundred thousand pounds. Anthony Summers and Tom Mangold, *The File on the Tsar* (New York, 1976), p. 78.
4. *Ibid.*, p. 49.
5. Alexandra, *Last Diary*, p. 197, note.
6. In 1918, arsenic was at times prescribed for both nervous disorders and rheumatism. Though arsenic was notorious as a poison, arsenic compounds were also ingested as a tonic, and in some parts of Austria arsenic was eaten regularly. Alix's strong pains are noted in *Last Diary*, pp. 192–3, 195–6.
7. Victor Alexandrov, *The End of the Romanovs* (London, 1966), p. 217.
8. Buxhoeveden, p. 327.
9. *Lifelong Passion*, p. 633.
10. *Ibid.*, p. 634.
11. This account of the Romanovs' final hour is taken from Yurovsky's description of what happened, in *Nicholas and Alexandra: The Last Imperial Family*, p. 381. Other accounts differ in details.
12. Tatiana's Pekinese Jimmy perished with the family in the early morning of July 17. Alexei's spaniel Joy was found at the Ipatiev house on the day following the executions, and was taken in by one of the guards. Summers and Mangold, p. 53. Of the third dog, Ortipo, which the family brought from Tsarskoe Selo to Tobolsk, and perhaps to Ekaterinburg, there is no record. Many secondary books give erroneous information about the family dogs.

List of Works Cited

Note to the reader: The following brief bibliography includes only works cited in footnotes.

Alexander Michaelovich. *Once a Grand Duke*. Garden City, New York: Doubleday, 1932.

Alexandra Feodorovna. *The Last Diary of Tsaritsa Alexandra*. ed. Vladimir A. Kozlov and Vladimir M. Khrustalëv. New Haven and London: Yale University Press, 1997.

—— *The Letters of the Tsaritsa to the Tsar*. London, 1923. Reprint Stanford, California: Hoover Institution Press, 1973.

Alexandrov, Victor. *The End of the Romanovs*. London: Hutchinson, 1966.

Almedingen, Edith von. *An Unbroken Unity: A Memoir of the Grand Duchess Serge of Russia*. London: Bodley Head, 1964.

—— *I Remember St Petersburg*. London: Longmans Young, 1969.

—— *The Empress Alexandra, 1872-1918: A Study*. London: Hutchinson, 1961.

Battiscombe, Georgina. *Queen Alexandra*. London: Constable, 1969.

Benckendorff, Count Paul. *Last Days at Tsarskoe Selo. Being the Personal Notes and Memoirs of Count Paul Benckendorff Telling of the Last Sojourn of the Emperor and Empress of Russia at Tsarskoe Selo from March 1 to August 1, 1917*. trans. Maurice Baring. London: Heinemann, 1927.

Billington, James. *The Icon and the Axe*. New York: Knopf, 1966.

Botkin, Gleb. *The Real Romanovs*. New York: Revell, 1931.

Buchanan, Sir George. *My Mission to Russia and Other Diplomatic Memoirs*. Boston: Little Brown, 1923.

Buchanan, Meriel. *Dissolution of an Empire*. London: Murray, 1932.

—— *Queen Victoria's Relations*. London: Cassell, 1954.

Bulygin, Paul. *The Murder of the Romanovs*. London: Hutchinson, 1935.

Buxhoeveden, Baroness Sophie. *The Life and Tragedy of Alexandra Feodorovna, Empress of Russia. A Biography*. London, New York and Toronto: Longmans Green, 1928.

Bykov, Paul. *The Last Days of Tsardom*. London: Martin Lawrence, 1934.

Dehn, Lili. *The Real Tsaritsa*. London: Thornton Butterworth, 1922. Reprint by Royalty Digest, 1995.

d'Encausse, Hélène Carrère. *Nicholas II: The Interrupted Transition*. trans. George Holoch. New York and London: Holmes and Meier, 2000.

Dumas, Alexandre. *Adventures in Czarist Russia*. trans. and ed. A.E. Murch. London: Peter Owen, 1960.

Epton, Nina. *Victoria and Her Daughters*. New York: Norton, 1971.

Gilliard, Pierre. *Thirteen Years at the Russian Imperial Court*. trans. F. Appleby Holt. London: Hutchinson, 1921.

Iroshnikov, Mikhail P. *et al. The Sunset of the Romanov Dynasty*. Moscow: Terra Publishing Center, 1992.

King, Greg. *The Last Empress: The Life and Times of Alexandra*. New York: Carol Publishing Group, 1994.

Kokovtsov, Count. *Out of My Past*. trans. Laura Matveev. ed. H.H. Fisher. London: Oxford University Press and Stanford, California: Stanford University Press, 1935.

Kurth, Peter. *The Lost World of Nicholas and Alexandra*. Boston: Little Brown, 1995.

Levine, Isaac Don. *Eyewitness to History*. New York: Hawthorn Books, 1973.

Marie Pavlovna. *Education of a Princess*. trans. Russell Lord. New York: Viking Press, 1931.

Massie, Suzanne. *Land of the Firebird: The Beauty of Old Russia*. New York: Simon and Schuster, 1980.

Maylunas, Andrei and Sergei Mironenko. *A Lifelong Passion: Nicholas and Alexandra: Their Own Story*. New York: Doubleday, 1997.

Mossolov, Alexander. *At the Court of the Last Tsar*. London: Methuen, 1935.

Mouchanow, Marfa. *My Empress: Twenty-Three Years of Intimate Life with the Empress of all the Russias from Her Marriage to the Day of her Exile*. New York: John Lane, 1918.

Moynahan, Brian. *Rasputin: The Saint Who Sinned*. New York: Random House, 1997.

Mironenko, Sergei. *Nicholas and Alexandra: The Last Imperial Family of Tsarist Russia.* New York: Harry N. Abrams, 1998.

Packard, Jerrold M. *Victoria's Daughters.* New York: St Martin's Press, 1998.

Paléologue, Maurice. *An Ambassador's Memoirs.* 3 vols. New York: Doran, 1924-5.

Pares, Bernard. *My Russian Memoirs.* London: Jonathan Cape, 1931.

—— *The Fall of the Russian Monarchy.* New York: Vintage, 1961.

Poliakov, Vladimir. *The Tragic Bride: The Story of the Empress Alexandra.* New York: Appleton, 1927.

Pope-Hennessy, James. *Queen Mary.* New York: Knopf, 1960.

Radzinsky, Edvard. *The Rasputin File.* trans. Judson Rosengrant. New York: Doubleday, 2000.

Rasputin, Maria. *My Father.* Reprint. New Hyde Park, New York: University Books, 1970.

Salisbury, Harrison. *Black Night, White Snow: Russia's Revolutions 1905-1917.* New York: Doubleday, 1978.

Sazonov, Serge. *Fateful Years.* New York: Stokes, 1928.

Summers, Anthony and Tom Mangold. *The File on the Tsar.* New York: Harper and Row, 1976.

Victoria, Empress of Germany. *The Empress Frederick Writes to Sophie: Letters 1889-1901.* ed. Arthur Gould Lee. London: Faber, 1955.

Victoria, Queen. *Advice to a Granddaughter: Letters from Queen Victoria to Princess Victoria of Hesse.* Selected by Richard Hough. London: Heinemann, 1975.

—— *Letters of Queen Victoria from the Archives of the House of Brandenburg-Prussia.* trans. Mrs J. Pudney and Lord Sudley. ed. Hector Bolitho. New Haven: Yale University Press, 1938.

—— *Queen Victoria in Her Letters and Journals: A Selection.* ed. Christopher Hibbert. New York: Viking Penguin, 1985.

Vorres, Ian. *The Last Grand Duchess.* New York: Scribner, 1965.

Vyrubov, Anna. *Souvenirs de ma Vie.* Paris: Payot, 1927.

Yusupov, Prince Felix. *Lost Splendor.* trans. Ann Green and Nicholas Katkov. New York: Putnam, 1953.

Index